CHASE!
A Tribute to the Keystone Cops

Compiled and Edited by
Lon & Debra Davis

With a Foreword by Sam Gill

CHASE! A Tribute to the Keystone Cops
©2020 Lon & Debra Davis (compilers and editors)
No part of this book may be reproduced in any form or by any means, whether electronic, mechanical, or digital, or through photocopying or recording, except for brief excerpts included in reviews, without permission in writing from the publisher.

Published in the USA by:
BearManor Media
4700 Millenia Blvd.
Suite 175 PMB 90497
Orlando, FL 32839
www.bearmanormedia.com

BearManor Media, Albany, Georgia
Printed in the United States of America

Library of Congress Cataloguing-in-Publication Data:

CHASE! A Tribute to the Keystone Cops / Edited by Lon & Debra Davis
Paperback ISBN 978-1-62933-543-8
Case ISBN 978-1-62933-544-5
Keystone Cops (comedy team) 2. Keystone Cops films—history and criticism.

Front cover illustration by Mark Leneve.
Frontispiece: The Keystone Cops set out to quell a riot. *Keystone Hotel* (Vitaphone-Warner Bros., 1935). Photo courtesy of Bison Archive.
Back cover: Reproduction of one-sheet for *Cinders of Love* (Keystone-Triangle, 1916).
Book design and layout by Robbie Adkins.
Line edit by Mark Pruett.

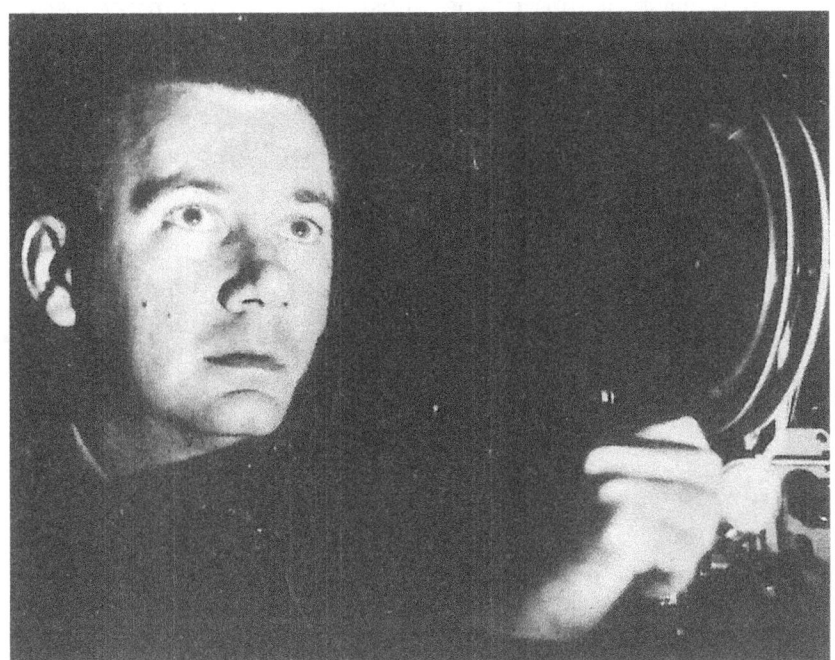

In memory of
Kalton C. Lahue
(1934–1993)

An important author to those of us who first discovered silent comedy in the sixties and seventies, he provided an unprecedented history of that bygone era.

In honor of Mr. Lahue, all proceeds from this book will be allocated to silent film preservation.

About the Front Cover Illustration

A familiar picture of the Keystone Cops (from the 1939 Warner Bros. production *Hollywood Cavalcade*) has been rendered in pen and ink for this book's front-cover illustration.

The talented artist is Mark Leneve, a British citizen who, it just so happens, was once a police officer himself.

At our request, Mark added some recognizable faces to the anonymous stunt men replicating the players, including Roscoe "Fatty" Arbuckle, Hank Mann, and Jimmy Finlayson.

Nearly every one of us lives in the secret hope that someday before he dies he will be able to swat a policeman's hat down around his ears. Lacking the courage and the opportunity, we like to see it done in the movies.

—Mack Sennett, 1918

Table of Contents

Acknowledgments vii
Foreword: A Walk Down Memory Lane, or "Where's the Nearest Police Station?" . . . xi
    by Sam Gill
Chapter 1: Parody and the Rise of the Cops, by Rob King. 1
Chapter 2: Keystone in 1913: Slapstick and the Art of Ensemble Acting, ... 17
    by Mark Pruett
Chapter 3: Lost and (Partially) Found: *In the Clutches of a Gang*, by Lon Davis. 28
Chapter 4: Fate and a Flea Market: How a Fortuitous Find Rewrote Keystone 34
    Cops History, by Paul E. Gierucki and Chris Seguin
Chapter 5: *Tillie's Punctured Romance*: Then and Now, by John Bengtson 45
Chapter 6: *The Show Off*: Ford Sterling Revealed, by Mark Pruett. 52
Chapter 7: The Sennett Story: The Unwritten Rules for Writing Physical Comedy, . . . 63
    by Joe Adamson
Chapter 8: Fact, Fiction, and Folly: The Mythology of the Keystone Cops, ... 100
    by Lea Stans
Chapter 9: When Keaton Met Keystone: Kops, Custard, and Reality Run Amuck, . . . 114
    by Chris Seguin
Chapter 10: Cops for (Re)Sale: Reissuing the Keystone Comedies, ... 127
    by Michael J. Hayde
Chapter 11: The Keystone Cop and the Missing Briefcase, by Lon Davis. 142
Chapter 12: Cops, or Kops: Kolliding into Kontemporary Kulture, ... 159
    by Randy Skretvedt
Chapter 13: Mack Sennett and Keystone in Print and Home Entertainment, ... 185
    by Rob Farr
Chapter 14: Top Cops: Fifty-five Profiles of Original and Honorary 200
    Keystone Cops, by Lon Davis and Brent E. Walker
Chapter 15: The Keystone Cops on Film, Television, Radio, and Stage, ... 246
by Brent E. Walker and Lon Davis
Appendix A: Keystone, an Illustrated Chronology, 1912–1917, ... 298
    by Marc Wanamaker
Appendix B: "Putting the Key in Keystone" by Stanley W. Todd, ... 308
    Motion Picture Classic (January 1917)
Index. 314

Acknowledgments

It has been a distinct pleasure to work with our fellow authors on this, the first full-length book devoted exclusively to the immortal Keystone Cops. In alphabetical order, they are:

- **Joe Adamson**, the award-winning author and filmmaker, who contributed a detailed examination of Mack Sennett's evolving approach to storytelling in comedy films.
- **John Bengtson**, about whom Kevin Brownlow said that "had it not been for his researches [pinpointing locations used in countless silent films], virtually all traces of the silent era would likely have been erased." John has written a fascinating comparison study of locations used in American cinema's first feature-length comedy, *Tillie's Punctured Romance* (Keystone, 1914). He has also contributed an endless stream of requested screencaps.
- **Rob Farr**, film history professor and founder of the annual Slapsticon Film Festival, who used his vast knowledge to sort out all the books and DVD/Blu-rays that have been devoted to Mack Sennett's *oeuvre*.
- **Paul E. Gierucki**, noted historian and producer, whose Blu-ray sets of vintage comedies present them at their apex, sat down for his first-ever in-depth interview concerning his rediscovering the lost Chaplin/Keystone Cop film, *A Thief Catcher*.
- **Sam Gill**, the legendary film historian noted for his documentation of silent comedy shorts, who was gracious enough to provide the deeply personal foreword to *Chase!* We film buffs of a certain age cut our teeth on the book he co-authored with Kalton C. Lahue, *Clown Princes and Court Jesters*, back in the early seventies. As Sam recently told us, "Little did we know that our completed work would contribute so much to the delinquency of a whole generation of young historians."
- **Michael J. Hayde**, whose dogged research on silent film reissues and revivals made him the perfect choice to write about the Cops films that have been duped, reduped, recut, and retitled, thereby making them available even today, more than a century after they were shot.
- **Rob King**, film professor at Columbia University and award-winning author, who contributed a scholarly treatise on Sennett's use of parody, particularly of the films of his visionary mentor, David Wark Griffith.

- **Tim Lussier**, author and longtime webmaster, who has faithfully maintained the popular Silents Are Golden site since 1998. Tim pored over his sizable collection of trade magazines for articles about the Keystone studios. We have reproduced one of these vintage profiles in the appendix. Tim was also kind enough to provide a blurb for the book's cover.
- **Mark Pruett**, novelist and author of probing articles about celebrity and censorship in the silent era, who has written an outstanding analysis of ensemble acting in the earliest Keystone films. He has also contributed a well-deserved tribute to Ford Sterling, the seminal comedy star best remembered for his role as Keystone's chief of police. Mark was a constant source of encouragement and help throughout the entire process. He even did a line edit of the completed manuscript.
- **Chris Seguin**, the comedy programmer for the Toronto Silent Film Festival, who has given us a fresh look at the 1939 20th Century-Fox Technicolor extravaganza *Hollywood Cavalcade*, the film Mack Sennett called his "autobiography." Chris also conducted the fascinating interview with Paul E. Gierucki, which makes its debut herein. Chris was always available for wise counsel and provided an endless stream of facts and images.
- **Randy Skretvedt**, the world's leading authority on the wonderful team of Stan Laurel & Oliver Hardy, who proves that he is just as knowledgeable about the Keystone Cops, particularly when it comes to their timeless effect on popular culture. Randy, whose home is a storehouse of movie and music history, was characteristically gracious in his assistance with this project.
- **Lea Stans**, webmistress of the fine Silent-ology site (and our token millennial), who penned an interesting, accessible chapter that separates the facts from the myths associated with the Cops. Lea's kind demeanor and scholarly knowledge are greatly appreciated by the editors. It was she who supplied the Keystone Cops' obituaries displayed in the final chapter.
- **Brent E. Walker**, author of the exhaustive *Mack Sennett's Fun Factory: A History and Filmography of His Studio and His Keystone and Mack Sennett Comedies, with Biographies of Players and Personnel* (even the title is exhaustive), who spent a total of thirty years making that indispensable reference book a reality. Despite his particularly demanding schedule, he took the time to collaborate with Lon on the filmography, as well as on the chapter "Top Cops."
- **Marc Wanamaker**, curator of Bison Productions/Archives in Los Angeles, who sent along pristine, high-resolution scans of dozens of photos of the Keystone Cops in every incarnation. He also supplied an illustrated chronology of the Keystone studio.

Additional thanks to
- **Ben Ohmart,** the benevolent founder and president of BearManor Media, who is taking yet another chance on us by publishing this book.
- **Edda Manriquez,** the charming public access coordinator at the Academy of Motion Picture Arts and Sciences, who made it possible for Lon to view long-lost footage of the Keystone Cops from 1914.
- **Robbie Adkins,** noted book designer and layout artist extraordinaire, whose mad skills helped us realize this highly personal project.
- **Stuart Oderman,** the late author and brilliant silent film accompanist at the Museum of Modern Art in New York City, who was kind enough to make available to us his interviews with Sennett veterans Minta Durfee Arbuckle, Chester Conklin, Gloria Swanson, Babe London, and Frank Capra.

And, finally, to
- **Scott H. Reboul,** our good friend in South Carolina, who was a constant source of encouragement from the inception of this project. Scott, incidentally, went in search of this book some fifty years before it was written. We hope it was worth the wait!

Lon & Debra Davis
Portland, OR

Lon & Debra Davis have been writing together for forty years. In the early eighties, they worked in tandem with Francis X. Bushman's widow to pen her late husband's authorized biography, *King of the Movies,* which was published to critical acclaim by BearManor Media twenty-five years later, in 2009. Their other book collaborations include *Silent Lives: 100 Biographies of the Silent Film Era* (2008), *Stooges Among Us* (2008), and *Flirtation Act: The Story of a Boy, a Girl, and Vaudeville* (2016). In addition, the Davises have edited hundreds of academic books on the performing arts, American history, and literature.

A Walk Down Memory Lane
or "Where's the Nearest Police Station?"
A Foreword by Sam Gill

Being asked to write the foreword to a book dedicated to Kalton C. Lahue is a great honor. Kal was a major influence on my life from the first time we corresponded until he decided he'd had enough of film history and walked away from his dream. That dream, as he related it to me, was to make a living by writing books on film history. At the time of his decision, Kal was giving special attention to subjects long ignored by most film historians—serials and comedy shorts. After nearly a dozen books had been published, he said the financial return for all his work was inadequate to make a living and had put a severe strain on his marriage. Kal walked away from film history for good. But before this sad turn of events, there was freshness and excitement when everything was new and the future bright. It's that wonderful time that I will write about, and the many incredible individuals who peopled Kal's and my lives—*our* lives.

By the time I first met Kal in person, he had already gone page by page through a near-complete run of *The Moving Picture World*, taking notes on everything that was of interest to him. He was especially interested in the business end of the motion picture industry and how it functioned. He wanted to know—and indeed spent the time necessary to better understand—the corporate histories of the companies that made up that industry. I'd say the ones that fascinated him most were the film exchanges and the film distribution system. And within that, Kal had a special fascination, as did I, for motion pictures of the 1910s. On that subject, we had many, many discussions and exchanges of information, both in-person and through correspondence. The masthead of Kal's stationery was printed in color and contained the logos of six famous early-day film companies—Pathé, Kalem, Vitagraph, American, Essanay, and, last but not least, Keystone. The beauty of his stationery said more about Kal than he would ever admit. That was due to the fact that Kal tended to have a dark view of human nature, along with a sardonic sense of humor. But I came to realize he was a softie at heart who could, and did, use his sometimes abrasive personality as a shield.

Kal's 1966 book *World of Laughter* is the only film history I am aware of that presents an overview with much interior detail about the motion picture comedy short in the American silent screen era, covering the years 1910 to 1930. In one of our first meetings just before the book came out, over a cup of coffee at our usual hangout—the Copper Skillet diner on the southwest corner of Sunset and Gower—Kal told me he was expecting serious criticism for organizing each chapter chronologically and by distribution company. I tried to reassure him that I was very impressed that he had done that. To my knowledge, it was the first time any film historian had arranged a book in this way, at least one dealing with the subject of the silent film comedy short. I told Kal that, having organized a massive amount of often-unwieldy subject matter, he had provided a fresh look at an important aspect of the film industry, one that no film historian had attempted before.

As Kal worked on every one of his books, I tried to help as much as I could, as did others who liked his approach to different subjects. Especially helpful were John and Dorothy Hampton, who ran the Silent Movie Theater on Fairfax (the first place I visited when I arrived in Hollywood!), where John held special screenings just for Kal. Also very supportive was Kent D. Eastin, of the Eastin-Phelan Corporation, the parent company of every film collector's best friend, Blackhawk Films. Mr. Eastin would ship countless film prints from Davenport, Iowa, to wherever Kal was living at the time; this included both coasts and many places in between.

Kal, very wisely in my estimation, felt that to get a more accurate picture of how the early film industry functioned, he needed to approach the men and women who had been there. It was this desire to track down and interview the actual participants, especially those who had slaved away in the making of comedy shorts and serial chapters, that brought Kal and me together. My primary field of interest was the comedy short; Kal's was the serial. But what we both soon discovered was that contacting one person inevitably led to the contacting of another, which led to a third, then a fourth, then a fifth, and so on. The challenge for Kal and me, to be brutally frank about it, was to track down and interview every person we could before they died on us. It was a race against time.

One area that absolutely fascinated us was the Keystone Film Company, its director-general Mack Sennett, and all of his employees in front of and behind the camera. Keystone was located in a place we thought had a somewhat humorous name and is populated to this day by citizens who are loyal to their town and its unique history—Edendale. We were on the hunt for every person we could find who had worked for Keystone, a company launched in 1912 and furiously active for five years until Sennett presented his walking papers and founded, in 1917, the company that would bear his own name—Mack Sennett Comedies. Sennett was convinced that his name had greater drawing power than the name Keystone, which limped along for a few more years before it collapsed, and by all accounts, he was right. A most formidable challenge Kal and I faced, however, was identifying the people we wanted to find, and then hardest of all, finding them!

In the 1960s there were very few sources available to aid researchers in finding anybody, let alone getting a mailing address or phone number—and preferably both. Even genealogical sources were scarce and nearly impossible to search. Sometimes it seemed like the deeper one would dig, the more people one would find who had simply disappeared. Comedienne Babe London once said that she met up with more people she had worked with at funerals than anywhere else. Funerals of silent film veterans, it was sad to realize, were occurring in ever-increasing numbers due to the incessant march of time, whisking away a whole generation of incredible, fascinating individuals, many of whom—in fact, *most* of whom—had never been interviewed. These people were not stars—they represented everybody else, and they were the ones Kal and I most wanted to find. Babe said she was always sure to take her address book along with her whenever she attended a funeral, so that she could get contact information on those who "remained." Babe London, as everyone who knew her will recall, was very generous with her address book, bringing together many people who would otherwise never be found.

After Lon and Debra Davis approached me about contributing a foreword to a book about the Keystone Cops (and dedicated to Kalton C. Lahue), I spent a solid year fretting and stewing: writing six different drafts, all of which became increasingly autobiographical and increasingly boring. It's amazing how one's own story can be so much less interesting than that of someone you actually care about—and whose story you want to read. Thus, out went the autobiography and in went the endlessly fascinating accounts by endlessly fascinating people of an endlessly fascinating subject: the Keystone Cops. Much of what follows would never have happened without the encouragement, support, and help of someone who remains as much an inspiration today as he did fifty-five years ago. So, with the anecdotes that follow, I would like to make, with Lon and Debra's indulgence, my own dedication-within-a-dedication to a friend I loved, admired, and will miss forever: Kalton C. Lahue.

What I soon discovered was that everyone I managed to track down had already given their photographs to George Gray, the stills chairman of the Hollywood Museum. Hearing this so often, I concluded that maybe I needed to track down this George Gray myself. I'm glad I did. He had a wealth of information, seemed to know everybody in the business, and best of all, as I soon learned, had worked at Keystone in the early days. George first joined Keystone in 1914 as a stunt man, then left for a year in vaudeville, then returned to Keystone in 1916 as a stunt man and double, then an actor, then a writer, then a co-director of one film, then an actor once again, and then—for the rest of his life—a makeup man. There didn't seem to be much that George Gray hadn't done in a lifetime in the movie business. I soon learned that anything he was willing to share was pure gold, and I was the lucky prospector.

As I was starting to do more and more interviews, I took along a few photographs and a book or two containing scene stills from Keystone films. The players in the photos were either partially identified or totally unidentified. One of the stills I brought along to George's home turned out to be a candid photo taken on the set of the 1916 Triangle-Keystone Comedy *The Winning Punch*. In the photo were eight men standing in a boxing ring. I asked if he could identify anyone in the picture. He studied it, then pointed to each person in the photograph, left to right, and replied: "Tommy McFarland, Walter South, Slim Summerville, James Rowe, Al Kaufman, Bobby Dunn, James Donnelly, and Len Lauder." Not only did he recognize all eight players, he personally *knew* each one.

George Gray was a modest, soft-spoken individual with a rather unusual nickname—"Sloppy Weather." As he explained, "It was given to me at the time I was working with Dr. Carver's Diving Horses act. I got it because I used to delight in landing in the water and splashing everyone within several yards of the tank. It was Bobby Dunn—he also worked for Dr. Carver—who brought the nickname 'Sloppy Weather' to Keystone." George then explained that, once he was on the Keystone lot, Sennett gagman Johnnie Grey took him aside and suggested he come up with a more dignified nickname than "Sloppy Weather." Grey said that most likely everyone at the studio would shorten it to the even less dignified "Sloppy." Johnnie Grey, a wag if there ever was one, announced his suggested name change: "*Mr.* Sloppy." George laughingly added, "As it turned out, everyone at the studio shortened it to 'Sloppy' anyway!"

George Gray and Bobby Dunn were great friends, which interested me because Bobby Dunn had died so many years before, in 1937, and very little had been written about him since. I thought he was an excellent comedian and enjoyed any film of his that I had the good fortune to see. One time, George and Bobby went out on a drinking binge and time got away from them. Finally, looking up at the clock over the bar, they saw that it was four thirty in the afternoon—much too late to return to the studio. Sennett was quite strict and did not like his employees to drink. So, the next day, after Sennett was informed of this infraction, he gave George and Bobby a week's suspension. I neglected to ask if they did any drinking during their suspension. However, George did add that one suspension was enough and that, in the following fifty years in the film business, he never missed another day of work.

During one of our discussions, the subject of Andy Clyde came up. I told George how much I'd love to meet him because I had seen all of his Columbia shorts on television when I was a kid, and also enjoyed the few silent comedies I had bought from Blackhawk Films of Andy Clyde and Billy Bevan when both comics were with Sennett. Without saying a word, he walked over to the telephone, picked up the receiver, and dialed a number.

"Andy, there's a fellow here from Kansas who'd like to meet you." He turned to me and asked, "Can you go now?"

"Boy, *can* I!"

"Andy, we'll be right over."

And that's how I got to meet Andy Clyde, which was one of the most enjoyable visits I ever had.

Practical jokes, as everyone who worked at Keystone would tell you, were rampant. Having a bucket of water dumped on one's head or sitting on an electrically wired toilet seat were not uncommon occurrences. One of the funniest examples of a Keystone practical joke was told to Kal and me by George W. Stout, who had been an accountant and, later, the studio manager. Mr. Stout was in his office, discussing business with a newly married young assistant director. The fellow was sitting on the edge of his desk, and very absorbed in the topic under discussion. Mabel Normand, a renowned imp, walked in and saw the young fellow. He was wearing a brand new pair of spiffy white pants, a look very much in style at the time. Mabel went to him, leaned over, and kissed the young man right on his fly, leaving the very obvious mark of her bright red lipstick. Mabel laughed, then told the young man, "Now explain THAT to your wife!" Kal and I laughed out loud, but apparently George Stout didn't like what Mabel had done and was still visibly annoyed at her fifty years later. His stern reaction caught Kal and me by surprise, making us laugh even louder. So, as it turned out, Mr. Stout was amused neither by Mabel nor by us!

Roscoe Arbuckle was someone I would love to have known, but his death in 1933 robbed the world of one of the silent screen's greatest comedians. Everyone I talked to who either knew or worked with him said he was a great practical joker but added that you *never* wanted to be on the receiving end of one of his jokes. Later, of course, he and Buster Keaton joined forces in perpetrating some of the most legendary practical jokes that were to be talked about throughout Hollywood, and in fact, still are!

Minta Durfee was Roscoe Arbuckle's first wife, and it was always enjoyable to attend events at which she was present. No one I ever met was as fond of the Keystone days as she. Whenever I heard her tell a story, she always couched her words in the phrase, "*My* Keystone." I think Minta Durfee is at long last coming into her own and being reappraised as an extremely skillful comedienne. It always seemed to me that she was overlooked and, sometimes, downright ignored. She could be very funny, but in an understated way. Minta even had her own production company in the late teens after leaving Sennett. It was called Truart Pictures and was located in Providence, Rhode Island, of all places. There seems to be only one film that survives from that period, one in which she is joined by comic Billy Quirk. It's titled *His Wife's Union* (sometimes referred to as *The Wife's Union*) and was shown to me by Florence Moore St. John during a visit to my home in Sterling, Kansas, in October 1965. She was performing nearby in what was called a "Hollywood Hillbilly" show featuring cowboy star Tim McCoy. At her request, I spent a few weeks promoting her show before she reached Kansas to ensure that she would get a good reception.

Flo Belle, as she was also known, stayed overnight at my home, and had brought along several films that starred or featured her husband, Al St. John. One we screened was *Buzzin' Around* (1933), which seemed to me to be a loving farewell tribute to Roscoe and Al in a sound film, showcasing gags similar to ones they first performed at Keystone (or even, possibly, on the stage), then at Comique, Educational, and finally Warner Bros., where *Buzzin' Around* was made. I very much wished I could have met Al St. John, one of my all-time favorite comedians, but he had died just two years before I met his widow. Perhaps my favorite quote of Al's was something reported in a Georgia newspaper shortly before his death in 1963. Being a superb acrobat, he was asked if he could still perform stunts. He replied, "Well, I can get down just as good as I always have, it's just that I can't get back up." At my current age, I know exactly how he must have felt.

Now, briefly back to Minta Durfee. She was very generous with her time and was more than willing to answer the many questions I had. It was Minta, incidentally, who explained to me just how tight a friendship Roscoe had with two gentlemen from Keystone—Jimmy Bryant and Joe Bordeaux—as well as with his nephew Al St. John and, beginning in 1917, Buster Keaton. Another close friend to Roscoe and Al was the versatile comedian Glen Cavender, who seems to have worked for every studio, making comedy shorts and playing any kind of part to which he was assigned. Minta verified that Glen Cavender would sometimes serve as assistant director on Arbuckle films. Charles Avery served as a director on many of Roscoe Arbuckle's earliest films and was well remembered by everyone who had worked with him. Avery was another Keystone alum who died in 1926, long before I made it out to California.

Among the most fascinating "couples" I ever met were the sisters Dixie and Hazel Chene. They lived next door to each other in Hollywood and had stories galore about the Keystone company and everyone who worked there. In fact, in their youth when they were "soubrettes" on the stage, before entering pictures, they lived with Al St. John's mother and father. Al's mother was Nora St. John, Roscoe's sister. Al's parents managed an apartment building located near 3rd and Figueroa, where the Chene sisters resided as well. While living there, Al fell head over heels in love with Dixie. She recalled that when she arrived for her first day at Keystone, she was introduced as "Al's girl." She also recounted that she was accompanied by Glen Cavender, who at the time was her sister Hazel's husband. As Glen accompanied his sister-in-law onto the studio lot, all the young men lined up and took turns kissing Dixie.

"Oh, Al was mad about that!" she recalled laughingly.

The Chene sisters said Al could always be found in the wardrobe department or on the street, practicing tricks on his bicycle. He was spending so much time in wardrobe, in fact, that Sennett once asked him sarcastically, "You going to *live* back there?" Al told Sennett he was picking out a wardrobe. Sennett's reaction to this was to order Al to straighten up the area. "That's how Al St. John came to 'hang wardrobe' at the Keystone studio," Dixie explained, using an old film industry term.

Dixie stated that virtually every male at Keystone was "on the make." However, there were two women who took it upon themselves to keep the men at bay, particularly at the entrance to the women's dressing rooms: Alice Davenport, who was called "Mother" Davenport by everyone, and Blanche Payson, an ex-policewoman who stood six-four and weighed 234 pounds. Both ladies were formidable and not to be trifled with.

Another player remembered fondly by the Chene sisters—Rube Miller—is described by Lon Davis and Brent Walker in the "Top Cops" profiles that can be found in Chapter 14. Rube, they said, was one of the most talented and well-liked comedians at Keystone. Neither sister could understand why he had been so forgotten. I suggested that the reason might be that Miller often appeared in Sennett's one-reel and split-reel comedies, of which relatively few survived. But it does seem to this author that he deserves more attention, not only for his work at Keystone and in the circus as a producing clown, but later at Kalem, Vogue, L-KO, and Comique before he disappeared into the void. Brent Walker, in his massive study *Mack Sennett's Fun Factory*, a reference work unrivaled in every way, from its organization and completeness to its accuracy and accessibility, sheds more light on the elusive Rube Miller than anyone has before. Brent never gives up, and his determined spirit tracked down this odd-looking but intriguing gentleman who seemed to work hard at hiding himself. Now that he has been "found," perhaps there can be a more balanced and reasoned appraisal of his talents.

When it comes to the delightful Charles Murray, everyone I interviewed who had worked with him attested to the fact that he was one of the most beloved comedians in the business. He seemingly had not a single enemy and, by all accounts, was the greatest storyteller ever. Since the early film companies relied upon the sun for their light, at least for any outdoor scenes, when it would rain (yes, even in the Eden of Edendale it could rain), it would bring production to an abrupt halt. Everyone who worked at Keystone in the early years said that as the diffusers would be filling up with water, looking like they were about to collapse on everyone and drench the sets, the costumes, and the people on and in them, Charlie Murray could always be counted on to come to the fore and entertain everyone with songs, jokes, and stories, in essence to provide his own special brand of sunshine on an otherwise dark and dreary day. Charlie Murray was another of the Keystone alumni I most wish I could have known, but he was taken away in 1941 at the age of sixty-nine.

Of Mack Sennett himself in the early years of Keystone, everyone laughingly agreed: when he was directing, he looked like a bum in one of his own comedies, and when he was acting, he looked like a country bumpkin. While everyone agreed that he might have been a stubborn penny-pincher, he was also an astute businessman who would give a virtual unknown a chance at stardom. He might lose one of his starring comedians due to his relatively low salaries, but more often than not the actor would come back when the going got rough. Everybody also agreed that when it came to "knowing" comedy and judging what the public wanted, Sennett had no peer. Minta Durfee had some interesting insights into Mack Sennett that she shared with me in one of her more reflective moods: "Mack Sennett may not have been any 'creative talent,' but he knew comedy. There are different kinds of intelligence—his was not the educated type—but no one had a finer sense of comedy." And regarding Sennett's well-known and oft-mentioned scowl, which literally frightened some people who worked for him, Minta had a different slant: "He seemed very gruff, but there was a rough Irish kind-heartedness about Mack Sennett."

Since stars didn't want their fans to know they were not doing their own stunts, and with the film producers adamant that stunt people not go public with the specifics of what stunts they were performing, it is extremely difficult to get reliable information on just who did what stunts in a given picture. George Gray told me that he had doubled for Ben Turpin in his first year at Keystone, 1917. Since Turpin was clearly capable of doing difficult stunts himself, it must have been a dangerous one indeed for Sennett to disallow Ben from doing it. As some stunt men wryly say, describing a typical producer's innermost but unspoken thought: "If someone is going to be killed doing a stunt, it certainly isn't going to be my star!"

Some of the most interesting and revealing background information on stunt work at Keystone came from the widow of Grover Ligon. Ligon was one of the Keystone regulars, popping up in countless Keystones, and very identifiable because of his prematurely bald head. He died just one year before I made my first trip to Los Angeles in the summer of 1966. I never had the pleasure of meeting him but his widow was extremely generous with her time, and was very knowledgeable about her late husband's film work. They had been married in 1910 and, at the invitation of William Beaudine, who was just a prop boy at the time, Grover Ligon started in pictures at Biograph in 1911.

I asked about her husband's baldness and she explained that it was a result of his having malaria while serving in the Marine Corps, just prior to entering films. He first worked for Biograph, interestingly, doing stunts with motorcycles. He was also a good swimmer and diver, as well as an adept boxer, as were many of the Keystone Cops. Also, it was at Keystone, according to Mrs. Ligon, that her husband joined forces with the greatest stunt man in early film: Bill Hauber. As Brent Walker points out in his Sennett book, if you spot Bill Hauber in a film, you could expect an incredible fall to soon occur. In other words, just wait, and you'll soon see something that only Bill Hauber could do.

Mrs. Ligon also explained that her husband and Bill Hauber became a stunt "team," of sorts. They looked out for each other in what is arguably the most dangerous vocation in motion pictures. Both Ligon and Hauber also worked together at Vitagraph in Larry Semon's wildly physical comedies. After that, the dynamic duo went to Warner Bros. Ligon was not with his friend, however, on July 17, 1929. That was the tragic day Bill Hauber and cameraman Alvin Knechtel were killed in an airplane crash.

Mrs. Ligon, at the end of a letter she wrote to me dated June 18, 1973, made a statement that I believe is a most fitting sentiment for this book and a kind of wave goodbye to an era and the people who made it so special.

I hope I have helped with all that followed the Keystone Cops.
It does seem they deserve a memorial of some kind.
They worked hard, had a lot of fun and in the early years
were young and could do so and enjoy the work and companionship.

And so ends my walk down memory lane. So long, Kal.

Sam Gill
Niles, CA

Sam Gill was born and raised in Sterling, a small town in Central Kansas. While still in high school, he began writing a series of career profiles on Larry Semon, Mack Swain, Charley Chase, Lloyd Hamilton, and other comedy greats in a column titled "The Funny Men," which appeared in *8mm Collector Magazine* (known today as *Classic Images*). In 1964, upon graduation from high school, Sam entered college at the University of Kansas from which, in 1968, he graduated with a Bachelor of Arts degree in English & Humanities 20th Century. While in college, during the summers of 1966, 1967, and 1968, Sam traveled to Los Angeles where he worked for the Academy of Motion Picture Arts and Sciences, organizing and inventorying the Mack Sennett Collection. From 1968 to 1971, he served in the United States Army in Military Intelligence. In 1970, while Sam was still in the Army, A. S. Barnes published *Clown Princes and Court Jesters*, a groundbreaking book about the lesser-known silent comedians, co-authored by Sam and Kalton C. Lahue. Following his honorable discharge in 1971, Sam returned to Los Angeles where he resumed work for the Academy. In 1974, he took a leave of absence and traveled to Jacksonville, Florida, where he began researching the once-flourishing silent film industry of that city. While in Jacksonville, Sam was hired by David Shepard of Blackhawk Films in Davenport, Iowa, to provide written introductions for Blackhawk's extensive selection of silent film comedies. In June 1974, Sam returned to Los Angeles, where he began his work of twenty-five years, first as director of the Academy's National Film Information Service, then as archivist for the Academy of Motion Picture Arts and Sciences. Upon his retirement, he relocated to the Niles district of Fremont, California, where he serves as a board member for the Niles Essanay Silent Film Museum.

Chapter 1
Parody and the Rise of the Cops
By Rob King

Photo courtesy of Bison Archives.

Any attempt to name the first appearance of something is a mug's game. This is not just because any hypothetical "first" is always provisional, subject to revision, but because the supposed "first" never quite resembles or fits with what hindsight expects. Case in point: the Keystone Cops. What is *their* first appearance? Most historians of the Keystone Film Company trace the idea of the bumbling, frenetic cops back to the influence of the French firm Pathé Frères and, in particular, the 1907 chase comedy *La Course des sergents de ville* (*The Policemen's Little Run*, dir. Ferdinand Zecca), which Mack Sennett seems to have known. Sennett himself admitted in his autobiography that "[i]t was the Frenchmen who invented slapstick and I imitated them," and claimed to have been excitedly hawking the idea that "cops were funny" more or less as

soon as his film career began at Biograph in 1908. Yet historians' efforts to unearth the first appearance of "funny cops" in Sennett's own films fail to come up with anything that remotely resembles the gallivanting police of the Pathé film, nor indeed anything really worthy of an idea to get excited over.

Thanks to the remarkable archaeological work of Brent Walker, for instance, we know that there is a funny policeman in the Sennett-directed Biograph film *Algy the Watchman* (June 1912) and that three policemen show up at the end of *Katchem Kate* (also June 1912)—although, as Walker notes, their appearance there is "not especially comedic." We also know—based on the evidence of a surviving still—that the third Keystone film ever released, *Riley and Schultze* (September 1912), revolved around two policemen, played by Mack Sennett and Fred Mace, who are rivals for a girl. *At It Again* (November 1912) is the "first verifiable Keystone comedy to feature a *group* of cops" (Walker) as well as the first in which Ford Sterling takes the police chief role; that, nonetheless, Sennett more commonly

cast himself as chief in the studio's early months, in films like *A Temperamental Husband* (November 1912), *Pat's Day Off* (December 1912), and *Hoffmeyer's Legacy* (also December 1912); and that *The Stolen Purse* (February 1913) has two cops (Sennett and Mace again) in a chase after a tramp—but none of these films is extant, and, again, none of this has the ring of comic legend.

Yes, cops appear; and yes, some of the pieces are moving into place (a chase here, a police chief there, etc.), but we still seem to be lacking an "inception moment." It is the argument of this chapter that that moment came only when Sennett's proclivities for funny cops crossed paths with another comedic tendency in Keystone's early output—specifically, the impetus to parody the kind of rescue melodramas made popular by Sennett's former mentor at Biograph, D. W. Griffith. In this respect, documenting first appearances may be less significant than understanding the larger comedic strategies that worked to thrust the cops into the popular imagination.

What, after all, are we actually looking for? Not just the onscreen presence of a cop or cops will do, but more specifically a group of cops *involved in some sort of frenetic pursuit*. This, after all, is the "classic" role of the cops, as it would be enshrined at Keystone over the course of 1913. The template is a familiar one: the first half of the film will lead up to some situation of danger or peril—Mabel Normand tied to a railroad track in the path of an advancing train in *Barney Oldfield's Race for a Life* (June 1913), or sweethearts Normand and Charles Inslee stuck in a rowboat while a lake is drained in *A Muddy Romance* (November 1913)—the police are in some way summoned, and a parallel-edited race to the rescue ensues, the film cutting between the madcap police officers, various other frenzied pursuers, and the imperiled victims.

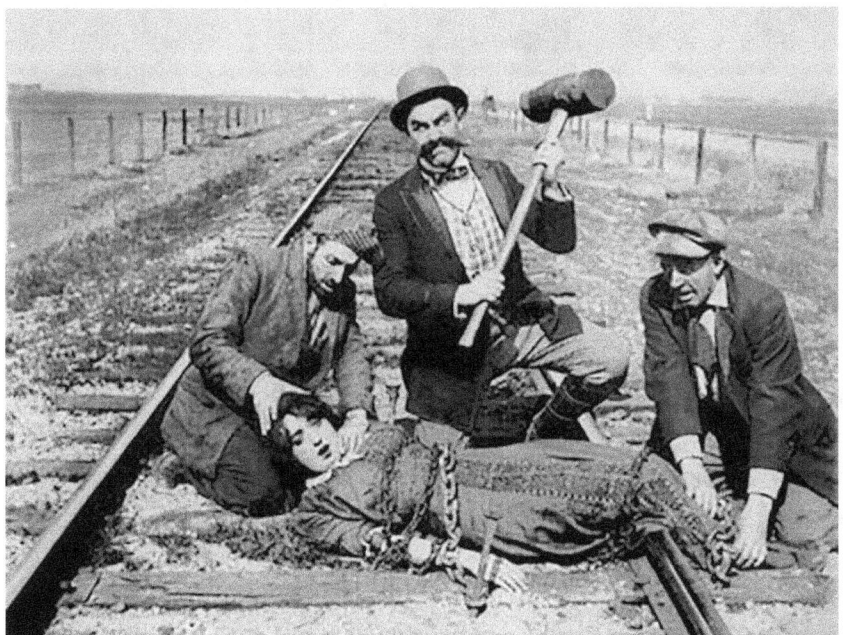

In a direct parody of a Griffith Biograph melodrama, the villainous Ford Sterling (center) cruelly chains Mabel Normand to the railroad tracks. The identity of the henchman on the left is uncertain; the henchman on the right is Raymond Hatton. In an excitingly photographed climax, Mabel is rescued in the nick of time by Mack Sennett and real-life racecar driver Barney Oldfield. Barney Oldfield's Race for a Life *(1913).*

The Man Next Door is the earliest-known Keystone Cops film known to exist. Left to right are an unknown player in the background; Bill Hauber; Charles Avery, and Dave "Andy" Anderson. Frame enlargement courtesy of the Library of Congress.

It is thus a particularly choice coincidence that the very first extant example of a parallel-edited race to the rescue in a Keystone film is also the very first extant appearance of funny cops in the Keystone catalog: the Sennett-directed *The Man Next Door*, a split-reel comedy released on March 17. As per the template above, the opening of the film establishes a situation of (apparent) peril when a wife and her lover (Dot Farley and Ford Sterling) trap the wife's husband (Nick Cogley) in a parlor-room trunk, mistakenly believing him to be a burglar. The wife then phones the police, setting up a parallel-edited climax as follows:

Shot 36: Exterior police station. Four policemen (played by Dave "Andy" Anderson, Charles Avery, Bill Hauber, and Edgar Kennedy) rush out in a disorderly group.

Shot 37: Parlor. The lover sits on top of the trunk as the husband struggles to get out.

Shot 38: Hallway. The wife ends her call to the police and exits to the parlor.

Shot 39: Parlor. The lover hands a gun to the wife and, setting her atop the trunk, exits to the hallway.

Shot 40: Hallway. The lover picks up the phone.

Shot 41: Road. The police attempt to flag down a speeding automobile. The car races past them, knocking them down.

Shot 42: Hallway. The lover puts down the phone, exiting to the parlor.

Shot 43: Puddle. The police stand before a large puddle blocking the road.

Shot 44: Parlor. The lover enters.

Shot 45: Puddle. As they wade through the puddle, the police are knocked into the water by another speeding car.

Shot 46: Road (as in shot 41). A separate group of policemen unsuccessfully attempts to flag down another passing automobile.

Shot 47: Puddle (closer view). The soaked policemen get to their feet and run out of the puddle the way they came.

Shot 48: Parlor. The lover is sitting atop the trunk. The trapped husband manages to lift the lid and stick out his hand, which the lover promptly bites.

Shot 49: Interior trunk. Close-up of the husband lying in the trunk cradling his wounded fingers.

Shot 50: Parlor. The lover remains on top of the trunk.

Shot 51: Road (a different location from shots 41 and 46). The policemen rush down the road. One finds an abandoned bike and rides out of shot.

Shot 52: Parlor: The wife is sitting on the trunk. The lover hears the approaching police and exits.

Shot 53: Exterior house. The lover rushes outside and leads the policemen into the parlor.

Shot 54: Parlor. The police pull the husband from the trunk, much to the embarrassment of the wife, whose adultery is now revealed to all.[iv]

"This half-reel picture is full of rapid-fire situations, which fortunately are easily understood and bring shouts of laughter," *Moving Picture World* noted.[v] Soon the association of comic policemen and rescue climaxes became standard strategy at Keystone: of at least seventeen extant prints ending with a parallel-edited rescue released in 1913, thirteen feature Keystone's roughhouse cops as the would-be rescuers.[vi] The popularization of the cops in 1913 was in this way closely tied to Sennett's introduction of race climaxes. Any attempt to account for the former must, then, include an archeology of the latter as well.

A word, then, on a crucial distinction: a chase vs. a race to the rescue. By the time Keystone arrived on the scene, the chase was an established trope of film comedy, dating back to 1904, when the Biograph Company had released three widely emulated chase comedies in quick succession—*An Escaped Lunatic* (January), *Personal* (June), and *The Lost Child* (October), all directed by Wallace McCutcheon. The format established there was a straightforward one: a character is chased by a group of characters from one location to the next. Each shot presents a single location and is held until first the pursued, then the pursuers exit the frame; only then does the film cut to the next location, where the action repeats. This pattern served as a template for scores of films from 1904 to 1908, by which time, however, it was becoming passé: "Time was when a chase, a fall into water, the upsetting of wagons and pushcarts, the stumbling over sticks and fences, made up a very considerable portion of the funny moving picture," wrote one critic in 1908, looking back on the cycle of chase films that Biograph's innovations had inspired.[vii]

A race to the rescue is a very different entity, whose full fruition depended on the editing innovations that D. W. Griffith began to popularize shortly after his hiring at Biograph in 1908 (the exact moment, in other words, when the simple chase format was falling out of favor). What typifies the style of race-to-the-rescue melodrama developed by Griffith is the use of crosscutting or parallel editing, which refers to the technique of cutting between simultaneous and converging lines of action—most characteristically between characters in peril and their would-be rescuers—according to an alternating a-b-a-b pattern (or a-b-c-a-b-c, etc., depending on how many lines of action are introduced). Formally, the style of race-to-the-rescue melodrama deserves to be thought of less as a simple embellishment of the chase film than as the latter's converse. The chase stretches a *single* line of action over a number of shots; parallel editing uses shots to *multiply* lines of action. The chase treats each shot as a *container* for an action that must be completed before a cut can be made; parallel editing *interrupts* an ongoing action to show what is happening, simultaneously, elsewhere.

But parallel editing also imparts a kind of moral dualism, pitting heroes against villains, villains against their victims, which Griffith exploited as a means of bringing the tenets of Anglo-Saxon moralism to the screen. As Soviet director Sergei Eisenstein showed in his famous critique of Griffith, parallel editing expresses a vision of society "perceived *only as a contrast between the haves and the have-nots*, ... [as] reflected in the consciousness of Griffith no deeper than the image of an intricate race between two parallel lines."[viii] Visualized as what Griffith called the "battle of human ethics common to all consciousness," the parallel-edited rescue thus served Griffith as the vehicle for a social conception aligned with the ideology of America's genteel middle class.[ix] Time and again, in Griffith's films, the "battle of human ethics" centered upon the shattering of the genteel order by an outside intruder, usually a figure marked as socially or racially different. The climactic race to the rescue of Griffith's 1908 *The Fatal Hour*, for example, is precipitated by the violent abduction of two white women by a Chinese villain and his henchman.

Chapter 1: Parody and the Rise of the Cops

Before slapstick became his obsession, Mack Sennett appeared in dramas directed by D. W. Griffith and photographed by G. W. "Billy" Bitzer at Biograph. For The Lonely Villa (1909), Sennett even wrote the scenario, for which he was paid twenty-five dollars. Based on the French play Au Telephone, by André de Lorde, the story concerns a wife and mother (Marion Leonard) who frantically calls for help when her home is invaded by a gang of thieves. The tallest of her children (huddled in the background) is Mary Pickford, in what was only her second film. Sennett also played two roles in this split-reel drama, a butler and—what else?—a policeman. (Note the insignia for American Biograph, AB, painted on the backdrop. This was an early means of preventing another movie company from claiming the film as its own product.)

In Bangville Police (1913), Mabel Normand calls for help when she overhears what she believes are the voices of intruders in the barn on her father's farm.

Responding to the call, the Chief (Fred Mace) revs up the engine of his peculiar-looking police car.

In the end, the mysterious voices turned out to have been two farmhands discussing a newborn calf. Screencaps courtesy of CineMuseum, LLC.

In a similar vein, *The Lonely Villa* (June 1909) exploits parallel editing to arouse identification with a white suburban family whose home has fallen under attack from ear-ringed immigrant burglars.[x] Parallel editing was, in Griffith's hands, a vehicle of a social conception centered upon the conflict between Anglo-Saxon middle-class culture and its would-be assailants, and the device figured prominently in around a quarter of the over four hundred films he went on to direct at Biograph.

Mention of *The Lonely Villa* returns us to Mack Sennett, a Biograph actor at the time, who later claimed authorship of the film's story idea.[xi] It was around this time, in fact, that Sennett struck up what appears to have been a fairly one-sided friendship with Griffith, seizing on the director's habit of taking evening strolls as an opportunity to advance his own ambitions: "When Griffith walked, I walked. I fell in, matched strides, and asked questions. Griffith told me what he was doing and what he hoped to do with the screen, and some of what he said stuck. I thought things over. I began to learn how to make a motion picture." The walks, Sennett admitted, were "my day school, my adult education program, my university" in picture making. But while he admired the expressive value of Griffith's storytelling techniques, he remained skeptical about Griffith's genteel ambitions for the screen. "I did not see these factors in the same terms as Griffith. . . . He saw stories as mass movement suddenly pinpointed and dramatized in human tragedy." In contrast, "What I saw in his great ideas was a new way to show people being funny."[xii]

Sennett also realized that Griffith's techniques could be used to parody the very themes that his tutor took so seriously. As Sennett explained to a journalist in 1916, his "natural tendency to burlesque every serious thing that Griffith did" became the "turning point" of his career.[xiii] That tendency seems first to have expressed itself in Sennett's half-reel comedy *Help! Help!* (April 1912), released while both he and Griffith were still at Biograph. An overt burlesque of *The Lonely Villa*, the film illustrates a fundamental tactic of parody, namely, the comic effect achieved through structural incongruities between an original text and its parodic imitation.[xiv] *Help! Help!* achieves this through a direct, dialectical engagement with *The Lonely Villa*'s parallel-edited format, evoking the Manichean melodrama of Griffith's film only to reveal, in the closing moments, that all is not as it seems: the moral dualism of Griffith's dramatic conception is dissolved in a humorous twist.

The film begins with "Mr. and Mrs. Suburbanite" (as a title puts it) at breakfast in their middle-class suburban home. The wife (Normand) is reading a newspaper report about a spate of local robberies, to which she draws hubby's attention. The husband (Mace) reassures her that all is well and leaves for work. Alone and apprehensive, Mrs. Suburbanite espies two tramps outside her home and, fearful that they are the burglars, locks herself inside her husband's study. The sudden movement of a curtain convinces her that the tramps are jimmying the window, and, in a state of exaggerated terror, she phones her husband for help. What follows is a burlesque race to the rescue in which Sennett cuts between the husband's comic mishaps in his dash homeward and the wife's increasingly absurd displays of fear, even to the point of locking herself inside a trunk.

While both Griffith's original and Sennett's parody thus use parallel editing to dramatize basically similar situations, the structure of *Help! Help!* contains a crucial difference. *The Lonely Villa* had conveyed its drama through a three-pronged editing pattern—cutting between threatened family, intruding burglars, and desperate husband. With the exception of two early shots in which the tramps are seen outside the Suburbanites' home, *Help! Help!* excises the intruders from its structure, focusing on only two narrative trajectories—the wife's panic and the husband's pursuit. This careful transformation sets up the final twist—the discovery, upon the husband's arrival, that there were no burglars after all, just a dog playing behind the curtain. Whereas, in *The Lonely Villa*, the home invasion had been real, the urgent rescue justified, here the invasion is imagined, the rescue a waste of time. As such, Sennett's reworking offers a pointed subversion of the moral terms of Griffith's drama. If *The Lonely Villa* derives its intensity from the struggle to protect the middle-class family,

Help! Help! offers a desacralized vision of suburban paranoia: the "Angel in the House" of sentimental cliché is revealed as a gibbering fool.

It should not have escaped our attention, at this point, that *Help! Help!* and *The Man Next Door* are, structurally, more or less the same film: a misapprehension of danger, a bungling race to the rescue, the embarrassing revelation of foolishness or impropriety—only with the cops substituting for the husband as rescuers in the latter film. But this, in turn, begs the question: is *The Man Next Door* a parody, too? The comedic intent of both certainly seems to be the same: replicate the form of Griffithian race-to-the-rescue melodrama but gut it of its moral and moralizing meanings (in *The Man Next Door*, for example, by turning middle-class domesticity into a site of comic adultery). Certainly, too, the film was produced at a time when Sennett had parody on his mind. Shortly after *The Man Next Door*'s release the studio took the unusual step of announcing burlesque melodrama as company policy. As reported in *Moving Picture World* on March 29, 1913: "Mack Sennett, Fred Mace and the rest of the members of the Keystone company are engaged in putting on a new line of pictures—that is, Sennett says he is producing 'comic melodramas' which is [sic] an entirely new form of art."[xv]

That announcement seems to have been timed to coincide with the March 27 release of *At Twelve O' Clock*, a lost film that directly parodied Griffith's *The Fatal Hour*. Griffith's picture—the first of his films, incidentally, to include a parallel-edited finale—had featured as its central attraction the kind of technological contrivance common to the "sensation scenes" of low-priced stage melodrama. While on the trail of a gang of white slavers, a woman detective is captured and tied in front of a gun rigged to fire when a clock strikes twelve. A race to the rescue ensues, in which she is saved just before the eponymous "fatal hour." It was the contrivance of the timed gun that Sennett borrowed for his film, in which a "big Mexican bruiser" (Mace) ties the erstwhile object of his affections (Normand) to a post, directly in the sights of a revolver.[xvi] But where Griffith's film propelled its narrative trajectory through the precise and irrevocable advance of the clock's deadline, Sennett used the Keystone Cops to subvert this temporal momentum. According to *Moving Picture World*'s summary, the film derived much of its humor by intercutting between the woman's urgent situation and the interminable incompetence of the policemen, who "have all manner of mishaps in reaching the scene."[xvii] This temporal playfulness seems to have culminated, in the film's climactic moments, in a physical symbol of time's inversion: the woman's boyfriend (Sennett) "finally secures a big magnet, which he sticks through the barred window at one minute of twelve, and ... pulls the hands back."[xviii] Time, dramatized by Griffith in its unstoppable forward movement, is, in the Keystone film, rendered comical by its apparent reversibility.

Sennett's former working relation with Griffith shines through in his knack for taking aim at specific titles from his mentor's back catalog, as would be the case in the next Sennett-directed burlesque, A *Life in the Balance* (April 1913), which spoofs the rescue of a toddler from a window's ledge in Griffith's *A Miser's Heart* (November 1911)—and which again provides a notable early appearance of the Cops. As other directors took up the reins at Keystone, however, the target of the studio's parodies became more generalized—less specific Griffith titles than the "idea" of rescue melodrama, with all its clichéd character types and plot formulas. Subsequent entries in this series also saw a return to *Help! Help!*'s device of false danger. A case in point, for example, is the Henry Lehrman–directed *Bangville Police* (April 1913), which adapts the premise of *Help! Help!* to one of the most characteristic tropes of 19th-century sentimental literature, the idealization of rural life as an unspoiled moral economy.[xix] Here, a simple country girl (Normand) overhears a conversation between two farmhands and, believing they intend to rob her, barricades herself inside a farmhouse and calls the police—cueing a distinctly rustic version of the Cops to commence their pursuit. Once again, the mistake is revealed only in the final moments, after the woman has been "rescued." And once again, as in *Help! Help!* and *The Man Next Door*, the joke is at the woman's expense. From the perspective of the film's conclusion, Normand's country maid seems more a dimwitted rube than an embodiment of pastoral innocence. In other films from the cycle, by contrast, the viewer is in on the mistake from the outset, as in the split-reeler *Hide and Seek* (April 1913). In a comic twist on the climax of the stage melodrama *Alias Jimmy Valentine*, office workers mistakenly believe that a child is trapped in a time-locked vault, resulting in a madcap race to the rescue involving firemen and police chief Ford Sterling. Interspersed among images of speeding fire trucks and anxious office workers, director Sennett inserts a series of shots that reveal to the audience what none of the characters know—namely, that the little girl has simply wandered off to a nearby playground. Parallel editing thus establishes an ironic narrative omniscience, deflating the melodrama before it has begun to get off the ground.

"It is our conviction that there never was a single strictly straightforward genre, no single type of direct discourse . . . that did not have its own parodying and travestying double, its own comic-ironic *contre-partie*."[xx] So claims the great Russian theorist of language, Mikhail Bakhtin, whose work on parody can give some conceptual traction to the history we have been tracing. What Bakhtin argues is that any culture is by definition *dialogic*—that culture is shaped by a tension between those forces that would seek to control the meanings of things and make them univocal, trimmed to their own worldview, and a reality that is too plural and messy to admit such limitations. Culture in Bakhtin's view thus becomes a continually waged struggle over the meaning of things, and parody is a significant weapon in that struggle, a way of contesting and changing those meanings. "Parodic-travestying literature," he writes, "introduces the permanent corrective of laughter, of a critique on the one-sided seriousness of the lofty direct word, the corrective of reality that is always richer, more fundamental and most importantly *too contradictory and heteroglot* to be fit into a high and straightforward genre."[xxi]

This model of culture finds one illustration in the American cinema of the period covered in this chapter, when gentrifying forces within the industry worked to repackage what had once been a "cheap amusement" into respectable entertainment that conveyed middle-class values to filmgoers. If those forces fueled the efforts of high-minded filmmakers like D. W. Griffith, who once described his intent to "reform the motion picture industry," they also called into being their own laughing reflection in the form of Mack Sennett and his fellow Keystoners.[xxii]

Four influential directors: (left to right) Thomas Ince, Charles Chaplin, Mack Sennett, and D. W. Griffith, 1914.

As I have argued elsewhere, the Keystone Film Company was, from its inception, a kind of comic double of the burgeoning American film industry's main lines of development in the early 1910s.[xxiii] At a time when supposedly reputable motion picture companies aligned themselves with Anglo-Saxon culture and values, Keystone's founding members were predominantly from working-class or immigrant backgrounds.[xiv] At a time when most studios were rationalizing filmmaking under the Taylorist watchword of "efficiency," Sennett cultivated an image of the Keystone lot as a space of chaotic play. And at a time when filmmakers like Griffith were refining techniques for cinematic storytelling, Keystone subverted those techniques to comic ends. The burlesque melodrama was, in this sense, the most explicit gesture in Keystone's positioning as carnivalesque mirror to an increasingly self-serious film industry.

But this has consequences for how we should interpret the Cops. In his autobiography, Sennett explained at some length his ideas on the comic treatment of the police as symbols of authority: "[P]olicemen are natural foils for comedy. They have dignity, and wherever there is dignity, comics can embroil it, embarrass it, flee from it, and thumb their noses at it. Like me, I imagine, the average citizen is a little afraid of policemen. He enjoys reducing the cops to his own level. I wanted to take a giant step and reduce cops to absurdities."[xxv] But Sennett here underrates his own achievement. What he describes seems to be the kind of archetypal comic effect of, say, the buffoonish baron who falls into a muddy puddle or the society lady who belches—the degree-zero humor whereby our abstract ideals of social authority or dignity get undermined, for our amusement, by intrusions of material reality. But that's not all that gets undermined in the race-to-the-rescue climaxes in which the Cops began to feature in 1913; also at stake, this chapter has suggested, is a system of cinematic signification through which filmmakers like D. W. Griffith sought to turn film into a handmaiden for a genteel worldview. The runaway Cops were, in this sense, the motor force of a satire that was not only *social* but *social-cinematic*.

By the end of 1913, Mack Sennett's policemen were on their way to becoming comic icons. The first use of the phrase "Keystone Cops" in the trade press appears to have been in scare quotes in the title of the 1914 *Motion Picture News* article "Keystone 'Cops' Cause Excitement," which reported on the location shooting of *His Sister's Kids* (December 1913). As the article explained, the filming of that picture had involved the comic cops running down Broadway in downtown Los Angeles, to the confusion of an actual traffic officer on the scene who "mistook a fleeing player for an escaped lunatic."[xxvi] The first reference to the "Keystone Kops" (with the *Kops* spelling) seems to have come a few months later, in an exhibitor's report from Watseka, Illinois: "The Keystone

Kops have become so well known," the report states, that local press were protesting "the action of the city in buying a two-seated automobile for the police department on the ground that, when filled, the rig will look like the comedy moving picture officers."[xxvii] A little later still, the term began its evolution as a derogatory reference to actual police or byword for incompetent law enforcement, which sense it retains to this day. In 1916, the *New York Times* reported that the police guards given to strike-breaking oil workers in Bayonne had been disparagingly nicknamed the "Keystone cops," although their "work in the danger zone was anything but comic."[xxviii] In all these (admittedly sometimes dubious) reports, real cops confuse Keystone Kops for the real thing, or run the risk of looking like Kops, or are insulted as Kops. Sennett's merry band of madcap officers had clearly taken hold of the era's cultural imagination.

This chapter has argued that the Cops' popularization was inseparable from their roles in Keystone's parodies of race-to-the-rescue melodrama. The burlesque melodrama was, inarguably, among the studio's most influential contributions to American film comedy during its first year and it was the platform for the Cops' success. As late as 1916, advertisements were still promoting burlesque melodrama as Mack Sennett's "special formula," proven "to get desired results at all times." "Take one perfectly good dramatic plot," one ad explained, "soak in several gallons of fun and laughter, pour in one villain and mix thoroughly, add one favored sweetheart, and stir the contents until it is completely twisted out of shape into a hilarious tangle of fun and frolic."[xxix] Throw in a clumsy troupe of police officers in chaotic pursuit, too, one should add.

By this time, the institutionalization of the format had, as might be expected, all but annulled its original parodic force, and Sennett's playful mockery of Griffith's Biograph films came to be beside the point. But the Cops and the format remained, having long outstripped their original parodic mark. In this, perhaps, they betray one of parody's seemingly perplexing properties—its capacity to detach from and outlive its target. But this is strange only if parody is thought of as a "merely" parasitic form, not as itself productive. To make one final reference to Bakhtin: what parody in fact does is to release the targeted tropes and conventions from the prison-house of a singular meaning; it snatches those conventions away under cover of laughter and frees them for alternate uses and appropriations. Writing of Roman literary culture, Bakhtin describes how parodic forms "liberated the object from the power of language in which it had become entangled as if in a net; they destroyed the homogenizing power of myth over language; they freed consciousness from the power of the direct word, destroying the thick walls that had imprisoned consciousness within its own discourse, within its own language."[xxx] This is how we should understand Keystone's burlesque melodramas, too: they broke the parallel-edited rescue climax apart from the genteel ethical precepts that Griffith made it serve and found in the device a novel comedic premise that reenergized the old-fashioned chase comedy. Griffith's worldview would soon come to seem outdated, too, of course, but Mack Sennett's Cops just kept on running.

This chapter reworks parts of my 2009 book *The Fun Factory: The Keystone Film Company and the Emergence of Mass Culture*. I am grateful to the University of California Press for permission to do so.

Sources:

i Mack Sennett, with Cameron Shipp, *King of Comedy* (San Jose: toExcel, 2000 [1954]), 65, 53.

ii Brent E. Walker, *Mack Sennett's Fun Factory: A History and Filmography of His Studio and His Keystone and Mack Sennett Comedies, with Biographies of Players and Personnel* (Jefferson, NC: McFarland & Co., 2010), 22.

iii Advertisement for the Keystone Film Company, *Moving Picture World*, September 21, 1912, 1140; Walker, *Mack Sennett's Fun Factory*, 270 (emphasis added).

iv Shot numbers refer to the Library of Congress's incomplete 35mm print (missing the opening).

v "Comments on the Films," *Moving Picture World*, March 22, 1913, 1222.

vi The films are *The Man Next Door* (March), *Hide and Seek, A Life in the Balance, Bangville Police* (all April), *Mabel's Awful Mistake, A Little Hero* (all May), *Barney Oldfield's Race for a Life* (June), *Love and Rubbish, A Noise from the Deep* (all July), *The Riot, Mabel's New Hero* (all August), *A Healthy Neighborhood, Two Old Tars* (all October), *A Muddy Romance, Cohen Saves the Flag* (all November), *The Gusher*, and *His Sister's Kids* (all December). Of these, *Hide and Seek, A Little Hero, A Healthy Neighborhood*, and *Cohen Saves the Flag* do not feature policemen as the rescuers: *A Little Hero* is a novelty film with an animal cast, while *Hide and Seek, A Healthy Neighborhood*, and *Cohen Saves the Flag* feature firemen, doctors, and soldiers as the respective rescuing groups.

vii W. Stephen Bush, "The Place and Province of Humor in the Moving Picture," *Moving Picture World*, November 28, 1908, 420.

viii Sergei Eisenstein, *Film Form*, ed. and trans. Jay Leyda (San Diego: Harcourt Brace Jovanovich, 1942), 234.

ix Griffith quoted in Lary May, *Screening out the Past: The Birth of Mass Culture and the Motion Picture Industry* (Chicago: University of Chicago Press, 1983), 77.

x Most notorious of all is the parallel-edited climax to Griffith's blockbuster twelve-reel *Birth of a Nation* (1915), in which the "heroic" Ku Klux Klan ride to rescue a white woman from the clutches of a mixed-race villain.

xi Sennett, *King of Comedy*, 60. According to his autobiography, Sennett regularly submitted story ideas at Biograph to supplement his five-dollar-a-day actor's salary.

xii Ibid., 51-52, 54-55.

xiii "Sennett Has Big Army at Laugh Factory," *The Triangle*, March 11, 1916, 3.

xiv See Margaret A. Rose, *Parody/Meta-Fiction: An Analysis of Parody as a Critical Mirror to the Writing and Reception of Fiction* (London: Croom Helm, 1979), 25-26.

xv "Doings at Los Angeles," *Moving Picture World*, March 29, 1913, 1323.

xvi "Comments on the Films," *Moving Picture World*, April 5, 1913, 49.

xvii "Independent Film Stories," *Moving Picture World*, March 29, 1913, 1364.

xviii Ibid. A fuller discussion of *The Fatal Hour* in relation to Griffith's use of parallel editing is offered in Gunning, *D. W. Griffith and the Origins of American Narrative Film: The Early Years at Biograph* (Urbana, Ill.: University of Illinois Press, 1993), 95–106.

xix See Ann Douglas, *The Feminization of American Culture* (New York: Knopf, 1977), esp. chapter 4.

xx Mikhail Bakthin, "From the Prehistory of Novelistic Discourse," in *The Dialogic Imagination: Four Essays*, trans. Caryl Amerson and Michael Holquist (Austin: University of Texas Press, 1981), 53.

xxi *Ibid.*, 55.

xxii D. W. Griffith, "Unfinished Autobiography" (MS, Museum of Modern Art, New York), quoted in May, *Screening out the Past*, 71.

xxiii See my *The Fun Factory: The Keystone Film Company and the Emergence of Mass Culture* (Berkeley: University of California Press, 2009), chapter 1.

xxiv Vitagraph, for instance, seems to have hired predominantly white, middle-class employees and was described in a late article as "the only one of the original motion picture companies that was founded entirely by Anglo-Saxons." William Basil Courtney, "History of Vitagraph," *Motion Picture News*, February 7, 1925, 342, quoted in Siobhan B. Somerville, "The Queer Career of Jim Crow: Racial and Sexual Transformation in *A Florida Enchantment*," in Jennifer M. Bean and Diane Negra, eds., *A Feminist Reader in Early Cinema* (Durham, NC: Duke University Press, 2002), 258.

xxv Sennett, *King of Comedy*, 53.

xxvi "Keystone 'Cops' Cause Excitement," *Motion Picture News*, January 3, 1914, 24.

xxvii "Exhibitors News," *Moving Picture World*, July 11, 1914, 293.

xxviii "American Workers Break Oil Strike," *New York Times*, October 20, 1916, 7.

xxix Advertisement for the Keystone Film Company, *Motion Picture News*, June 17, 1916, 3704–3705.

xxx Bakhtin, "From the Prehistory of Novelistic Discourse," 60.

ROB KING is a professor at Columbia University's School of Arts and author of the award-winning book *The Fun Factory: The Keystone Film Company and the Emergence of Mass Culture* (University of California Press, 2009). His most recent tome is 2017's *Hokum!: The Early Sound Slapstick Short and Depression-Era Mass Culture*, also published by the University of California Press.

Chapter 2
Keystone in 1913:
Slapstick and the Art of Ensemble Acting
By Mark Pruett

Were early Keystone comedies—madcap Cops and all—artful? Did they demonstrate technical facility, show an attention to detail, reveal an eye for composition? Is it even possible to ask these questions with a straight face, or should we simply apologize, as many have done, for having thought the Keystones worthy of a second look?

When we talk about the art of filmmaking in the early years of the last century, we must acknowledge that few people living then thought movies had anything to do with art at all. But they did watch an awful lot of movies. It wasn't unusual, when storefront theaters were rotating programs of one- and two-reel westerns, dramas, and comedies throughout the day, for regular patrons to take in a dozen films in a week's time. If you were making the rounds of your neighborhood cinemas in the waning years of the nickelodeon era, you were likely seeing Keystone productions. But you weren't watching them in a vacuum. For the storefront exhibitor, variety was the key to successful programming. What else might you have seen, and how would the Keystones have compared?

Let's drop in on two short films that were showing in the summer of 1913, the first a drama from Biograph, the second a comedy from Keystone.

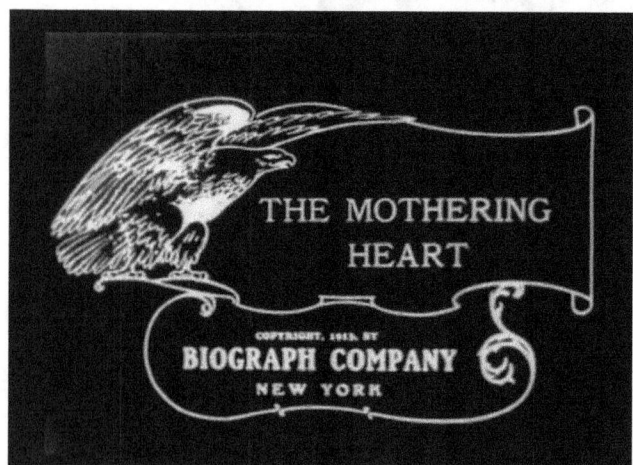

D. W. Griffith had already directed hundreds of films for Biograph, and the opening minutes of *The Mothering Heart* gave no hint that something extraordinary was about to occur onscreen. Those who caught the beginning of the two-reel drama recognized its principal characters immediately. The patient, loving wife, the straying husband, the other woman—all were conventional figures in popular fiction and the movies. If the actors were convincing, audiences were prepared to respond with sympathy or disapproval as they saw fit. They were not prepared to be moved to tears by a tree.

Well, not exactly by a tree, but by the vision, wholly in their minds, of what that tree concealed. The character played by Lillian Gish, married and with child, discovers a single white glove in her husband's coat. The possibility that her husband is involved with another woman bewilders her. She tries to laugh it off but is soon overcome by doubt, and her expression turns grave. When her husband leaves the house on some pretext, she follows him out to the front yard, taking refuge behind the trunk of a large tree. All we can see of her are the fingers of her left hand, her fluttering scarf, and, when she leans around the tree to take stock of the situation, her face, now empty of expression. We watch with her as the husband hurries to a waiting taxi, where he is welcomed by the stylish gold digger who, in an earlier scene, had made eyes at him as he sat with Lillian in a bustling cabaret. As the taxi pulls away, the camera returns to the tree and to Lillian's impassive face.

Then something magical happens. Lillian moves back behind the tree so that, once again, our view of her is restricted to her resting fingertips and the trailing scarf. The trunk of the tree fills the screen, and the camera continues to gaze at it. Two, three, four long seconds of nothing—but that nothing produces, as Griffith knew it would, a flood of emotion. He achieves this, astonishingly, by leaving out the very thing audiences had come to expect of wronged wives on the screen: visible "emoting," or passion writ large, replete with theatrical gestures and appeals to heaven. Gish's sensitive portrayal of the young wife during the film's first reel has made the emotional aftershock of her husband's betrayal—now proved beyond doubt—unnecessary to dramatize. We know her so well that the tree can show us nothing and yet tell us everything about the depth of her anguish.

If *The Mothering Heart* has moved us with its daring and innovative camerawork, it has done so despite our relative ignorance of film technique. Nevertheless, the experience may have convinced us that subtlety and sophistication are no longer the exclusive province of the fine arts. We leave the theater with a renewed confidence in the burgeoning artistry of the moving picture. And it is with this confidence that we look in on our second short film from the summer of 1913.

Mabel's New Hero, directed by Mack Sennett at Keystone, is less than half the length of the Griffith film and unreels at a brisker pace. At the midpoint, Roscoe "Fatty" Arbuckle and Mabel Normand go to the beach, where Fatty gets into a fight with a masher who has taken liberties with his girl. Fatty throws a wriggling fish at the masher but hits a Keystone Cop, who falls down. The Cop tries to intervene to stop the fight but takes a blind punch and falls down again. Later, when Mabel becomes stranded in a hot-air balloon, Fatty telephones the police in a panic. A Cop on foot tries to flag down a passing auto and is knocked down. He races back to join four other Cops and, like a bowling ball striking tenpins, knocks down all four of them—and himself. Three Cops run onto the road; a car passes, knocking down all three. When another car passes in the opposite direction, five Cops go down. The entire force eventually joins Fatty to aid in rescuing Mabel, still suspended in a basket high above ground. Five Cops pull on the drop line in a tug-of-war with the balloon, and all five fall down at once. They try again—and again they fall down.

Before the Cops show up, it is generally Fatty who falls down (or who causes others to fall). We see Fatty fall onto his back, feet in the air, when he collapses a table in Mabel's parlor. At the beach, he trips upon entering the bathhouse and falls headlong through the doorway. Getting up, he loses his balance and takes a pratfall in the same spot, to Mabel's embarrassment. Leaving the bathhouse minutes later, he knocks down a dandy who is jeering at his striped bathing costume—and again falls down in the doorway. On the beach with Mabel, he loses his balance and topples backwards onto the sand. Minutes later, two of Mabel's friends, one of whom has just knocked down the masher, discover Fatty buried in the sand where they are sitting. Fatty leaps to his feet and instantly pitches forward onto his face. He takes another fall during his subsequent fight with the masher. And when Mabel, appealing for help, is joined on the sand by six concerned bystanders, all but Mabel are knocked down when Fatty is flung backwards into them. Fatty falls down too. During the balloon sequence that follows, he falls down again—twice.

Arbuckle's ten falls are elegant, even spectacular, compared with those of the Cops. But of the approximately forty-four falls that occur in *Mabel's New Hero*, the Cops accumulate twenty-six in the final four minutes. While making a mess of Mabel's rescue, they also wreak havoc on the film's storyline, which all but evaporates as we watch them hurtle from one place to the next, stagger, collide, fall down—and do it again.

Are we disappointed by what we have seen? Convinced that Sennett has made a mockery of the art so meticulously practiced by Griffith? Not a bit. In 1913 we would likely have pronounced both of these films rousing successes, the drama deeply affecting and the comedy riotously funny. We would not have known what we know today—that the Griffith film pointed to the future of cinema while the Sennett film did not.

This is not to denigrate the Keystone comedy in any way. Griffith's Victorian sensibility, certainly, was old hat even in 1913, but his skill at delineating character—at probing subtle gradations of feeling though a succession of images—was ahead of its time. Sennett, on the other hand, busy managing an efficient but closed system of interchangeable Cops and minimally motivated chases, collisions, and falls, was about to experience the unexpected cataclysm that was Charlie Chaplin.

Chaplin arrived at Keystone knowing next to nothing about filmmaking. By the time he moved to Essanay at the end of 1914, he had become the most celebrated—and bankable—performer on the studio's roster. Sennett, who had once doubted his own wisdom in hiring the intractable actor, claimed that he offered to split his one-third ownership of Keystone with Chaplin if he would stay on the lot. But money was not the only prize Chaplin was after. He wanted a more leisurely production schedule, one that would allow him time to devise situations in which the Tramp's quirks and foibles could be revealed naturally. As David Robinson has written, Keystone's comedy was imposed upon its characters, who remained at a distance from the audience. Chaplin's comedy emerged from a recognizable, all-too-human personality, which established an immediate kinship with the audience.

Chaplin's popularity surged following his appearance in the feature-length *Tillie's Punctured Romance*, released in November 1914, less than two months before his departure from Keystone. That he represented a potential gold mine had been clear to Sennett as early as August, when, despite the expense, the producer added a second two-reel comedy to Keystone's monthly release schedule (with one-reelers still being issued every Monday, Wednesday, and Saturday). Chaplin's exit was a blow, but Sennett had already survived the loss of Ford Sterling and would invest his confidence in many other engaging performers, including Ben Turpin. More critical than shifting personnel was the changing landscape of comedy itself. At Keystone, the business of slapstick no longer looked like business as usual.

Chaplin had upped the ante. It was around this time, Rob King has shown, that the construction of Keystone's plots began to attract the favorable notice of reviewers. The move toward a more carefully paced zaniness, King points out, was largely born of necessity: the two-reel comedy, soon to be standard at the studio, demanded more elaborate scaffolding and greater attention to the integration of gags.

But the reviewers' approving nods came at a price. Among those who promoted moving pictures for a living, the new interest in "character comedy" was often linked to a perceived backlash against slapstick. An ad for George Kleine's *The Fixer* (1915) in *Moving Picture World* insisted that its comedy contained no hint of "vulgarity or slapstick." The same promise was made in *Motion Picture News* on behalf of two chimp comedies, *Napoleon the Great* and *Sally*, the Fox comedies *Social Pirates* and *Chased Into Love*, and the Kleine-Edison series *The Mishaps of Musty Suffer* (all 1916). Mutual's Strand Comedies, like *Kleptomaniacs* (1917), were publicized in *Moving Picture World* as "polite" comedies that were "free from slapstick and vulgarity." *Exhibitor's Trade Review* used nearly identical language to describe the Hunt Stromberg comedy *The Foolish Age* (1921). And the *Exhibitors Herald* ad for *Number, Please?* (1920), featuring Harold Lloyd, was careful to distance the film's star—who had worked briefly for Sennett in 1915—from any association with "vulgarity" and "crude slapstick."

Slapstick did not go away, despite the best efforts of its detractors. Its value as entertainment was challenged repeatedly, however, as widespread appeals for refinement and good taste settled like a fog over the motion picture industry. Chaplin himself was routinely chided for coarseness during the silent era, and as late as 1950 the Catholic Film Institute's journal *Focus* was still finding fault with the "vulgarity" in *City Lights* (1931). But the cheerful reception given 1939's *Hollywood Cavalcade*, with its reenacted Keystone Cops sequences, showed that public disapproval of slapstick, if it had ever existed in fact, had long since given way to nostalgic indulgence. Reenactments, of course, whether of chaotic chases, tossed pies, or cavorting beauties, may simulate the tumult of the originals but miss their spirit entirely. To grasp the peculiar art that evolved at the Keystone studio, we must return to its pre-Chaplin days.

Of the many myths that cling to Keystone's early history, the most persistent is that the Sennett crew simply made things up as they went along. We are forced to acknowledge the kernel of truth in this myth whenever we watch the Cops careen and collide in scenes of clearly improvised mayhem, like those in *Mabel's New Hero*. But mayhem is seldom all there is to a Keystone Cops comedy. The Cops' impromptu buffoonery is often set against quieter scenes that have been carefully constructed to advance the story or to reveal character.

Such scenes depict a style of ensemble acting that, to modern eyes, seems quaint and stage-bound. The coming star system, with its single-minded focus on distinctive personalities, would do away with this unique brand of group performance in short order. But the glimpses we have of it in early Keystones reveal a lovely melding of form and function. In the Cop comedies, it serves as a counterweight to pandemonium.

In *Bangville Police* (1913), directed by Henry "Pathé" Lehrman, the ensemble scene occurs near the end. The buildup consists of expert crosscutting between Mabel Normand (as a damsel in distress) and the Cops who cannot come to her aid because they keep getting in their own way. As the daughter of farmer Nick Cogley, Mabel believes that the two men she has discovered in her barn are burglars. Frightened, she takes refuge in the house and telephones Fred Mace, the sheriff of Bangville. From the moment Mace takes the call—from bed, where he alerts his men by firing four shots into the ceiling—the film's scenes alternate between the agitated Mabel and the hopelessly disorganized police force. The Cops—Mace, Charles Avery, Rube Miller, and Edgar Kennedy—race back and forth in a kind of panic, brandishing not only guns and handcuffs but a pitchfork, a shovel, and a baseball bat. Mace and Avery set off in a dilapidated police vehicle while the other Cops attempt to reach the farm on foot. Thanks to a series of violent collisions and falls—and one explosion—it takes them the remainder of the film to get there.

When they arrive, Sheriff Mace leaves his deputies at the barn and approaches the front porch of the house with Avery in tow. Both are petrified that they might encounter actual burglars. By now, Mabel has been joined by her father Nick Cogley and her mother Dot Farley. Hearing noises outside, Cogley opens the door to confront the intruders, his pistol at the ready. There is mutual shock and surprise as the Sheriff and Cogley recognize each other. As they are recovering, Mabel steps between them, pointing in the direction of the barn, and holds up two fingers (a gesture that Cogley and Avery repeat). The Sheriff, finally comprehending, puts one finger to his lips (with Avery following suit) and sets off for the barn.

The brief scene on the porch is beautifully composed, showing us all five players at once in character-defining poses. Starting at the doorway on our left, we see Mabel, her hand on Cogley's back; Dot Farley, her face visible between Mabel and Cogley; Cogley and Sheriff Mace facing each other on the same horizontal plane; and short Charles Avery crouched low beside Sheriff Mace. Our eye is led in an arc from top left to bottom right.

Next, Mabel moves between Cogley and Mace, joining the horizontal arrangement. We very briefly see Dot's eyes dart toward the camera from behind Cogley's hat. She is making sure that the camera can still see her. Effort

was made, in other words, to keep all players visible within the crowded frame.

Though the scene provides relief from the preceding ruckus, it is in no sense a tableau. There is movement within the frame, in particular a choreographed rearranging of performers that leads the eye naturally from one to the next. No actor becomes wallpaper; all are performing throughout the scene. The horizontal arrangement is not an instance of stage-bound cinema but a deliberate attempt to engage many actors at once in a moment of needed exposition. (In contrast, virtually all of the action scenes in *Bangville Police* show Lehrman's adroitness at using depth within the frame, with sets angling offscreen and performers approaching the camera or receding into the distance.) The scene on the porch is a fleeting moment of calm before the final storm of exasperation, when the ragtag police force—with the Sheriff in front, now bursting with self-importance—discovers that the barn harbors no evildoers but merely Mabel's hoped-for newborn calf.

Group performances—all players acting at once and in concert—are easy to distinguish from mere clusters of individuals. In *Barney Oldfield's Race for a Life* (1913), five "villagers" appear out of nowhere to encourage Mack Sennett's suit for Mabel. They are merely back-slapping supporters, without identity or backstory. In this they resemble the six anonymous bystanders who respond to Mabel's calls for help during the beach sequence of *Mabel's New Hero*.

We witness ensemble acting at its 1913 peak in *Fatty Joins the Force*, directed by George Nichols. Nichols himself plays the police commissioner who puts Fatty in uniform after learning that he has saved the commissioner's little daughter from drowning. (We know, though the commissioner doesn't, that Fatty's girlfriend had to push him into the lake to effect the rescue.) Nichols comes down from his front porch when he sees Minta Durfee, the nursemaid, carrying the child into the front yard. She is accompanied by a drenched Fatty, Fatty's girl Dot Farley, and jealous Cop Edgar Kennedy, who glowers at Fatty from the rear of the group as Minta describes the rescue to the commissioner.

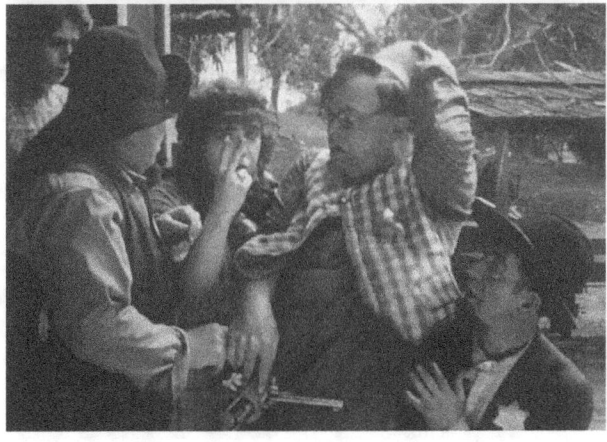

The scene that transpires is an exceedingly skillful demonstration of group pantomime. Ranged horizontally across the frame, Fatty, Dot, Minta, and Nichols remain fully visible to the audience, making it possible for soundless dialogue to be easily understood: "She fell in the water and this man saw her. He dove in the water, pulled her out, and saved her!" As it happens, the actors' expressions are so revealing and their gestures so precise that dialogue is unnecessary. With the exception of the passive child, all of the players are performing at every moment. Minta tells what happened at the lake, using extravagant gestures to dramatize the rescue, while Nichols leans back, awestruck. Fatty, at first uncomfortable in the presence of the commissioner, now puts his thumbs in his suspenders and assumes a goofy smirk, puffing out his chest as he listens to Minta's flattering—and inaccurate—account. When Nichols, incredulous, looks Fatty up and down, Dot affirms the truth of the nursemaid's story, causing the commissioner to throw out his hand. Initially flummoxed, Fatty finally clasps it in an exaggeratedly manly way—man to man!—while Dot beams and

Edgar Kennedy scowls. When Dot points at Kennedy's uniform and then at Fatty, the commissioner slaps Fatty on the chest (Fatty recoils) and offers him a position on the force. Grinning like a kid who has been promised a candy apple, Fatty wrings his hand—gleefully this time—and, arm in arm with Dot, follows the commissioner and the still-fuming Kennedy offscreen.

This is ensemble playing at its most disciplined. Though Arbuckle is posed at the edge of the group, he is central to the scene's comic business, as he is to the film as a whole. But as the scene is conceived, all of the actors perform simultaneously, their individual turns meshing like gears. Upstaging—stealing the thunder of another actor by diverting attention to oneself—has no meaning in such a setting. Every player's bit is essential for Arbuckle's performance to have its comic effect.

Unlike the ensemble scene in *Bangville Police*, this scene takes place near the beginning of the film. Yet it provides a similar counterbalance to the tumultuous Cop chases and pratfalls to come. More important, it artfully assembles the house of cards that will come tumbling down on Fatty at the picture's end, when, exposed and humiliated for having disgraced his uniform, he is cast into jail while his fickle girl flirts openly with the chief of police.

A number of Sennett's performers, including Ford Sterling and Charlie Murray, had circus backgrounds—ideal training for the job of Keystone Cop. Those with vaudeville experience were as knowledgeable about stagecraft as about clowning, and nowhere did that knowledge serve them better than in the superlative ensemble pantomimes of early Keystone comedies. Despite their antique flavor today, these ensemble performances were modest works of art, constructed for efficiency—a means of propelling events that were already moving at breakneck speed. How lucky we are, more than a century after these films unspooled for a nickel, to be able to gather a few friends, turn down the lights, and join in the laughter again.

Mark Pruett has written about Ford Sterling, Baby Peggy, and Maurice Tourneur for *The Silent Film Quarterly*. His appreciation of Chaplin's *The Vagabond*

Screencaps from Fatty Joins the Force *(1913) are courtesy of* The Forgotten Films of Roscoe "Fatty" Arbuckle *DVD set, © 2005 Laughsmith Entertainment, Inc./Mackinac Media, Inc.*

is online at www.silentsaregolden.com. "Extras," a short story set during the heyday of Hollywood movie serials, appeared in *Thuglit*, issue #8. *Dead Wax*, a novel, has nothing to do with the movies, but it should definitely be turned into one. Keep bidding.

Chapter 3
Lost and (Partially) Found: *In the Clutches of a Gang*
By Lon Davis

There are a number of iconic images from silent comedies: Harold Lloyd hanging from the hands of a huge clock, high above Los Angeles... Charlie Chaplin shuffling down a lonely country road... Buster Keaton being chased through the streets of Los Angeles by an entire police force.

Few images, however, have been published as frequently as the one featuring the Keystone Cops from *In the Clutches of a Gang* (1914). You know the one I mean: the cross-eyed Chief Teheezel (Ford Sterling) sits at his desk, listening intently on the receiver of his candlestick telephone. Observing him with rapt attention is a lineup of sorry-looking men in uniform. I first saw this photo when I was in the fourth grade, on page forty-three of Daniel C. Blum's *A Pictorial History of the Silent Screen*.

In the Clutches of a Gang, a two-reeler, was completed for the Keystone Film Company in December 1913 and released on January 17, 1914. It was produced by Mack Sennett, directed by George Nichols (who also essayed the role of The Detective), Virginia Kirtley was The Girl, and the Cops (listed alphabetically here, but unbilled in the film) were

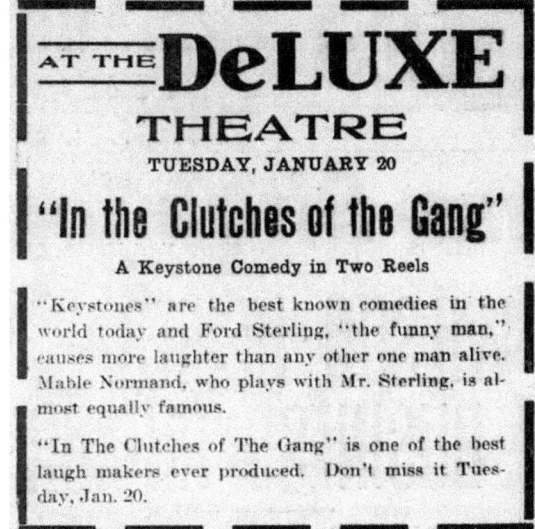

Roscoe "Fatty" Arbuckle, Robert (Marvin) Cox, Bobby Dunn, George Jeske, Edgar Kennedy, Hank Mann, Rube Miller, and Al St. John. But *where* is the actual film? Since its original release, more than a century ago, it has been considered one of the estimated thousands of silent films lost to time and nitrate decomposition.

For whatever reason, I have always wondered if one day a print of this film might turn up. A ray of hope came when I was reading *World of Laughter: The Motion Picture Comedy Short, 1910-1930* (University of Oklahoma, 1966) by Kalton C. Lahue. On page seventy-four, he wrote that *In the Clutches of a Gang* "to this day remains the funniest comedy ever to feature the Keystone Cops." Based on that one sentence, I figured the film must exist *somewhere*. Why else would Mr. Lahue imply that he had first-hand knowledge of it?

As the decades flew by, I would occasionally ask a fellow film geek if he knew if that particular short was among the lucky survivors of the Keystone oeuvre. My late friend Cole Johnson, the owner of *Slapstick!* Archive, had a logical response to my query: "If it was still around, wouldn't it be available on video?" Alas, it was not.

Fast forward another decade or so. The internet had invaded virtually every home in America. Suddenly, obscure information (some of it even true) could be quickly accessed on the Internet Movie Database (more commonly known by its acronym, IMDb). Included in the entry under *In the Clutches of the* (sic) *Gang* was the highly questionable claim that the film was "the eighth of the twelve movies that starred the Keystone Cops." (As Lea Stans makes clear in her chapter on the myths surrounding the Cops, they neither starred in a film, nor did their names appear in the opening credits.) The Cops' primary purpose was to show up at the end of the film and manage *not* to save the day.

Now virtually forgotten, *In the Clutches of a Gang* was something of a blockbuster upon its initial release. A contemporary review from the *Moving Picture World* (January 14, 1914) enthused:

> Another of those thoroughly enjoyable burlesque pictures, in which nothing occurs that is to be taken seriously. Ford Sterling as Chief Teheezel has more than the usual amount of trouble. The arrest of the mayor and the scenes on the raft are highly amusing. A very successful nonsense offering.

And then, this truly remarkable tidbit, listed under the heading "Trivia":

> A fragment of this long-missing film was discovered in the New Zealand Film Archive in 2011; it had been donated in 1989 following the death of local film projectionist and collector Jack Murtagh.

Now I was even more determined to see "the funniest comedy ever to feature the Keystone Cops." It took a few years before I found the time to take a break from my day job as a book editor, but I finally made the trip from my current home in Portland, Oregon, to Los Angeles, California, in August 2019. I had made special arrangements to view the 35mm fragment at the Academy of Motion Picture Arts and Sciences, located at 1313 Vine Street in Hollywood. This rare opportunity was made possible by the Academy's public access coordinator, a delightful young lady named Edda Manriquez. She welcomed me into the spacious, modern lobby, one entire wall of which was decorated with a vintage advertisement for *Little Annie Rooney* (1925), a William Beaudine–directed feature starring Mary Pickford. How appropriate, given that America's Sweetheart was one of the original founders of the Academy in 1927.

Edda led me to a room equipped with what is known as a KEM 16mm and 35mm flatbed (please see accompanying photograph). Already threaded up was the answer print made from the original 35mm preservation print of the approximately five-minute film. What struck me immediately was that several of the surviving shots featured the exact lineup from that famous still, only the formerly still figures were moving animatedly, standing, saluting, raising their truncheons in unison, and performing other bits of business. Ford Sterling, Keystone's leading comedian before the arrival of Charlie Chaplin, was clearly the film's star (after all, his is the only character sporting an actual moniker, as opposed to The Detective, or The Girl.) Sterling, known at that point in his career for his exaggerated mugging, simply outdid (and perhaps overdid) his well-rehearsed schtick. The one genuinely funny bit occurs when he is alone in the station, pacing frantically with his hands behind his back. Just then he makes a jerky sort of leap in the air, his legs splayed exaggeratedly in opposite directions. I actually laughed out loud when I saw it.

According to James L. Neibaur's fine book *Chaplin at Essanay* (McFarland & Co., 2008), in 1918, Charles Chaplin signed a lucrative contract with First National after having created what many consider his greatest work—twelve brilliant two-reelers for the Mutual Film Corporation. Meanwhile, one of his former workplaces, the Essanay

Film Manufacturing Company, which had lured him away from Keystone in late 1914, decided to exploit Chaplin's meteoric box-office appeal by editing together some snippets from his Essanay films *Work* (1915) and *Police* (1916), along with some unused footage of a Dickensian flophouse scene he wrote and directed for an uncompleted film with the working title "Life." This incomprehensible mishmash was meaninglessly dubbed *Triple Trouble* and included newly shot

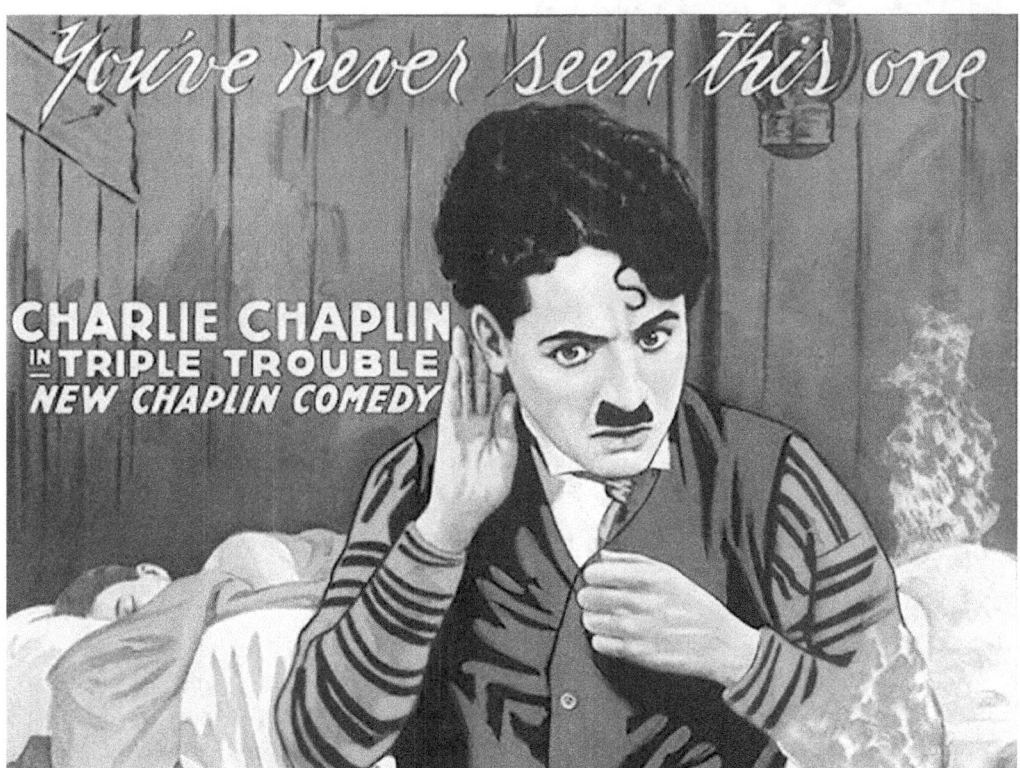

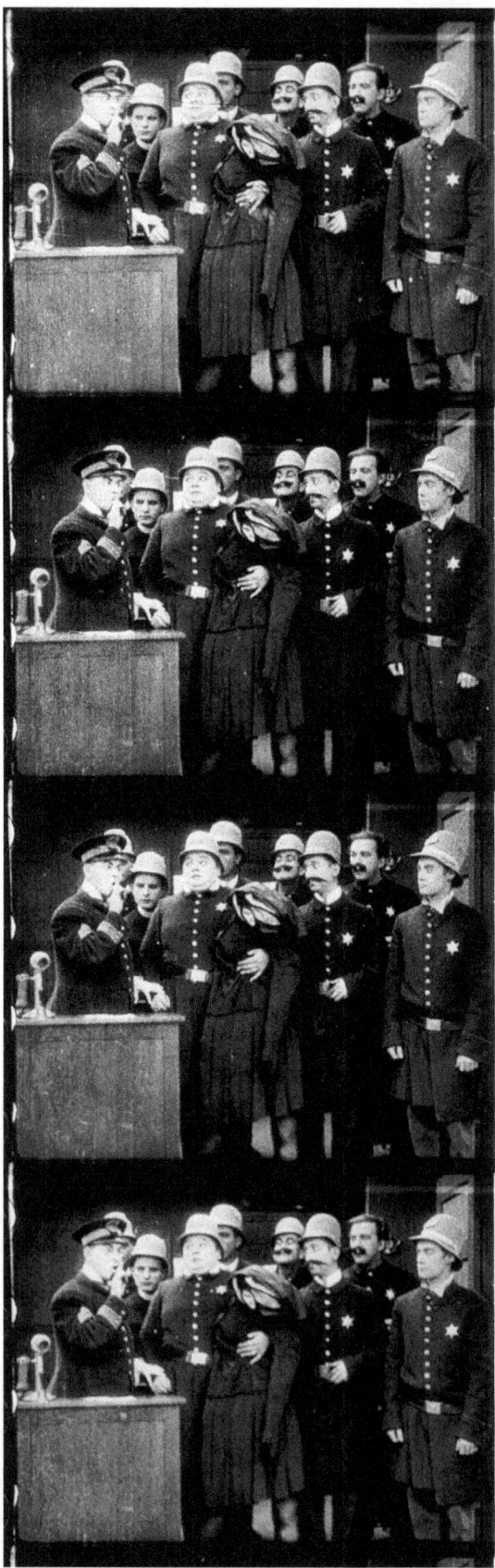

scenes directed by Leo White. Some fly-by-night producer decided to do the same thing with one of Chaplin's 1914 single-reel Keystones, *The New Janitor*. Combining it with scenes from random Keystone comedies, this 1917 three-reel "comedy sensation of the season" bore the title, *Charley* (sic), *the Gang Leader*. The misspelling of his first name may well have been this low-rent company's attempt to avoid copyright infringement.

Film preservation is indeed vital, but in the case of *Charley, the Gang Leader*, the absence of the majority of this revised contrivance may not be such a tragedy after all. The film haphazardly combines scenes not only from *The New Janitor*, but *In the Clutches of a Gang* and *Fatty and Mabel Adrift* (1916). Although all three films were shot by the same company within a two-year period, there is a marked difference in the prints used; the scenes from *The New Janitor* and *Fatty and Mabel Adrift*, in fact, are battered looking and somewhat out of focus, while the footage from *In the Clutches of a Gang* is much cleaner. Worst of all is the utter lack of continuity. Scenes shift in a way that can only be described as jarring. A few examples: the Cops are at the station, looking deeply concerned about their potential case; just as suddenly, interspersed is some grainy footage of the Cops battling the ocean waves in a

The Cops stand in a different order than that of the famed photograph. Film strip courtesy of The Academy of Motion Picture Arts and Sciences.

rowboat. Cut back to the station and the Cops are not the least bit damp from their oceanic voyage; they also look every bit as worried as they had been only a moment before. From there, we see a few more seconds of Charlie (or Charley, as the ads insist his name be spelled), and then right back to the station with Sterling, doing his pacing bit or mugging exaggeratedly, either on the phone or in the confines of a dark closet.

And just like that, the film ends, or more accurately, runs out.

My viewing companion and I sat silent for a moment after the monitor went black. Looking for something positive to say, Edda pointed to the still I had featuring the police lineup and said of Roscoe Arbuckle, "That guy has a great face for comedy!" There was no denying *that* observation.

The sole purpose of re-running the film was to pick out an image that could be used for inclusion in this chapter. Fortunately, Edda has experience as a director of short films and therefore has a good eye as to what the best composition of the shot should be. It is that sequence of frame enlargements which are used to illustrate the look and feel of the actual film. Unfortunately, the favored scenes of the critic from *Moving Picture World*, involving the mayor's arrest and some undoubtedly frantic activity on a raft, have apparently disappeared forever.

The entire experience was over all too soon, but it is one I shall never forget. I mean, how often do you receive an invitation from the historic Academy to view a film you've had on your bucket list for more than half a century?

Lon Davis sits expectantly at the KEM 16mm and 35mm flatbed at the Academy of Motion Picture Arts and Sciences in Hollywood, in August 2019. Photo by Edda Manriquez.

Chapter 4.
Fate and a Flea Market:
How a Fortuitous Find Rewrote Keystone Cops History
By Paul E. Gierucki and Chris Seguin

There was something about the otherwise unremarkable trunk that caught Paul E. Gierucki's attention. Screencap from The Property Man (1914), *Lobster Films for the Chaplin Keystone Project.*

In the annals of silent film research, certain long-lost "Holy Grail" titles are referenced constantly—Laurel & Hardy's *Hats Off*, Lon Chaney's *London After Midnight*, Theda Bara's *Cleopatra*, and the forty-two-reel version of Erich von Stroheim's *Greed*. The search for these titles is relentless—and, to date, fruitless.

However, fate occasionally smiles and it puts the right person in the right place at the right time. One who discovers the holiest of all grails—a heretofore unknown film appearance by one of the greatest and most famous artists of the silent screen, Charles Chaplin.

In this case, the right person was producer, director, historian, and preservationist Paul E. Gierucki. (Gierucki is the former president of Laughsmith Entertainment and the co-founder of CineMuseum, LLC.) The right place was a traveling antiques show in the suburbs just outside of Detroit, Michigan. The right time was just another Saturday.

The film itself was *A Thief Catcher* (1914), the only existing proof that Charlie Chaplin was once indeed a Keystone Cop. Who knew? It was a remarkable find—and its chance discovery is an even more remarkable story. But let's allow Paul himself to tell us about it, in conversation with fellow film buff Chris Seguin.

Chris: Paul, you wrote, produced, and directed an award-winning primetime television documentary (*Stooges: The Men Behind the Mayhem*) for A&E, restored over three hundred classic comedies, contributed to fifty-odd film history books and dozens of documentaries, produced several of the highest rated home video collections of the last two decades (*The Forgotten Films of Roscoe "Fatty" Arbuckle, Industrial Strength Keaton, The Mack Sennett Collection, Vol. I, The Round Up*), saved the Educational Pictures sound short-subject library from destruction, recovered large collections of rare Hollywood memorabilia, and worked alongside several icons of the classic film community. You are a literal giant in your field [Gierucki is six-five] but are perhaps best known for rediscovering seven short minutes of film. So, how did it feel to rewrite the history of the world's greatest comedian?

Paul: Humbling, Chris. Deeply humbling. I have been fortunate to recover several interesting and notable titles over the years, but nothing quite on the order of a completely lost Chaplin film. Frankly, I was not at all prepared for the flood of calls, emails, or the intense international response. And there is no way to describe how bizarre it was to see news video of oneself dubbed to be speaking Italian, Spanish, German, Chinese, Russian, Urdu . . . Dzongkha (*laughs*). The discovery was fun and exciting, of course, but it also came with a tremendous sense of responsibility.

Chris: I remember sitting with you at the bar during Cinefest in Syracuse, New York, back in 2010, and you hinted at a "new" Chaplin find. You were being super coy. How hard was it to keep it a secret, knowing just how big this discovery was?

Paul: Coy? Well that doesn't sound like me at all (*laughs*). Seriously, we work with rare and sole-surviving film materials on a regular basis, and while always fascinating—it really is just a part of the job. I understood and appreciated the historical significance of the find but had not fully considered thebroader implications. During the lead-up to the announcement, someone casually said, "Well, you've just forced them to change all of the history books." It was a pretty sobering moment. That's where I was when we first spoke about it. Ten years on, I am *still* amazed by the continuing interest.

Chris: Okay, tell us the whole story of how you stumbled across this film. Start with what you had for breakfast that morning. It was bacon, right?

Paul: We're brothers in nitrate and nitrites, Chris (*laughs*)! In late 2009 or early 2010, I went to one of the antique shows held at the Gibraltar Trade Center in Taylor, Michigan. It was a small show, mostly furniture and home goods, nothing in the way of film or memorabilia, so I decided to leave. As I was heading for the door, I spotted an old steamer trunk out of the corner of my eye...

Chris: When I'm at a flea market, I'm always scanning for film reels, etc. *Luggage*, not so much. What made you look at that specific trunk?

Paul: Honestly, I don't know. I've never collected or even had any particular interest in them either. I can only say that I stopped dead in my tracks, turned, walked over to the trunk, flipped open the lid, and was thrilled to find a huge pile of film inside! It was just one of those incredible instances of being in exactly the right place at precisely the right time. Anyway, none of the reels were marked, so I sat on the concrete floor and spooled through them by hand. There were some industrial films, a few cartoons, a bunch of commercials, several sound comedies, a few silent Keystone shorts, and lots of odds and ends. After examining everything, I picked out a handful of reels, haggled for the lot, took them home, and put it all on a shelf for repair at a later date. That was it.

Chris: So they just sat on a shelf? For *months*?

Paul: Yes, completely untouched until March of 2010 when I read a blog post about Chaplin's lost short *Her Friend the Bandit* by Sennett historian par excellence Brent Walker. That film is widely believed to have been reissued as *Mabel's Flirtation* and *The Thief Catcher*—the title of the Keystone reissue which I had picked up at the show several months earlier! Or so I thought.

I immediately pulled the film, gave it a quick inspection, and then set up an Elmo 16CL projector because it is generally easier on older film. It was late, three o'clock in the morning, so rather than battle with a screen at that hour I opted to project it directly onto the wall at about one-foot wide. Not exactly ideal viewing conditions, but it was adequate for a quick run through. Sure enough, the print was a Tower Films reissue, which was retitled *His Regular Job*, but incorrectly billed as formerly being The Thief Catcher rather than A Thief Catcher. As the film progressed, I realized that it was not *Her Friend the*

Bandit—rather, it was a lost Ford Sterling comedy! A great find, just not quite what I was expecting.

It was at that point, approximately five minutes in, when a pair of Keystone Cops walked into the scene—the lead figure looking suspiciously like Charlie Chaplin . . .

Chris: Okay, you have to be *really* specific about your reaction to seeing Chaplin. I mean details—amazement, cold sweats, a Jimmy Finlayson double-take—tell us *all*.

Paul: Initially I was more confused than anything else, so I stopped the projector and checked the various Chaplin reference books and standard web sources—found nothing. There were some small references to an interview where Chaplin had casually mentioned appearing on screen as a Keystone Cop, but he gave no specific title or supporting details. At that point, I restarted the projector and watched the scene again. And again. And again. I simply could not believe what I was seeing but there it was—Chaplin as a Keystone Cop!

My first thought was, "Who the hell can I call? It's four o'clock in the morning!"

I needed some additional, unbiased verification, so I snapped a few photos and fired off an email to several associates with a note which read: "Is this who I think it is?" but nothing else.

I immediately received a call from historian and fellow night-owl Richard M. Roberts, who said "Yep, could be, but I've gotta see him move." So I sent a rough video and he agreed, as did everyone else, that against all odds it *was* indeed a lost Chaplin appearance! It took a while to sink in but, ultimately, I was elated to be able to add this title back into the filmography.

Chris: You're talking about the H. D. Waley filmography, from the late thirties, right?

Paul: Yes. Subsequent research revealed a few interesting things: *A Thief Catcher* was released by Mutual in 1914. By 1915, Chaplin's popularity was such that when Tower Films reissued this Ford Sterling vehicle it was instead being billed as a comedy starring Charlie Chaplin. After its initial run and reissues, all known prints and negatives for *A Thief Catcher* were eventually lost, incinerated for silver reclamation, or destroyed by nitrate decomposition.

In the spring of 1938, Hubert D. Waley, technical director of the British Film Institute, compiled the first detailed list of Chaplin's Keystone films for a *Sight & Sound* magazine article titled "Is This Charlie?" There, Waley detailed the difficulties of creating a definitive Chaplin filmography, and listed the UK Chaplin releases, which were compiled from a page-by-page search of contemporary trade journals containing the Keystone Company's release announcements. It was in this article that Waley first included *A Thief Catcher as Chaplin's fourth appearance at the studio*. However, the title was dropped from the subsequent filmography published in a *Sight & Sound* supplement from 1945. It was this revised version of the list which served as the base for Theodore Huff's long unchallenged filmography in his monumental book, *Charlie Chaplin*, which was published in 1951.

Chris: Wait up. Why, if it was in Waley's listing, did it disappear in subsequent filmographies?

Paul: No one seems to know for sure. One possibility is that the still-missing short subject *Her Friend the Bandit* was also reportedly reissued as *The Thief Catcher*. It is easy to see how a pioneering researcher could be confused by two nearly identical titles, particularly so when original documentation was sparse and the actual films were no longer available for reference. Too, those early filmographies were fluid and generally considered to be works in progress. Chaplin was still a working artist in 1938!

Chris: Yes, it must have been nearly impossible for anyone to come up with a comprehensive filmography under those circumstances. A good example of this is John McCabe's early error-ridden Laurel & Hardy filmography. It continued to evolve over many years.

Paul: Exactly. So whatever the reason, *A Thief Catcher* was removed from the official list, so it was all but forgotten and considered completely lost—until 2010.

Chris: Okay, you're sitting on this amazing find. It's super-secret. How did you decide to share it with the world?

Paul: I decided to re-premiere the short at Slapsticon, which was an annual festival dedicated to screening rare silent and sound comedies. Slapsticon was founded by Rob Farr, organized and produced by Richard M. Roberts and Linda Shaw, regularly contributed to by myself, several major archives, as well as other friends and colleagues in the classic comedy community. It was an easy choice. From there, Brittany Valente (co-founder of CineMuseum) and I planned to tackle a proper restoration for home video, and then eventually prepare a new negative for long-term preservation.

The event took place at the Spectrum Theater in Arlington, Virginia, on Saturday, July 17, 2010. We dedicated that screening to the memory of Hubert Waley, the first historian to believe *ATC* belonged in the filmography. It only took sixty-five years and an unplanned trip to an antique show to discover that he was right.

Chris: I was *there*! I remember watching its debut in the packed house. I see "new" footage of old comedians all the time—but this time I literally got chills. How did you feel seeing it with an audience for the first time?

Paul: It was incredible! And the anticipation palpable! The theater was filled to capacity and that short one-reel comedy completely rocked the house with laughter. That screening was unlike anything else I have ever experienced, truly the event of a lifetime. Of course, once it was over I received numerous tongue-in-cheek confirmations, in true Slapsticonian form, that it was indeed a great new Billy West discovery (*laughs*).

Chris: Richard M. Roberts's comment of "I've gotta see him move" is really telling. Because *nobody* moved quite like Chaplin.

Paul: Agreed! And Chaplin had only made three films before this—yet he was already commanding the screen. Even in this relatively brief appearance one can see his growing mastery of the art and the seeds of a style that would eventually make him one of the most famous men in the world. He was born for the camera.

Chris: Around the same time, a fellow in the UK had purchased a "lost" Chaplin film called *Zepped* on eBay for a few quid but convinced himself he'd hit a goldmine and got all sorts of press about it. Reports had it up for auction at Bonhams with an opening bid of £100,000. You were in the news too, but you took an entirely different route. Why was that? Shouldn't you be a billionaire by now?

Paul: (*laughs*) It's difficult to quantify just how thrilling it is to find lost or previously unknown material, but the notion that anyone has ever made a fortune by locating one is pure fantasy. In reality, the costs involved with finding, shipping, transferring, restoring, preserving, storing, promoting, and releasing a film are astronomical. And regardless of *A Thief Catcher* being called one of the most historically important discoveries of its kind, when all was said and done, I just about broke even. Almost.

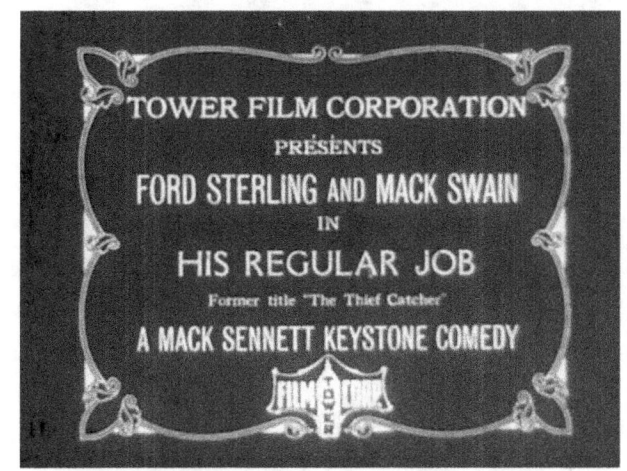

Cops confusion! The endless reissues and retitling of the Keystone films can make researching them a baffling ordeal. All screencaps from A Thief Catcher are courtesy of Paul E. Gierucki and CineMuseum, LLC.

For me, and for the small handful of producers who are still doing this work outside of the archive and studio systems, the real reward is in being able to save a small bit of our cultural heritage and then sharing it again with others. To that end, I made arrangements to include the short in our next release, *The Mack Sennett Collection, Vol. I*. At least that was the plan—until fellow historian and preservationist David Shepard (owner of the Blackhawk Films collection/ Film Preservation Associates) called to ask if he and Serge Bromberg (owner of Lobster Films in Paris) could use the short for their comprehensive *Chaplin at Keystone* DVD set. David had been a good friend and collaborator, generously providing access to some really wonderful master materials for our Sennett restorations and other projects, so how could I say no? Since *A Thief Catcher* was already slated for our release, we worked up a plan to include part of the film on their set and they would in turn use that fragment to help promote our Sennett release. In the end, the cross promotion was great for both productions and we were able to get the film into the hands of eager Chaplin fans everywhere.

"I gotta see him move!" Even as early as this fourth film, Chaplin's body language was so distinct it was the only way to absolutely identify him.

Chris: Do you believe in destiny? Straight up, how weird is it that you, of all people, would find this film?

Paul: Absolutely. My entire life has been a series of bizarre, unbelievable, surreal, and otherwise unexplainable events. Call it what you will—fate, providence, karma, predestination, whatever—there is a strange order to the universe and I find myself at the crux of "right place and right time" far more often than one might imagine possible. Yeah, this was weird in the extreme. Never a dull moment!

Chris: So, I have to ask—we're positioning this as "Charlie Chaplin is a Keystone Cop," but there's not all the jumping up and down or exaggerated antics generally associated with the Cops. What defines a Keystone Cops film to you?

Paul: Historian Brent Walker makes a critical point in his book *Mack Sennett's Fun Factory*—the Cops did not really "star" in any films as a unit. Nor were they composed of one specific group of individuals. Rather, it was an ever-changing entity with a revolving-door cast. The Cops would frequently show up *en masse* toward the end of a film, give chase, wreak havoc, execute some breath-taking

Ultimately, the Keystone Cops show up to do typical Keystone Cops things.

stunts, and provide big laughs before the fade-out, but there was never a proper Keystone Cops series. There *are* some instances where they are more central to the plot—*Bangville Police* being a good example. And, of course, Chief Ford Sterling had starring roles in some notable entries.

Chris: And Roscoe Arbuckle in *Fatty Joins the Force*. He even takes a pie in the face in that one!

Paul: Precisely. Beyond those exceptions, the legend of the Cops is perhaps greater than their actual participation in the totality of the Keystone Studios output. That said, when one thinks Keystone today one cannot help but picture the Cops first!

Chris: You've been tracking down, restoring, and releasing the films of Mack Sennett for home video and broadcast on Turner Classic Movies since 2012. Do you think the Keystones get a bad rap based on the "cliché" of Keystone Cops?

In June 2011 the internet was abuzz with the news that a Charlie Chaplin film purchased off eBay for a mere £3.20 in 2009 was a previously unknown Charlie Chaplin film, titled Zepped. The film was, in fact, a pastiche of old Chaplin Keystone and Essanay clips, a few alternate takes, and a great deal of new animation and footage cobbled together, resulting in a World War I propaganda film whose purpose was to assuage fear of zeppelin attacks over England.

Paul: I do think that the Keystone comedies are underappreciated—but not because of the visual conjured by the Cops. When pioneering historians like James Agee, William K. Everson, Kalton C. Lahue, etc., first started revisiting these works in the fifties and sixties, a goodly portion of the films were unavailable for viewing or considered lost entirely. There was no single source from which one could view more than a handful of titles—it was catch-as-catch-can. And the prints which *did* survive were often edited, retitled, choppy, incomplete, jerky (because they were running at the wrong projection speeds), and reprinted to the point of being unwatchable. How can anyone properly evaluate the worth of a film if it no longer exists as it was originally intended to be seen? This was precisely why Brittany and I decided to take on 100 Sennett restorations for the 100th anniversary of the Keystone Studios. It is our hope that these restorations, carefully crafted from the best surviving materials, will lead to a proper re-evaluation by a new generation of authors, historians, and

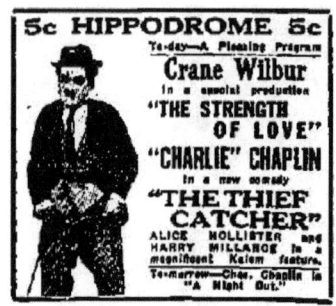

What a difference a year makes. By 1915 A Thief Catcher *was being unashamedly promoted as a Charlie Chaplin film. Image courtesy of Michael J. Hayde.*

fans. The hard-working Sennett crew and artists deserve nothing less.

Chris: Do you think there's the chance of other "lost" Chaplin discoveries? I mean, this came out of nowhere.

Paul: We are ninety years beyond the silent film era, yet lost and unknown material continues to resurface all over the world. We recently recovered a 35mm nitrate negative of Lee de Forest's first tests of the Phonofilm sound process from the early 1920s. Today—*today!*—I took possession of two original 35mm nitrate prints of Roscoe Arbuckle's *A Reckless Romeo* and *The Rough House* (both 1917), co-starring Buster Keaton. So, *why not* more Chaplin? I certainly intend to keep looking.

A Thief Catcher, a one-reel Keystone comedy, was released by the Mutual Film Corporation on February 19, 1914. It was produced by Mack Sennett and directed by the film's star, Ford Sterling.

Chapter 5
Tillie's Punctured Romance:
Then and Now

By John Bengtson

Long recognized as Hollywood's first feature-length comedy, *Tillie's Punctured Romance* (1914) is best remembered today for helping to launch Charlie Chaplin's meteoric film career. But while Chaplin and fellow Sennett studio luminary Mabel Normand co-starred in the production as a couple of con artists, famed Broadway star Marie Dressler played the eponymous lead, her transition from stage to screen presented with her literally bowing before a theater curtain at the opening and closing of the film. Nearly every studio cast member played roles (or multiple roles) in the movie, barring only Roscoe "Fatty" Arbuckle, whom Marie reportedly excluded from the production over concern that his appearance, as a fellow "heavyweight" comedian, might detract from the laughs for her role. The movie provides brief glimpses of early

Hollywood and the Keystone production methods, and as such, a representative—if not exhaustive—study of the Keystone Cops filming on location.

Marie portrays Tillie, a naïve farm girl who is mistaken by Charlie to have inherited a fortune. When Mabel and Charlie steal Marie's money early in the film, she becomes drunk and has several run-ins with the Keystone Cops. Here above they assist Marie in the middle of Hollywood Boulevard, looking west from the corner of Cahuenga.

It's hard to imagine how open and undeveloped Hollywood was back in 1914. At the time this commercial corner, perhaps the most developed in town, was surrounded for miles by acres of orchards, vacant lots, and expansive home sites.

The C. E. Toberman Building, still standing at 6410-6146 Hollywood Boulevard, appears at back. Known as "Mr. Hollywood," Toberman would

The Toberman Building today.

later build many local landmarks, including the Hollywood Bowl, Grauman's Chinese Theater, and the Roosevelt Hotel.

The Hollywood National Bank building on the left nominally remains standing, although two additional floors and a new Art Deco tile façade were added in 1931, completely altering its appearance. With few other choices available then for local filming, this corner appears in many early films.

Looking west at the same bank corner, Mabel flirts with a suspicious Cop.

The same barber pole and hardware store sign from the prior shot of Mabel on the boulevard appear in the background. I am intrigued by the woman at back seen peeking through a screen door. Filming on location was once far more casual, and bystanders commonly appear at back, or reflected in windows, during early Keystone films. Mabel's Edwardian-era full-length skirt would soon give way to the flapper fashions of the Roaring Twenties.

Standing on the porch of the Hollywood Hotel, Marie flirtatiously waves to a Cop across the street.

Once situated on the northwest corner of Hollywood and Highland, the Hollywood Hotel was one of Hollywood's most prominent landmarks.

It was built in 1903, and by 1914 it had become the center of Hollywood social life. The Hollywood Hotel was demolished in 1956, and the site is now home to the Hollywood & Highland Retail and Entertainment Center, known for its towering Babylon Court shopping mall, patterned after the Babylon set from D. W. Griffith's 1916 masterpiece *Intolerance*. The site is adjacent to the Dolby Theatre (2001), home to the annual Academy Awards ceremonies, and the TCL (Grauman's Chinese) Theatre (1927).

Above, two Cops bring an inebriated Marie into the police station for questioning. Notice the word POLICE painted on the sidewalk. Comparing the identical door and window features with the vintage photo reveals that this scene was filmed using the Keystone Studio entrance door as an exterior set. In this frame from *Fatty's Plucky Pup* (1915), Fatty Arbuckle rides a bicycle towards the same studio door, where the word POLICE still appears painted on the sidewalk. A prop Police Station sign has been added to the wall for effect. Chaplin used the same studio doorway as a dentist office entrance in *Laughing Gas* (1914).

Built in 1909 as the first permanent studio in Los Angeles, the Selig Polyscope Studio stood at 1845 Allesandro sandwiched between Clifford and Duane Street corner. The Selig studio was enclosed by a distinctive stucco wall, decorated with miniature turrets, and stepped sections where the far ends of the walls rose uphill.

When Charlie flirts with a pretty girl here in *Those Love Pangs* (1914), the matching turrets and stepped sections of wall confirm this was filmed looking west uphill from the Duane Street corner of the Selig studio.

Released from jail, Marie flirts with a Cop in *Tillie* further uphill on Duane Street beside the back corner of the Selig studio wall. The short lattice fence beside the children in the *Love Pangs* frame appears clearly here. The two homes at back were 2212 and 2216 Duane Street, now the site of modern apartments. Without Cops or stars, two other minor scenes from *Tillie* were filmed beside the Selig studio on Allesandro.

While King Vidor's celebrated "everyman" drama *The Crowd* (1928) caused a minor stir for daring to show a flush toilet in the background of one domestic scene, often cited as the porcelain appliance's screen debut, it appears *Tillie* beat this record by more than a dozen years. There must have been a hardware or plumbing store near the small restaurant where Marie works during the movie, as the Cop pictured here is obliviously standing in front of a commode, apparently promoted for sale as a sidewalk display.

Incorrectly assuming she has inherited her uncle's fabulous estate, Charlie and Marie meet at the entrance gate to Castle Sans Souci, formerly located in Hollywood at 1901 Argyle above Franklin.

Another view of Charlie and Marie at her uncle's estate reveals a broad view of the former mansion, owned by Dr. A. G. R. Schloesser, a prominent Hollywood booster, capitalist, and art connoisseur. Responding to anti-German sentiment during the First World War, Schloesser (meaning "castle" in English)

 legally changed his name to Dr. Castles. Castle Sans Souci was demolished in 1928 to make way for the aptly named Castle Argyle Apartments, still standing now perilously close to the later Hollywood freeway. The exotic castle home appeared frequently in early film, including Lois Weber's *The Dumb Girl of Portici* (1916).

A closer view of Marie, still inebriated, flirting with a Cop at the Castle Sans Souci front steps.

The movie ends with a wild chase as gun-toting Marie, furious she has been deceived, races after Charlie, and the frantic Cops race after Marie. Here above, a band of Cops stumble over themselves near Mohawk Bend on Sunset Boulevard, within a few blocks of the Keystone Studio. Looking west, at back appears the original Los Angeles Fire Engine Co. No. 20 at 2144 Sunset.

The station appears in a later Keystone title *Dirty Work in a Laundry* (1915), also looking west, and in Chaplin's *Cruel, Cruel Love* (1914), looking east. A modern fire house replaced the original station building in 1953. The climax of the film has Marie and the Cops falling off the Venice Pier into the Pacific Ocean.

John Bengtson is a business lawyer and film historian whose books *Silent Echoes*, *Silent Traces*, and *Silent Visions* explore the early Hollywood history hidden in the background of the films of Buster Keaton, Charlie Chaplin, and Harold Lloyd, respectively (see silentlocations.com). John's work has been hailed by the *New York Times* as a "Proustian collage of time and memory, biography and history, urban growth and artistic expression." John has lectured at over fifty events hosted by the Academy of Motion Picture Arts and Sciences, the Turner Classic Movie (TCM) Channel Film Festival, and The Museum of the Moving Image in New York, among others. John serves on the Board of Directors of the San Francisco Silent Film Festival.

Screencaps from *Tillie's Punctured Romance* (1914) courtesy of the Lobster Films Chaplin Keystone Project.

Chapter 6
The Show Off:
Ford Sterling Revealed
By Mark Pruett

Ford Sterling disapproves of his son Bobby Vernon's relationship with Juanita Hansen. His Pride and Shame *(1916) Photo courtesy of Bison Archives.*

Everyone remembers Ford Sterling. The circular goatee, the wire-rimmed spectacles, the shabby top hat and frock coat—these spring to mind at the mere mention of Mack Sennett's Keystone comedies. But what do we know of the gifted actor who brought such vitality to the Sennett ensemble? Despite his steady presence onscreen for nearly two decades after his final parting with Sennett in 1920, Sterling's later work—most of it in feature-length films—has a weaker hold on our collective memory than those early knockabout shorts.

As Brent Walker explains in *Mack Sennett's Fun Factory*, by the time Sterling moved from short comedies to features in the early 1920s, he had already discarded the stereotypical getups and caricatures familiar to his audience. But that antic legacy would prove surprisingly durable. Fifteen years after Sterling's death in 1939, Sennett was still honoring him as "the first real comedy star in motion pictures." At Keystone, Sterling had endowed his bunglers and charlatans with elastic physiognomies and boundless nervous energy, from the Chief of the Keystone Cops to a shifting array of philanderers, mountebanks, and villains. A single widely-published photo of his grimacing, cross-eyed Chief, telephone receiver at his ear and a ragged line of Cops behind him, was soon recognized the world over by people who had forgotten, if they ever knew, the title of the two-reeler it came from (*In the Clutches of a Gang*, 1914).

There was an intelligence in Sterling's grotesque portrayals that belied their vaudeville underpinnings. Behind the leaps and leers and gesticulations lay a sensibility keenly attuned to the value of self-parody. Sterling would burlesque not only hackneyed plots and conventional characters but also the tools of theatrical artifice that were every actor's stock-in-trade. To call attention to greasepaint eyebrows, or to false hair clumsily applied, was to bring audiences in on the joke. In *Barney Oldfield's Race for a Life* (1913), the sheer outlandishness of Sterling's makeup is central to his performance (and by far the funniest thing in this race-to-the-rescue comedy). Sterling is a stock villain

whose pasted-on mustache is unevenly applied—and conspicuously so, one extension appearing to grow from his left nostril while the other covers more than half of his upper lip. It's hilarious. By the second reel, the mustache has migrated to his lip's outer edges. The broader his sneer, the more fraudulent—and comical—his villainy. Sterling even ridiculed the patent phoniness of his most familiar guise—the "Dutch" makeup of the Chief. In *Our Dare-Devil Chief* (1915), he discovers a photo of himself that the jealous mayor has torn in half. Offended, he manipulates the two halves in an effort to restore his image—and his dignity. But in raising the bottom half of the picture, he settles the black disk of his chin beard just below his staring eyes. His portrait now resembles a dog with an oversized snout. Though the rearrangement is entirely the Chief's doing, he reacts as if to a second insult.

It wasn't until his last two years with Sennett that Sterling abandoned his characteristic guises and garb. Envisioning a career in features, he trusted that skills sharpened by years of experience would offset the loss of instant recognition onscreen. He had his work cut out for him.

Few patrons who wandered in late to a showing of King Vidor's *Wild Oranges* in 1924 would have recognized in the levelheaded Paul Halvard the scowling Chief of the Keystone Cops. Even when audiences knew who he was, Sterling was seldom the actor they had come to see. His principal challenge throughout the 1920s was to get his name on the marquee, but in features he was typically cast in supporting roles. *He Who Gets Slapped* (1924) belonged to Lon Chaney, *Stage Struck* (1925) to Gloria Swanson. Sterling gave solid performances in both pictures, but his parts were secondary to those of two world-famous stars.

A glorious exception is *The Show Off*, released by Famous Players–Lasky in the summer of 1926. Mal St. Clair, who had directed Sterling in *The Trouble with Wives* (1925) and *Good and Naughty* (1926), believed him ideally suited to play the self-important windbag Aubrey Piper in the screen adaptation (the first of several) of George Kelly's 1924 Broadway hit. His hunch paid off. The actor whose outrageous mugging had once been his signature—as a circus clown, on the vaudeville stage, and at Keystone—brought an unexpected depth to his portrayal of the unsympathetic Aubrey. "I saw the screen succumbing to subtlety," Sterling told the writer Malcolm Oettinger. "The obvious was getting the gate. So I decided not to be one of the victims. It was time to strike out in new pastures..." (*Picture-Play Magazine*, April 1926).

Aubrey Piper is detested by every other important character in *The Show Off* but one: his sweet, clueless fiancée Amy, played by Lois Wilson. Known to his co-workers as Carnation Charlie (for his ever-present boutonnière), the conceited Aubrey struts and preens about the offices of the Pennsylvania Railroad as if he owned the company, when in fact he is just one among dozens of low-level clerks. He maintains the façade when he visits Amy's family, the Fishers, but they are no more taken in by his boisterous self-promotion than his co-workers are. Mom and Pop Fisher are humble people, however, and they endure his bluff pronouncements and back-slapping conviviality with a weary resignation, only now and then letting go of their manners and telling him off in the baldest terms. True to his mostly opaque sense of self, Aubrey treats these outbursts as trifling aberrations. That the Fishers are distraught at the prospect of their Amy marrying an insufferable poseur never crosses his mind.

And marry they do. The event quickly punctures the hot-air balloon of Aubrey's grandiose promises. Stuck in a small apartment, with no money to pay the rent coming due, Amy puts her faith in Aubrey's insistence that their lot is about to improve. Then Pop Fisher dies, and Amy, in a spiral of disappointment, is forced to accept the inevitable: she and Aubrey must move back into the Fisher household. Even Aubrey's momentary good fortune—he wins a car in a raffle—is squandered in a characteristic display of pride. Refusing to admit that he can't drive, he careens wildly through traffic, goes the wrong way down a one-way thoroughfare, and finally crashes the car, injuring a policeman. At his

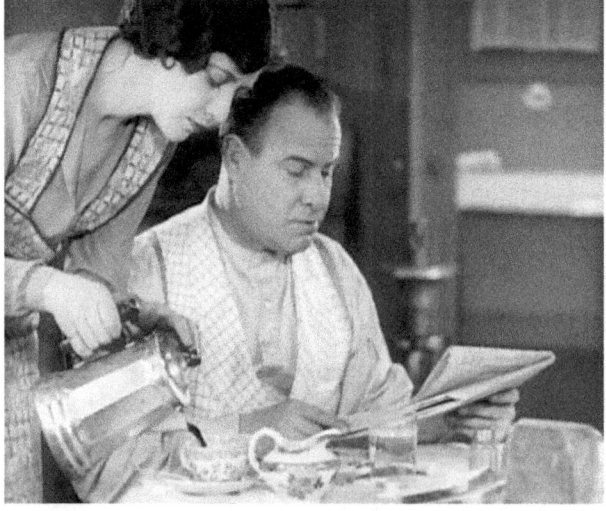

trial, he so offends the judge that his fine is doubled on the spot. To save him from jail, Amy's brother Joe pays Aubrey's fine, using the family's mortgage money which Pop Fisher had given to Joe to promote his new invention.

In lesser hands, *The Show Off* might have surrendered to sentimentality. When genuine sentiment does intrude, it merely throws into relief the showboating behavior of Sterling's Aubrey Piper. In an astonishingly controlled performance, Sterling never breaks character, never invites the audience to warm to Aubrey by pretending that beneath his puffed-out chest beats a heart of gold. As he lounges at breakfast in their small apartment, Aubrey asks Amy for more coffee. Amy leaves her ironing board and goes to the breakfast table to pick up the coffee pot, which is sitting only inches from Aubrey's hand. She pours, she replaces the pot, she returns to her ironing. Such moments—and there are many—attest to Aubrey's supreme egotism. And Sterling does nothing in the way of gesture, mannerism, or expression to soften their effect. As Aubrey watches Amy labor at the ironing board in her limp housedress and apron, a look of concern crosses his face. For an instant we are taken aback, hoping against hope that a selfless impulse has broken the surface of Aubrey's narcissism. "Amy," he says, "I ought to have a new suit. You know the boys at the office look to me for their styles."

The collaboration between Mal St. Clair and Ford Sterling left the director bubbling with enthusiasm. With *The Show Off* in release, he was cited in *Picture-Play Magazine* (Sept. 1926) as believing that Sterling was "the greatest pantomimist on the screen." According to *Picture-Play*, the opinion was shared by Allan Dwan, who had directed Sterling in *Stage Struck*.

Reviewers had mixed feelings. Some praised Sterling but disliked the film, pronouncing it inferior to the stage play. Others found the film amusing but wondered why anyone should devote a moment's attention to an obnoxious blowhard like Aubrey. Surely there were funnier, nobler, more uplifting, or more exciting portrayals onscreen that summer. And in truth the competition was stiff. When *The Show Off* opened at the Rivoli on August 16, the other movies playing on Broadway included *The Big Parade*, *Battling Butler*, *The Scarlet Letter*, *Mare Nostrum*, *The Black Pirate*, *Ben-Hur*, *Variety*, and *Don Juan*. Complicating the jobs of publicists everywhere, the gravely ill Rudolph Valentino, reported by *The Film Daily* to be "practically beyond danger" on August 22, died on August 23. The paroxysm of grief that rocked the film world reverberated for weeks in the press, not only in somber

Screencaps courtesy of Image Entertainment's 2012 DVD release of The Show Off/The Plastic Age.

newsreel footage of the funeral but in movie magazines that printed heartfelt remembrances of Valentino by friends, fellow actors, and fans. One fan, still meditative a year after the star's death, captured the prevailing mood: Valentino, she wrote, was "the reincarnation in the modern world of an ideal hero of olden times" ("What The Fans Think," *Picture-Play*, Nov. 1927).

Who had the patience to endure, much less make sense of, the flamboyant posturing of an unrepentant braggart, bluffer, windbag, and liar?

Mal St. Clair had worked on both sides of the camera. From the outset he was convinced that a cinematic reimagining of *The Show Off* could sharpen the edge of George Kelly's satire. To achieve that end he relied on the expert assistance of screenwriter Pierre Collings, cinematographer Lee Garmes, and master pantomimist Ford Sterling.

Collings's scenario opened up Kelly's set-bound stage play. In the play, the action never strays from the Fisher family's sitting room. Thanks to Garmes's seamless blending of interior and exterior photography, St. Clair puts the wider canvas of Philadelphia onscreen. We see neighborhoods, busy streets, the downtown plaza, an office, a park, an apartment, a courtroom, and a boardroom, as well as the Fisher home. The sudden spaciousness transforms the play, dramatically enlarging the scope of its satire. It is one thing to see Aubrey Piper against the backdrop of the humble Fisher household, and quite another to see him in the context of that world he longs so desperately to inhabit: the world of the big shot.

The first minutes of the film expose this elite realm—and Aubrey's lowly status within it—with an incisiveness that the play cannot match. Titles invoke the names of Betsy Ross, Abraham Lincoln, and William Penn, lauding Philadelphia as "an arena for the deeds of great Americans." The inheritors of that arena, we are quickly told, are "the Commercial Giants of the modern age." Aubrey Piper, emerging from a subway, is introduced as one of "the thousands" who toil in the service of commerce. He is, in other words, a typical wage earner, undistinguished, uncelebrated, unknown.

Except that Aubrey refuses to be typical. On his way to work, he is dressed as if for a stroll along the boardwalk. He sports a light-toned glen plaid suit, spruced up with a straw boater, a tattersall vest, a bow tie, and a pocket handkerchief. As he enters the office building he falls in step with an older, gray-haired man in a silk hat and a black topcoat. Observing him closely, Aubrey affects the older man's bearing, even holding his cane at an identical angle. He notices the man's boutonnière and samples the fragrance of his own. The man stifles a yawn; Aubrey does the same. The older man becomes aware of Aubrey as he reaches the door of his office, which is labeled "Vice President."

Turning from the door opposite, Aubrey nods affably and offers a greeting. The vice president, clearly affronted to have been addressed by a subordinate, regards Aubrey with distaste and pushes on into his office.

Puzzled by the snub, Aubrey enters the other office—and here St. Clair drives the point home. Aubrey's outlook on life—his optimism, his unselfconscious good humor—differs from his co-workers' solemnity as thoroughly as his cheery glen plaid suit differs from the vice president's funereal dress. As he strides past the other office workers, all of them preoccupied (and all dressed, like the boss, in somber shades), he claps one on the back. The man responds with a cross word, to Aubrey's seeming amusement. At his desk Aubrey opens his newspaper to the stock listings, shakes his head dismissively, and turns to the "Barney Google and Spark Plug" comic strip, which immediately piques his interest. All at once he throws back his head and laughs uproariously, his mouth wide open.

His co-workers react with shock and disapproval. Aubrey tries to share the strip with the man sitting behind him, but the other is incensed at his breach of office protocol and tells him off. (The cadaverous actor selected for this bit makes a truly repugnant sourpuss, his twisted mouth bristling with bad teeth.) After Aubrey is reprimanded by a superior, the man snarls, "Now maybe you'll learn this *is* an office—not a bird-house!" Aubrey looks about the room, bewildered by the reaction, then turns back to the comic strip—and suppresses another laugh.

We delight in this scene precisely because we side so completely with Aubrey against the other office workers—dour, stiff-necked drones whose only joy is a joyless embrace of uniformity. (This is two years before King Vidor's *The Crowd* would depict the modern office as a soul-killing hive of monotony and anonymity.) In barely five minutes of screen time, St. Clair has set the tone of the film and provided the prism through which to view our hero's antics. By the end of the picture, Aubrey will save the Fisher family from ruin. To sell Joe's invention, a rustproofing paint, to a steel manufacturing company, he will deliver a sales pitch in which he is every bit as confident, pretentious, and patronizing as the corporate big shots he must persuade. The skills he calls upon to close the deal, it is clear, are skills that the unassuming Joe does not possess.

At the beginning, however, it is enough to recognize that Aubrey is the polar opposite of the ill-tempered co-worker who self-righteously berates him (and whose scowl mimics the scowl of the haughty vice president). Aubrey may impersonate pompous bigwigs, but his true personality—expressed in his buoyancy, his exuberant laugh, his flashy clothing—is an open invitation to fun. Above all, it reveals a readiness to drop pretense in the very act of putting on airs. It is, perhaps, what Amy saw when she fell in love with him.

Reviewing *The Show Off* a few weeks after the film's premiere, Epes W. Sargent wrote, "The discerning will thoroughly enjoy the subtle humor of Ford Sterling" (*Moving Picture World*, Sept. 4, 1926). Brilliant acting tends to hide its own machinery, however, and the complexity of Sterling's performance is generally overlooked even today. Thus the cover art for both the Kino and the Image DVD releases of *The Show Off* imply that the star of the film is Louise Brooks (well-cast in a supporting role as Clara, the Fishers' acerbic but appealing neighbor and Joe's girlfriend). Both covers feature the same stunning closeup of the actress, with Image going so far as to place her name alone above the title. It is fitting, then, that one of the fairest modern assessments of the film is to be found on the Louise Brooks Society website, directed by the prolific Thomas Gladysz: "While remembered today as a Louise Brooks film," Gladysz writes, "*The Show-Off* is really a vehicle for Ford Sterling, a comedian best remembered for his starring work as a member of the Keystone Kops."

And it was to the Keystone Cops, if not to Sennett, that he would return. While 1926 proved a banner year for Sterling, with the completion of eight features in addition to *The Show Off*, the offers slowed with the coming of sound. He found work in short comedies again, usually for Christie or

In Big Moments from Little Pictures *(Roach, 1924), Will Rogers hilariously imitates Chief Ford Sterling's pointless ritual prior to answering an emergency call. Screencaps courtesy of Image Entertainment's Slapstick Encyclopedia.*

RKO. Shorts, in fact, accounted for half of the films of his final decade. His last features for First National (*Kismet*, 1930 and *Her Majesty, Love*, 1931) and Paramount (*Alice in Wonderland*, 1933) were followed in 1935 by two crime dramas for Mascot, a poverty row studio. In *Behind the Green Lights* and *The Headline Woman*, as in many of his recent shorts, Sterling did comic turns speaking English with a faux-German accent, a sound-era realization of the "Dutch" characters from his silent days. (Billy Gilbert and Sig Ruman had their own wonderful versions of this voice.) He used the nominally Teutonic, not-quite-classifiable accent to best advantage in his reprise of the Chief in *Keystone Hotel*, a frenetic and hugely popular Keystone Cops two-reeler, also released in 1935. The short was produced by Warner Bros./Vitaphone without the participation of Sennett, who had long since given up the rights to the Keystone name. Looking a bit heavier in his Chief's uniform, Sterling is nonetheless instantly in character. Some part of him, we feel, has come home. Working with old friends and former Keystone stalwarts Ben Turpin, Chester Conklin, Hank Mann, Bert Roach, and Marie Prevost, Sterling gives an energetic performance—a last performance—as the blundering Chief, adding, to our delight, the delicious lunacy of a multinational accent heard nowhere on earth but in the movies.

In 1927, Mack Sennett paid homage to his own greatest contribution to American comedy in Love in a Police Station. *Andy Clyde captured the likeness of Ford Sterling's Chief with a skillful combination of makeup and mimicry. Photo courtesy of Bison Archives.*

Older but no wiser: former Sennett stars Marie Prevost, Ben Turpin, Ford Sterling, and Hank Mann reunite for the Vitaphone two-reeler Keystone Hotel *(1935). Photo courtesy of Bison Archives.*

The Media History Digital Library provided invaluable scans of the magazines referenced above. I am also indebted to Lon Davis, *Silent Lives* (Albany, GA: BearManor Media, 2008); Thomas Gladysz, "The Show-Off (filmography page)," *Louise Brooks Society* (http://www.pandorasbox.com/films/show_off); Simon Louvish, *Keystone: The Life and Clowns of Mack Sennett* (London: Faber and Faber, 2003); Mack Sennett, *King of Comedy* (Garden City, NY: Doubleday, 1954); Brent E. Walker, *Mack Sennett's Fun Factory* (Jefferson, NC: McFarland, 2010); and Wendy Warwick White, *Ford Sterling: The Life and Films* (Jefferson, NC: McFarland, 2007).

A shorter version of this article appeared in the Fall 2016 issue of *The Silent Film Quarterly*.

Chapter 7
The Sennett Story:
The Unwritten Rules of Writing Physical Comedy

By Joe Adamson

Mack Sennett animatedly shares a story idea with an unidentified writer. Photo courtesy of Bison Archives.

One morning in 1913, Mack Sennett opened his newspaper and discovered that Echo Park Lake, right down the street from his studio, was going to be drained that very day! He saw the opportunity for some mud-slinging comedy and, as he put it later, "The Cops put on their uniforms and we whistled up

a carful of writers and went out.... We made up the gags and story as we went along."

The story they came up with stuck Mabel Normand and Charles Inslee in a small boat in the middle of the lake, with a minister between them frantically attempting to read them their wedding ceremony while Ford Sterling stood by on the shore firing guns at them and letting loose with a steady stream of German-English (or "Pennsylvania Dutch") gibberish, which, were this not a silent comedy, would have to be censored. The "gags" consisted chiefly of a series of not particularly well-motivated pratfalls in the increasingly muddy lake bottom and on the dirt roads surrounding it. Later story development situated Normand and Sterling as next-door neighbors and presumably sweethearts, with Inslee turning up as an alternate suitor at Mabel's front door while she makes goo-goo eyes at Sterling out the back window—in footage collected in tranquility. Shots of the police being called, pandemonium in the station house, Sterling turning a large wheel that presumably empties the lake, and so on, could be cut in ahead of the shots initially grabbed as the lake was drained, and appear to be building up to the grand spectacle. In fact, the number of actual shots taken on Echo Park Lake's muddy bottom is relatively small; the harvest of that first frantic day appears to have been modest but priceless, granting Sennett hundreds of dollars worth of production value in exchange for little more than quick thinking.

The result was released November 20, 1913, as *A Muddy Romance*, and reissued and recycled many ways from many Sundays since, but the story of its making has grown a beard as a cross-section of Sennett anarchy, of Keystone as a fly-by-the-seat-of-the-pants, just-wing-it-and-we'll-fix-it-in-post, Devil-take-the-hindmost operation. But this only muddies the water: *A Muddy Romance* is just as illustrative, for those who care to dig a little deeper, of Mack Sennett's genius for running a film comedy studio, of the talent for mass-producing canned lunacy that made him the comedy sensation of the theatrical world in 1912 and 1913, and established for him the reputation that stands (albeit in misunderstood and misrepresented form) to this day.

To accomplish what he did (in a prehistoric era BLT—Before Looney Tunes—and before there was even One Stooge, let alone Three), Sennett had to know two things so well that he could fuse them together into an alloy that struck everybody else as pure magic: he had to know comedy and he had to know film—at a time when few people really understood either, and no one else had actually gotten anyone to stake them to a studio based on a synthesis of the two.

Sennett's schooling in comedy didn't happen in school; it happened on the boards, out in front of audiences on the musical comedy and burlesque stage, and it all added up to an insider's glimpse at the perennial point of view of all humorists.

As for film, Mack Sennett was there when the art form was born. As an actor and writer for D. W. Griffith, he learned when Griffith was going to be walking where, and just happened to be going his way. Sennett said later, "His story for a picture usually consisted of one or two typed sheets of paper—the outlines of the theme and the motivations for the main situations; the rest of the story came out of his head as he directed the scenes."

A synthesis of these two elements was the Keystone of Sennett's studio, his art, his oeuvre, his life. So stories, scripts, and writing were an important part of what he did. Sennett said himself, "I found the more money I put into writing a picture, the cheaper it was to shoot and the better it came out. The ill-prepared films were the ones that cost a lot of money."

But a script for Sennett functioned just as it did for Griffith: as a springboard, not as Scripture. "The written word awed but did not frighten him," as Gene Fowler put it. "He held that pictorial action, like music, is of itself a universal language, one designed to address the eye, just as music addresses the ear." Sennett himself perpetuated the musical analogy when he maintained, "Whatever it was that we created, we played it by ear as we went along."

"You had to understand comic motion," Sennett once said to an interviewer, and pushed him into a swimming pool, insisting "*That* is comic motion."

So how do you write "comic motion"?

His Prehistoric Past

According to Charlie Chaplin, as soon as he arrived at the Keystone lot at the tail end of 1913, Sennett told him, "We have no scenario—we get an idea, then follow the natural sequence of events until it leads up to a chase . . ." Chaplin considered this method "edifying," but either he or Sennett was exaggerating: scenarios—or at least story outlines—were in existence for nearly every Keystone picture, but the director was given free rein to follow it or depart from it as he saw fit, free rein to "follow the natural course of events"— or what passed for natural when surrounded by clowns like Ford Sterling and the Keystone Cops.

What they obviously didn't have at Keystone was a detailed shooting script, with each shot sequentially numbered and the whole thing stamped "Shoot As Written" (as Thomas Ince was supposed to have done—not that anybody could ever prove he did it, but anyone working at a studio with that policy—like anyone working at a studio today—would understand the game plan: they wouldn't need a stamp). The plot for *Mabel's Dramatic Career* is simple, but it left room for a lot of frantic improvisation by Mabel Normand, Roscoe Arbuckle, Ford Sterling, and Sennett himself.

Chaplin created his Little Tramp character at Sennett's studio, and he did it at Sennett's suggestion when a one-reel comedy eventually to be called *Mabel's Strange Predicament* was going into production. The "scenario" this picture was based on still exists—three paragraphs on a single piece of paper

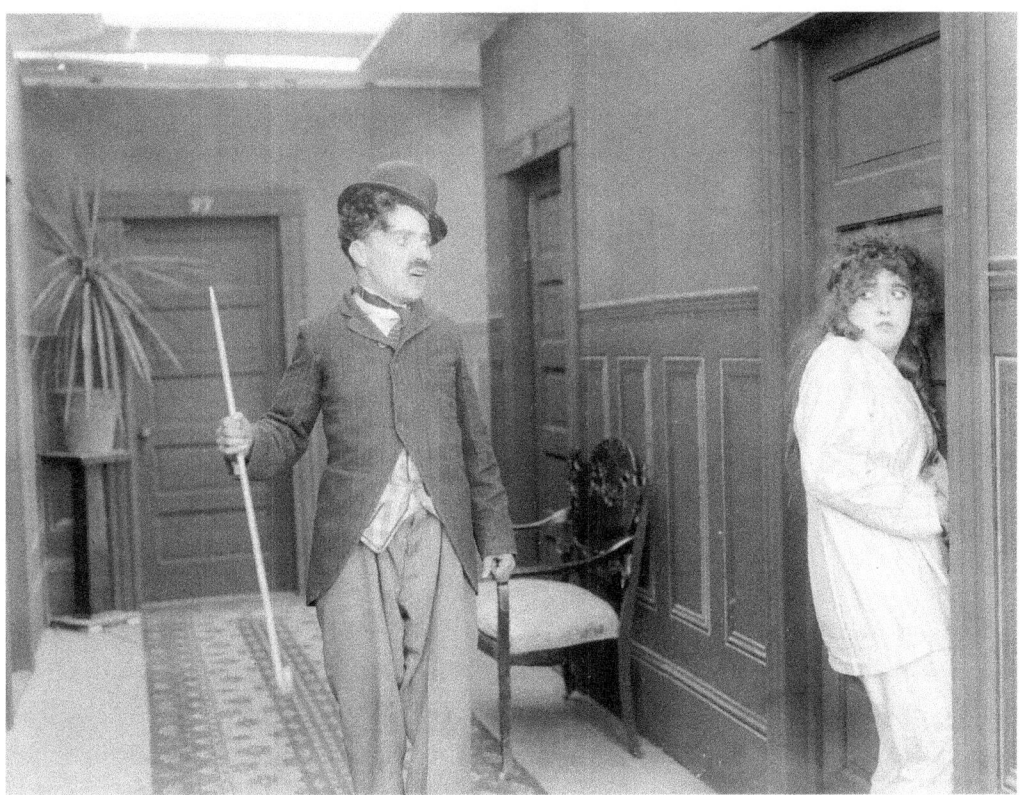

Charlie is definitely the instigator behind Mabel's Strange Predicament *(1914)*. Photo courtesy of Bison Archives.

covering "the outlines of the theme and the motivations for the main situations," basically telling, Griffith-style, the story to be told by the film itself: Mabel Normand plays a girl living in a hotel whose "strange predicament" is that, while playing innocently with her dog in her pajamas, she's managed to lock herself out of her own room and ends up hiding under the bed in the room next door—which, since it's being occupied by a married couple, leads to predictable Keystone chaos (or, as the scenario describes it, "Consternation etc."—on which note the scenario discreetly closes). The main characters total exactly four: Mabel; the couple next door, played by Chester Conklin and Alice Davenport; and Mabel's boyfriend, who also turns out to be a friend of Conklin's, and who is played by Harry McCoy. The part Sennett had in mind for Chaplin is covered, in its entirety, in two sentences: "At this point drunk comes along and tries to flirt with Mabel. In a panic she tries the next rooms door and enters husbands room." (*sic*)

As Chaplin himself remembered it, in *My Autobiography*, he had finished one film and was watching the company at work: "I was in my street clothes and had nothing to do, so I stood where Sennett could see me. He was standing with Mabel, looking into a hotel lobby set, biting the end of a cigar. 'We need some gags here,' he said, then turned to me. 'Put on a comedy make-up. Anything will do.'"

Harry Geduld (*Chapliniana: A Commentary on Charlie Chaplin's 81 Movies, Volume I: The Keystone Films*), later jumped to what must have seemed a logical conclusion: "Close examination of the film's plot dispels the notion that Chaplin's role was inserted into the picture 'at short notice'—as he himself maintained. His drunken masher character is clearly integral to the complicated chain of events. Not only does Charlie provide most of the film's comedy, he also aggravates Mabel's predicament by forcing her to hide in a married man's bedroom, and he is inextricably involved in all the madcap activity that follows. The most reliable assumption, therefore, is that for this Keystone film at least, Charlie interpreted a role rather than created it."

In fact, both things are true: Chaplin's "interpretation" of a walk-on part amounted to the "creation" of one of the screen's most indelible characters. And he does, as it turns out, "provide most of the film's comedy"—mostly an onslaught of pestiferous business on the lobby set (which barely figures at all in the original story) and in and around the various rooms and hallways—the kind of inventiveness Sennett knew his star was capable of before he even invited him to the studio. None of this is mentioned in the "scenario" because this is not what the scenario was for; once it had suggested a "natural sequence of events" and created a couple of situations presenting comic possibilities, the scenario's work was done. The hotel lobby set has no real purpose in the scenario except to allow Alice Davenport to seek out the hotel's manager to complain about Mabel's boisterous behavior. Only after it was built and populated did it (apparently) occur to Sennett that it presented comic possibilities of its own.

What Chester Conklin remembered of Chaplin's contribution was, "It wound up that he stole the picture from us." But that wasn't all:

Chaplin, on the basis of his success at getting laughs from audiences, progressed rapidly from comedian to director of his own films and writer of his own "scenarios." "I began to offer suggestions which Sennett readily accepted," he recalled. "Thus grew a belief in myself that I was creative and could write my own stories. Sennett indeed had inspired this belief. . . . His manner of working had given me confidence; it seemed right.

"For instance, in *His Prehistoric Past*, I started with one gag, which was my first entrance. I appeared dressed as a prehistoric man wearing a bearskin, and, as I scanned the landscape, I began pulling the hair from the bearskin to fill my pipe. This was enough of an idea to stimulate a prehistoric story, introducing love, rivalry, combat and chase. This was the method by which we all worked at Keystone."

He and Chester Conklin worked up a story taking place in a combination bakery and café—leaving room for lots of pie-throwing, cake-throwing, flour-spattering, and tumbling down the stairway to the kitchen. Sennett told them, in effect, end it with an explosion and you've got a picture, so strikers were introduced and a bomb detonated, and the result was released as *Dough and Dynamite*—which proved to be explosively funny and explosively popular for many years thereafter.

In one long, semi-improvised single take on a posh restaurant set, *The Rounders* allows Chaplin and Roscoe Arbuckle to cut loose as a pair of Dueling Clowns, obviously trying to steal the scene from each other. Neither one looks directly at the other, but neither can perform a gag without the other trying to top it.

In his book *Charlie Chaplin*, Theodore Huff's plot synopsis for *His Musical Career* is typical mistaken identity: "Told to deliver a piano to Mr. Rich at 666 Prospect Street and bring back one from 999 Prospect Street, they get the signals mixed, dragging the piano upstairs to the 999 address and proceeding to remove the one at the other place . . . ." But what Chaplin makes of this—oiling his joints and ears with an oil can in preparation for the task ahead, then riding the piano while Mack Swain does the moving, then reacting violently when the piano falls on Mack, even climbing under the piano with him to give him counsel, before he gets around to giving him any assistance—is an onslaught of gags building up to the kind of "pandemonium" Sennett was aiming for.

The average film made before Griffith, Sennett, and Chaplin simply *was* its own synopsis—a literal, prosaic, usually perfunctory re-enactment of whatever events the written scenario called for. By the time Chaplin made *His Musical Career* in the fall of 1914, he was proving the written text insignificant: his films *were* his performances, and everything else became window dressing.

"We worked together in developing the comedy action, taking a basic idea and constantly adding new gags," as Mabel Normand described it. "Each day Charlie would come to the set brimming with new ideas, which he would act out for me. I would add my suggestions, and soon we were ready for a take."

It's now clear that many of those "new ideas" Chaplin came to the set brimming with were in fact whole sketches or routines lifted bodily from the repertoire of music hall comedians like Fred Kitchen. Europe had a comic tradition at least as old as the *commedia dell'arte*, where a comic scenario was nothing but a starting-off point for comedic interpolation ("Pedrolino, from Isabella's house, learns from Olivetta how she has come to talk to Isabella on Orazio's and the Capitano's account"). So Chaplin took pretty easily to fashioning his films on the boards in front of the camera, and as he gained power and independence in his moves from Keystone to Essanay, to Mutual and to First

National, that is, more and more, exactly what he did: he developed his character and his style out of the non-regimented, improvisational Sennett method.

Film Editors Adrift

Chaplin learned filmmaking from Sennett, who had picked up the D. W. Griffith technique while Griffith was developing it. If you weren't using standard-issue shooting scripts with numbered shots, and you weren't keeping track of the number of takes per shot, how were you identifying the individual shots as you took them, and how were you organizing the shots once they showed up in the cutting room? Chaplin's method, once he was running his own studio, was to number each successive exposure, whether it was another take of the previous shot or a whole new shot.

Gloria Swanson (seated within the tripod) and Bobby Vernon (far right, conferring with director Clarence Badger) were teamed in a series of successful romantic comedies between 1916 and 1917. Josef Swickard, the distinguished-looking gentleman standing just behind Bobby, was one of the original Keystone Cops. (Note the slate used by cameraman J. C. Bitzer [Billy's younger brother] with the initials NG and OK, signifying whether or not another take was needed.) Photo courtesy of Bison Archives.

At Sennett's studio, things got even looser than that. As William Hornbeck, probably the most famous of Sennett's editors, remembered it:

"At the end of a scene, the director might say, 'Well, I think that was a good one.' So the cameraman would grind a few more frames, making the OK sign with finger and thumb. If the director said 'NG,' he would make the NG sign—the hand held out like a traffic cop. Later, the director might decide to use an NG take; that was why the cameraman had to go into the laboratory and break his material down into the print takes. We had our own laboratory. They would screen the rushes first for the director, then Sennett would get a special running, either at the studio or at his home, in the evening, where he had projection equipment.

Everyone is pretty well agreed that when Sennett ran footage he said little but worked up an elaborate body language that spoke volumes. If he squirmed to the right, that meant one thing; if he squirmed to the left, that meant another. If he spat tobacco juice, you knew you were in trouble.

This may explain why Sennett set up a system that allowed him to be selective when it came time to put the final version of each film together and ship the negative to New York.

Stuart Heisler, another Sennett editor from the early days, remembered: "The script girl would give you a little outline; that's what you worked from, the script girl's notes. But you never had to follow them. If you could make it better by switching stuff around, that was permissible, that was part of your job.

Roscoe, Mack, and an unidentified writer discuss ideas for the latest Arbuckle vehicle.
Photo courtesy of Bison Archives.

Keystone Writers, 1915. Left to right are Harry Williams, Hampton Del Ruth, Clarence Badger, Frederick Palmer, Jean Havez, Vincent Bryan (with his arm on the table), Harry Wulze (above/behind), and Charles "Chuck" Reisner. This photo originally appeared in the October 9, 1915 issue of Motion Picture News. *Photo courtesy of Bison Archives.*

You would ask a director, 'Why did you do this?' and he would tell you, and it was usually because it would make sense somewhere farther on in the picture. You wouldn't talk only to the directors; you'd talk to the writers. If you could build a story so that one incident led to something else in the story, that was considered good construction. Something may happen in the very first scene they shot for that picture. It wasn't necessarily on the little card that the director had from the Story Department. But somebody would do something, and it led to something else, and if they hit a key anywhere along the line, they would pick up the key and develop it. They never let it die. . . . You just put together everything the director had done to the best of your ability. This is what they call the first cut. . . . There were many more scenes than would be in the final picture."

Journalist Harry Carr visited the studio for an article in 1915, and Sennett told him that only about 25 percent of the footage shot for a comedy would end up making the final cut. When Kalton C. Lahue wrote *Mack Sennett's Keystone*, he figured it came closer to 20 percent by the end of 1916.

"The fellow who wrote that idea would be assigned to write the titles," Heisler explained. "We would work with him, and we'd be swapping thinking with the guy who wrote the story. Writers, title writers, property men, cameramen or actors—whoever came up with an idea they felt would make a funny picture, they would tell it to somebody, or go to the Story Department and say, 'Is this a good idea for a picture?' Then in that department they would put it on paper and try to develop it enough so that the director had something to go on. In a comedy studio, every time somebody got something they thought was funny, they went around and tried it on everybody, and lots of that stuff got into the films. The writer would put an idea on paper, and if the director liked the idea, then he would make his own notes on it, and go out and shoot it."

A measure of just how vague this idea could be can be gleaned by reading the outline for *Mabel's Strange Predicament*, or the beginning of "Aeroplane Elopement Story," which is reproduced in *Mack Sennett's Keystone*: "Roscoe leaves aeroplane near clump of bushes and goes to girl. Establish a love affair in opening scene between Roscoe and the girl—get over that her father is trying to marry her off owing to her ferocious temper or something." (Shades of *The Taming of the Shrew*—a connection the writer apparently considers best left unstressed.)

Keystone's state-of-the-art cutting room, circa 1916. Future director William Watson was that department's supervisor at the time. Photo courtesy of Bison Archives.

The "SYNOPSIS OF (WORKING TITLE) 'FATTY AND MABEL ADRIFT,'" prepared by the Story Department for the comedy that would later go out with its working title intact, is no less vague in its particulars, but does succeed in telling a coherent story and in spelling out for the production crew what their key challenge is going to be: creating the illusion that Roscoe Arbuckle (the credited writer, as well as director and star comedian of the eventual film) and Mabel Normand are put out to sea in a house that takes on water but manages to stay afloat (finally achieved by alternating shots of a house-shaped vessel floating on the real ocean with separately photographed shots of Roscoe and Mabel swimming for their lives in a flooded interior set—probably situated in the studio pool).

The synopsis supplies the basic story and much of the casting in five paragraphs:

1: "Fatty, a farm boy, noted principally for his strength, good-nature (*sic*) and affection for his dog Fido, loves and is beloved by Mabel, his employer's daughter." But "the son of a neighboring farmer" turns out to be a rival for Mabel's hand, who "swears vengeance ... on the announcement of the wedding." Mabel's father gives the couple "a little cottage by the seashore" for a wedding present, and off they go with Fido to that very spot for a honeymoon, "followed by the vengeful rival."

2: The rival is discovered prowling around the cottage, only to get chased away by Fido. Then, "falling in with a band of robbers he (*sic*) hires them to help him destroy the little cottage." The synopsis bundles the couple off to bed and into a sound sleep, then allows "a terrible storm" to come up—at which point it declares, "[W]hile peacefully sleeping inside the rival and the robbers knock the underpinning from the cottage and float it out to sea." (*You* know what they mean!)

3: Fatty and Mabel wake up to discover they are "far out to sea"—"As a last hope of getting news to shore, they tie a note to Fido's collar and send him out the window, as (once again, *sic*) Noah sent the dove from the Ark." (Cecil B. DeMille might've gotten at least a subtitle out of this quaint Biblical touch, but it hasn't got a snowball's chance at Keystone.) Though he's, strictly speaking, Fatty's dog, Fido goes straight to Mabel's parents and awakens them. Alerted to the new couple's peril by Fido's note, the folks call the "harbor police," then "mount their old tandem bicycle" and head for the wharf, where they manage to run into "the real-estate man who had sold them the little cottage," who takes everyone on his private yacht to begin the rescue operation.

4: Fatty and Mabel have by now climbed out on the roof of the floating cottage and "are rescued by the yachting party."

5: "In the meantime the rival and the robbers return to the cave" (though the cave they "return to" is making its first appearance in this scenario). They quarrel over cards and accidentally manage to drop a lit cigar into a keg of powder, which blows up "and they are all destroyed. Fatty and Mabel return with her mother and father to their happy home" for a happy ending.

Nothing has been said about the harbor police ever getting there, being of any use, or, in fact, doing anything whatsoever. Just about everything you see in the film—the business with the cow's udder, Fatty's fight with Al St. John, the struggle with the oversized fish, the tough biscuits, the "Phantom Kiss," the harbor police tumbling around as Keystone Cops, the heart-shaped graphics, the fact that Mabel's father is a farmer himself, so that much of the action will logically take place on a farm—all of this is pure filmmakers' interpolation, and part of what directors did to earn their paycheck.

This is probably what was meant by Sennett veterans (including Chaplin) who would cavalierly say, "We had no script in those days." Much of what a later scriptwriter would be compelled to nail down on the page before production could begin would still, at this point, be left up in the air to be

In this tender domestic scene, newlyweds Roscoe and Mabel sit down to breakfast with their faithful dog Luke (named Fido in the scenario). Unfortunately, neither Roscoe nor Luke is particularly fond of Mabel's homemade biscuits, much to the poor girl's sorrow. Fatty and Mabel Adrift (1916). Photo courtesy of Bison Archives.

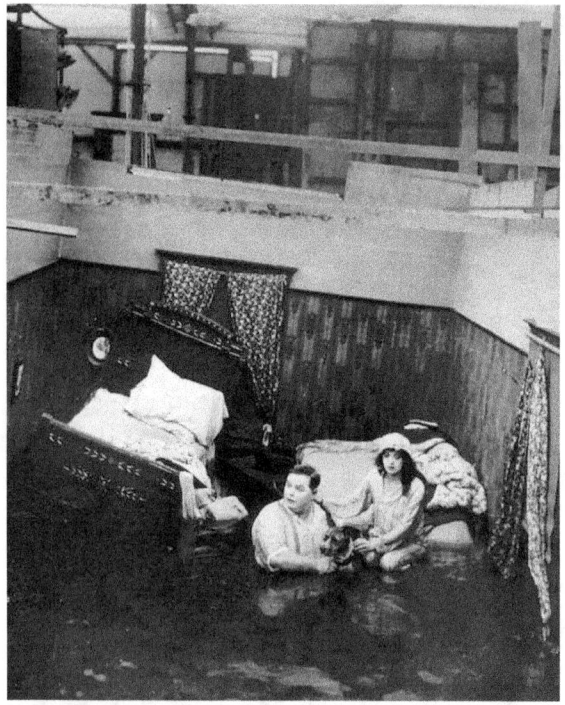

This fascinating production shot shows just how the flooded house scenes were filmed. Fatty and Mabel Adrift *(1916). Photo courtesy of Joseph Adamson III.*

worked out on the set while the camera crew awaited the cue to start cranking.

The subtitles that bracket all this frenetic action are content to be connective and descriptive (THEY LIVED IN SLEEPY HOLLOW), possibly cute (FULL OF HOPE AND FRECKLES), but never competing with the visuals for comedy honors. They might be explanatory ("IN SEARCH OF A PENCIL"), but, since there's no one onscreen saying this, the quotation marks are pointless. All the punctuation, in fact, is casual at best: one subtitle has a period and the next one doesn't. The subtitles appear in the film exactly as they are typed on a separate title list, with errors and inconsistencies intact.

Bright Ideas

By the 1920s, gag subtitles, of the kind H. M. Walker was writing for Harold Lloyd at the Hal Roach studio, had come into fashion, and Sennett stayed on top of the trend. Once a first cut was assembled, the Sennett studio gagmen

This slide for Ben Turpin's 1922 Sennett-Pathé two-reeler Bright Eyes *was used as a coming attraction notice in movie theaters. Photo courtesy of Joseph Adamson III.*

went to work on the subtitles that would pepper the finished film. This process began by making a list of title "spots" (place and story purpose for each title) based not on the script but on the existing cut of the film, then coming up with a list of possibilities for each spot, trying out alternate gags and alternate wordings until the one that got the most laughs won.

So when it came time to establish that Billy Bevan was playing a two-faced butler in the 1922 comedy *Bright Eyes*, the writers suggested subtitles saying, "The butler never let his right hand know what his left was doing" and also "The conceited butler whose every move had a double meaning." They even tried "The butler might have been twins," which could have proved confusing to those members of the audience who had failed to attend any of the story conferences. Sennett's choice for optimum clarity was "The butler was so suspicious he kept a sharp eye on himself."

When Bevan emerges from the kitchen's walk-in refrigerator, the gagmen hazarded "It's a great place to spend the summer" and "I think I'll put a stove in there next winter" before Sennett approved "Heaven help those who have no home on a night like this." (Sennett never missed a chance to lampoon anything that took itself too seriously.)

The line "If your face was your fortune, you'd be arrested for vagrancy" or its alternate, "I think you could chop wood with that face," gave way to the streamlined "That face of yours is hard on furniture."

When the action shifts to a golf course and Ben Turpin starts keeping score on Bevan's shirt front, the written dialogue included "If you can't keep the score on your mind, perhaps you can keep it on your chest" as well as "An evening shirt should be good for something in the afternoon" and "If we play long enough, you may have to go home for another shirt," before everyone finally settled on "If we stop for lunch be careful with the soup."

Bright Eyes was based on a six-page original story called "Wedding Days," which went through several permutations, but essentially concerned Budd Ross and Dot Farley as an ambitious couple hoping to marry off their daughter, played by Harriet Hammond, to a "Titled Imposter" being played by Jack Richardson, then suddenly thrown into a quandary when Ben Turpin shows up at their front door on the wedding day, heir to an oil fortune and hoping to marry Harriet himself.

Faced with literate subtitle options like "In financial distress, Mr. and Mrs. Rossmore had planned to marry their daughter to the first unattached bank account" and "In financial distress, the Hurley family had thrown their daughter at the first titled suitor that loomed up," Sennett finally went for the snappy: "A family of social climbers who were on their uppers."

In the same way, Harriet Hammond's introduction could have gone "The bride's only consolation was looking forward to the day when she might become a widow" or "The bride had beauty while there was room for improvement in the groom" or even "A match that had not been made in heaven," but finally ended up as "The bride's only objection to the wedding was the groom."

When Turpin appears, he's bearing a letter from his father reminding Budd Ross that the two families' original plan was for their children to marry when they grew up, and that Turpin owns forty oil wells in Texas and is worth $50 million (or, as the title writers later put it, "owns nearly all the oil wells West of the Rockies and has a heart as big as a watermelon"). When Dot Farley sees this, she immediately alters her daughter's plans and (apparently more impressed by the oil wells than the watermelon) makes excuses to Jack Richardson's disappointed bridegroom (their daughter "is too young to be married, but that sometime in the future, etc. [sic] and that he will always be a welcome guest to dinner, etc.") The subtitle writers tried handling this line directly: "We'll have to postpone the wedding for a couple of weeks; I'm afraid my daughter is too young to marry." They also tried getting creative: "We'll have to postpone the wedding again, your Lordship; I forgot this is Friday" and "I think we ought to postpone the wedding until next week when it may be cooler." But Sennett finally decided the funniest rendition of this line was the bluntest: "I'm sorry, your Dukeship, but we have a better proposition."

The letter explaining all this is dropped on the floor, so the Jack Richardson character can eventually discover it, and when he finds out what's really going on, he tells the family off publicly, protesting, according to the original scenario, that "they didn't want a husband but a bank roll." What the title writers made of this ranged from "Friends this poor girl (sic) is being forced to marry a freak who has money and oil to burn" to "Friends, the wedding has been called off to force this poor girl to marry a rich oil man who could never look her straight in the face" and to "Folks, I've been chucked aside by this cow-faced fortune hunting (sic) female, so she can sell this poor girl to a cock-eyed cartoon who smells of kerosene oil." None of these were strong enough for Sennett, or possibly for preview audiences, so the writers knuckled down to their typewriters till they came up with "Folks, I'm being canned by this dame so she can slip Flossie to a crooked looking guy (sic) who made a couple of dollars selling kerosene."

It turns out that Turpin is too busy falling for Phyllis Haver, the maid of the house, even to look in Harriet Hammond's direction. But Haver, before Turpin ever came on the scene, was being fought over by Billy Bevan as the house butler and Kalla Pasha as the chef. One look at Ben Turpin is enough to send Harriet Hammond screaming into the arms of Jack Richardson, but she's really less interested in either of these prospective husbands than she is in George

O'Hara as the family's chauffeur. The whole episode on the golf links seems to have been written into the story for the purpose of allowing all these unions and rivalries a chance to play out, first in the cars on the way to the country club (father and mother in the first car, Harriet and Ben coupled in the back seat of the second—till the first car is out of sight, when Harriet climbs into the front seat with chauffeur George, and Ben now comes between Phyllis Haver and Billy Bevan, physically as well as romantically), then on the golf course itself (Ben sending his ball into a stream so that Bevan, as his caddy, has to go look for it while Ben makes time with Phyllis—Harriet driving her ball into available bushes where she and O'Hara, as her caddy, are compelled to disappear together). Budd Ross and Dot Farley go looking for their daughter and their chauffeur "and every time they find them, they have just found the ball. (Chance for love scenes.)" The written scenario has chauffeur George tell Harriet, on one of their expeditions into the wilds of the shrubbery, of his plan to send a fake telegram to the house declaring that Turpin's wells have gone dry and he's a penniless imposter, to save her from this second arranged marriage.

But once the production unit actually got out on the golf course, physical comedy took over, and Billy Bevan and Ben Turpin, along with director Mal St. Clair, had enough fun working up sight gags (Bevan getting down on the green and holding the ball with his fingers so Turpin can run up and kick it, as if this were a football game; Turpin digging an ever-deeper hole with his club in a futile attempt to hit the ball which, if the subtitles are to be believed, goes on well into the night) to remind us that this was, after all, a Mack Sennett two-reel comedy and not a soap opera.

The original story goes on providing complications after this: Jack Richardson goes for the safe and steals the family jewels, but the writers suggest an additional wrinkle where the safe is empty except for a note saying that Harriet has hidden the jewels in a desk or somewhere, so Richardson finds them anyway. Later it's planned to have Richardson put the jewels back in the safe, but a parenthetical note wonders, "Wasn't it decided that he didn't get them in the safe?"

Eventually the revelation that George's telegram is a fake is moved to after it arrives and is accepted by everyone as gospel. In some prints, Dot Farley's reaction when the telegram arrives just as they are about to marry Harriet to supposed millionaire Turpin (turning to her daughter and hissing, "Faint! He's broke!") gets on the screen before we've even seen the telegram come to the door.

An uncle of Turpin's shows up to talk about Ben's new oil wells and assure everybody that his balance sheet is doing fine, but another writer's note reminds us "He starts out as father."

Turpin runs away with Phyllis Haver, and Billy Bevan and Kalla Pasha race after them to get Phyllis back, at which point, according to the scenario, "Ben goes to plank, Bevans and Kali (*sic*) follow and try to knock him in the falls." The writers maneuver Turpin into the middle of this plank, and Bevan and Pasha on either side, with Phyllis trying to join Ben in the middle—but if everybody gets on the plank, it will break and they'll all end up in "the falls."

The final version of the film skips over most of this, and simply races from sequence to sequence, stopping just long enough to reach the punchline of a joke, so that a gag subtitle can take us to the heart of the next sequence. A short script for the pursuit of Ben Turpin and Phyllis Haver, specifying what action takes place on what set, is followed fairly closely (with Bevan and Pasha tying their car to a phone pole with a rope, then getting beaned by the pole when a train hits the car, sending Ben and Phyllis in the wheel-less body of the car skidding down the street and up a loading platform into a hay wagon)—even to the point of turning a tortuously written piece of action for Ben and Phyllis as they stand on the railroad tracks ("Switch camera angle—they still talking to themselves—another train coming close up from behind them—they hear—see—and make a wild jump to the other tracks as the train hits the switch and follows them over—they get into the road this time, as the train roars past") into a neat little sight gag. Ben Turpin is identified onscreen as "An Oil Magnet," but it's not clear whether this is a pun or a simple misspelling.

When *Bright Eyes* was screened in Italy at Pordenone's *Giornate del cinema muto* in 1994, film archivist Paolo Cherchi Usai described as its main attraction to the festival something totally unrelated to anything written for the film: "The routine of a golf tournament turns a standard gag in(to) a havoc of epic proportions."

The Maudlin Circus

In 1925 the studio put out a statement attributed to Sennett himself, which claimed, "The greatest advance in comedy making in the past year, in my opinion, has been in the stories. We at our studios firmly believe that the basic foundation of a two reel comedy is the story, just as this is true with drama. . . . A five reel story boiled down to two reels is what we are striving for in our comedies. And because the story element in our comedies is stressed, the comedians must be different. The trick moustache and 'muff' are fast disappearing . . . a real story needs more or less real characters—believable characters. . . . Story, gags and believable characters are the fundamentals of the new type of two reel comedy."

Thirty years later, Vernon Smith, one of Sennett's story editors, said virtually the same thing: "As a matter of fact those comedies were fundamentally sound in plot structure and characterization. Each comedian had a definite character and a definite range. The stories and the gags were custom-tailored to fit Ben Turpin, Harry Langdon, Billy Bevan, Charlie Chaplin, Mabel Normand, or whichever funny person the story was for . . . Mack Sennett supplied most of the basic ideas. Then he and I would kick most of these basics around until we were satisfied that we had the springboard for a good comedy. Then I would assign two writers to develop it. All they did was tell a story—no gags. They made no attempt to conform to any kind of pattern or even to stay within the limits of the footage required for two reels. . . . When we decided that a yarn was good enough, it went to the gag room."

By this time, Sennett's studio had dropped the name Keystone and articulated its new formula as "Speed, pretty girls, and spectacular effects." But by now Sennett tailored his films more closely to the dimly perceived but nevertheless saleable star personalities of Ben Turpin, Billy Bevan, and a few others, as opposed to his approach in the late teens and early twenties, when the ensemble was everything. Pictures like Ben Turpin's *The Dare-Devil* clearly

Billy Bevan shows off his mighty physique for some pretty (albeit disinterested) female onlookers. Gymnasium Jim *(1922). Photo courtesy of Bison Archives.*

show the influence of Sennett's competitors in the way he had progressed beyond the Keystone technique: Its story is simply two Chaplin Keystones (*The Masquerader* and *A Film Johnnie*) spliced together, but its gags are constructed in the Buster Keaton manner. When Turpin runs toward a doorway, the shot is framed from behind him, so that we perceive it's really a painted flat at about the instant he slams into it.

Sennett considered Del Lord to be "the best" of his directors at delivering the freewheeling, nonsensical kind of footage the times and Sennett's reputation demanded. In heady romps like *Lizzies of the Field*, *The Halfback of Notre Dame*, and *Wandering Willies*, filmic and comic logic took precedence over sense. Lord would receive a carefully structured narrative from the story department, and, as he scavenged it for comic possibilities, it would tend to unwind as the picture unspooled. *Wandering Willies*, as written, involves a clearly delineated love triangle between hero Billy Bevan (slinging hash at a hash house), Kewpie Morgan (as the owner of the place) and Ruth Hiatt as the girl who works there (in whom they are both interested), all of which gets intensified when the girl inherits a fortune in time for everything to be resolved by a big chase. The finished film, as it gallops from one marvelous gag sequence to the next, is, from the evidence, about nothing at all.

In the original story, a letter informing Hiatt she's an heiress motivates the climactic chase. But the subtitle identifying this single piece of paper went through multiple permutations, including "He was stealing my diploma as winner of the beauty contest!" "He was stealing the deed to my Florida apple sauce orchard!" "Look! This proves he is president of the Kidnappers Corporation!" and "The big clam was trying to get a corner on Muscle Shoals." Once you've seen the variant they finally chose to remain in the film ("Look! a mortgage on Niagara Falls!—we must stop it before he shuts off the water!"), try to figure out what it has to do with any of the others, or to the situation depicted on the screen.

But no matter, the theaters and their patrons ate it up. "Here is a real comedy," said the manager of the Empress Theatre in Grundy Center, Iowa, when he ran *Lizzies of the Field*, then added, "All Sennetts are good." An exhibitor in Cullom, Illinois, called *Lizzies* "[t]he best comedy we have ever shown." When *The Halfback of Notre Dame* came to Iowa City, Iowa, the reaction was "Here is a knockout of a comedy." *Halfback* starts out with sight gags on the gridiron, then, once it's worn that out, runs to the campus dental lab for a few sight gags there, slips quickly into the hall for one quick sight gag from the chemistry department, before letting the characters graduate and do sight gags at work and sight gags at play (with some Sennett Bathing Beauties), before tying it all up with a breathless chase and rescue in the air (using a bicycle with propellers), and caps it off with a gag on trolley wires that has nothing to do with any of the previous gags. It is a "knockout" chiefly in terms of inventive gagging, which it provides in abundance.

Frank Capra arrived on the Sennett lot in mid-1924 and immediately concluded that writers had clout: "You could give a director three words, he gets a five-minute routine out of that! The guys who came up with just a few words that could give you a whole routine were looked up to. . . .Gagmen get big money." He also appreciated the story process at work at the Sennett studio: "...the building of a gag, the surprise heaping of 'business on business' until you top it all off with the big one—the 'topper.'"

The nonsensical intertitle above provided enough motivation for a wild chase with the Keystone Cops, proving that logic was unnecessary when making a classic silent comedy. Wandering Willies (1926).

Capra introduced the value of understatement to the Sennett looney bin, and Sennett appreciated it. He was so impressed by Capra's work on the story

Ben Turpin as Rodney St. Clair is caught in a wild automobile chase when he attempts to rescue Madeline Hurlock from her kidnapper, villainously played by Aaron Byrd. The Marriage Circus *(1925). Photo courtesy of Joseph Adamson III.*

that became *Super-Hooper-Dyne Lizzies* that he felt it should be gagged and played a little less wildly than usual, advising his actors, "Don't burst a blood vessel at the beginning of a situation, save it for the iris." But, in its final form, the film's protracted Halloween climax and its most famous scene—in which Billy Bevan pushes an entire line of autos up a hill—made it one of Del Lord's gag-filled comedies, and blood vessels were burst in the usual style.

"Three Men," the story Vernon Smith wrote with Frank Capra which became the Ben Turpin comedy *The Marriage Circus*, may be, as Capra biographer

The dashing Rodney St. Clair (Ben Turpin) in the opening sight gag from The Pride of Pikeville *(Sennett-Pathé, 1927). This type of surprise reveal was used by all the major comedians, including Chaplin, Lloyd, and Keaton. Screencaps courtesy of CineMuseum, LLC.*

Joseph McBride has called it, "a pure, undisguised scream from Capra's heart, an outcry at all the women who had ever mistreated him, beginning, of course, with his mother . . .," or it may have been just what Sennett and Smith said they were looking for: a good, solid, serious story that could be used as the basis for a gagged-up two-reel comedy.

The basic story of "Three Men" is simple: On the day of Turpin's scheduled wedding to Madeline Hurlock, he discovers that she loves one of the two other men who make last-ditch efforts to talk her out of this union. Amid great breast-beating, Turpin (now playing a recurring character called "Rodney St. Clair") first attempts to kill the other man, then, when Madeline pleads for his life, gives her up to him. When he announces to the wedding guests that there will be a switch in bridegrooms, "He is smiling, but his great heart is breaking." Turpin suffers and the third man gnashes his teeth as the ceremony is performed, and when the couple is pronounced man and wife, Ben "goes into hysterics," whereupon he is rushed upstairs and given chiropractic treatment.

In the second version of the story, the same events are gagged up a little and also developed dramatically. The more melodramatic things get, the more likely Turpin's pants are to rip. When he's given a gun to avenge this crime of the heart, he has to be talked out of his first thought, which is to shoot himself. Seeing that Madeline truly loves the other man, he declares, "What right have I, with my cockeyes, to want such a beautiful thing as you." Turning to a full-length mirror, he compares himself to the other man, and the stage directions read, "Ben in his torn pants presents a ludicrous appearance alongside of the handsome Babe [William C. Lawrence]." He declares simply, "He shall take my place at the wedding, you shall marry him." Madeline thanks him, and Turpin kisses her tenderly; since this is a Mack Sennett comedy, this show of emotion causes Turpin's coattails to rise in the air and quiver, and his pants to drop.

This is where the story calls for Turpin to go to his mother and lay bare his soul in the manner that so impressed Mr. McBride: "Mother, you are the cause of me losing my lovely bride. . . . Why did you give me this face and this body? Why must I go through life only to be laughed at and unloved?"

His mother's response to this outburst is to roll up her sleeves, point to a picture on the wall looking exactly like Turpin, and exclaim, "You little runt, I've told you for the 15th time that I'm not to blame, it was your father. . . . This is the last time you'll accuse me of being responsible for you." She chases him around the room swinging a carpet sweeper at him. This scene ends with both mother and son weeping in each other's arms.

As the wedding progresses with a change of bridegrooms, Turpin cries bitter tears "so hot that they catch on fire when they land on the floor, like burning drops of oil"; his heart pumps visibly; he takes out a bottle of smelling salts, sniffs it, and drinks it dry; his visible heart now proceeds to pump faster. When the ceremony is concluded and the couple kiss, "the shock is so great that Ben's heart explodes with a bang." He falls on the floor in a fit of the "Heebie-jeebies."

Taken upstairs for the treatment, he is given a bottle of whiskey by Billy Bevan, drains it, and revives; irritated, Bevan knocks him over the head with it, and he passes out again. The third man, identified as "the heavy," proceeds with the chiropractic treatment, consisting of "twisting Ben's head round and round, getting toe holds on his feet and twisting them round and round, shaking him as a terrier would a rat, beating him with Indian clubs, and finally when all else seems to fail, taking Ben by the heels and swinging him around over the heavy's head. Ben's shoes come off in the heavy's hand and Ben flies out of the window."

Rather quickly, it's explained that he lands in a sand truck and a chase ensues, concluding with Ben being dumped in the ocean and drowning. The End.

As the story is developed, melodrama and absurdity are built up around each other. A gag about laundry being delivered late (by Keystone Cop Heinie Conklin) is introduced, so that Turpin can yell, "Hey, mamma, hurry up with that shirt. I'm getting married in three minutes." When it finally arrives, a string breaks, and the clothes spill out all over the floor and get stepped on; Turpin is forced to attempt to white out a footprint on his one and only dickey with chalk. In a gesture toward giving the original marriage plans some kind of plausibility, the plot point is introduced that, up until now, Hurlock has never seen Turpin out of his military uniform. Trying to tie Ben's tie, his mother lifts him off his feet by the neck and nearly strangles him to death. When he makes his bitter accusation to his mother, the scenario notes ominously that "she takes a horse-whip, such as mothers use on children," and proceeds to chase him and beat him all over the upstairs of the house, then down where the guests are assembled, saving the worst beatings for those he attempts to hide behind. A bizarre fantasy is added in the middle of the wedding ceremony, in which Turpin imagines his astral body floating out of his physical body and flying to Heaven with Hurlock's astral body.

On the set, under joint direction by Reggie Morris and former Keystone Cop Edgar Kennedy, new gags and subplots were introduced. Turpin lands on a Victrola's turntable and gets spun out of the house. It was decided that the heavy should attempt to kidnap Madeline Hurlock, motivating another chase prior to the climactic chase (though the heavy is still permitted to attend the wedding and take part in Ben's treatment, as if this unpleasantness hadn't occurred). While the kidnapping is going on, Turpin's beating at the hands of his mother extends out into the street, with his attempting to escape her wrath by hopping passing automobiles, and her catching up with him on a streetcar. After production, Felix Adler and Al Giebler, two of Sennett's deftest word-smiths, wrote the dozens of possible subtitles. As to why Hurlock agreed to marry Rodney St. Clair in the first place, it was suggested that she "said 'Yes' to Rodney because she didn't have the heart to say 'No'"; that she "won Rodney when she lost an election bet"; that she "accepted Rodney because he had given her his seat in a street car"; or that she "accepted Rodney when she mistook his messenger boy's suit for an admiral's uniform," along with several other possibilities. It was finally decided that she "accepted Rodney while under the influence of a nut sundae."

For the melodramatic moment where Turpin compares himself to the other man in the mirror, the gagmen went baroque: "Take him and I'll bust the mirror!" "Take him and let me save my face!" "Take him, this glass pains me deeply!" "Take him—his picture will look better in the paper than mine!" "Take him, I give up after a moment's reflection!" "Take him, this is the first time I've ever looked in a mirror!" "Take him, I might have had a chance in a bathing suit!"

And the winner? "He's yours without a second look." Let the image get the laugh.

Where the story suggests that Turpin needed a line to the effect that "I will go away so that you two may be happy," the suggestions ran from "Goodbye, it's a bitter pill, but a St. Clair always takes his medicine!" to "Goodbye, I should never have let you see me in the daytime!" and "I'll go West, you go East—and never the trains shall meet!" The end result was "You'll never know where I am, but if you need me—write!"

When it was suggested that he make a philosophical declaration to the effect that it was better to have loved and lost than never to have loved at all, it came out "I've lost in the game of Hearts but thank Heaven I'm still a good pinochle player!"

For the heart-wrenching exchange with his mother, none of the laugh-lines sounded very funny, so Sennett went for the simple and direct, "It's your fault she doesn't like my face!" His mother's answer could have been the smirky "She's right! I divorced your father on the day he shaved!" but is finally pared down to "Don't blame me—look at your dad!"

Only at the preview stage did it occur to anybody to give Turpin a comeback to this argument, closing off the discussion with "Out of a hundred million men you had to pick him!" *The Marriage Circus* was put together in a version that satisfied itself with the first chase and dropped scenes already photographed; once Hurlock was kidnapped and returned, and Turpin's mother had finished beating him and reconciling with him, the maximum level of excitement had been reached, and the picture ended there.

Then a "Re-vamped" version of the film was put together, with the wedding scene, the looney fantasy, Turpin's breakdown, and the final chase reinstated, and everything else moving along more quickly, without stopping to milk any situations with lines like "Out of a hundred million men you had to pick him!" Then the "Re-vamped" version was revamped, with "Out of a hundred million men . . ." restored and "He's yours without a second look" dropped, and with a brand-new opening in a barber shop getting the whole thing off to a better start. When the film was released, San Francisco's *Call* and *Post* called the Turpin comedy "one of his best."

Broken Comedy

By the time the Sennett studio started work on the Ben Turpin comedy *Broke in China* in 1926, it had surrendered to the inevitable and was drafting its scenarios in the standard shooting-script format—with separate gags or stages in the story singled out as specific "scenes" and numbered—that is still in use today. The studio was also keeping better records than before, so we know exactly who was working on the comedy and when they were doing it. It was Arthur Ripley who worked all day on Wednesday, March 24, with Earle Rodney at his side. On Friday and Saturday the 26th and 27th, the ball was passed to Clarence Hennecke. On Monday and Tuesday the 29th and 30th, Hennecke got together with Ripley, Rodney, and Grover Jones. This team spent half the day on Wednesday the 31st huddling on the story with Phil Whitman, then on Thursday April 1 and Monday April 5, Ripley, Rodney, and Jones hashed it out without the other two, bringing Hennecke back into the group on Tuesday the 6th, along with Harry McCoy. On Wednesday and Thursday April 7 and 8, it was Ripley, Rodney, Hennecke, and Jones without McCoy, and on Friday and Saturday the 9th and 10th it was Ripley, Rodney, and Jones without Hennecke—though they brought him back on Monday the 12th, along with English writer Randall Faye, to finish up the story.

The first version of "Turpin Story #241" centers on Turpin as a millionaire and manages to revive the fake-telegram-claiming-he's-bust gag from *Bright Eyes*—not once, but twice! As the story opens, he's preparing for a gala dinner—replete with a small orchestra and a young girl dressed as Cupid hiding inside a massive cake—at which he plans to announce his engagement to Madeline Hurlock, and the guest list of which has been strictly limited to all of his other girlfriends. Ben kicks this charming meal off with a blast on a trumpet, the cue for Cupid to rise from her cake, which she does with jam on her face, since she's already started sampling the goodies. Turpin begins to intone solemnly that he can marry only one of his many girlfriends, "and I hope the losers will act like ladies . . ." As he drones on in this vein, a servant enters with the incriminating telegram, which is soon seen by one of the girls, prompting her unceremonious exit. The next girl to read it follows suit. Soon one entire side of the table has been vacated, while Ben goes on lecturing solemnly to the other side. While Ben is noticing that the first side has been emptied, the other side is in the process of emptying. When there is no one left at the table but Ben and Madeline Hurlock, he says to her, "Poor dears—instinctively they knew you were the chosen one and could not stand it." But once Madeline lays eyes on the telegram, she's gone too. Finally Ben reads it, reacts, and drops it, so that it finds its way to the musicians, who realize they're not going to get paid and head for the door themselves. Ben cries out, "Oh, Cupid—hast thou forsaken me?"—whereupon Cupid emerges from the cake again, fires an arrow into Ben's rear, and exits herself, but not before pilfering "some delicacy" from the table.

Ben's best friend Reggie enters at this point and reveals that he sent the telegram himself because he wished to prove that Madeline was a gold digger and, sure enough, got his wish. Ben (who is seen from the back) just goes on heaving his shoulders, so Reggie suggests he hie himself to a small country village like Meadowbrook—but anonymously, as a poor man, so he can "find someone there who will love you for yourself alone." Ben turns to reveal the shoulder-heaving arises from the fact that he is gobbling corn from a series of cobs. (Chaplin devotees will recognize this as a variation on a gag from *The Idle Class*).

Thus Reel Two finds Ben in Meadowbrook working as a soda jerk at the local drugstore. Without the slightest hint that he's a millionaire, the cleaning girl at the drugstore is madly in love with him, but he's too busy looking for a girl "who will love him for himself alone" to notice. It turns out the name "Meadowbrook" wasn't just pulled out of a hat—it's the home of Reggie's brother, whose little family includes a daughter of marriageable age being played by Ruth Taylor. But she's got a beau of her own, and not only are they happy with each other, but her parents are both happy with the two of them—until Reggie's telegram arrives saying the town's soda jerk just happens to be worth $10 million and "is looking for an old fashioned girl . . ." Suddenly Ruth's boyfriend gets the bum's rush, and she is told to head directly to the soda fountain and to go as "a little demure country girl." At the drugstore, Ben is scouring his customers for likely prospects, but all he sees are men ("rustic types"). Once he learns that all the girls in town work for a living and will dutifully troop into the soda fountain when the noon whistle blows, he watches the clock till the noon hour, anticipating the appearance of a bevy of beauties—but what he sees is a row of stools occupied by Louise Carver types (Ben to druggist: "Are those them?" Druggist to Ben: "...them's those"), and he hangs up his jacket and quits on the spot. At this point Ruth Taylor walks in ". . . with her hands folded Quaker fashion in front of her" and with an order on perfumed note paper for ice cream to be hand delivered by no one but Ben. He falls for her, though she's not so sure about him ("I won't have anything to do with that guy in there"). The cleaning girl must be pressed into service to bicycle Ben to the right house. Once there, he orders her to bicycle around the house while he takes the ice cream in. She ends up wearing a rut around the house while Ben and Ruth make each other's acquaintance—Ruth playing on a pump organ in the living room and Ben singing along, getting one foot stuck in a decorative planter and, while kicking it off, sending it through the window and knocking the cleaning girl off her bicycle. Soon Ruth's parents decide that she and Ben are compatible enough to draft wedding plans, and Ben outdoes himself in that department, enlisting a battery of press photographers to document the occasion. But in the meantime Madeline Hurlock has shown up with a brunette wig, passing herself off as her own sister, and sent that second fake telegram evaporating Ben's fortune. Unfamiliar with this ruse at Ruth's house, they fall for it without question. The wedding plans are not canceled but Turpin is, and Ruth is married to her first love before Ben even gets there. Madeline gets nowhere because Reggie appears and gives her plot away to Ben. He turns to the cleaning girl in desperation, but she says Tough luck, she's teamed up with the druggist. THE END.

All this went before the cameras under the direction of Eddie Cline (who started at Sennett's as an actor and Keystone Cop in 1914 and is best known for collaborating with Buster Keaton on the direction of his great two-reelers and the feature *Three Ages* in the early 1920s and with W. C. Fields on his Universal feature comedies of the late 1930s and early 1940s) and underwent the usual process of having some situations developed and others abbreviated or dropped. The fact that Turpin falls for Ruth Taylor while attending a soda fountain is communicated by getting one of his fingers stuck in a bottle of syrup, not to be extricated without smashing the bottle with a hammer. While crooning in the Martin living room, Turpin (who was best known as a wiry little acrobat before Sennett decided to exploit his lazy eye) finds a spittoon to get his foot stuck in rather than a planter, and—supporting his body with nothing more than a single elbow on the organ top—swings both legs in the air to kick it off, where it beans Andy Clyde (playing Ruth's father) rather than exiting the room. Probably the funniest interpolation Cline and Co. came up with occurs on the morning of the wedding day, when Ben has his team of journalists assembled in his bedroom to watch him primp at his dresser. The photographer fills his tray with flash powder and strikes every note of appropriate caution before igniting it—whereupon the resulting explosion knocks everybody in the room over and propels Turpin clean out of the room and onto the sidewalk (a dummy takes the fall).

Al Giebler, Sennett's most prolific title-writer in the twenties, came up with his usual assortment of zingers to spice up the action, describing Reggie as a man who lived by his wits, which was why he was always broke. To set up Meadowbrook, he came up with "Reggie Martin's brother lived in Meadowbrook—where the fast trains stop—when a cow gets on the track" and "Reggie Martin's brother lived in Meadowbrook—where you can spend a week—any afternoon" and, if you didn't like those, "Reggie Martin's brother lived in Meadowbrook—Where lots of good people have come from—and never went back." To set up Ruth's parents, he proposed "'Squire' Martin and his wife—the kind of old fashioned couple you meet in books—of fiction." But Sennett actually approved "'Squire' Martin practiced a little law—and a lot of economy." To introduce the drugstore, it was "Pillsbury's Drug Store served the best crushed turnip sundaes in Meadowbrook." Ben Turpin's dialogue of dismay with the druggist could always go: "Are those the village belles?" "Yep, but they've stopped ringing!" When Andy Clyde tells Ruth to look rural and demure, he might say, "Go put on the dress your Aunt Hetty wore—before she went in the Follies!" When she's not impressed by Turpin's attempts to serenade her, Giebler suggested "That kind of singing will sour the milk—" Ben's instructions to the press photographers potentially included "See that my picture is broadcasted on the radio—" and "You may send my pictures everywhere—but not to the comic papers!" but the final choice was "Make me look as much like John Barrymore as possible." And when Madeline Hurlock makes her appearance in the second reel, the final, approved subtitle was succinct: "The news that Roland was still rich reached Helen Hardcastle one day—and she reached Meadowbrook the next."

What to call this laugh-jerker? Writers wrote Love's Sweet Taffy, Ladies Prefer Dough, and Gentlemen Prefer Ladies. They tried Love Laughs at Soda Slingers and Love Laugh at Soda Fountains (sic—those up on their Buster Keaton will recognize these as variants on the opening subtitle of Cops). They came up with When Sweeties Turn Sour, Blistered Hearts, Lukewarm Lips, Hungry For Wedding Cake and Too Many Cookies. Previews were held. Del Lord directed a day's worth of retakes on June 19 with Ben Turpin, Andy Clyde, Ruth Taylor, and Thelma Hill, who was cast as the cleaning girl, at one of the local movie ranches.

But in the last analysis, Sennett finally decided that the only way to save this picture was to make it two pictures, and to give each one of them something exotic enough to pep it up. So now Production #241 would combine "Country Scenes" (meaning Meadowbrook footage from Reel 2 already in the can) with a "Chinese Set," and a whole new film, Production #261, would be called into being blending the "Turpin in Evening Clothes (Engagement Party)" sequence, or Reel 1, with some "Theatrical Scenes," giving the proceedings a taste of Broadway.

The "Chinese Set" created for the original production, #241, was first called The Shanghai All Nations Café and was imagined as an Oriental night spot where Turpin and another actor (turned out to be Don Maines) could visit as American sailors and tell the Meadowbrook story as a flashback. They start out with Ben on the dance floor doing a solo dance which is received with approval by Don Maines, his monkey, and no one else. At length the character designated as "Head Waiter, Manchu Type Chinaman" (to be played by Tiny Ward, with the suggestion "Have Andy Clyde make him up"—acknowledging that one of the studio's star comedians doubled as its resident special makeup expert) proposes to Ben that he vacate the dance floor and take his seat. Ben has no more than a single dollar bill to spend, which he wields conspicuously enough to catch the monkey's attention, and the monkey decides that a good place for it is #36 on the roulette table, and soon Turpin has a lot more than a dollar to spend—he even has a half-dollar to drop carelessly back on #36. When the Proprietor of the place sees Turpin pocket his winnings, it prompts him to get bargirls Louise Carver and Alice Belcher and tell them to "get that wad of dough back from them or out you go." Soon Louise and Alice have got Turpin pouring his heart out to them, cueing completed Meadowbrook footage to be cut in as flashbacks—and all the while he's accumulating a stash on #36 and the Proprietor is getting increasingly agitated. Through the discovery of birthmarks and family connections, and a brand new flashback to 1880 showing Don Maines walking out on Louise Carver and Carver carrying her baby (who is described as "Ben in baby clothes," with no explanation of how this is to be accomplished), to the steps of the "Sailors' Mission," it is revealed that Don Maines is not only Carver's ex-husband but Ben's real father. When, in the midst of these revelations, the Proprietor tells Turpin that he's won a bunch of money on the roulette table, he doesn't have the time or attention to deal with it. Having nothing else to stake against Ben's winnings, the Proprietor sees no alternative to wagering his entire café. Next thing he knows, he's notifying Turpin that he owns the place. Ben's reaction to this news is to say, "Well, if this is my café, now I can dance and no one can stop me"—which he proceeds to do. THE END.

Again Eddie Cline took the story to the stage and shot it, and by the time he was through the Chinese nightclub (now simply "The All Nations Café" located in Shanghai) is beautifully appointed and beautifully photographed, but never does get turned over to Ben Turpin—and never surrenders to the

Mack Sennett madness either. Turpin's appearance as an infantile version of himself is achieved through the stratagem of two sets for the same "Sailors' Mission" front door: a regular-sized set to which Louise Carver can carry a doll or a dummy she keeps well wrapped and hidden from camera, and an outsized replica of the same set toward which Ben Turpin—shorn of moustache and sailor's uniform and adorned only in swaddling clothes—can tread softly as if on little baby feet in a separate shot (and in a pallid imitation of Harry Langdon's impersonation of his own baby at the end of the Sennett feature *His First Flame*). Turpin's sailor character does acquire a hefty fortune at the gaming table, and in exactly the accidental way called for by the original script, but the Proprietor never does stake his entire establishment against Ben's winnings, so the small amount of high-stepping Turpin does on the dance floor in the opening scene never leads to the planned resolution.

And again the title-writers went to work. The introductory title for the rechristened locale might read "The Café of All Nations—Where wine flowed like water—and tasted about the same." Ben Turpin's introduction could go "Donald Drake, sailor—anxious to spend a pleasant evening—and one dollar." ("Donald Drake" would later be used as an early name for a Walt Disney character before it was simplified to "Donald Duck.") Or, just as easily, "Joe Flotsom, a high spirited sailor with his bank roll at low tide" (*sic*). Louise and Alice were given an assortment of alternative identities, including "Molly and Polly—broke hearts in the café—and dishes in the kitchen." When Turpin gets a look at the menu and realizes his dollar won't go very far, his reaction finally boiled down to "At these prices, we can't even smell a cork!" Once he samples the drink he can actually afford, the writers came up with "Tastes like disappointed cider!" And when they needed a new line for a customer to hand Ben at the Meadowbrook soda fountain, their best shot was "I want a nut sundae with no wise cracks!" No other options were offered and none was needed.

The new main title could have been Romance and Chop Suey, A Drug Store Cowboy, Fate's Football, or Chinese Hiccups, but finally, with a Christie comedy starring Bobby Vernon called *Broken China* in current release, the natural lampoon follow-up was *Broke in China*—and with that title, Production #241 reached theaters on April 24, 1927.

For the theatrical footage, it was decided to send Turpin to a grand Broadway theater on performance night to break the news to one of his rejects, to be played by Alma Bennett, and to have her respond with a spectacular series of suicide attempts. (Silent comedy buffs familiar with *Haunted Spooks* and *Hard Luck* are accustomed to the idea of suicide as an acceptable basis for a comedy routine.) Beginning in her dressing room and proceeding to Turpin's mansion, the actress turns hardcore drama queen and stages a spectacular series of phony suicide attempts, with empty vials of poison and guns with empty chambers, just as Ben is trying to make nice with Madeline Hurlock (still his real fiancée) and her expansive mother, to be played by Sunshine Hart. Bearing the brunt of most of this is Turpin's valet, who suffers falls into filled bathtubs, teeth being punched out of his mouth, and a host of other indignities—and only partially compensating for the punishment is a passionate kiss planted on the same mouth by Alma Bennett in the dark when she mistakes him for the Master of the House. The scripted action was to climax when Bennett finds an ancestral battle axe in the house and goes after everybody with it, jabbing Ms. Hart in the behind through a door. The butler finally sends for the police, who herd the motley crowd into a paddy wagon, and the script ends when Hart sits on one side of the wagon, causing the whole thing to list at a 45 degree angle.

Once Eddie Cline had turned this concept into workable footage, sight gags got added and subtracted, and other modifications were made: the battle axe was reduced to a baseball bat, which is broken over Sunshine Hart's head, saving her posterior for another day, and the valet's indignities came to include getting brained with it when Turpin ducks Bennett's swing.

Then the title-writers went to work again—taking their second shot at some of the same spots. One stab at an opening went "The story of a gilded youth who loved not wisely—but too many times" (with no visible apologies to *Othello*). Two tries at introducing Ben Turpin were "Of all society's upper crust—Courtney Crumpett was the sweetest crumb" and "Virgil Vancourt, a sweet crumb from the social pound cake" (making it clear that somebody was impressed by Harry Langdon's introduction in *Saturday Afternoon*, "Just a crumb from the sponge cake of life." After several different tries, Alma Bennett's introduction became "Alma, Virgil's former flame—who doesn't know she is about to be put out." Turpin's extravagant dinner now happens "[a]t the Hotel Highattan," where he might announce, "One of you will be picked for my wife—the others will please not weep in the clam chowder!" When the other girls have left the dinner, Turpin's line to Madeline Hurlock might go "The darlings have probably gone after rice and old shoes!" Another possibility they conjured up was "They're so polite—they know two's company—and twenty's a crowd!" When Alma gets the bad news just before her big entrance, her title could read "Stop the show, or give me a sad song to sing—" (Marx Brothers fans will recognize variations on those lines used later in *A Night at the Opera* and *Duck Soup*.) Attempts to turn suicide into comedy extended to lines given to Reggie such as "She says she'll shoot herself in two minutes—hurry or you'll miss it!" and "... she commits suicide every time she's turned down!" as well as

Alma's spiteful line to Turpin "If you are a gentleman—you'll shoot yourself to keep me company!"

The writers came up with an imposing array of main titles for this mélange, but only Marriage or Your Life got so much as a stray mark from Sennett's pencil. Finally, on another go-round, they dreamed up *The Jolly Jilter* and Production #261 was released by Pathé under that title on March 13, 1927. The Sennett editors had in the end managed to create a version of this story that dispensed with Turpin's grand dinner (and "the Hotel Highattan") altogether, and the single story that had started life with two fake telegrams declaring Ben Turpin a pauper had morphed into two separate stories and no fake telegrams at all.

As the years went by and success after success had made Sennett a wealthy, important figure in the movie business, he also became less accessible to his employees. Here he is, in his so-called "Ivory Tower," in conference with an unidentified writer. Photo courtesy of Bison Archives.

The Depression and Beyond

When sound came in, Sennett (like most Hollywood producers) reverted to the theatrical mode, wherein writing a scene became a matter of filling the page with dialogue, and filming a scene became a matter of actors learning their lines and cameramen obscuring the microphone. But, like John Ford, Howard Hawks and Alfred Hitchcock, Mack Sennett was one of the silent-era filmmakers who struggled to keep the silent film traditions alive in the era of synchronized dialogue. Bing Crosby's memories of working with Sennett involved his attempting to motivate a chase in every instance, which squares with Chaplin's memories, and the Sennett talkies do succeed in incorporating action sequences more often than was the general short-comedy norm. The studio's best talkies were probably the W. C. Fields shorts, and Fields was his own best writer; even he was never content with his own written dialogue, and was notoriously free with notes, revisions and spontaneous improvisations—to the extent that no two takes of any one of his scenes contained the same action or dialogue. But Fields, like Sennett, had worked with D. W. Griffith himself, and needed no help in the creativity department.

It was a W. C. Fields short, *The Barber Shop* in 1933, that became the last film produced by the Sennett studio to go into theatrical release. But in the twenty-two years of the existence of the Keystone and Mack Sennett studios, they had created a tsunami of an impact that continued to be felt for decades afterward. Charlie Chaplin and Harry Langdon, having created their screen characters at Sennett's studio, went on to use them to great effect in creating their worldwide fame.

Stories, gags, and techniques that got their start at Sennett's studio went on to active life all over Hollywood. In *Hold Everything*, a 1923 Christie comedy with Bobby Vernon, a lake is drained as soon as the bad guy is thrown into it, for no clear reason other than it happened in *A Muddy Romance*. The 1932 Sennett short *The Loud Mouth* was remade at Jules White's short comedy unit at Columbia, once in 1940 as *The Heckler* with Charley Chase, then again in 1946 as *Mr. Noisy* with Shemp Howard. Conscious references to and parodies of the Mack Sennett style, such as Will Rogers's *Big Moments from Little Pictures*, Vitaphone's *Keystone Hotel*, 20th Century-Fox's *Hollywood Cavalcade*, and Universal's *Bud Abbott & Lou Costello Meet the Keystone Kops*, poured forth from studio after studio and became a staple of early television. Billy Bevan's contretemps with a live oyster in his oyster stew in the Sennett comedy *Wandering Willies* was revived by Clyde Cook in *Thundering Taxis*, George Sidney and Charlie Murray in *The Cohens and Kellys in Trouble*, Jerome "Curly" Howard in *Dutiful but Dumb*, Shemp Howard in *Shivering Sherlocks*, Larry Fine in *Income Tax Sappy*, and Lou Costello in *Here Come the Co-eds*. Sennett studio footage itself was recycled in features put together by Robert Youngson, such as *The Golden Age of Comedy* and *When Comedy was King*.

Harold Lloyd's description of story development with his gag writers sounds like a typical Sennett story's evolution: "'How about a railroad picture?' one suggests. We canvas the idea, agree and set to thinking in terms of railroading. Let's have the boy a country station agent, baggage man and telegrapher, but the telegrapher suggests a lineman and the lineman suggests a telephone story. A bank robbery is written into the telephone story as an incident. It grows until railroad, telegraphy and telephone all are crowded out and the boy who started to be a country station agent winds up as a bank clerk."

Possibly the single-most visible effect that Sennett and his methods had on the filmmaking process in general lay in the roster of talented behind-the-scenes personnel who cut their cinematic eyeteeth at his studio. Even the obvious cases, like Chaplin, Capra, Eddie Cline, Mal St. Clair, and Eddie Sutherland, account for a hefty portion of classic Hollywood. William Hornbeck eventually edited for Capra, as well as George Stevens and Alexander Korda, and became one of the best-known and most authoritative film editors in the business. Del Lord helped fashion the filmic personality of the Three Stooges and guided them through most of their best comedies. Cameramen like Fred Jackman, Elgin Lessley, and Hans Koenekamp did some of the finest and most innovative cinematography in Hollywood. And Sennett veterans like Stuart Heisler, his friend Ray Enright, and Tay Garnett, William Beaudine, Frank Lloyd, Victor Heerman, Lloyd Bacon, Clarence Badger, and Roy and Hampton Del Ruth entered the ranks of the industry's most creative, prolific, and reliable directors. Most of these men were not shy about the benefit their Sennett experience had given them—as when Capra admitted, "What a thing that was, to have that experience of spreading a gag and playing it out, getting more laughs, more laughs, more laughs—with Sennett! When sound came in, I brought that experience with me. I had a great head start on these things."

Anyone who'd had a chance to practice filmmaking the way D. W. Griffith had really envisioned it—developing a film out of the contributions of many people, rather than mass-producing it out of an ironclad script, budget, and schedule—understood that a screenwriter's function was, ideally, to create a ballpark estimate of what a film's story would be, and to allow good performers to play in that ballpark.

Sources:

My key source for this article was the story files contained in the Mack Sennett Papers held at the Margaret Herrick Library of the Academy of Motion Picture Arts & Sciences in Beverly Hills—particularly the files for *Mabel's Strange Predicament, Fatty and Mabel Adrift, Wandering Willies, Super-Hooper-Dyne Lizzies, The Marriage Circus, Bright Eyes,* and *Broke in China.* Three Stooges scripts in the Jules White Papers at the Margaret Herrick Library were compared to their filmic counterparts. I also consulted such books as Mack Sennett and Cameron Shipp, *King of Comedy* (Garden City, New York: Doubleday & Co., Inc., 1954), Brent E. Walker, *Mack Sennett's Fun Factory* (Jefferson, North Carolina and London: McFarland & Co., Inc., 2010), Gene Fowler, *Father Goose* (New York: Covici Friede Publishers, 1934), Kalton Lahue, *Mack Sennett's Keystone: The Man, The Myth, and the Comedies* (South Brunswick and New York: A. S. Barnes and Company, 1971), Kevin Brownlow, *The Parade's Gone By . . .* (New York: Alfred A. Knopf, 1968), Charles Chaplin, *My Autobiography* (New York: Simon & Schuster, 1964), Theodore Huff, *Charlie Chaplin* (New York: Henry Schuman, 1951), Harry M. Geduld, *Chapliniana: A Commentary on Charlie Chaplin's 81 Movies, Volume I: The Keystone Films* (Bloomington, Indiana: Indiana University Press, 1987), Harold Lloyd and Wesley Stout, *An American Comedy* (New York: Longmans, Green & Co., 1928), Frank Capra, *The Name Above the Title* (New York: The Macmillan Co., 1971), Joseph McBride, *Frank Capra: The Catastrophe of Success* (New York: Simon & Schuster, 1992), Randy Skretvedt, *Laurel & Hardy: The Magic Behind the Movies* (Beverly Hills: Moonstone Press, 1987), and Chuck Harter and Michael J. Hayde, *Little Elf: A Celebration of Harry Langdon* (Duncan, Oklahoma: BearManor Media, 2012)—I have drawn on many of the same sources as the authors of this last book, but a decade or two earlier. Many biographical and career details have been culled from various editions of the *Motion Picture Studio Directory and Trade Annual*, *The Film Year Book*, *Motion Picture Almanac*, and *The American Film Institute Catalog of Motion Pictures Produced in the United States: Feature Films* before the Internet Movie Database came along, but since then I have consulted that as well.

Periodical sources include Bob Thomas, "Sennett Recalls Past Glory," *Los Angeles Mirror-News*, 1/23/59, Jeff Davis, "Mack Sennett, Serene at 80, Recalls Glory," *Los Angeles Mirror-News*, 6/20/60, and the unsigned "Satrap of Slapstick," *Newsweek*, 11/14/60. There are many quotations from the "Short Subjects," "Newspaper Opinions on New Pictures," and especially "What the Picture Did for Me" sections of *Exhibitors Herald*, from March 29, 1924 through October 24, 1925.

I also drew on my interviews with Stuart Heisler, which were done in Carlsbad, California, in 1977 and 1978 for an oral history which is being edited for the Directors Guild of America, and the interview with Frank Capra and Walter Lantz I did with Paul Maher in Silver Lake, California, June 5, 1981.

JOE ADAMSON is an award-winning writer/filmmaker known for his witty books *Groucho, Harpo, Chico, and sometimes Zeppo*; *Tex Avery: King of Cartoons*; *The Walter Lantz Story*; and *Bugs Bunny: Fifty Years and Only One Grey Hare*. He also played a major role in the creation of three acclaimed documentaries: *The Marx Brothers in a Nutshell*; *W. C. Fields Straight Up*; and *The Chaplin Puzzle*. A longer version of his in-depth essay "The Sennett Story" originally appeared on the Blu-Ray set of CineMuseum's *Mack Sennett Collection, Vol. 1*.

Chapter 8
Fact, Fiction, and Folly:
The Mythology of the Keystone Cops
By Lea Stans

Photo courtesy of Bison Archives.

Of all the famous names of American silent comedy, from Charlie Chaplin to Buster Keaton to Laurel & Hardy, few performers embody the zaniness of the era more thoroughly than Mack Sennett's Keystone Cops. Decades after they ran and tumbled and took pratfalls past the hand-cranked cameras, these hapless policemen have become icons of classic slapstick. Who among us isn't familiar with their round helmets, flying coattails, and sudden spills out the back of rickety patrol cars?

Or rather, who among us isn't familiar with them . . . in theory? For aside from glimpsing a few heavily edited clips of Keystone films, not too many people nowadays will actually sit down and enjoy Sennett's century-old shorts.

Florida-based political cartoonist Bill Day takes on the state's "Keystone Cops," otherwise known as the Florida Department of Law Enforcement (FDLE), in 2015. Bill Day drawing courtesy of Cagle Cartoons.

Still, it's clear that virtually everyone knows of the Cops, or at least has a misty idea of what the Cops were supposedly like in that long-ago era. Think of how often inept modern authority figures are deemed "a bunch of Keystone Cops" in newspaper op-eds alone.

If you asked your general man-on-the-street to describe the Cops, you would likely hear something along these lines: they were a zany group of bumblers; they had their own series; they were always trying and failing to save the day. And yes, he might say that they probably threw a lot of pies. (After all, isn't that what silent comedy was all about?)

But a closer look at the Sennett shorts reveals that the way the Cops were used in the original one-, two-, and even split-reelers was somewhat different from this popular mythology. (For one thing, precious few pies can be found.) One of the joys of exploring silent comedy is uncovering forgotten tropes, trends, and trivia that can clarify our understanding of this giddy era and deepen our appreciation of it. And who couldn't benefit from deepening their appreciation of the Keystone Cops?

When he first started using policemen characters at Keystone, Mack Sennett was aiming at a general kidding of authority, a popular theme in both silent comedy and burlesque theater. His imagination was sparked by memories of 1900s burlesque shows in particular. "Their approach to life was earthy and understandable," he told his biographer Cameron Shipp. "They whaled the daylights out of pretension. . . . They reduced convention, dogma, stuffed shirts, and authority to nonsense, and then blossomed into pandemonium . . . I thought all this was delightful."

He certainly wasn't the first director to use comic cops, or even the first to involve cops in comic chases. A good example is the early short *The Unfortunate*

Policeman (1905) by English director and film pioneer Robert W. Paul. The policeman in question is shown flirting with a woman, to the ire of his romantic rival who dumps a can of paint on the policeman's head and then bolts. The angry cop proceeds to chase him all over town, looking like a buffoon in the process.

Sennett also wasn't the first to use an entire bumbling police force. Georges Méliès's *The Scheming Gambler's Paradise* (1905) is set in an illegal gambling hall that's quickly transformed into an innocent dry goods store, just before a police force enters. (Later, when the lights are out, the cops bust in again and mistakenly start fighting one another.) An even better example is the charming French one-reeler *Policemen's Little Run* (1907) by Ferdinand Zecca, involving a particularly inept force trying to capture a dog that's stolen a leg of lamb from a butcher shop. The dog leads the cops on a whirlwind chase through the streets of Paris, and thanks to their cowardice, *he* starts chasing *them*.

Sennett loved French comedies in particular, reportedly working with a translator at one point so he could enjoy them at his Edendale studio. Their gleeful kidding of authority would not only be mirrored in his own films but amplified. Somewhere along the way he decided that if the exploits of one or two police officers was funny, regular appearances by the pack of Cops was

Algy on the Force (1913) was one of the first films to feature the Keystone Cops. In the front row (at far left) is Charles Avery; standing just behind him is a young Edgar Kennedy; Nick Cogley is the pompous man at the right. Photo courtesy of Bill Cassara.

guaranteed to be a riot. (Similar logic was applied to the attractiveness factor of the Sennett Bathing Beauties.)

But there was at least one major difference between those 1900s one-reelers and the Keystone comedies: the Sennett Cops were not the main stars. And here's where we address the biggest myth about the Keystone Cops: that they starred in their own series.

In reality, it was rare for the Cops to be the main focus of a film—and no Sennett short ever had "Keystone Cops" in the title. Police did, in one way or another, make regular appearances in Sennett's films almost from the second he started creating them in 1912. His third Keystone release, split-reeler *Riley and Schultze*, was about a constable and a sergeant vying for the same girl's attention, and *At It Again*, released a few weeks later, contained the first verifiable appearance of an entire police force. (It was also advertised as "an uproarious 'cop' picture.") Contrary to popular belief, *Bangville Police* (1913) wasn't the first "Cops" film—not by a long shot—although it may have been the first release in which police have major roles, albeit with "rural yokel" characterizations (and the attention is still centered on Chief Fred Mace).

The Keystone Cops take on the case of The Stolen Purse, *filmed in November 1912 and released in February of the following year. From left to right are Mack Sennett himself (holding the purse in question), Henry "Pathé" Lehrman (wearing a derby), Ford Sterling, and Fred Mace. Chester Franklin (who later became a successful director) can barely be glimpsed behind Sterling, and Arthur Tavares (later an editor of feature films) is the desk sergeant at the far right.* Photo courtesy of Bison Archives.

However, these early Keystones don't necessarily contain the best examples of the Cops as we know them today. Sennett's signature tropes took time to evolve, especially since cinema itself was still evolving nearly simultaneously. While we can point to a few examples of police-oriented Keystones like *Bangville Police* or *In the Clutches of a Gang* (1914), those still revolve mostly around the character of the police chief.

Once the Sennett style was in place, many of the Keystone shorts displayed a formula that started with a foundation of bold farce, added a generous heaping of slapstick, and frequently built up to a fast-paced chase sequence at the end. And it was this chase sequence that was the lifeblood of the Keystone Cops. In many shorts, the sequence went as follows: mayhem is caused by one or more of the main characters; someone telephones the police; the chief answers the phone and then orders his clumsy force to rush to the rescue; the force tumbles out of the police station and either runs or drives to the rescue, showing up too late, in most instances, to be of use to anyone. Shots of their frantic running and their packed patrol car zooming through the hilly Edendale landscape are interspersed with shots of the main frenzy taking place—the famed "parallel editing" that masters like D. W. Griffith used so well. Sennett's editors arguably turned it into a science.

In short, the Cops provided extra mayhem on top of the mayhem already being caused by the main characters. This might sound a bit strange to anyone who wholeheartedly believes the second-biggest Keystone Cops myth: that they were an ensemble cast of wacky characters. While they were popular with audiences and certainly made a strong impression on the screen (they were basically the Sennett mascots), the Cops were in truth more of an impersonal jumble of ill-fitting coats and helmets than vivid personalities. Membership in the force was on a "revolving door" basis, usually dependent on whichever actors were handy at the time.

Sennett, who never minded playing along with the legends about his studio, would claim in his autobiography that there were seven specific actors who were the "original" Keystone Cops: Edgar Kennedy, Bobby Dunn, Slim Summerville, George Jeske, Charles Avery, Hank Mann, and the unverifiable Mack Riley. However, "original" was used very loosely, especially since not all of these gentlemen were actually working on the lot in the beginning. In reality, the number of actors who pop up as Cops just in the first few years of the studio's existence is vast: Nick Cogley, Roscoe Arbuckle, Mack Swain, Raymond Hatton, Grover Ligon, Arthur Tavares, Fritz Schade, Al St. John, Chester Conklin, Bill Hauber, Marvin Cox, Rube Miller, Billy Gilbert, Dave Anderson, Fred Mace, Dick Smith, Harry McCoy, James Bryant, Frank Hayes, Glen Cavender, Eddie Cline, Joe Bordeaux, even Charlie Chaplin himself—to name a bunch.

On one of the rare occasions when members of Sennett's police force were identified by name, eight actors were pictured in a program for the 1914 "Picture Player Camera Men's Ball." In panel one are G. G. (Grover) Ligon, M. G. (Robert Marvin) Cox, Billy Gilbert, and Al St. John. Panel two has Geo. W. Jaeschke (Jeske), W. D. (Hank) Mann, W. C. (Bill) Hauber, and Bert Hunn. Photos courtesy of Brent Walker.

In general, the rule for getting to play a Cop was simple: if you were willing, weren't afraid of stunt work, and could pull off a few pratfalls, you were in. (Mastery of the tricky "108," where the performer does a forward flip and lands on his back, was a bonus.)

Buster Keaton and Al St. John are, to all intents and purposes, Keystone Cops in the Comique Roscoe Arbuckle short The Rough House *(1917).*

Buster Keaton expertly demonstrates a variation of the "108." In a filmed 1976 interview with Kevin Brownlow, former stunt man Harvey Parry described a "108" as "the old fall where you walk along the street and you step on a bar of soap. You go up in the air like that—flat—then boom, you come down, flat on your back. Of course, the flatter you land the better it is for you because it's not a one-point landing, it's an all-points landing."

A new actor might try his luck as a Cop in hopes of getting larger roles down the line, although at Keystone you might play a lead one week and next week show up in a slightly dented helmet again. Frequently, supporting actors and extras in a short would do double duty as Cops in the same film, their faces sometimes disguised with crepe hair mustaches.

All this isn't to say that the Cops lacked personality—far from it. Many of the actors who portrayed Cops had backgrounds in acrobatics, helping them tough out the regimen of crashes and falls with carnivalesque style. Watching their rapid-fire sequences closely shows that some actors tried to drop in their own gleeful comedic touches whenever possible. In a shot where the force rushes past the camera one actor might do a crazy pratfall, and when many are packed into the patrol car one might try mugging a little more than the others or improvise with the Cop next to him. And, of course, there was usually a hardy soul who volunteered to cling to the back of the car and get dragged along the ground (this feat was done "safely" by using a low, well-hidden kind of skateboard).

Then again, *all* of the Cops were expected to be hardy souls, performing whatever stunts came into the director's head. One short might feature them bouncing around in the patrol car as it zigzagged on soaped-up streets, nearly tipping over; another might show the car teetering on the edge of a cliff, as a flailing Cop or two dangled from the back. Many shorts reveled in water stunts, where the whole force usually plunged off one of those high, Southern California piers into the chilly ocean. Contrary to breathless legend, precautions would be taken whenever possible (although today's insurance companies would probably raise their eyebrows). For instance, stunts involving heights relied on optical illusions, the camera placed so the ground (or nets and mattresses below) wouldn't be visible. Some actors likely wore padding to help protect them during the more back-breaking pratfalls. Still, even simpler stunts, like the Cops tumbling out of the police station in an unwieldy

pile, probably resulted in more than a few bruises. No doubt the adventurous actors also saw them as opportunities to show off more acrobatics.

The "Keystone hop," as demonstrated in this publicity shot for Bud Abbott & Lou Costello Meet the Keystone Kops *(1955).*

A new generation of Cops imitate the originals: Eddie Quillan (saluting), Andy Clyde (as Ford Sterling's Chief character), and the towering "Tiny" Lipson (as Mack Swain). Love in a Police Station *(1927). Photo courtesy of Bison Archives.*

While they might not have had distinct characters of their own, as a group the Cops had a specific performance style that could be spotted from a mile away. They ran with batons flailing and knees lifted high, creating a cartoonish effect. Their scrambles were often punctuated with what former child actor Coy Watson Jr. called the "Keystone hop"—"a jump straight up into the air; pulling their feet and knees up high and then back on their feet a bit off balance." (Buster Keaton would later master the tropes in the 1917 Arbuckle comedy *The Rough House*, where he and Keystone veterans Al St. John and Glen Cavender race to the rescue in Cops garb.) And the shots of Cops running single file along a roof or a hilltop have taken on their own iconic status.

If they appeared comic as a group rather than as individuals, they were also particularly inept as a group. In one priceless sequence from *The Knockout* (1914), they attempt to capture Roscoe "Fatty" Arbuckle with a rope and he single-handedly drags the entire force across the ground. In *Tillie's Punctured Romance* (1914), groups of Cops pursue a rampaging Marie Dressler on foot, in a two-seater car, by speedboat, and finally, even by rowboat. Each group, of course, fails to stop her.

If any single Cop got to be a little more character than caricature (so to speak), it was the police chief, most famously portrayed by Ford Sterling in his famed chin-whiskers-and-round-glasses getup ("Chief Teheezel" was his moniker). While in later years Sterling was strongly identified with the role of "police chief," that was just one of the many characters he portrayed during his 1912-1914 reign as one of Sennett's biggest stars.

We could, if we like, get even more detailed in our dismantling of the Keystone Cop mythology and examine the most fundamental detail of their legacy: the alliteration in the spelling of their name. The Cops weren't always the "Kops"—up until the mid-1910s, they were commonly called "the Keystone police force" or simply "Keystone cops (with the lower case 'c')." One early example of the creative spelling appears in the July 1914 *Moving Picture World*, which reported: "The Keystone Kops have become so well known that the Rock Island Argus protests the action of the city in buying a two-seated automobile for the police department on the ground that, when filled, the rig will look like the comedy moving picture officers." The jollier "Kops" spelling grew more common during the 1920s and was cemented throughout the following decades, particularly when classic comedy nostalgia set in during the fifties and sixties.

At least one group of savvy performers pounced on the alliteration early on: in 1915, a small vaudeville troupe billed themselves as the "Keystone Komical Kops" (never mind the alarming acronym) and toured the East Coast and parts of the Midwest. Setting their act in a "burlesque police station," they subtly advertised themselves as a "kwintette of komical kusses in kutups and kapers."

So why have these particular myths about the Keystone Cops become so ingrained? Even during the silent era itself they gained steam rapidly, along with other generalizations about Keystone comedies. It's undeniable that certain images, characters, and gags seemed to stick with viewers more than others. A prime example is the near-obsessive fascination with pie throwing. Writers invariably described Keystones as "custard pie comedies" throughout the 1910s and 1920s, and in later years Sennett actors invariably reminisced about their days throwing the gooey desserts. As it happens, relatively few examples of pie throwing in Keystones can be verified today, and are matched, or even dwarfed, by scenes of the comedians hurling bricks or other projectiles.

In hindsight, any analysis of Keystone mythology needs to consider the fact that Mack Sennett produced a staggering number of films in his career, well over a thousand in all, and most of them shown for a brief window of time before being tossed or put in storage. The mythology of the Cops seems almost inevitable when we consider the sheer number of gags, chases, fights, and other mayhem that for years hit the cinemas on a regular basis. After all, were audiences more likely to remember Keystone's many "romantic rivals quarreling in a park" one-reelers, or the sight of overstuffed patrol cars spinning wildly on greased-up pavement?

If we try to study the Sennett filmography objectively today, we get a clearer picture of the Keystone Cops' role in his comedies. The force was very much in tune with the era of wild, unpolished Edwardian farce. Up until the late 1910s, Keystone was a distinctly clownish place, as many comedy studios were. The thick makeup, fake mustaches, and manic characters handed down from vaudeville and burlesque were the norm. Top actors were given specific character names and personas: Mack Swain was "Ambrose," Chester Conklin was either "Mr. Droppington" or "Walrus," Louise Fazenda was briefly "Maggie," and Charlie Murray was "Hogan." The deliberately broad acting styles were matched by the comic chases and out-of-control fights that highlighted many of the films, with the cameras undercranked to produce dizzying speed. Considering how quickly (and cheaply) many Keystones were filmed, the care taken to piece together those montages is remarkable—and also helped associate the Cops' appearances with frenzied bursts of action.

As the Edwardian era came to an end, the studio astutely picked up on different trends and let go of those that were no longer fresh or in vogue. Slower and more logically plotted two-reelers replaced the freewheeling old one-reelers, and the popularity of "grotesque" performances began to decline. Many comedians eased up on the greasepaint and started adopting normal attire, and familiar gags began to look passé. By 1915 even the Cops had traded their old helmets for more contemporary visors. (Helmets had been de rigueur for American policemen up until the late 1900s, when visors were introduced, which meant the original look of Sennett's Cops was deliberately outdated). Being so firmly identified with fast-paced slapstick, the Cops were essentially temporary casualties of these changing tastes, and they were more or less retired by the early 1920s.

Sennett would revive the Cops somewhat in the mid-1920s, a good example being *Wandering Willies* (1926), which featured the whole police force getting wrapped around a pole, and *Smith's Family* (1926), which included a number of Cops in a rowboat. But most intriguing—and surprising—of all was the satire *Love in a Police Station* (1927), which was Sennett's own wink at the mythologizing of his world-famous Cops. Partly a vehicle for youthful star Eddie Quillan and former Bathing Beauty Madeline Hurlock, it also featured Andy Clyde in a chin beard and spectacles, imitating Ford Sterling's Chief Teheezel, and a comic police force in the familiar helmets-and-tailcoats attire. Members of the force were made up to resemble Roscoe Arbuckle, Chester Conklin, Mack Swain, Charlie Murray, and other famous former Cops. The plot involves Quillan and the police chief vying for the hand of a wealthy widow while the force tries to track down a robber. The sight of the familiar Cops, however, is the real draw—one of the lobby cards simply shows the whole force standing at attention, billy clubs in hand.

It wouldn't have been surprising if *Love in a Police Station* had been single-handedly responsible for the myths about the Keystone Cops, being the sort of broad satire destined to be misinterpreted by modern audiences as an authentic Cops farce. But, unfortunately, the short has been forgotten for many decades. However, we can point to an earlier film as a likely culprit for much of the mythology: *In the Clutches of a Gang* (1913), a Ford Sterling vehicle originally packaged as a two-reel "special." A still photograph from the short, showing Sterling's police chief answering a call while his force stands by expectantly, became one of the most famous images in silent comedy. The still may have been used for lobby displays initially and started circulating in later decades as *the* visual representation of the Keystone force. Roscoe Arbuckle, Edgar Kennedy, and Al St. John are a few of the Cops that can be identified. The familiar uniforms, goofy expression by Sterling, and pleasing composition combine to make the photo an iconic image. Brent Walker notes in his monumental book *Mack Sennett's Fun Factory*: "Later claimants to the mantle of 'Keystone cop'. . . felt duty-bound to identify themselves as one of the cops in that still, whether or not their own Keystone tour of duty corresponded with the period in late November 1913 when that film was being produced."

Indeed, as nostalgia for the "good ol' days" of slapstick took hold during the early television era, many former silent film performers claimed they most definitely had been Keystone Cops. Various families also passed down slightly vague tales of a granddad or great uncle once being a Cop—usually one of the "original" members, mind you. Of course, to have truly been part of the force, an actor would have had to live in or at least near Los Angeles during the silent era, and be verifiably active at the Sennett studio, specifically around 1912-1915, the prime Keystone Cop years—but, admittedly, such details are only known by a few historians today.

It's an enlightening fact that although Los Angeles County alone was host to a number of early comedy studios, some of which clearly imitated Sennett's brand, it wasn't L-KO, Selig, Joker, or Christie where everyone claimed to have worked—it was the Keystone Film Company. It's an ongoing testament to the Fun Factory's unshakeable status in cinema history.

It's also a testament to the foothold the Keystone Cops still have in the public imagination. Even as talkies took over and memories of the rich silent era faded; even throughout the indignities of 1960s shows like *The Funny Manns* and *Fractured Flickers*, which added goofy commentary to battered prints of old silents; even after many of the slapstick veterans passed away, taking their memories with them; even after silent films were mainly remembered as scratchy, old-fashioned relics your great-grandparents used to enjoy—throughout all this and into the brave new digital era, the Cops have retained their charm.

In a sequence from *A Hash House Fraud* (1915), Hugh Fay and Louise Fazenda are in an automobile being pursued by the Keystone Cops in their rickety patrol car. They lead the Cops on your typical "merry chase" through a neighborhood, and the two vehicles end up facing each other on opposite ends of a long street. They start speeding toward one another in an apparent game of chicken, but pass each other harmlessly. Again the vehicles turn, and again they pass each other—the confrontation turning into a decidedly modern joust. So close is this enthusiastic police force to catching the culprits, and yet—eternally—so far. This is the essence of their humor, and why just their name can still cause an involuntary smile today.

Sources:
Books
King, Rob. *The Fun Factory: The Keystone Film Company and the Emergence of Mass Culture*. Berkeley and Los Angeles, CA: University of California Press, 2008.

Massa, Steve. *Lame Brains & Lunatics: The Good, the Bad, and the Forgotten of Silent Comedy*. Albany, GA: BearManor Media, 2013.

Sennett, Mack (with Cameron Shipp). *King of Comedy*. Garden City, CA: Doubleday & Company, Inc., 1954.

Walker, Brent E. *Mack Sennett's Fun Factory*. Jefferson, NC: McFarland & Company, Inc., 2010.

Watson Jr., Coy. *The Keystone Kid: Tales of Early Hollywood*. Santa Monica, CA: Santa Monica Press, 2001.

Periodicals
Exhibitors Herald
Los Angeles Times
Moving Picture World
Motion Picture News
Motography
Reel Life
Variety

Lea Stans is a born-and-raised Minnesotan and a graduate of the University of St. Thomas. She blogs about silent films at her site Silent-ology, where she covers any and every subject pertaining to that fascinating era of cinema. Aside from her regular blogging, she has written for *The Keaton Chronicle*, *The Silent Film Quarterly*, and *Classic Movie Hub*. Her great enthusiasm for the silent era is largely Buster Keaton's fault.

Chapter 9.
When Keaton Met Keystone:
Kops, Custard, and Reality Run Amok
By Chris Seguin

December 25, 1932 delivered a disastrous Christmas present to Mack Sennett: instant obsolescence.

On that day, the one-time King of Comedy released *Hypnotized*—a swing-for-the-fences feature film that was the nail in the coffin for Mack Sennett Productions. Starring the blackface comedy team of George Moran and Charlie Mack, a.k.a. The Two Black Crows (with Moran interacting with Mack for a total of, oh I don't know, about twenty seconds—what's that about?), it's a sloppy, helter-skelter mess full of such Sennett tropes as crazed hypnotists, falls into swimming pools, cross dressers, and runaway lions. Here, in a sloppy sixty-six minutes, and five years after Sennett optimistically exited the silent era, is a film that can only be seen as the ultimate embodiment of what a "Mack Sennett Production" had become by the early thirties: quaint, old-timey, yesterday's news. Sennett, who directed as well as produced, had nobody to blame but himself.

But it didn't have to be that way. Mack Sennett entered into the talkie era full of high hopes, big dreams, and major ambitions. This ex-boilermaker was going full steam ahead into the future, dammit. In 1927, he commenced work on a mammoth, state-of-the-art studio, moving from outdated Edendale to mass acreage at the corner of Ventura Boulevard and North Radford Avenue. Sixteen buildings, two massive steel and concrete stages (wood was so 1912), revolving panoramic backgrounds, and "the largest plate-mirror glass swimming pool in the world" . . . the new Mack Sennett Studios would have everything—including, very quickly, sound. "Here is a new science that lends itself marvelously to screen comedy," he told *Motion Picture News*. Note the use of the word *science*.

Even though he embraced the future—beating arch rival Hal Roach to the talkie screen by a full five months and developing sumptuous Sennett-Color to bring more prestige to his productions (and to better showcase his Bathing Beauties), technological innovation didn't necessarily translate into comedic inspiration. Soon Hal Roach would no longer see Sennett as a true competitor.

Which returns us to the fiasco of Christmas Day 1932. As 1933 began, Sennett still had two pretty big stars on his roster—Bing Crosby and W.C. Fields—but they were destined for much, much, *much* bigger things, and pronto. Beyond those two, there was crooner Donald Novis, Marjorie Beebe, Nora Lane, Franklin Pangborn, and an increasingly sickly Lloyd Hamilton. Not the names you want to hang your future on, even with science on your side. When production wrapped on W. C. Fields's *The Barber Shop* in early May 1933, the Sennett Studios shut their doors. Iris out.

Now what?

Rewrite your history, that's what. Better yet, create a new mythos, one much larger than the man. And do it fast.

One quick year later, 1934, saw the publication of Gene Fowler's *Father Goose*, a boisterous, romanticized rags-to-riches biography that would form the foundation for every Mack Sennett bio to come. Even today, it's impossible to untangle fact from fiction in the Sennett story—nor does there seem to be a real desire to do so. Certainly Sennett would see no need for that. Why not concoct a tale of a cockeyed optimist, driven by a simple love of what's funny . . . oh, and

In The Barber Shop *(1933), Cornelius O'Hare (W. C. Fields) attempts to give a haircut to an endlessly be-hatted girl (Gloria Velarde) while her overprotective mother (Fay Holderness) looks on. This was the last of four sound two-reelers written by and starring W. C. Fields; it was also the last of the estimated one thousand films produced by Mack Sennett.* Photo courtesy of Jerry Murbach (www.doctormacro.com).

a girl. We need a girl. A girl who'd look equally fetching in a bathing suit as she would with custard on her face. Let's call her Mabel. Mabel Normand. And the lovers? Simply, Mack and Mabel.

What a movie this would make.

Except let's not make it a biopic of Mack Sennett. Let's make it a biopic of *all* of Hollywood. And let's not call them Mack and Mabel. Let's call them Mike and Molly. And we'll get Don Ameche and Alice Faye to play them. That's it. And it'll be a prestigious Darryl F. Zanuck production in glorious Technicolor. And we'll call it . . . (cue the 20th Century-Fox fanfare) . . . *Hollywood Cavalcade*.

But make no mistake, *Hollywood Cavalcade* is the Mack Sennett story . . . or pretty close to the story Sennett would tell if Sennett were telling the Sennett story. And in case there's any question, there's this exchange during Sennett's promotional appearance for the film on radio's *Texaco Star Theatre*, December 13, 1939, between announcer Jimmy Wallington and singer Kenny Baker:

Wallington: We're ready to give you the lowdown on the bathing beauties, the chase, and the custard pie, made famous by Mack Sennett many years ago.

Baker: Many years ago? Why I saw all that stuff in a picture the other night. *Hollywood Cavalcade!*

Wallington: Well, naturally Kenny, that's the story of Mack Sennett's life!

The opening-night audience at the film's gala premiere no doubt applauded nostalgically when the following title card (in a font patterned after an old-fashioned typewriter) flashed on the screen:

```
         We also wish to thank
      Buster Keaton    Ben Turpin
     Chester Conklin    Hank Mann
      Jed Prouty    Snub Pollard
       for their contribution to
      the silent screen sequences
              which were
              Directed by
          MALCOLM ST. CLAIR
           and supervised by
           MR. MACK SENNETT
```

As the film unfolded in all its Technicolor brilliance, Wallington was proven right—or half right. The first 50 percent of the tale indeed follows Sennett's story arc, before the lead character morphs into what is essentially D.W. Griffith meets Cecil B. DeMille. Ameche plays Michael *Linnett* Connors (that middle name gets extra oomph when they really want to emphasize the Sennett connection), an up-and-coming Hollywood go-getter who discovers the lovely Molly Adair (Alice Faye) and—in shockingly rapid succession and for no other reason than "because he does"—invents slapstick comedy, seaside bathing beauties ("C'mon Marie, Gloria, Mabel, Phyllis!") and, of course, Komedy Kops. Ben Turpin is there for good measure, as is Chester Conklin, and astonishingly, in a charming homage, Roscoe "Fatty" Arbuckle ("Hiya, Roscoe!"), seen from the back and embodied by portly actor Marshall Ruth. And just to make the connection crystal clear, and to add an extra dollop of credibility to the whole endeavor, the cherry on top of the whipped cream on top of the custard pie is the ultimate seal of approval—an appearance by Mr. Mack Sennett (emphasis

Buster seems to be in his own world in the presence of Michael Linnett Connors, the director (Don Ameche) and Pete Tinney, the cameraman (Stuart Erwin). Hollywood Cavalcade.

In one of Hollywood Cavalcade's *more authentic moments, a silent-era open-air stage is shown. Chester Conklin is the two-gun shooter in the mock saloon, the bar of which is attended by Ben Turpin (not pictured).*

on MR. in the opening credits, as befitting an elder statesman) as, of all people, *himself*. Which leads to one of filmdom's most curious moments.

Late in the film, at a black tux fête for Alice Faye's character Molly Adair, Mack Sennett is invited to stand up and say a few words. But wait a minute. Isn't Linnett Sennett? And if Linnett is Sennett but isn't Sennett . . . and if Sennett isn't Linnett but Sennett . . . *who is Sennett*? Isn't he the man who invented slapstick comedy, bathing beauties, and Kops? Nope, he can't be. We just saw Linnett invent *everything*. I keep expecting the real Mack Sennett to vanish into a puff of smoke the moment he realizes he can't possibly coexist with Linnett in this alternate universe.

Meanwhile, *this Mack Sennett is introduced as "a star maker." And seated next to him at the soirée is another man whose history is about to be rewritten by Hollywood Cavalcade (pretty much rewriting the entire history of silent comedy in one fell swoop)*: Buster Keaton.

Like Sennett at this time, Keaton was pretty much considered a relic of bygone days. Out of work after a magnificent fall from grace from MGM (which needn't be regurgitated

Buster Keaton, Lona Andre, and Stanley J. "Tiny" Sanford cavort for an unseen Mack Sennett, manning the megaphone. The Timid Young Man *(Educational Pictures Corporation, October 25, 1935).*

Hollywood Cavalcade, *released on October 13, 1939—the day Ford Sterling died—features Jed Prouty stepping in for the late Chief of Police. Also pictured (left to right) are Hank Mann, James Finlayson, Heinie Conklin, and newcomer Eddie Collins.*

Buster Keaton laughs as Alice Faye takes one for the team in this delightfully candid outtake.

The Great Stone Face actually smiles between takes of Hollywood Cavalcade. *After years of personal and professional turmoil, Keaton appears to have found happiness at last.*

Mack and Mabel flirt for the camera in 1913. In 1921, Sennett produced Molly O', *starring Normand in the title role of Molly Odair. Mabel's counterpart in* Hollywood Cavalcade *is named Molly Adair. A coincidence? We think not.*

here, but it was seriously ugly), Buster spent the mid-1930s slumming at Educational Pictures. (Sennett was too, but to a lesser extent, returning to Educational to produce/direct a handful of modest two-reelers in what might be seen as a charity move by Educational's president and Sennett's old distributor, Earle W. Hammons.) It was at Educational that, for the first and only time, The Great Stone Face was directed by the King of Comedy, in *The Timid Young Man* (released October 25, 1935). And if you ever wanted to see a film where Buster Keaton catches fish with the help of Mexican jumping beans (go ahead, raise your hand, nobody's judging you here), this is the film for you.

But in *Hollywood Cavalcade*, the Sennett-Keaton connection is forever cemented as "fact," and establishes the legend that both Mack and Buster would take to their graves—despite Buster's assertion in his autobiography, *My Wonderful World of Slapstick:* "[T]here is one guy who never worked for Mack Sennett, although practically every screen historian insists he did. That's me, Buster Keaton," we know that *Cavalcade* has zero interest in actual history.

So let's switch reels to the silent comedy recreations in the film. Just as Sennett isn't Sennett, this Buster Keaton isn't Buster Keaton. Not by a long shot.

We first see Buster as "the romantic lover" in what seems to be a Molly Adair meller-drammer. Faced with a rival, Buster is momentarily at a loss: *What do I do next?* As director Linnett bellows, *"Hurry, Buster! We're running out of film!"* this alternate reality Buster scans the set, picks up a conveniently

Former silent film comedy director and Buster's past collaborator Malcolm St. Clair helmed the lively chase sequences.

located custard pie, and hurls it *smack* into Molly's face. The crew bursts into riotous laughter. Thus, pie throwing is born. Thank you, Buster.

So who—or *what*—is this "Buster Keaton" supposed to be? An inept dramatic actor who's gone up in a scene? A comedian who happens to have no idea of how to be funny? An accident just waiting to happen? What he *is* is the incarnation of what Buster would officially become in the public eye from then on. It's at this moment that Buster Keaton reaches the point of no return—officially defining himself as a slapstick pie-thrower and little more, a role he would fully embrace a decade later with the advent of TV.

Now, with the Sennett-Keaton connection complete, let's cut to the chase. Literally. The ersatz Keystone Kops film-within-the film titled "Help! Murder! Police!" directed by former Sennett megaphoner Malcolm St. Clair (who, like Sennett and Keaton, had seen better days) and "supervised by MR. MACK SENNETT" (per *Cavalcade*'s title card). Populated by Sennett veterans Heinie Conklin, Hank Mann, and Jimmy Finlayson, with Jack Cooper as a shifty crook and *Hypnotized*'s female lead Marjorie Beebe, the eight-and-a-half-minute homage to the Kops tries hard, awfully hard, to recreate the old days. But what it does instead is say to the audience, "This is what a Keystone Kops comedy was. Remember? Now remember that for the next forty years."

With much leaping up and down, flinging of stunt men and dummies, spinning around in soapy intersections, near misses, and grimacing in front of rear-projection screens, "Help! Murder! Police!" is more like Vitaphone's recent

The original (and actual) motorcycle chase sequence as directed by Buster Keaton in Sherlock Jr. *(Metro Pictures, 1924).*

For Hollywood Cavalcade, *Buster recreates the thrilling motorcycle chase, this time with a game Alice Faye."*

reunion film *Keystone Hotel* (Warner Bros., 1935) than a bona fide Keystone Kops one-reeler.[1]

Despite the presence of Mann, Conklin, and Finlayson, the scene is dominated by two Fox contract players: Jed Prouty (of Fox's Jones Family series) filling in for Ford Sterling as the Chief, and ersatz Kop Eddie Collins, who mugs and mugs mercilessly in a way that even Sennett might have said, "Take it down a notch, Eddie." With Prouty and Jones behind the wheel, the legit Keystoners literally take a back seat to those two.

As the Kops rush to the rescue, Buster takes a parallel path, manning a motorcycle while Molly rides double. The inspiration for the motorcycle seems to come largely from Buster's 1924 silent classic *Sherlock Jr.*, but with one big difference—the "real" Buster Keaton, the one of *Sherlock Jr.*, would *never* have relied so heavily on rear projection. (And one wishes that Buster had taken the fall for Alice Faye off the back of the motorcycle, as he had for Ford West in *Sherlock Jr.* But nope, that job went to a stunt man instead. "And stunt men," Buster often said, "don't get laughs.") Buster does manage to get some typical Keatonesque touches in there: a marvelous slide off the skidding bike followed by a splendid neck-deep dunk into the mud puddle Molly's fallen into, as well as some manhandling of Molly reminiscent of his treatment of Marion Mack in *The General*. (Kudos

---

1   Mal St. Clair obviously studied *Keystone Hotel* carefully. He would later lift the Kops' wild ride on an amusement park roller coaster in the 1935 Keystone tribute film when he directed Laurel & Hardy in their 1943 20th Century-Fox feature *The Dancing Masters*.

should be given to Alice Faye for being such a good sport.)

Hollywood Cavalcade was considered one of 20th Century-Fox's premier offerings of 1939, a year that has frequently been called the greatest in movie history. It was enjoyed by undiscerning, pining-for-the-past audiences, but the critics weren't necessarily buying it. Frank Nugent, in an unenthusiastic write-up about the principal players for the *New York Times*, stated:

On March 10, 1938, W. C. Fields and Frank Capra (at that time the president of the Academy) presented their former boss with an honorary Academy Award. It is inscribed: "For his lasting contribution to the screen, the basic principles of which are as important today as when they were first put into practice, the Academy presents a Special Award to that master of fun, discoverer of stars, sympathetic, kindly, understanding comedy genius—Mack Sennett."

> [T]he real talent, of course, and *Hollywood Calvacade*'s first line of defense against cynical criticism belongs to the boys of the slapstick brigade—to Keaton, Jed Prouty, Eddie Collins, James Finlayson, Hank Mann, Chester Conklin, and Ben Turpin. We have no case against them.

Oddly, Nugent overlooked Mr. Mack Sennett who, with this major film appearance, had fearlessly conquered obsolescence. *Variety*, in their much more positive review on December 31, 1938, wouldn't make the same mistake:

> In addition to a brief personal appearance, Mack Sennett plays an important off-screen role in the film, principal novelty of which is the successful and amusing introduction of oldtime Sennett comedy routines and formula.

There's that word again . . . oldtime. Despite that, for both Mack Sennett and Buster Keaton, *Hollywood Cavalcade* was a success.

From that point on, Mack was no longer a has been. He was officially a living legend. With a movie lionizing all things Keystone and a recently received honorary Academy Award under his belt, he would drink deep from the cup of his newly established mythos. Mack now eased into a life of semi-antsy retirement, secure in his exalted place in film history, making periodic appearances,

The Keystone Cops celebrate their fiftieth anniversary (or fifty-second, since the first films to feature the Cops were released in 1912) with the help of Buster Keaton at the Movieland Wax Museum, Buena Park, California, on May 3, 1964. The most recognizable Cops are Eddie LeVeque (far left), Tom Kennedy (directly behind Buster) and Eddie Gribbon (wearing a scowl instead of a mustache). Not surprisingly, this nostalgic occasion devolved into a messy pie fight.

usually in the presence of various Kops and onetime Bathing Beauties. (Nineteen-fifty-four was a particularly banner year for him, with the publication of his autobiography *King of Comedy*, an appearance on Ralph Edwards's weekly televised ambush *This Is Your Life*, and a cameo appearance, again as himself, in *Bud Abbott & Lou Costello Meet the Keystone Kops* [1955]. Keystone nostalgia was back in full force.)

And he'd never give up peddling new ideas—even if it meant recycling old ones. Nineteen-forty-nine saw him return to the movie theaters in *Down Memory Lane*, showing up to help Steve Allen and Franklin Pangborn peddle his past accomplishments in a highly entertaining clip show. TV offered new possibilities, and just a few months before his death on November 5, 1960, Sennett was regaling UIP reporters with upcoming plans:

> "It'll all be shot new—no old film clips. . . . My show will have one purpose only—to make people laugh. There'll be beautiful girls to look at and plenty of action. And with a young fella like me around, things will keep hopping."

Some things never change.

Hollywood Cavalcade provided Mack with something he never found in real life: closure. No doubt Mabel Normand's premature death haunted him till the end of his days. But *Cavalcade* gave audiences—and Mack and Mabel, through their cinematic proxies Mike and Molly, a near-deathbed moment of reconciliation:

> "Look Molly, I know what it is to be tired, the way that you're tired. When your whole world topples and nothing seems to matter any-

more, it can lick ya, that feeling, if you let it. You gotta fight back. Get well. Then things'll look different, Molly. What happened to you wasn't your fault. What happened to me, *I* was to blame for. I was wrong, Molly. About you, about everything, I guess. Bull-headed and blind. Through all those years the only thing that really mattered to me was . . . you."

As for Buster Keaton, *Hollywood Cavalcade* didn't bring him the comeback he desired and deserved . . . at least not immediately. He'd stumble through the 1940s, returning to cheap two-reelers and bit parts, supplementing his acting income with work as a gag writer at his old haunt, MGM. Fortunately, he'd found lasting personal happiness with his third wife, Eleanor Norris. Professional salvation would have to wait until 1947, first with a successful personal appearance at Paris's famed Cirque Medrano and then, to everyone's surprise, with that newfangled invention, television. (Keaton, like Sennett, was keen on "science" and a first adopter of new technology.) He established himself almost immediately as slapstick's sole survivor, fully embracing his porkpie-hatted, slapshoed persona of yore, first on Ed Wynn's *Camel Caravan*, where he reprised his 1917 screen debut in *The Butcher Boy*, and then in a custard-infused appearance with some actual Keystone Kops of bygone days. Of that performance, Keaton proudly wrote in his autobiography:

> I had been a guest star several times on Ed's show, but this was an impromptu appearance.
>
> Ed asked, "Where do you keep your stage wardrobe? ... I have no finish for tonight's show, I thought if you come on you might think of something."
>
> [Wynn] quickly explained that he had lined up four of the old Keystone Cops to demonstrate custard pie throwing. "Why I never thought of getting the champ," he added, "I'll never understand." Everybody loved the finish I improvised—except Chester Conklin, Hank Mann, his brother Heinie, and Snub Pollard, the four Keystone Cops involved.[1]
>
> "I got the finish *I* wanted," Ed Wynn whispered to me. "You saved the show for me tonight."

---

1 Contrary to widespread belief, the Conklins—Chester and Heinie—were not real-life brothers, and neither were Hank and Heinie, as Buster inadvertently claimed. In addition, there were five Kops on the show, not four; the one Buster failed to mention was the biggest of them all, six-foot-seven-inch Tiny Ward.

For the next two decades, Buster Keaton would be saving the show for Ed Sullivan, Donna Reed, game show hosts, Eastman Kodak, Alka-Seltzer, Simon Pure Beer, the Ontario Construction Safety Board, even Frankie & Annette and the *Beach Blanket* crew—anywhere there was a pie to be thrown or a chase to be had. He even threw back to his so-called Keystone Kop days, playing a Kop on *The Rosemary Clooney Show* and being pursued by Kops in a Ford Econoline commercial. But when Buster shuffled off this mortal coil—no doubt exhausted—on February 1, 1966, genuine Sennett-slapstick died with him. Yes, a few stray Kops would carry on into the 1970s, but with the loss of Mack Sennett and then Buster Keaton, their legacies intertwined for a quarter century, the real Hollywood *Cavalcade* came to an end—an anything-is-possible era that *Cavalcade* tried so hard, so earnestly, to recapture, and a time (to borrow a chapter title from Buster's *My Wonderful World of Slapstick*), "When the world was ours."

Chris Seguin is a Toronto-based writer and researcher of classic comedy film. He is Comedy Programmer for The Toronto Silent Film Festival and has contributed to numerous book and DVD/Blu-ray projects, including All Day Entertainment's *Harry Langdon Lost And Found* and *Becoming Charley Chase*, the British Film Institute (BFI)'s restoration of Laurel & Hardy's *Atoll K* (1951), and the upcoming CineMuseum release *Blue Collar Buster Keaton*.

All photos in this chapter are courtesy of the author's collection.

Chapter 10.
Cops For (RE) Sale:
Reissuing the Keystone Comedies

By Michael J. Hayde

Mack Sennett was unquestionably the creative guiding force of Keystone, but he didn't create the company. That honor goes to Adam Kessel, Charles Kessel, and Charles O. Baumann of the New York Motion Picture Company (NYMP), which until the summer of 1912 had been releasing their product through Universal, for which Baumann was president. When he was unceremoniously ousted from that position at the close of June, Baumann and the Kessel brothers moved distribution to the Mutual Film Corporation, run by Harry E. Aitken.

While with Universal, NYMP had no need to supply a comedy series, but as a provider for Mutual they were expected to have a complete program. Baumann and the Kessels turned to Sennett, then making comedies as a salaried employee of the American Biograph Film Corporation. When they offered him his own studio, one-third ownership of Keystone, and full creative control, Sennett couldn't sign fast enough. Had he not done so, or had NYMP remained with Universal, this volume might be focused on the Biograph Cops.

Keystone comedies swiftly became Mutual's hottest property. NYMP's original agreement, commencing in September 1912, was for one comedy reel per week. Before the close of 1913, that had been upped to three reels per week, plus one multi-reel "special" per month. And the Keystone Cops, while not as omnipresent as legend would have it, were certainly a major component of that output, appearing just often enough during the closing chaos to be as welcomed by audiences as a favorite performer or vaudeville routine.

NYMP also brought producer-director Thomas Ince and Ince's leading star, William S. Hart, to Mutual. In 1913, Aitken lured D. W. Griffith, Biograph's top director, into the fold by giving Griffith *his* own company, Reliance. Aitken invested in Griffith's *The Birth of a Nation* (1915) to unprecedented critical and box-office acclaim. Its success convinced Aitken that colossal pictures by top talent would soon be the norm. He and his NYMP associates thus formed the Triangle Motion Picture Company, so named for its three "points": Griffith, Ince, and Sennett. In June 1915, Aitken resigned from Mutual to run the new company.

On paper, Triangle looked like a winner, but Aitken's ambition far outweighed his resources. His idea to lure top Broadway stage stars into pictures with weekly four-figure salaries proved disastrous; of this group, only Douglas Fairbanks found wide favor among moviegoers. He was unable to coax the movies' two unquestioned leading lights, Mary Pickford and Charlie Chaplin, to join Triangle; adding insult to injury, Chaplin signed with Mutual. Griffith's second super-spectacle, *Intolerance* (1916), failed to recoup its massive cost. Aitken's plan to fashion a circuit of theaters, which would have made Triangle a pioneer in the vertical integration business model that became the norm by the following decade, had to be abandoned. Tiring of sparse distribution and irregular income, Griffith, Ince, and Sennett all left by mid-1917, as did Hart and Fairbanks.

In order to save their shirts, Aitken, Baumann, and the Kessels needed to monetize their assets—specifically, their film library. This ultimately led to the creation of a new company in September 1917 to handle states-rights distribution of reissues. Aitken, owner of a European-based exchange circuit called Western Import Company, leased negatives from NYMP, then brought in two of his Western Import officers, Hyman Winick and Winick's brother-in-law Joseph Simmonds, to run the new concern. Simmonds became president and, as he later claimed, named the company W. H. Productions by reversing Winick's initials. W. H. would pay Western Import a modest fee for the negatives, plus 50 percent of all company profits.

W. H. officially opened for business in December with a slate of seventeen William S. Hart two-reelers, three five-reel Hart features, and twenty-eight Keystone two-reel comedies. The following May, they added twenty of Charlie Chaplin's Keystones and twenty-

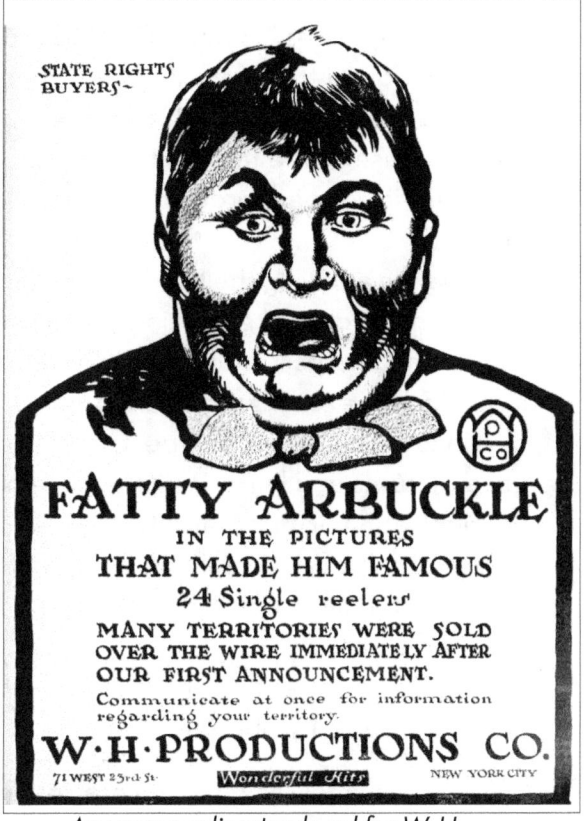

An unappealing trade ad for W. H. Productions' Arbuckle reissue package of 1918.

four one-reel Keystones starring Roscoe "Fatty" Arbuckle, along with sixteen two-reel Broncho westerns starring Shorty Hamilton. In January 1919, they reissued another fifty-six Keystone one-reelers in two series of twenty-eight: Keystone Liberty and Keystone Eagle, plus thirty Kay-Bee western two-reelers. For the 1919–20 picture season, Simmonds and Winick formed a new subsidiary, The Tower Film Corporation, to handle a revival of *Tillie's Punctured Romance* (1914); along the way, they reissued another fifty-six Keystone one-reelers, including a dozen starring Arbuckle and at least three with Chaplin. All of the films, except *Tillie*, were given new names, and a goodly percentage of the Keystones included the Cops.

From the start, W. H. publicity claimed they were in business to assist the independent film exchanges and exhibitors, backing it up by pricing the Keystones at eighty dollars per reel, and not as a lease but as an outright purchase. "This price assures to the exchange man the greatest galaxy of comedies and stars on the screen today at a price that will bring to them bigger profits than they have ever made before. It will also assure a reasonable rental price for the exhibitor."

"In many cases," Simmonds told *Motion Picture News* in December 1918, "we have found that were it not for these productions, a number of the independent exchanges and exhibitors would have been obliged to go out of business because of the fact that they could not make a profitable investment on the majority of new productions released today, on account of the inflated prices.

"We are applying the Ford and Woolworth methods to our basic principles. We intend to do a large business at a small margin of profit, so that the public can be made a part of our organization. We are creating in the minds of the independent exchange man and the exhibitors a desire to come to W. H. Productions Company for the best, because they are assured of good treatment, good pictures and fair prices. We have been able to purchase our various productions at a fair price, and have been successful in choosing box-office winners, so that it can readily be seen that we can well afford to dispose of our product at a fair profit and still give the benefit to the independent exchange men and exhibitors."

The independents were indeed grateful, as implied in these testimonials culled for publicity purposes:

"We can safely say that we are serving 60 percent of Michigan theatres with your re-issues." —*D. Mundstuk, Strand Features, Detroit MI*

"The Mack Sennett two reelers and the Arbuckle single-reel comedies are meeting with more favor generally than we had even anticipated. We handle a large variety of newly produced short subjects... and W. H. Productions Co. re-issues are far superior as a money-maker for us or a box-office asset to the exhibitor." —*J. Lannon, Greater Features Co., Seattle WA*

"In most of the towns hereabout the representative houses are our regular customers for these re-issues, and it is quite frequently that we are told that these pictures are appreciated more than many of the new comedies of today." —*A. A. Weiland, Standard Film Exchange, Pittsburgh PA*

"W. H. Productions Co. have established a reputation for re-issuing only pictures that prove satisfactory to all classes of patrons. Our exhibitors all over the state are more than satisfied and from them I gather that their patrons also are." —*R. C. Cropper, Bee Hive Exchange, Chicago IL*

"We are meeting with phenomenal success in the New England territory." —F. B. Murphy, Boston Photoplay Co., Boston MA

"Proving to be box-office assets. We are not experiencing any trouble in booking them to the leading exhibitors." —H. Charnas, Standard Film Service, Cleveland OH

Simmonds also liked to point out that the films would be new to most patrons. "It is a well-known fact that the motion picture going public has increased almost 1,000 percent within the past two years, so that the productions we are now releasing were never seen by the new film fans." One W. H. trade ad boldly proclaimed, "More than 75 percent of the moving picture fans of today never saw them, because they did not attend picture theaters when these subjects were originally released."

There was, of course, some opposition to W. H.'s existence. Even before the company launched, Mutual's president, John R. Freuler, had filed an injunction and $400,000 damages suit in Superior Court of New York against NYMP to block any plans they had to sell the pictures to other distributors. "The contracts covering these pictures," said Freuler in November 1917, "provided that the Mutual Film Corporation was to have exclusive right of distribution in the United States and Canada, and that the Mutual was to be supplied with additional positive prints of any of the pictures at any time. We now charge that the defendants are engaged in circulating a number of these pictures through obscure channels, and unlawfully." Unfortunately for Mutual, the following February Superior Court Judge Whittaker disagreed and denied the injunction, stating that Mutual was entitled only to the original releases.

More critically, lawyers for William S. Hart filed a complaint with the Federal Trade Commission regarding W. H.'s retitling of his films, asserting that exhibitors were being duped into thinking they were his new productions. Hart also alleged

William S. Hart.

that *his* initials had more to do with the company's name than Hyman Winick's. The western star was especially vexed that one of his Broncho two-reelers, *The Conversion of Frosty Blake* (1915), had been padded to five with the addition of new material allegedly of his character as a child. The resulting feature had been christened *Staking His Life*. It took the FTC until August 1919 to make it official: Simmonds was directed to "cease forthwith issuing old films with new titles [unless] he informs the public and exhibitors clearly and unmistakably that they are old films with new names."

Simmonds believed he'd been doing that all along, although the original titles were emphasized more distinctly on poster art than on the films themselves. (See example at the top of this chapter.) He also believed it was up to the exhibitor to so inform their patrons, and W. H. publicity did not skirt the issue: "If you pretend that these are new pictures, you are going to offend patrons who would have enjoyed them all the more for the fact that they

Sheet music from Mickey *(1918)*.

were reissues if you had told them that. People resent being fooled, and they will buy pictures, as anything else when you are frank.

"Most of these pictures have been re-edited and retitled, but the old titles have been retained as well so that anyone *looking at the paper* (emphasis mine) will not be deceived into thinking that they are new pictures. *We repeat that the exhibitor will get more money by making this fact mighty clear* (emphasis theirs)."

Why retitle at all? Simmonds claimed that the new names were part of "reconstructing each one of these [pictures] in their entirety, so that when they go to the public they will be as modern, as interesting, and as new as it is possible to make them." There was another reason, however: most of the backlog had never been copyrighted in the first place. Keystone, for one, did not begin regularly copyrighting its releases until the end of 1914, after dupes of their Chaplin titles started turning up with alarming frequency. By giving the films new names and intertitles, along with a lower price point, they hoped they were protecting themselves from pirates; but by selling to small independent exhibitors, many of whom were less than honorable, the company eventually saw profits sink into a sea of bootlegged prints.

During its four years of existence, W. H. Productions also distributed Mabel Normand's first starring feature, *Mickey* (1918), which Sennett was forced to surrender to Western Import upon leaving Triangle. The company, and its sister concern Tower Film Corporation, took on other independent features and serials but failed to score as big a hit as the Normand film.

A trade ad for Tower Film Corporation's revival of Tillie's Punctured Romance.

Eventually both firms faded out and the principals moved on, but their legacy is secure, and the Keystone Cops owe them a debt of gratitude. "Many of these films exist today only because of the W. H. Productions reissue," wrote Kalton C. Lahue in 1971. "Had the subjects not been re-released, only a slender record of the Ince and Sennett productions of the 1912–15 period would still remain on film."

The two Kessels and Baumann had bowed out of Triangle by May 1919, having sold their backlog outright to Aitken's Western Import. Desperate for cash, in April 1920 Aitken licensed 150 of Sennett's Triangle Keystones to a new concern, Majestic Pictures, Inc., which was headed by Triangle's former sales manager, J. J. Unger. By 1921, Triangle was nearly bankrupt, and shareholders voted in a new board of directors, which promptly filed a fraudulent practices lawsuit against Aitken and his brother Roy. The pair settled out of court in 1922, surrendering their shares while maintaining ownership of Western Import and its assets.

In late 1923, Aitken was again trying to monetize his library. He and Oscar Price, formerly with United Artists, created Tri-Stone Pictures, Inc. to reissue Triangle features and Keystone Comedies. They opened for business with a dozen Keystone two-reelers (including three of Chaplin's) and engaged Charlie's brother, Syd Chap-

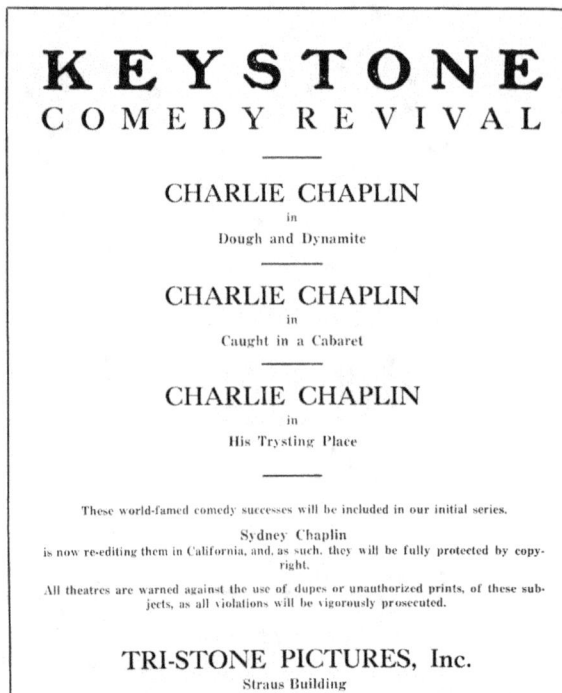

Trade ad for Tri-Stone Pictures' initial releases.

lin, to re-edit and dress them up with new intertitles. Trade ads promised that the Doug Fairbanks Triangle features would shortly follow, and that everything would be "sold on a business basis that makes a profit all around."

But 1924 was a decade and countless cinematic advances removed from 1914, and only the smallest of small-town theaters weren't tied up with a major producing company. It didn't help that the films were an embarrassment for all concerned. "A very bad picture and re-issuing did not do much good," wrote one Kansas exhibitor about *His Trysting Place*, also summing up Syd Chaplin's contribution: "Rather crude, vulgar jokes in titles." A Kentucky theater owner griped about *Caught in a Cabaret*, "Perhaps we laughed at these a decade ago, but my crowd did not seem to see anything funny about this reissue." By 1925, Tri-Stone had petered out.

The following year, the Aitken brothers formed a new Triangle Film Corporation, and talked about reissues and a new film to be written by Thomas E. Dixon, author of *The Clansman*, upon which *The Birth of a Nation* was based. Nothing happened, and the brothers spent most of the next thirty years attempting to raise the financing for a sound remake of *Birth*. Harry Aitken also held negatives for a few vintage Keystone comedies, at one point leasing them to Blackhawk Films for home use, but the vast majority of survivors were those that had been duped and re-duped over the years.

As discussed elsewhere in this volume, various conglomerations of "Keystone Kops" turned up in shorts and feature films well into the talkie era, but the comedies in which they made their reputation pretty much vanished from theater screens by the late 1920s. There would always be fast-buck producers peddling one or more of the Chaplin Keystones, and B-factory Monogram Pictures even trotted out *Tillie's Punctured Romance* in 1941, but for the most part the vintage Cops were AWOL from the picture palace for over thirty years. Yet their legend never died—indeed it only grew larger thanks to the advent of home movies, television, and Robert Youngson's compilation documentaries.

Surprisingly, vintage Keystones never appeared in the Kodascope libraries of the 1920s and 1930s, perhaps because the 16mm safety film company had a wealth of more recent titles, from such still-active producers as Hal Roach and Al Christie, at its disposal. In 1942, a company called Cope Studio announced a slate of "laugh-provoking Keystone Comedies," but the only title to emerge was from a later era: the Sennett-produced Ben Turpin two-reeler, *Step Forward* (1922). The earliest known home movie release of a vintage Keystone arrived courtesy of Castle Films; serendipitously, it also included the Cops. *A Muddy Romance* (1913), which starred Ford Sterling and Mabel Normand, was retitled *Muddled in Mud* and released in September 1946 in both 8mm and 16mm cut-down and complete formats. "Old-time comedy stars of Keystone slapstick era cavort!" read the blurb in Castle's new release announcement. "Famous comedy cops foil villain who drains lake to halt wedding in rowboat! Laugh riot of mud and merriment . . . a historic classic of slapstick to spice your collection!"

In 1954, a Hollywood company called Olde Time Movies released

Castle Films releases A Muddy Romance *(1913) under a new title in 1946.*

Ad for the short-lived Olde Time Movies Company.

five early Sennett titles in both 16mm and 8mm versions. One of these, *The Love Riot*, was a one-reel cut-down of *Tillie's Punctured Romance*, in which "Marie Dressler tangles with the Keystone Kops." Olde Time Movies advertised in *Home Movie* magazine during the year but disappeared soon after.

For the serious film collector, there was Blackhawk, which specialized in vintage silent material as clear and complete as possible and which, as noted

Yankee Doodle In Berlin

A Sanitarium Scandal

Love, Speed And Thrills

Spanking Breezes

previously, had obtained several Keystones from Harry Aitken. Among the earliest of the company's "Collector's Series" offerings were *Barney Oldfield's Race For a Life* (1913) and *Mabel's Dramatic Career* (1913, under its W. H. reissue title *Her Dramatic Debut*), both of which included the Cops. Over the years, Blackhawk added other "Keystone Cops" titles, most prominently *Bangville Police* (1913), *Our Dare-Devil Chief* (1915), *Love, Speed and Thrills* (1915), *Love, Loot and*

Crash (1915), *A Hash House Fraud* (1915), *Wife and Auto Trouble* (1916), *A Desperate Scoundrel* (1916), *Dollars and Sense* (1917), and, naturally, *Tillie's Punctured Romance*.

For the average consumer, there were Castle and Ken Films, the latter of which licensed Warner Bros. short subjects like *Keystone Hotel* (1935) and the compilations *Happy Times and Jolly Moments* (1943) and *Good Old Corn* (1945). There were also minor concerns like Atlas and Carnival that released anything they could lay hands on, regardless of condition, mainly in fifty-foot "Kiddie Movie" cutdowns. Up to the mid-1970s, Atlas was literally the dollar bin of 8mm. For them, Keystone comedies were a natural, and some could even "star" the Cops, something that never happened when the films were new.

Television was hungry for material in its early days, and nearly all silent comedies, including the Keystones, were pressed into service. Sometimes they'd be presented respectfully as part of a nostalgic look back at the past; sometimes they'd be cut

Keystone Cops in home movie format for both the serious film collector and the average movie fan.

up into segments for children's shows; sometimes they'd simply appear without fanfare if a local station had a half-hour that needed filling. Inevitably, just as they had in the earliest cinemas, the Cops would turn up in these shows from time to time.

Robert Youngson had started his career at Warner Bros., which held a library of films Sennett had produced for First National Pictures in the early 1920s; he created two-reel compilations from these and other silent comedies beginning in the late 1940s. In 1958, he released *The Golden Age of Comedy*, the first of a series of semi-documentary features that would highlight the silent work of Sennett, Hal Roach, and other comedy creators. The Cops appeared in some of these as well, particularly in a chase sequence assembled from several shorts and used in *The Days of Thrills and Laughter* (1961).

As early as 1919, trade magazines and exhibitors waxed nostalgic about the Keystone Cops. Today, beautifully restored Keystones that include its hyperkinetic police force appear in several excellent home video releases from boutique companies like CineMuseum, Flicker Alley, and Kino, while dupey, splicey versions turn up for the undemanding curiosity seeker on the internet and in budget line video releases. Google the phrase "Keystone Cops" and (as of this writing) you'll get 244,000 results. Even in this century of on-demand multimedia options, the Keystone Cops have currency.

For that, we can thank Harry Aitken, Joseph Simmonds, Castle and Blackhawk Films, Robert Youngson and, of course, Mack Sennett.

Sources

Much information about Triangle, Western Import and W. H. Productions was obtained from *Hollywood Vault: Film Libraries Before Home Video* by Eric Hoyt (2014, University of California Press).

The following articles and publications were referenced for this chapter:

"Baumann Bolts Universal," *Motography*, July 6, 1912.

"Bison With Film Supply," *New York Dramatic Mirror*, July 31, 1912.

"H. E. Aitken Forms New Combination," *The Billboard*, June 26, 1915.

"Ince and Sennett Both Out; W. S. Hart Also Gives Notice," *Variety*, June 22, 1917.

"W. H. Productions Announces Prices," *New York Dramatic Mirror*, Date Unknown

"Who Said Failures?" *Motion Picture News*, April 13, 1918.

"'Hula Hula Dance' Chaplin Reissue," *Moving Picture World*, May 4, 1918.

"W. H. Official Speaks Regarding Market Conditions," *Moving Picture World*, May 25, 1918.

"Simmonds Speaks of 'Mickey'," *Moving Picture World*, August 3, 1918.

"Says Production Curtailment Enhances Value of Reissues," *Moving Picture World*, November 2, 1918.

"Reissues—And They Are Proud of Them" (W. H. Prods. Trade Ad), *Motion Picture News*, December 14, 1918.

"Special Service Section on Keystone and Kay Bee Re-issues," *Motion Picture News*, December 14, 1918.

"How to Appeal to Every Picture Fan in Your Section," *Motion Picture News*, December 14, 1918.

"'Old Timers Night' Will Help Put Them Over," *Motion Picture News*, December 14, 1918.

"W. H. Productions Teaches Reissue Exploitation," *Motion Picture News*, December 28, 1918.

"Good Bookings Reported on Keystone Reissues," *Moving Picture World*, March 1, 1919.

"Final Hearing This Week In Matter of Reissues," *Variety*, March 21, 1919.

"Trade Commission Closes Case in Reissue Investigation," *Variety*, April 4, 1919.

"Hart Wants Name Protected," *New York Clipper*, April 23, 1919.

"Kessels Out of Triangle," *New York Clipper*, May 28, 1919.

"Federal Trade on Reissues," *Variety*, August 8, 1919.

"Must Stop Retitling Films," *New York Clipper*, August 13, 1919.

"'Tillie's Punctured Romance' Is a Revival, Not a Reissue. Make It So," *Moving Picture World*, January 24, 1920.

"Company Formed by Hammell and Unger Will Reissue Mack Sennett Comedies," *Moving Picture World*, April 17, 1920.

"Triangle Company Makes Virulent Charges Against H. E. and R. E. Aitken," *Moving Picture World*, March 5, 1921.

"Triangle Suit Defendants Answer With Counterclaims," *Variety*, March 18, 1921.

"Aitkens Answer In," *Variety*, March 25, 1921.

"Law And The Theatre," *Variety*, December 30, 1921.

"Aitkens Surrender 15,000 Shares to Stop Triangle Suit," *Variety*, June 16, 1922.

"Keystone Comedy Revival" (Tri-Stone Pictures trade ad), *Film Daily*, January 11, 1923.

Exhibitor review of "His Trysting Place," *Exhibitors Herald*, December 29, 1923.

Exhibitor review of "Caught in a Cabaret," *Exhibitors Herald*, January 5, 1924.

"If You Want a Film to Show: Keystone Comedies," *Home Movies*, April 1942.

Castle Films Advertisement, *Home Movies*, September 1946.

Blackhawk Films Catalog #26B, November-December 1952.

Olde Time Movies Advertisement, *Home Movies*, November 1954.

Blackhawk Films Catalog #50, Fall 1955.

Blackhawk Bulletin B-281, December 1976.

Michael J. Hayde is an author and a popular culture historian specializing in film, television, and radio history. His books include *Side By Side: Dean Martin and Jerry Lewis On TV and Radio*; *My Name's Friday: The Unauthorized But True Story of Dragnet and the Films of Jack Webb*; *Flights of Fantasy: The Unauthorized But True Story of Radio and Television's* The Adventures of Superman; *Chaplin's Vintage Year: The History of the Mutual-Chaplin Specials*; and (co-authored with Chuck Harter) *The Little Elf: A Celebration of Harry Langdon*. Mr. Hayde has consulted for and appeared on NBC-TV's *Unsolved Mysteries* and TV Land's *Myths and Legends*, and has hosted presentations at the Library of Congress, the Packard Canyon Theater, and the Mid-Atlantic Nostalgia and the Friends of Old-Time Radio conventions. He lives in Manassas, Virginia, with his wife and four children.

All images in this chapter courtesy of the author.

Chapter 11
The Keystone Cop and the Missing Briefcase
By Lon Davis

An alternate shot from In the Clutches of a Gang *(1914). Courtesy of Bison Archives.*

It looked like something you'd find in a thrift shop. Faux leather, cracked with age, the latch broken. The color had faded over time, but you would still say it was brown, or maybe just brown*ish*. It was an old briefcase, nothing more. But, oh, what treasures it contained! Artifacts of the richest period in film history—the silent era—collected by an authentic participant, someone who had been both in front of and behind the hand-cranked camera. There were autographed photographs of well-known actors and actresses; there were production stills and call sheets from major features helmed by important directors. It was like a time capsule.

Now granted, being an eye witness to the earliest days of Hollywood may not be the desire of every fourteen-year-old boy, but then, I was no ordinary fourteen-year-old boy. Instead, I was one of those rare misfits obsessed with silent films. As far back as grade school I was devouring every film-history book in the public library. I overstayed my welcome in local pizza parlors that showed silent films. I sought out veterans of the industry, some of whom lived not far from where I lived in Phoenix, Arizona, and others (including my great-uncle Ted Edlin) who resided at the Motion Picture and Television Country House and Hospital in Woodland Hills, California. And I was determined to share my passion with others. Possessing an ancient (and ridiculously heavy) TSI 16mm projector and a stack of Blackhawk film prints, I gave talks in high schools and colleges, showing my fellow students the kind of visual comedy that had put their grandparents in the aisles. Not surprisingly, these timeless films would have the same impact on them. When an article detailing my avocation appeared in the Teen section of the *Phoenix Gazette*, those I knew (and many I didn't) began associating me, a mere kid, with the black-and-white images of the past. And I, for one, could not have been prouder.

One day after returning home from school I received a phone call from an area podiatrist. He told me that one of his patients had been in silent movies and, for a time, had worked as a Keystone Cop—and that he had obtained permission from this patient to give me his number. Immediately upon hanging up, I had my doubts. Over the years, many actors (and many who were not) had claimed to have been Mack Sennett's original Cops, just as there were Our Gang and Sennett Bathing Beauty impostors. Maybe this old gent is just looking for attention, I thought to myself. "Oh, well," I said philosophically, "what have I got to lose?" I dialed the number and listened to the repeated rings.

"*HELLO?*" The high-pitched voice belonged to an old man, one who was just this side of crotchety.

"Pardon me, sir," I asked deferentially, "is this Mr. Cox?"

"This is Robert Cox. Who's *this*?"

I identified myself, told him of my interest in silent films, and asked if it was true that he had been one of the Keystone Cops.

"Sure," he said, "I was one of those guys." He sounded relieved that I wasn't a bill collector.

"Do you, by any chance, have any pictures—?"

"Got a whole briefcase full of 'em," he said, his tone now welcoming and friendly. "Why don't you come over and you can see for yourself?"

Armed with an official invitation, I made plans to visit Mr. Cox at his modest one-story home on Polk Street. Accompanying me was my neighbor Cheryl Lanning, a freelance feature writer who was hoping this meeting might lead to a human-interest story.

In his modest Phoenix home, Robert Cox displays some of the contents of his briefcase, including a personally signed portrait from his friend Roscoe Arbuckle. Photocopy from an article appearing in Arizona Magazine *on April 7, 1974.*

Our host was an ordinary-looking fellow, well along in years (he was seventy-eight, having been born on May 12, 1895). He was short (perhaps five feet tall), thin (no more than 120 pounds), and profoundly bent over (he bore the maladies of having stepped on a landmine while serving in France during World War I). His head appeared a bit too large for his frail body to support. His face was broad and not overly lined; his tuft of brown hair was neatly combed in a manner one might expect of a twelve-year-old boy whose mother had just tried to make him presentable. His puckered lips and small chin betrayed a lack of teeth. And his oversized glasses gave him a whimsical quality. He wore a blue-and-black-checkered Pendleton, black pants, and tan house slippers. Most noticeable of all was his ingratiating manner: he was crisp, to the point—but also sweet, even lovable.

Mr. Cox had been married and divorced three times and his home of twenty-three years clearly lacked a feminine touch. His kitchenette, visible from the front door, had an aluminum table on which stood—in a crowded island at the center—every possible condiment he could need during the course of any meal. The furniture in the living room was threadbare, sort of early Salvation Army, and every upholstered piece was covered by either a sheet or a blanket. Above a sunken arm chair was a large, dark painting, a genuine Van Gogh—at least that was what he genuinely believed to be the case. More interesting to his guests, however, was the aforementioned battered briefcase, which lay on his scratched laminate wood coffee table.

Mr. Cox emptied the contents—primarily original stills—and one in particular stood out to me: it was of the Keystone Cops. Not just *any* picture, mind you—it was *the* picture, the one taken for *In the Clutches of a Gang*, a two-reeler released on January 17, 1914. In that iconic shot, Ford Sterling (as the chief of police) is on the phone, cross-eyed with anticipation, while nine sorry-looking policemen stand by, ready for action. In addition to Sterling, several of the long-deceased actors would be recognizable to diehard silent film buffs: Roscoe "Fatty" Arbuckle, Hank Mann, Al St. John, Edgar Kennedy. But a

Looking dapper and somewhat severe, Mack Sennett supervises the shooting of a two-reel comedy featuring Chester Conklin while Hans F. Koenekamp cranks the camera. Photo courtesy of Bison Archives.

few individuals had never, to my knowledge, been identified in any film-history book. Could one of these unknowns have been our host?

"Yeah, that's me," he said, seeming to read my mind. "I'm right there between Bobby Dunn and Ford Sterling—I had to stand on an orange crate in order to be seen." Unlike many of his fellow Cops, Mr. Cox was clean-shaven, with no trace of the brush mustache then so widely in favor with Sennett's comedians. I asked him about it and he said, "Didn't wear a mustache; sometimes I had a beard, though." While those aforementioned poseurs had falsely identified themselves as being among this motley lineup, Mr. Cox spoke with such authority about his friends and co-stars that it was soon apparent he was what he purported to be. No impostor, this. And now, at this late date, he was about to be interviewed for the first time ever about his movie career.

I asked how, and when, he had gotten his start as a Keystone Cop.

"It was about 1912," he said. "I came out west with [movie producers] Kessel and Baumann. Mack Sennett was working on the same lot and when he decided to start his own company, I went with him. I was seventeen at the time."

Who made up the original Keystone company?

"Fred Mace was our leading man," he said. "Mabel Normand was our leading woman. Mack Sennett played the juveniles. And Mother [Alice] Davenport played the characters. Then there were about twelve of us Cops. We also had an electrician, a carpenter, and a cameraman."

What was Mabel like?

"She was as beautiful inside as she was out," he smiled in remembrance. "*Everybody* loved Mabel. Did you know that the Cops were her idea?"

The luminous Mabel Normand posed for this publicity shot for her starring vehicle Mabel at the Wheel *(1914). Photo courtesy of Bison Archives.*

Could he possibly describe the Keystone film studio in those embryonic days?

Pushing aside some photographs, he outlined a square area with his finger. "We were located in Edendale, California. Our first studio was shaped like this, with all bare ground and a house here. There was a great big room in the house and we all used it to make up. We threw up a big platform outside the overhead wires and pulleys and lightweight fabric of some kind. This was so we could pull the material back and forth, controlling the light for filming," he explained. "Indoor scenes were done there, but most of the time the Cops were on location in and around Los Angeles. It seems to me like I spent an awful lot of time walking on the bottom of Echo Park Lake, which was right near the studio.

"The thing I remember Mr. Sennett always saying was, 'Make me laugh.' If you made him laugh, he liked you. His philosophy, I guess you could call it, was to send the public

Mack Sennett is seen entering the studio by way of the Cops' dressing room. If you look very closely, you'll see the faded word Cops painted on the door behind him. Photo courtesy of Bison Archives.

The Cops look hot and tired after a day of hard-core slapstick. Slim Summerville, the tall man with the prominent nose, is the most recognizable Cop; Bobby Dunn (wearing a dirty suit) is next to him (the tallest and shortest Keystone players were teamed in a few shorts); mustachioed James Donnelly is wearing a derby and is seated on the ground, and George Gray is crouching below Summerville, his arms resting on his knees; Joe Bordeaux is at the far right, standing. Most likely, he and Gray were prop men on this particular shoot; Gray was also an accomplished stunt man. Photo courtesy of Bison Archives.

home from the theater laughing, and they'd come back for more. Now, most of the pictures at that time were melodramatic stories with dreary, depressing endings. He filmed the comedies to follow those dramas. You've got to give him credit. Mr. Sennett had vision."

Mr. Cox selected a yellowed snapshot from the table. "See this guy? This is my friend Slim Summerville, one of the original Cops, a real easygoing person. I'll never forget what happened to Slim the day we were shooting a lake scene with Mabel.

"Mr. Sennett explained to all of us what he wanted us to do. He never worked from a script," Mr. Cox insisted, pointing to his head. "His only script was up here.[1] He wanted to film a scene with Mabel out in a boat. He told her to yell for help and then instructed us to arrive on the scene, run off the dock and into the water to save her. It was pretty cold that day and Mr. Sennett had us doing so many antics in the water that Slim turned blue!

"Mr. Sennett told me to take Slim someplace to get him warmed up. I borrowed the Stutz Bearcat that Mr. Sennett had given Mabel and took Slim to a Turkish bath. I finally got him looking halfway human again and then I asked

Chester Conklin throttles his co-star Dale Fuller in this posed shot taken at Keystone in 1916. Photo courtesy of Bison Archives.

him if he wanted anything. He looked at me and said, 'Coxie, get me a clean collar, a pint of whiskey, and tell the Old Man to go to hell! I won't be back to work today.' And he wasn't, which was unusual for a Cop. We just didn't miss filming in those days unless we were injured, which wasn't very often. We worked from sunrise to sunset, and we weren't any of us temperamental. Mr. Sennett would have fired us if we had been."

Mr. Cox shook his head. "I always seemed to be changing into a dry uniform. We were issued two pairs of trousers, two coats, two white collars, one helmet, one truncheon, and one belt from wardrobe. I don't know how many outfits I wore out in those years. Must have been quite a few.

"Since Mr. Sennett didn't work from a script, whatever he thought was funny at the time was what we did. One day he asked us, 'Any of you ever been on roller skates?' We all looked at one another. My friend Al St. John, who was the only one of the original Keystone Cops who was a former stuntman, said he was pretty good on skates, but no one else knew how. It was my first time. So naturally Mr. Sennett sent over to a costume place and got twelve pair. "We

Al St. John, a born stunt man, managed to break into movies with the help of his aunt Minta Durfee Arbuckle. For whatever reason, Minta's husband Roscoe opposed this at first. Once Al proved his worth as a daredevil Keystone Cop, however, Roscoe took him under his wing, even inviting him to join him at Paramount where he would star in his own series. Photo courtesy of Bison Archives.

put 'em on and you should have seen the mess," Mr. Cox said, slapping the arm of his chair. "Cops all over the place, falling, reeling, sprawling on the floor, running into each other. Billy Hauber said later he was on his feet once in the whole scene. This was one time we didn't have to add any little business of our own to make the scene funny. It was genuine, every bit of it. And the Old Man—I guess Mr. Sennett must have about twenty-eight at the time—he ran around egging us on, calling out instructions to his cameraman and chewing on a cigar. He always had a big fifty-cent cigar in his mouth and in all the years I knew him I never once saw him light one.

"When we were all exhausted and black and blue all over, he let us stop. I was really bruised up. We all were except Al St. John, but Mr. Sennett said it was one of the funniest pieces of film he'd ever seen.

"I was always the littlest Cop there," Mr. Cox continued. "I couldn't have weighed more than ninety-five pounds. I usually brought up the rear or was the one swinging out on the ladder we used to use. One bit I especially liked was when Ford Sterling, the big man with [the Dutch makeup] who played the chief, would pound his gavel on the desk. Everyone but me would spring up from the bench, and naturally the bench would tip over and I slid onto the floor.

Ben Turpin looks to be on a sugar high in Love and Doughnuts *(1921).*

"Each comic at that time had some distinctive bit of business that was his alone. Ben Turpin used the cross-eyed bit. I've heard people say that he wasn't really cross-eyed. That's just not so. One time, Hank Mann, our prankster, got Turpin to direct traffic at a big intersection. You can imagine how he looked," Mr. Cox said, crossing his eyes. "It took several *real* cops a couple hours to straighten out the mess Turpin made. Mr. Sennett thought it was great, but of course he was used to making use of real events for his filming. The public never complained. They loved to watch us work."

He reached across the table and picked up a studio portrait of a heavily mustachioed, sad-eyed man, inscribed: *To Coxie, Lest we Forget the Old Keystone days, Your Old Friend, Chester.* "Conklin was in the original group, and so was Rube Miller. About that time—1913—we got Roscoe "Fatty" Arbuckle. You

A Sennett-like train gag, recreated for the 1955 Universal-International film Bud Abbott & Lou Costello Meet the Keystone Kops. *Photos courtesy of Bison Archives.*

know he was Minta Durfee's husband? We also got Charley Parrott and Mack Swain. Parrott later changed his name to Chase and was an actor and director for Hal Roach. With all the coming and leaving in the Cops we must've had forty or fifty guys that were Cops at some time or other."

He also recalled the Keystone Cops' legendary chase scenes. "Mr. Sennett had us using streetcars, horses, skates, Model T's. We lost one of those one day when the whole lot of us went off the end of a pier. We had one car that came apart for trick photography. We used real fire engines, bicycles, scooters, anything we could get our hands on to add fresh humor. Mr. Sennett generally rode with the cameraman in a Packard touring car.

"We always seemed to be on a collision course with a train. It wasn't as dangerous as it looked, because Mr. Sennett used trick photography and we'd trained ourselves to move in a jerky way that was characteristic of the comics of that day. All his

Charlie Chaplin, out of makeup, watches a shoot-in-progress. Popular comic Charlie Murray (wearing his trademark costume) is watching as well, 1914. Photo courtesy of Bison Archives.

film was shot at the speed used today.[2] We had gotten to be pretty adept stuntmen by that time. We used to extend ourselves out full length from the back of a moving object using just the strength of our arms. Many's the time I was sore all over because I hadn't fallen just right. It's hard to do pratfalls."[3]

"Money was what finally caused a lot of principals to leave Keystone," he explained. "Even the Cops were grumbling because we only made twenty-five a week. But Mr. Sennett couldn't pay more and so he lost people. Chaplin was one Keystone lost. Chuck was getting about a hundred-fifty a week with Keystone. When he went over to the Essanay Company, he was getting twelve-hundred-fifty a week.

"Before he left Keystone I got to know Chaplin pretty well. He was the type of man that if he liked you he would do anything for you, but if he didn't like you, *look out*. We roomed together at the Los Angeles Athletic Club. At night we would sit around and talk and he'd tell me about his plans and ambitions. One of them was to play Romeo. I said, 'You've got to be crazy, Chuck!' He was a funny guy, and at the same time, kind of sad and pathetic. And he played this to the hilt. He was also a perfectionist who was never satisfied with his performance. He was always reaching out to do better. You know, he even played a Cop in one of our pictures."[4]

"I knew he would make it. He knew who he was. You know, he used to keep his money under his bed in a box. He didn't trust banks. And he was a little tight with it. I'll never forget the time he wore out his derby. He couldn't find one to suit him here, so he ordered one from England. He was really put out when the studio made him pay for it."

According to the official records at the Margaret Herrick Library at the Academy of Motion Picture Arts and Sciences, Robert Cox (sometimes listed as Marvin Cox for some unknown reason) is one of the least documented Keystone players. One non-Cop role he had was in a two-reeler called *The Best of Enemies* (December 5, 1915), the first of only a few silent films starring the popular vaudeville team of Joe Weber and Lew Fields. In one scene, Mr. Cox played the team's uniformed chauffeur who becomes involved in a serious collision with a garbage truck.

The public's taste in comedy had begun to change, and Mack Sennett changed right along with them. As Mr. Cox explained. "He began bringing in bathing beauties along about 1917, and we all began to drift away from the Cops. I had a choice to make. Stay with the Cops or go with my friends when they left. When Harold Lloyd left Keystone he wanted me to leave with him and become his assistant. I turned him down. I'm not sure why. I guess I just wasn't ready to leave."

Joe Weber and Lew Fields were a tremendously popular Broadway comedy team known for their broken-English routines. They were less successful, however, when they attempted to make the transition to silent films, appearing in two Sennett comedies: The Best of Enemies *and* The Worst of Friends *(both Keystone-Triangle, 1915). Robert Cox had a small role as a chauffeur in the former film, which is now considered lost.*

"A few months later this job came up at Famous Players, Jesse Lasky's studio. I took it and was assigned to work as assistant to Jimmy Cruze, one of Lasky's directors. The first film I made with Cruze was *The Dictator* (1922) with Wallace Reid, Lila Lee, and Walter Long. It was a Mexican revolution comedy-drama. We filmed it in San Diego. I really enjoyed myself on that picture. I learned to speak pretty fair Spanish because as assistant I had charge of the extras." He held up several photographs. "See how authentic looking the Mexicans are in these pictures? We'd brought some of our people, but we'd had to wardrobe them, and the Mexicans had their own costumes. We paid them five dollars a day and a box lunch.

"I'd known Cruze quite a while when he announced that he was getting married. He built this great big house in Topanga Canyon and decided to have a housewarming party to celebrate. Everybody was invited. At that time I was living with Alan Hale and his wife. She was pregnant and since he was doing so much night filming, he wanted someone to be there with her.[5]

"Well, before we went to the party, Hale said, 'Coxie, we can't go up there empty-handed. We've gotta take something with us. I'll call my bootlegger and get us some liquor. He did, and so we went with four big bottles of gin. Of course when we got there, there was a big crowd, plenty to eat and drink. Hale wondered what we should do with the gin. If we left it in the car someone would steal it. So we decided to take it in with us and hide it in the oven in the kitchen. No one would ever think of looking for gin there."

He leaned forward in his chair and began to chuckle.

"Well, along about one or two o'clock in the morning, someone decided to make some coffee and have a bite to eat. We never thought anything more about the gin. When they lit the stove and the gin heated up, well, it exploded and blew a great big hole outta the back of Cruze's new house.

"Everybody came running and they all looked at the place where the wall had been, and they blamed it on the stove. Hale said, 'Let's get the hell out of here. We can tell him about it sometime when he's cooled down.' And we went home."

Mr. Cox found another snapshot on the table. "That's Cecil B. DeMille. I worked with him on *The King of Kings* (1927). I had been assigned to take care of twenty-five camels and about a hundred extras dressed as Arabs. Those camels. They spit food right back in my face a couple of times. Every time they were ready for a scene with the Arabs and camels, DeMille would pass the word, 'Bring out the camels!' and I'd say to myself, 'Oh, hell, here we go again,' and then I'd trot them all out and try to herd them in the general direction of the camera."

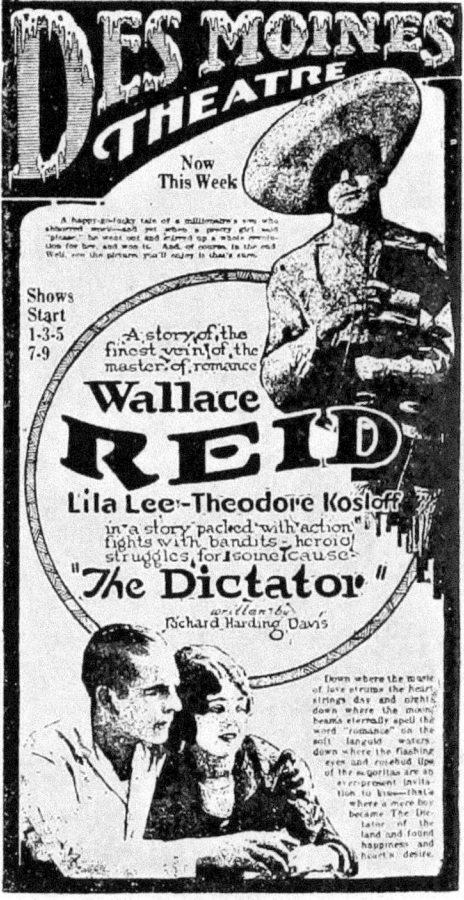

Cecil B. DeMille.

Rudolph Valentino.

Mr. Cox recalled working with director George Melford when he made *The Sheik* (1921), featuring Rudolph Valentino. "That dago about drove Melford out of his mind because he was so lazy and officious. This one morning Melford sent me over to where Valentino lived to see why he wasn't on the set when he should have been. He'd missed two days of filming. We worked around him, but this day he was needed. Was he sick? Too much to drink? *What?*

"Valentino had this Japanese valet. When he answered the door, he told me that Mr. Valentino was sleeping and could not be disturbed. I said, 'The hell you say! You get him up and tell him to get his ass over to the studio. He's wanted on the set.' And I left. Valentino showed up a couple hours later, yawning.

"And once you got him on the set, Medford had to tell him about six times how to play a scene. Valentino wasn't the brightest guy around. But I'll say one thing for him: he could sure dance."

He changed the subject. "I went over to work at Fox about that time. I can't remember, but I think they were paying me about three-fifty, four hundred dollars a week. I know I bought a seven-room house overlooking Hollywood, hired a housekeeper and a German butler named Bill, and bought myself a Cadillac roadster. I was really living."

He sorted through a pile of photographs and laid out a few. "All of these were taken during the filming of *The Iron Horse* (1924), which was directed by Sean Aloysius Feeney—you know him as John Ford." An epic western, *The Iron Horse* documents the building of a railroad into Nevada. It climaxes with a mammoth Indian attack on trapped locomotives, while the United States Cavalry races to the rescue. "This one was taken on February tenth," he continued, "the day the two crews of workers, played by actors of course, came together in the picture for the 'wedding of the rails.' You'll notice Ford here explaining

Legendary director John Ford (with his back to the camera) directs a scene for the mammoth production of The Iron Horse *(1924).*

something to his principals, George O'Brien and Madge Bellamy. This is the way he worked. He explained everything he wanted to his principals, then he ran through it a couple of times until they felt comfortable with it and then ordered a take. Anybody who ever worked with John Ford will tell you, you always knew what was expected of you. He was one of the great directors in the business.

"I always used to laugh at him, though. He had the darndest habit of chewing on his handkerchief. Always had one of the darn things in his mouth."

He reached over the table and picked up several typewritten sheets of paper. "These are shooting schedules and wardrobe needs for Clara Bow in 'The Fifth Wheel.'[6] Little Clara, 'The It Girl,' the people called her, was a sweet twenty-year-old actress who was a real professional. And do you know why? Because if she knew she was expected to be in make-up at such and such a time, she was there. If she was wanted on the set at six o'clock, she was there at six, ready to work. That's a real professional in my opinion.

"In 1925, 1926, the industry began to change," he said. "Rumors that talkies were the coming thing had us all worried. I wasn't worried because I'd learned to sway with the wind. But quite a few silent film stars were worried. Chaplin told me one time that he wondered if he could make it because

Clara Bow.

he had a strong British accent. Once *The Jazz Singer* with Al Jolson hit the theaters in 1927, most of us could see how big a change we were in for."

Mr. Cox picked up the briefcase that had been leaning against his chair and began refilling it with photographs and mementos from the coffee table. "When they started to make pictures where I couldn't see a plot, no reason for doing anything, why I knew it was time to quit, get out of motion pictures. I'd opened my big mouth a couple times and they didn't like it."

He waved his finger in the air. "I thought pictures should have a little more romance, a little more family life shown. I retired in 1933."

In the years that followed, the Keystone Cops would occasionally enjoy a comeback of sorts, usually in nostalgia-based Hollywood films about the silent era; former members also demonstrated pie-throwing techniques for live audiences at the 1940 World's Fair. There were even guest appearances on television programs, in nightclubs, and in parades. Mr. Cox never participated in any event of this kind. Leaving the past behind, he told us that he later joined the Narcotics Bureau and was stationed for a time in the Far East. Intriguing, certainly, but it wasn't film-related; besides, our heads were already spinning from all the inside information he had shared about the silent era. With handshakes all around, and mutual promises of future contact, the interview came to a satisfying end.

Cheryl Lanning wrote an outstanding feature article on Mr. Cox entitled, "Make Me Laugh," for which I was her research assistant.[7] The piece was published in *Arizona Magazine* on Sunday, April 7, 1974. That article somehow found its way to the New York City offices of the Mark Goodson–Bill Todman production company. For generations of network television viewers, these men's names were synonymous with such popular and enduring game shows as *Password*, *The Price is Right*, *Beat the Clock*, and *Match Game*. In no time, Mr. Cox was contacted by one of the Goodson–Todman's representatives and told that the company wanted to feature him as a guest contestant on an episode of *To Tell the Truth*.[8]

He was positively jubilant when he phoned me with the news, his already-high pitched voice now hitting dog-whistle levels. I was so happy for him. For the first time in his long life he was receiving some recognition as a motion picture pioneer. He was flown first-class to Manhattan, where he took part in the taping. The segment opened with a series of Keystone film clips, accompanied by live piano music. The studio audience responded enthusiastically to the Cops bumping into one another and skidding along the Los Angeles streets in their paddy wagon. When the lights came back on, three mature gentlemen were seen seated at the contestants' panel, each one claiming to be Keystone

Cop Robert Cox. The celebrity panelists (Kitty Carlisle, Orson Bean, Peggy Cass, and Bill Cullen) peppered the guests with questions in an attempt to determine who the *real* Robert Cox was. In the end, they all but unanimously believed contestant number one (Mr. Cox himself) to be the genuine article. He had, Bill Cullen observed, that distinctive air of a show business veteran: he was quick to relate an anecdote, drop a name, and crack a joke. At one point, Mr. Cox was asked how much his weekly pay was at Keystone, to which he responded, "*Big* money—thirty dollars per week!" (*Audience laughs.*) He continued: "We worked every day but Sunday; they let us go to church." (*Another roar from the audience.*) When it was time for the *real* Robert Cox to stand up, he did so with a big grin and a wink at the panel. The audience stood as well—and cheered. It was, he later told me, the thrill of his life.[9] To show his appreciation for my having nudged him into the spotlight at that late date, he said that, upon his death, he wanted me to have his briefcase and its historic contents. As I had actually done very little, I felt unworthy of this honor.

Basking in the limelight for the first and last time in his life, Robert Cox was a whimsical contestant on the popular television game show To Tell the Truth *in 1974. Screencap courtesy of Fremantle Productions.*

Mr. Cox's episode of *To Tell the Truth* was telecast on the last day of 1974, but he was not able to watch it. He had died suddenly of a heart attack a few months earlier, on September 8; he was seventy-nine years old and left no survivors. Perhaps even sadder than his passing was something that happened next. One of his bitter ex-wives was given the duty of clearing out his house. Seeing the battered briefcase among his belongings, she blithely threw it away.

Notes

1. In fact, Sennett did use scripts—quite detailed ones—but that was for the more complex films he shot in the 1920s. In the 1912-1915 period, Keystone comedies were indeed made with only a basic premise in mind. The gags were added during filming.
2. Sound film is shot at 24fps; silent film; particularly in the early Keystone era, was shot at 14fps. The fast-motion effect used in the Sennett comedies was achieved by undercranking the camera.
3. This is an understatement. Mr. Cox had broken his right arm so many times that he was barely able to bend it.
4. I recall thinking that he must have been misremembering; there was no record of Chaplin appearing as one of the Keystone Cops—at least not until 2011 when the 1914 one-reeler *A Thief Catcher* was rediscovered by Paul E. Gierucki at a garage sale in Michigan.
5. Alan Hale (whose actual name was Rufus Edward McKahan) was a prolific actor in both silent and sound films, with a filmography boasting some 235 titles. The baby being carried by Mrs. McKahan was born on March 8, 1921. Alan Hale Jr. eventually followed in his father's footsteps by becoming a character actor. He achieved lasting fame as the Skipper on TV's *Gilligan's Island* (1964-1967); he died, aged sixty-eight, on January 2, 1990.
6. There is no Clara Bow film by that name; this may have been a working title for *Dancing Mothers* (1926).
7. Several of the stories he told us are being retold in this essay.
8. Interestingly enough, Robert Cox wasn't the first Keystone Cops to be so featured on *To Tell the Truth*; Chester Conklin appeared as a contestant, in full uniform no less, in 1957.

Chapter 12.
The Keystone Cops, or Kops—
Kolliding Into Kontemporary Kulture
By Randy Skretvedt

A promotional shot for Hollywood Cavalcade *(20th Century-Fox, 1939).* Photo courtesy of Bison Archives.

Recently, someone I know who has a large portrait of *I Love Lucy*-era Lucille Ball adorning one of his walls, remarked that a thirty-something visitor had noticed it and said, "I *think* I know who she is." He wasn't sure, and he wasn't joking. A recent episode of *Jeopardy!* had three contestants in their forties who knew arcane trivia about Greek mythology and world geography but could not identify the movie *Casablanca*. The movie *Yesterday* presents a world in which nobody remembers any of the songs written and performed by the Beatles. Such a thing would seem impossible only a few years ago but sadly seems all too plausible today.

Which makes it especially impressive that the Keystone Kops (or Cops, if you prefer), who never had a proper film series, and whose most prominent appearances were in movies made over 100 years ago, are still regularly cited in our culture. Since the Kops' first flush of fame was between 1912 and 1917, subsequent reunions, tributes and citations far outnumber the original films. So strong was the impression they made that the stumbling, bumbling, leaping Kops with the runaway patrol wagon have remained an indelible image in our culture to this day.

What were the origins of the Keystone policemen? And is it Kops or Cops?

In his 1954 autobiography, *King of Comedy*, Sennett describes arriving in Los Angeles in September 1912 with Mabel Normand, Fred Mace, and Ford Sterling and notes, "We started making a picture within thirty minutes after we alighted at the Santa Fe station." The Shriners were on parade, and Sennett decided to make use of the spectacle by improvising a scene with Mabel and a baby doll. She played a mother looking among the Shriners for the father of her child, whom she believes is Sterling. Several real Shriners were rather embarrassed; actual Los Angeles policemen came into the scene and began chasing Sterling.

"The Shriners were good, but the best scenes we nabbed were the running cops," Sennett recalled. "I never got their names, but if there are any retired gentlemen of the Los Angeles Police Department who remember taking part in that incident, let them bask in fame: they were the original Keystone Cops." Unfortunately, no such film seems to exist, or ever has existed. Sennett did direct a split-reeler, *The Would-Be Shriner*, released July 25, 1912, which was filmed during a Los Angeles convention of the Shriners in May. A couple of actors are cast as policemen, but there's nothing to indicate a bunch of cops running after Sterling, who does not appear in the movie.

Sennett in fact had been inspired to enlist a squadron of funny cops for his films after seeing some of the early French comedies which were being released in the States. Says historian Steve Massa, "Both the Pathé and Gaumont Companies had a regular ensemble of clowns and acrobats who would often play cops and do the chasing and falls in the early French shorts. They seem to be the prototype for the motley crew that Sennett would assemble at Keystone. The group at Gaumont was called 'Les Poics' (bedbugs) and included people like Clement Mige and Gaston Modot (who worked in French films for over fifty years)."

As to whether the correct spelling is "Cops" or "Kops," it's officially both. Sennett in his 1954 autobiography consistently refers to them as "Cops," although the promotional copy on the covers of some editions of his book spell it as "Kops." That spelling would gain official status in the 1960s. More about this later.

A surprising addition to the Cops' filmography is *A Thief Catcher* (released February 19, 1914), which features a hyperactive Ford Sterling as "Suspicious John," who is bedeviled by crooks Edgar Kennedy and Mack Swain. To the rescue come Cops Rube Miller, George Jeske, Bill Hauber—and Charlie Chaplin! In a brief scene between Sterling and Chaplin, it's easy to see why, and how, Chaplin soon dethroned Sterling as Sennett's most popular comic.

Sterling is a whirlwind of constant action. His elbows are flailing, his chin twitches, his eyebrows dance up and down on his forehead. Chaplin, in helmet and "official" Keystone Cops costuming, looks at Sterling, not moving a muscle but just watching him with slight disdain. He then wiggles a finger as if to say, "cut that out." The economy of his motion draws our attention to him and makes him much easier to understand than Sterling, whose intent is obscured by the endless flailing and twitching. This film was long lost and was not known to be one of Chaplin's appearances until historian Paul E. Gierucki discovered a 16mm print at a Michigan antique sale.

Other notable films from the Cops' first flowering include *Fatty Joins the Force* (November 24, 1913), *Love, Speed and Thrills* (January 18, 1915), *Love, Loot and Crash* (April 24, 1915), *Wife and Auto Trouble* (March 5, 1916) and *Pinched in the Finish* (April 1, 1917).

The Cops had already become an indelible image in the popular culture by mid-1917 and had long since been breeding imitators at other studios. Essanay had a gaggle of funny cops, led by future Sennett comedian Ben Turpin, as early as 1914. A similar squadron was featured in at least one of the Apollo Comedies of that year starring former Sennett funnyman Fred Mace. Larry Semon used a platoon of bumbling policemen on occasion in his shorts for Vitagraph. In the July 1917 issue of *Motion Picture Classic*, one A. L. Handler wrote in his column, "Sob Stories of Sammy Screen," the following verse, which refers to performers for the L-KO, or Lehrman Knock-Out, company—headed by Henry Lehrman, one-time Sennett director:

> Theirs not to reason why,
> Theirs but to throw bricks or die—
> Into the Valley of Comedy rode the L-KO cops.

Those L-KO cops would include Billie Ritchie, Phil Dunham, Bert Roach, and Hank Mann, who had defected from Sennett in late 1914 and would return on several occasions.

A few of Henry "Pathé" Lehrman's L-KO Cops mug in this scene from Gertie's Gasoline Glide (1916).

The derivative Fox Cops pummel a helpless suspect. Photo courtesy of Bison Archives.

In another shot, they demonstrate a somber reason against parking a patrol wagon on railroad tracks. Photo courtesy of Bison Archives.

Also around this time, producer and studio mogul William Fox decided that imitation was the sincerest form of thievery by creating his own "Fox Cops," and stills attest to their ineptitude as well as the explosive nature of their patrol wagon.

The Cops even found themselves mentioned in popular songs of the time. "The Moving Picture Hero of My Heart," with lyrics by Roger Lewis and music by Ernie Erdman (published by F. G. A. Forster, Chicago, Il), is taken from a woman's perspective, one who romantically compares her boyfriend to the most recognizable stars of 1916. Its lyric read, in part:

> You've got the strength of Charlie Chaplin in your arm,
> When you embrace me
> And like a Keystone Cop you'll save me from all harm
> When villains chase me.

The Keystone Cops Band, made up of a group of minor comics, welcome Triangle star Douglas Fairbanks (front and center, wearing cap and overcoat) at Le Grande railroad station in Los Angeles in 1916. Photo courtesy of Bison Archives.

Also on sale in stores where sheet music was sold was a ditty entitled "Those Keystone Comedy Cops," by Charles McCarron (published by New York: Shapiro, Bernstein). The sheet music cover offers a heavily colorized photo of the Cops framed by silhouettes of cartoon cops and a mock-ancient

Grecian urn. McCarron had earlier written a hit song, "Poor Pauline," about actress Pearl White, the heroine of the popular serial *The Perils of Pauline*. His ode to the Cops deftly caught the spirit of the Sennett films:

> VERSE:
> Cops may come and cops may go,
> There's a bunch of cops I know,
> Working in the movie show,
> For the Keystone Comics.
> They must walk around the block,
> So their health won't fail;
> If they're not in at nine o'clock,
> They're locked out of jail.
> Poor dubs—their clubs—
> Are made of rubber hose—
> They sleep—like sheep,
> But when the whistle blows—
>
> REFRAIN:
> Nothing stops those poor old Keystone Cops,
> They're always on the job,
> When burglars break and rob.
> Just in time, up they bob,
> When you least expect them;
> Look! Look! look, they're gonna get that crook,
> There'll be some fun before the film stops—
> "He's Grizzly Pete from Idaho,
> Killed a dozen men or so,"
> Help! Help! [Whistle]
> Lord help those Keystone Comedy Cops.
>
> SECOND VERSE:
> Gee! The things that they must do,
> Just to earn a buck or two.
> Keep the coppers black and blue,
> But they do their duty—
> Soon a cry of "Fire!" rings out,
> Fact'ry's all ablaze,
> A thousand firemen stand about,
> But they're in a daze.
> "Away!"—they say—
> And everybody flees.

In there—is where—
They make Limburger cheese. (But)
SECOND REFRAIN:
Nothing stops those poor old Keystone Cops,
They're always on the job,
When burglars break and rob,
Just in time, up they bob,
When you least expect them;
Look! Look! look, they're flirting with the cook—
There'll be some fun before the film stops—
They land right on a barb-wire fence,
There's no padding in their pants,
Help! Help! [Whistle]
Lord help those Keystone Comedy Cops.

By late 1917, Mack Sennett had changed his distribution affiliation from Triangle to Famous Players-Lasky; this changed again to Associated First National. In this 1917-1922 period, Sennett was pursuing a more story-oriented brand of comedy, and the Cops appeared less frequently as plots and distinct comedy personalities gained prominence. *Love, Honor and Behave* (November 22, 1920) did feature Charlie Murray and three other actors as Cops, while *Be Reasonable* (October 31, 1921) had Billy Bevan pursued by practically an entire police force; in this one the cops were much more capable than their filmic predecessors, but just as intent on capturing their man. In this, Sennett and company were anticipating the huge swarms of very serious policemen who would chase after Buster Keaton in his 1922 comedies *Cops* and *Day Dreams*.

In 1923 Sennett began releasing his comedies through the Pathé Exchange, and a few of the films released by this firm through 1929 brought back the Cops—now wearing standard police caps instead of helmets—for some of their most elaborate chase sequences. *Nip and Tuck*, released August 12, 1923, has a wonderful finale in which Cameo, a little dog with a conscience, prompts a bevy of police to pursue Harry Gribbon, Billy Bevan, and Kewpie Morgan—and some gains that have been ill-gotten in a poker game. March 28, 1926 brought *Wandering Willies*, starring Bevan, Morgan, and Andy Clyde. The finale is a great chase scene in which Cops—who can't quite get into the speeding patrol wagon—form a sort of conga line and are pulled and then dragged down the street, at one point all twirling around a signpost. Thanks to its inclusion in many later compilations and documentaries, this is one of the best-remembered Cops sequences.

The climactic chase scene featuring Billy Bevan in Be Reasonable *(October 31, 1921).*

An identical chase scene featuring Buster Keaton in Cops *(February 15, 1922).*

By this time, the Keystone Cops, like the actual Keystone studio, had long since passed into the realm of legend, and the tributes to the films and performers of a decade earlier were beginning. Hal Roach produced one of the funniest and most authentic re-creations of a Cops sequence in a two-reeler starring Will Rogers, *Big Moments from Little Pictures*, released March 30, 1924.

Will introduces this sequence on a vaudeville stage, "speaking" this title while twirling his lariat: "The next will be Mr. Mack Sennett's great masterpiece, the 'Keystone Cops.'—Through personal friendship I got the entire original cast to come and work in this, with the exception of Ford Sterling who loaned me his clothes—I had to "do" him myself—." In a park, a thief steals a nursemaid's purse; she runs after him, abandoning her dog and the baby carriage she was minding. It sails down a hill and almost careens into a pond, but faithful Fido rescues it in the nick of time.

The nursemaid calls the police; Rogers does a great impression of desk sergeant Ford Sterling, twitching and fluttering before finally answering the phone. Eventually, the Cops bound into action—disappearing behind a stack of barrels and then emerging from one side of the barrels only in their wagon, thanks to a nifty split-screen shot. Sterling/Rogers takes a horse to the scene of the crime, doing a backward flip to mount the steed, while the Cops in their patrol wagon slip and skid along soapy streets. Ford/Will loses his horse but retains the saddle and is picked up for a wild ride by a Ben Turpin lookalike astride a motorcycle with a sidecar. Sterling/Rogers and the Cops crash into a bakery; some throwing of flour ensues. A pie naturally hits Ford/Will during the melee in the bakery. The thief escapes and cranks up a number of Model Ts, which, driverless, go careening across a field. Sterling/Rogers shoots at them, but they reverse direction and chase the Cops out of the scene.

Three- and one-half years later, Sennett showed that he could outdo Roach's satire of the Cops with his own parody-tribute, *Love in a Police Station*, released December 25, 1927. The character names of several Cops here are the surnames of performers from an earlier generation. Eddie Quillan is Officer Eddie Chase; Barney Hellum is Police Sgt. Conklin; Joe Kessel is Police Sgt. Arbuckle; William Armstrong is Police Sgt. Murray; Tiny Ward is Police Sgt. Swain. Bobby Dunn and Gordon Lewis are two other unnamed Cops. Although this is a Pathé release, the Cops are in a wagon marked "Police Patrol–Keystone," and the members of the force wear the old-fashioned helmets. Andy Clyde does an accurate imitation of Ford Sterling, with his trademark mannerisms. (The genuine article at this point was playing straightforward roles in Paramount feature films.) The highlight of the film is a wacky chase with the Cops in their police wagon, racing in hot pursuit of "Desperate

Nip and Tuck *(August 12, 1923)* spotlights Cameo (bottom left), the moralistic dog who leads the Cops to some law-breaking poker players (Billy Bevan, Harry Gribbon, Kewpie Morgan, none of whom are pictured.) Two identifiable Cops are the mustachioed Andy Clyde and the comically corpulent Marvin Loback. Photo courtesy of Bison Archives.

Big Moments from Little Pictures, *presented by rival producer Hal Roach in 1924, features legendary humorist Will Rogers portraying some of his screen contemporaries. In one memorable sequence, he salutes the Keystone Cops by channeling Ford Sterling as the chief. A Ben Turpin lookalike stands by with an unfortunate suspect.* Photo courtesy of Bison Archives.

Dan" and weaving around and between telephone poles as if they were a slalom course.

This would be the Cops' last hurrah in a Mack Sennett production. The producer survived the conversion to talkies surprisingly well, but the encroaching Depression and a dwindling market for independently produced short subjects would effectively end his career within a few years.

As the silent era drew to a close in 1928, director King Vidor made a wonderful feature-length comedy for MGM, *Show People*, loosely based on the life of Gloria Swanson. Marion Davies stars as Peggy Pepper, leading lady in slapstick two-reelers with Billy Boone (played by William Haines). She graduates to costume dramas, changes her name to Patricia Pepoire, and turns up her nose at her slapstick past, until she realizes that she was happier (and a bigger box-office draw!) in comedies. At one point, the slapstick unit is on location, doing a wild chase scene with some ersatz Keystone Cops; they intrude on a love scene being played by Miss Pepoire and her dashing leading man. (Billy recognizes him and says, "He used to serve me spaghetti over at Tony's!") This film was originally released with a synchronized music and effects score, but for Photoplay Productions' 1985 restoration, Carl Davis wrote a new accompaniment for the chase sequence, titled "Keystone Kops Theme (for orchestra)," which works to great effect.

Marion Davies, as slapstick queen Peggy Pepper, is uncomfortably surrounded by a group of faux, yet highly convincing, Keystone Cops in this publicity still for King Vidor's *Show People* (MGM, 1928).

Filmed tributes to the Cops, often including some of the veteran members, would continue into the thirties.

On April 4, 1931, Paramount distributed *The Stolen Jools*, an all-star two-reel comedy produced by the National Variety Artists, a New York–based guild of vaudeville performers. The film was made to benefit a sanitarium in Saranac Lake, New York, for older performers with respiratory diseases; originally called the NVA Lodge, it was later rechristened the Will Rogers Memorial Hospital. Ironically, the short was partially funded by Chesterfield Cigarettes! An early scene features Wallace Beery as the desk sergeant to a group of eight cops who behave in a recognizably Keystonian manner; they include Buster Keaton, J. Farrell MacDonald, and frequent Hal Roach bit player Jack Hill. (Meanwhile, Eddie Kane, Stan Laurel, and Oliver Hardy are plainclothes lawmen.)

Two months later, RKO-Pathé released a two-reel comedy produced by the Masquers Club, a fraternal organization of comedians formed in May 1925 who congregated in their clubhouse at 1765 Sycamore Street in Hollywood. *Stout Hearts and Willing Hands* was a parody of old-time melodramas, replete with virtuous Little Nell, a villain holding a mortgage on her old folks' family home, and a handsome idealistic hero. The bumbling lawmen rush in at one point to save the girl from certain death, tied to a log at a sawmill and awaiting a terrible fate from the buzzsaw. "The Original Keystone Kops"—with a "K"—were in this case Ford Sterling (as the desk sergeant), Mack Swain, Chester Conklin, Clyde Cook, James Finlayson, Hank Mann, and Bobby Vernon. (Several Sennett performers who hadn't been Cops in the initial films were now thought of as part of the official cadre. This would continue through the decades.)

The Cops' indelible image extended to animated cartoons. June 9, 1933 saw the release of Walt Disney's film *Mickey's Gala Premier* [sic] in which a bevy of Movieland celebrities show up at Sid Grauman's Chinese Theatre for the debut of Mr. Mouse's latest opus. The very first film personalities caricatured here are the Cops, in the persons of Ben Turpin, Ford Sterling, Mack Swain, Harry Langdon, and Chester Conklin.

Mack Sennett's career as an active producer of comedy shorts came to an end a month later, with the release on July 28 of *The Barber Shop*, a two-reeler starring W. C. Fields. However, Mack did not languish in obscurity for long. In October 1934, the legend of "the King of Comedy" really began in earnest with the publication of Gene Fowler's book, *Father Goose: The Story of Mack Sennett*. This became a best seller and solidified Sennett's reputation as a comedy innovator and discoverer of many future stars, from Mabel Normand to Chaplin to Bing Crosby. Like Sennett's own book twenty years later, it often bore faint relation to the facts but was an entertaining read and contributed mightily to the mythos of Sennett, Keystone, the Bathing Beauties, and the Cops.

Photo above courtesy Motion Picture Herald

BACK on the BEAT AGAIN

Remember the good old Mack Sennett days, when Desk Sergeant Ford Sterling used to receive the riot call and all the cops went piling into the trick Fords in pursuit of the scoundrel who peeked into Marie Prevost's boudoir? The cops had a re-union in Hollywood the other day, making a two-reeler, "Stout Hearts and Willing Hands," for the Hollywood Masquers Club. (Above, left to right) Roscoe Arbuckle, Bobby Vernon, Ford Sterling, Chester Conklin, Clyde Cook, Mack Swain, Jimmy Finlayson and (reclining) Hank Mann participated. Below, the boys concentrating. Left to right, Messrs. Finlayson, Conklin, Swain, Cook, Sterling, Vernon and Mann.

The Keystone Cops steal the show in Stout Hearts and Willing Hands, *the Masquers' 1931 salute to old melodramas. Standing left to right are James Finlayson, Hank Mann, Clyde Cook, Mack Swain, Bobby Vernon, Chester Conklin, and Ford Sterling. (Incidentally, although Finlayson and Vernon had worked for Sennett beginning in the late teens, they were not original Cops. Nor was Clyde Cook, a former silent film comedian who appeared in two-reelers for Fox and Hal Roach.)*

The popularity of Fowler's book may have inspired producer Ralph Staub to reunite as many Sennett veterans as possible for a new Vitaphone/ Warner Bros. two-reeler. *Keystone Hotel* was filmed in May 1935 and released on September 21. It brought back Ford Sterling (sporting a Cherman agzent) for a last hurrah as the police chief, with Joe Bordeaux, Bobby Dunn, Billy Engle, Jack "Tiny" Lipson, and a few others as the Police Patrol. Ben Turpin, Chester Conklin, and Hank Mann were prominent in other roles.

In this musical cartoon short, the singing Keystone Cops are represented by caricatures of (left to right) Ben Turpin, Ford Sterling, Mack Swain, Harry Langdon, and Chester Conklin. Mickey's Gala Premier *(1933).*

Keystone Hotel (1935) is a two-reeler made by Ralph Staub for Vitaphone that attempted to bring back as many Sennett players as possible, only with sound. In this promotional shot, Ben Turpin seems unfazed by his being apprehended by an entire platoon of Cops. From left to right, they are Billy Engel, Joe Bordeaux, George Gray, Grover Ligon, Billy Gilbert, and Bobby Dunn; the tall man at the right is Tiny Lipson; the three Cops standing behind Bordeaux, Gray, and Turpin are unknown. Photo courtesy of Bison Archives.

During the film's climactic two-and-a-half minutes, Sterling and his men make a frantic dash in their patrol wagon to the hotel to quell a pie fight. Some rather unconvincing rear-projection footage is intercut with some very impressive shots of the cops speeding into (and out of) streetcar tunnels and recreating the "slalom course" gag from *Love in a Police Station* at what looks to be the same location. *Keystone Hotel* was a talkie, but much of the final chase was shot silent and undercranked. It was so authentic that footage from it has been used in many subsequent documentaries as an example of genuine silent-era Keystone Cop comedy.

For his essential 1972 book *The Great Movie Shorts*, Leonard Maltin interviewed Ralph Staub, who recalled, "The picture, including all the chases, was made in seven days. I personally knew Ford Sterling, Ben Turpin, Chester Conklin, and others appearing in the film. I sold them on starting a new slapstick series. Jack Warner would only permit me to contract with the players for one picture. After the preview at Warner's Hollywood theater, Warner said 'sign them up for a series,' but this was not possible. Their agents were there at the preview and when I approached them, they wanted triple the salary they received in *Keystone Hotel*. Jack Warner wouldn't go for the hike in salary. I couldn't blame him."

October 13, 1939 was a bittersweet day in the history of the Keystone Cops. Ford Sterling, who had been inactive for two years because of diabetes complications, died at fifty-five of a heart attack. On the same day, 20th Century-Fox released *Hollywood Cavalcade*, starring Alice Faye (as a milder version of Mabel Normand) and Don Ameche (as a Sennett-like director) in a story of Tinseltown's early days. Buster Keaton joined a reconstituted Keystone force in a chase scene. Jed Prouty played the chief, made up with Sterling's traditional wire-rim glasses and chin whiskers. The

"Original Keystone Cops" Heinie Conklin, Chester Conklin, and Snub Pollard are at their most distinguished in this 1940 publicity photo for their joint personal appearance tour. Al St. John and Hank Mann (not pictured) appeared with them as well. Photo courtesy of Bison Archives.

Moonlighting as bakers, Hank Mann, James Finlayson, and Chester Conklin are armed and dangerous in this publicity still for Pearl White's fictionalized biopic, The Perils of Pauline *(1947).]*

other stalwart lawmen were Eddie Collins, Hank Mann, Heinie Conklin, James Finlayson, and Snub Pollard.

From this point on, most of the new films with the Keystone policemen were documentaries or compilations of silent comedy scenes. July 7, 1939 had brought an RKO two-reeler, *The Movies March On*, part of its series *The March of Time*. Jackson Beck narrated this collection of archival footage featuring the Cops along with other silent-era stars.

The novelty of promoting an event with original Keystone Cops, or at least comics who had worked in the silent era dressed up as the Cops, gained popularity as the 1940s dawned. Chester Conklin, Hank Mann, Snub Pollard, and Al St. John appeared for six weeks in 1940 as "Original Keystone Cops" at the New York World's Fair. The following year, St. John joined Heinie Conklin and a few newcomers as Cops at a police event held in the Los Angeles Coliseum. Sadly, 1940 marked the passing of Ben Turpin, and 1941 saw the demise of Charlie Murray.

Warner Bros., having turned down the idea of new Keystone-style comedies because of prohibitive salary demands, decided instead to make new shorts from the silent Sennett films they owned, originally distributed by First National. The *Broadway Brevities* series included *Happy Times and Jolly Moments* (1943), *Once Over Lightly* (1944), and *Good Old Corn* (1945), all of which featured Cop footage from earlier films such as *Married Life*, *Be Reasonable*, and the ubiquitous *Keystone Hotel*. Other such shorts featuring Sennett material without the Cops would continue to be released from 1948 through 1951.

A reunion of Sennett veterans was a highlight of Paramount's Betty Hutton musical *The Perils of Pauline*, released on July 4, 1947. Directed by comedy veteran George Marshall, the film didn't quite feature a Cops sequence, but did bring back Jimmy Finlayson, Hank Mann, and Chester Conklin as pie-throwing chefs and allowed us to see them in Technicolor. Snub Pollard and Heinie Conklin also appeared in small roles.

The Keystone Cops' enduring presence now extended to the Broadway stage, thanks to the hit musical *High Button Shoes*, which opened at the New Century Theatre on October 9, 1947. It was based on a novel by Stephen Longstreet, with a book by Longstreet and director George Abbott, music by Jule Styne, and lyrics by Sammy Cahn. The show starred Phil Silvers, Nanette Fabray, and Joey Faye, and featured a slapstick ballet choreographed by Jerome Robbins ("On a Sunday by the Sea"). This emulated silent film comedy, using a strobe light to approximate the flicker of old films, and prominently featured the Keystone Cops. The show transferred to two other Broadway houses before

Mack Sennett (left, seated) celebrates his seventieth birthday at a party held in White Oak Park in Simi Valley, California, on April 30, 1950. Joining in the nostalgic fun are such former Sennett players as (left to right) Charles Lynch, Max Asher, Hank Mann, Vera Steadman, Leo Sulky, Jimmy Finlayson, and Heinie Conklin. Photo courtesy of Paul E. Gierucki and CineMuseum, LLC.

closing on July 2, 1949 after 727 performances over nearly twenty-one months.

Mack Sennett turned seventy on January 17, 1950, but the event was celebrated on April 30 with a lavish party attended by dozens of studio alumni at White Oak Park in Simi Valley.

Virtually any male actor with a tie to Sennett's filmic past seemed to be recruited for appearances as a Cop at special events during the fif-

Although Hank Mann and Heinie Conklin were on hand in bit parts, the new set of Keystone Kops was made up of Universal's uncredited stunt men. Bud Abbott & Lou Costello Meet the Keystone Kops (1955).

ties. One was a benefit staged by the Masquers Club at the Pantages Theater in Hollywood on behalf of the Motion Picture Relief Fund. This program, held September 24, 1952, was coordinated by Eddie Gribbon and included Hank Mann, Heinie Conklin, Chester Conklin (no relation), Eddie LeVeque, and Jimmy Finlayson.

That event was likely Jimmy Finlayson's last public appearance, as he died of a heart attack at sixty-six on October 9, 1953. The next day, an obituary in the *Los Angeles Times* was headlined, "Jimmy Finlayson of Old Keystone Kop Fame Dies." Likewise, the *New York Times* obituary, also published on October 10, was headlined with "James H. Finlayson of 'Keystone Kops.'" Both articles highlighted Finlayson's work with Sennett instead of his now much better remembered affiliation with Laurel & Hardy. The Los Angeles notice called Finlayson "one of the zany Keystone Kops," while its New York counterpart instead referred to him as "the 'villain' in the 'Keystone Kops' movies of the silent screen era."

The next year was a brighter and more active one for Sennett and the former Cops, as the producer's autobiography (as told to Cameron Shipp), *King of Comedy*, was published. It was colorful, lively, and a great read although frequently wide of the mark historically. The book was successful; sales were likely bolstered by Sennett's being the surprise honoree on an episode of Ralph Edwards's NBC-TV series *This Is Your Life* on March 10, 1954. Cops who came in costume to bedevil their former producer included Andy Clyde, Chester Conklin, Heinie Conklin, Vernon Dent, Dell Henderson, and Hank Mann; director Del Lord also appeared.

On June 7, 1954, filming began on a new feature at Universal, *Bud Abbott & Lou Costello Meet the Keystone Kops*. Directed by silent comedy veteran Charles

Bud Abbott (left) and Lou Costello (above) try to infuse some energy in a rather static photo shoot with seventy-four-year-old Mack Sennett for their forthcoming feature Bud Abbott & Lou Costello Meet the Keystone Kops *(1955). Photo courtesy of Paul E. Gierucki and CineMuseum, LLC.*

Lamont, who had worked briefly for Sennett in 1926, the film has Bud and Lou buying the Thomas Edison movie studio from con man Fred Clark and his accomplice Lynn Bari. When the boys find out they've been swindled, they travel to Hollywood where they get jobs as stuntmen. Sennett himself appears briefly and throws a pie. Other alumni in the cast include Heinie Conklin as a studio guard and Hank Mann as a prop man. The final chase scene depicts a gaggle of Kops (by now the more frequent spelling) in a patrol car pursuing Clark and Bari's auto, with Bud and Lou following behind on a motorbike. The "slalom course" gag comes in again, this time in a grove of eucalyptus trees. Other gags involving collisions and a near-miss with a train are quite well done.

The late fifties and early sixties saw an increasing interest in Sennett's comedy, especially in films featuring the Kops. In 1955 British comedian Bob Monkhouse hosted an hour-long compilation film made in England, *All in Good Fun*, which included vintage footage of the Kops, and on December 26, 1957 Robert Youngson's feature film *The Golden Age of Comedy* debuted in theaters across the United States. Spotlighting excerpts of the Kops in *Wandering Willies* and *Nip and Tuck* as well as Will Rogers's sublime Kops parody from *Big Moments from Little Pictures*, Youngson's film became a surprise smash success and played theaters through much of 1958.

Two new syndicated television series debuted in the States in 1960—*Comedy Capers* and *The Funny Manns*, both of which used clips from many silent comedies, including an abundance of Sennett releases.

Indicating the growing interest in Sennett's films was the 1960 release of an album on Liberty Records, *Rides, Rapes and Rescues*—which originally was planned to have the more congenial title *Music to Watch Silent Movies By*. The opening track, "Keystone Kapers," was a perfect instrumental accompaniment to the Kops' antics and was used for years as background music in Disneyland's

Main Street Cinema. While the LP was credited to Hangnails Hennessey and Wingy Brubeck, its true author was revealed in the composing credit for the tunes—zany maestro Spike Jones.

No doubt Mack Sennett was pleased to see youngsters discovering his comedies; many of the kids from this generation would ultimately help preserve

The Shriners paid tribute to the Keystone Cops in an elaborate parade, circa 1960. Pictured from left to right are . . . oh, forget it!

his films and write about the history of his comic legacy. Sennett died at eighty on November 5, 1960, but the revival of interest in his films was just beginning.

Robert Youngson released three more successful theatrical feature-length compilations containing Sennett sequences—*When Comedy Was King* (1960), *Days of Thrills and Laughter* (1961), which featured an exciting montage of daredevil Kop chase scenes from several films, and *30 Years of Fun* (1963). Television's *Dupont Show of the Week* featured two hour-long episodes in September and October 1961 including Kops footage, and on September 17, Nat Hiken's TV comedy *Car 54, Where Are You?* debuted, bringing the idea of bumbling policemen into a new era.

A former Sennett actor named Eddie LeVeque, who was born in 1896 and thus a relative youngster when he worked on the lot in 1917, was very determined to keep the legacy alive. In 1961, he purchased the rights to the name "Keystone Kops" from the Mack Sennett estate and had it copyrighted and trademarked. He held a reunion on January 19 with a "coming out party." Eleven former Kops attended, including Eddie Gribbon; the event was covered in LIFE magazine. LeVeque would keep many of the older Sennett veterans frequently employed, as well as a new generation, in personal appearances throughout the sixties. Eddie Gribbon, Tom Kennedy, Chester Conklin, Pinto Colvig, Charles Diltz, Billy Bletcher, and several youngsters including Noble "Kid" Chisell, Stan Lawson, Jay Colonna, and "Slim" Ray Barnes would appear at venues such as the Movieland Wax Museum in Buena Park, California (where they hosted a pie fight with Buster Keaton), and at the Hueneme Bay town house complex, where they helped Joe E. Brown celebrate his seventy-second birthday.

LeVeque used the Kops as a way to enter the music business. He created a number of bands playing music in different styles: The Keystone Kops Dixieland

Band, the Kidstone Kops, the Keystone Kops Rockrollers, and a semi-psychedelic band called "Son's of the Keystone Kops" (note the unnecessary apostrophe), which released a record which has become a favorite among the rock cognoscenti, "Chain Gang Man"/ "I Laughed You Cried" on the Public Records label in January 1969.

Starting in the early sixties, another group of Keystone lawmen, unrelated to Eddie LeVeque's enterprises, had different squadrons all over the United States appearing in parades for charity events. The Ancient Arabic Order of the Nobles of the Mystic Shrine for North America—more popularly known as the Shriners—support a network of twenty-two children's hospitals to the present day with parades that feature marching bands, horse patrols, miniature cars, clowns, and the Keystone Cops (with a C).

Eddie LeVeque and the Shriners kept the Kops and Cops alive through public appearances in the sixties and beyond, while television continued to bolster their image. In 1963, Jay Ward—the producer of *The Adventures of Rocky and Bullwinkle*—debuted a new, twenty-six-episode syndicated series, *Fractured Flickers*. Hosted by the great comic actor Hans Conried, the program presented clips from silent movies; these were given soundtracks loaded with jokes both pointed and punning. Voices were provided by Paul Frees, June Foray, and Bill Scott. Many clips from Sennett films were included, and the Kops and their patrol wagon were prominent in the animated opening and closing title sequences.

Late in 1964, Buster Keaton starred in a one-minute TV commercial for the 1965 Ford Econoline van, in which several Kops chased after him. One of them was played by actor James Karen, who in 2017 told director/historian Peter Bogdanovich how impressed he was by Keaton's physical condition. Karen said, "He was in his late sixties, and he outran us."

The TV sensation of 1966 was ABC's *Batman*, based on the characters that had graced DC comics since May 1939. The episode of April 27, titled "Death in Slow Motion," co-starred Frank Gorshin as the guest villain, playing the Riddler. He and his henchmen crash a revival screening of a silent comedy hosted by Mr. Van Jones, a wealthy film collector (portrayed by an authentic matinee

Some now-elderly Kops stage a reunion on Friday, January 19, 1962, at 1219 North Vine Street in Hollywood. Pictured (up front) are Billy Bletcher and Chester Conklin; behind them are Clarence Hennecke and Glen Cavender (the latter of whom died a few weeks later); standing in back are Vance "Pinto" Colvig, Tom Kennedy, and Eddie Baker; seated in the driver's seat is Eddie LeVeque; standing next to Eddie Baker is writer John Grey (confusingly, this is the second John Grey who wrote for Sennett; the first worked only in silents and died in 1923; the second, John R., wrote scenarios for serials in the silent era and joined Sennett for talkies in 1932—he later wrote for Columbia shorts and various features); director Del Lord is at the back, wearing glasses. Photo courtesy of the author.

idol of the silent era, Francis X. Bushman). The Riddler is dressed as Charlie Chaplin's tramp character, while his cohorts in mischief are Keystone Kops.

Batman had been created by Bob Kane, and so was *Cool McCool*, a very funny Saturday morning cartoon show that ran on ABC-TV from September 10, 1966 through August 30, 1969. Each half-hour program had three segments—two of which starred the title character, an inept James Bond type who sounded like Jack Benny (thanks to Bob McFadden's vocal work). In between these was an adventure of Cool McCool's father, uniformed police officer Harry McCool, who back in the teens and twenties joined his brothers Dick and Tom as the Komedy Kops. The trio of lawmen often rode a three-seater bicycle in pursuit of lawbreakers; their efforts were somewhat hampered by the indecipherable mumblings of brother Tom, which would prompt brother Dick to ask, "Wha-wha'd he say, Harry? Wha'd he say??" Several of the cartoons were directed by Gerald Potterton, who in 1965 had directed Buster Keaton in a live-action short, *The Railrodder*, a welcome return for Keaton to silent comedy.

Eddie LeVeque, no doubt knowing about these animated films, secured a deal to make new Keystone Kop cartoons late in 1969. A press release in December noted, "In association with Estudio Macian, S. A. of Barcelona, Spain, the Keystone Kops are being produced in several languages in cartoon film animation and comic strips. LeVeque, one of the best gag writers in show business, writes the comic strip gags and some of the animation stories.

The "Komedy Kops," Tom, Dick, and Harry, were periodically featured on the 1960s Saturday morning cartoon show *Cool McCool*.

"Two theater scripts, 'The Keystone Kops Capture Virginia Richmond' and 'The Charge of the Keystone Kops,' a stage musical and three originals by LeVeque are being adapted by other writers." While these projects don't appear to have come to fruition, one has to admire Eddie LeVeque's enthusiasm and determination.

A memorable new appearance by the Kops graced TV screens in 1971—a color one-minute commercial for Shasta root beer. It features silent comedy veteran and occasional latter-day Kop Billy Bletcher in two roles, as the police desk sergeant and as a helmeted Kop on the beat. Set in the 1910s, a peaceful day in the town square is disrupted—a melee develops because Shasta root beer has such a foamy head that when you blow it off the glass it's just as gooey as pie filling. Many faces are thusly decorated. A foamy fight ensues, pasting everyone in the block, including four Kops. When the desk sergeant receives a call, he too is rewarded with a spray of foam through the mouthpiece of his candlestick telephone. This little gem of a film is extremely well staged and edited, and the art direction and costuming captures the period beautifully.

Another beverage saluted the Kops in 1971, as the Ezra Brooks brand of bourbon whiskey issued a ceramic collectable decanter, a sculpture of the Keystone Kops clambering over their patrol wagon.

In July 2015, the Chichester Festival Theatre in Sussex, England, produced a sumptuous restaging of Jerry Herman's 1974 Broadway show Mack and Mabel. *Jack Edwards is front and center as Roscoe "Fatty" Arbuckle. Photo by Manuel Harlan.*

In June through November 1974, a new musical with songs by Jerry Herman (who had written the scores for *Hello, Dolly!* and *Mame*) played on stages in San Diego, Los Angeles, and New York. *Mack and Mabel*, starring Robert Preston and Bernadette Peters as Sennett and Normand, attempted to depict their tempestuous romance in contrast to the wacky world of silent movie comedy. The Keystone Kops appeared in two numbers—the opening song, "When Movies Were Movies," and the second song in the second act, "My Heart Leaps Up." While this was not the long-running hit that *High Button Shoes* had been, subsequent productions in the U.S. and overseas from 1995 through 2018 have proven to be more successful than the original run.

And so the Kops have continued in many venues. The Hunt's Pier amusement park in Wildwood, New Jersey, featured an elaborate Keystone Kops "dark ride" in the late seventies and eighties. Many new documentaries and compilations, among them Kevin Brownlow's *Hollywood*, and others narrated by Steve Allen and Glenn Ford, have included the Kops among the saluted stars of yesteryear. In 1983, Activision released a video game, "Keystone Kapers," for the Atari 2600, 5200, MSX and Colecovision, bringing the Kops into the digital era. April 27, 1994 was the first day of issue of a twenty-nine-cent United States stamp with a drawing of the Kops by Al Hirschfeld, part of a "Silent Screen Stars" series. One can go to Amazon.com today and find complete Keystone Kops outfits available for sale, with the brass-buttoned tunic and helmet, and one company as of 2019 offers twenty different Keystone Kops cases to protect your iPhone.

Note that we haven't even mentioned the frequent use of "Keystone Kops" as a derisive description of inept politicians or sports figures. Those have been going on for decades and likely will for decades more.

A lot of comedy, especially slapstick, depends upon the deflating of dignity and authority. When Mack Sennett made his first movies with bumbling policemen, the neighborhood cop on the beat was an important contributor to everyday life. Sometimes he was loved, sometimes disliked, but always known as someone with power and command. Seeing these officials reveal their true ineptitude—and their humanity—was instantly appealing and laugh-provoking more than a century ago and still is today. The Keystone Cops, or Kops, will continue to embody and symbolize the bumbling behind the bravado for many years to come.

Randy Skretvedt, born in Long Beach, California, in 1958, first fell in love with silent comedies at the tender age of five, when late in 1964 a Los Angeles-based television station showed Robert Youngson's compilation film *The Golden Age of Comedy* each night for a week. Randy managed to catch every airing. By age twelve he was a member of the Way Out West Tent of Sons of the Desert, the Laurel & Hardy appreciation group. This venue allowed him to meet and interview some sixty-five associates of the beloved comedy duo. This research resulted in his definitive 1987 book, *Laurel & Hardy: The Magic Behind the Movies* (an expanded coffee-table version of which was published in 2016). Hardly limiting himself to that one topic, he also pursued his interest in animation and music, and for more than forty years has had his own radio show, *Forward Into the Past*, on which he spins records made popular in the twenties, thirties, and forties.

Chapter 13.
Mack Sennett and Keystone in Print and Home Entertainment
By Rob Farr

In its issue of April 5, 1919, the *Moving Picture World* published an obituary for the Keystone Cops and the company founded by Mack Sennett just seven years earlier.

The Keystone "Cops"—A Reminiscence

Where are the Keystone "Cops" of yesterday? The story of the troubles of the Louisville policemen outlined in our columns last week renews to memory one of the classics of the screen, or of the comedy screen—and if you won't stand for that denomination we'll say the slapstick comedy screen. For classics they were—and would be now—and the wide world laughed at the misfortunes of these misfit blue-coats. Otherwise staid and respectable citizens became convulsed with mirth when their caricatures of semi-suburban peace guardians were piled up in the waters of Eastlake Park or sprawled over the Hollywood landscape in their efforts to adhere to the speeding departmental flivver.

It was an indiscreet policeman who placed under arrest a boisterous youngster who in a spirit of fun had alluded to the former as a "Keystoner"; indiscreet because in court the opprobrious epithet was repeated in the giving of testimony. Three newspapers in the city are opposed to the local police administration. "Keystone" sounded good to the writers of all of them. Inevitably the town of Henry Watterson laughed with the newspapers and at the "Cops."

Which brings us back to our opening question. If a few twelvemonth (sic) ago you had asked a body of film men to state offhand the market value of the brand name of Keystone, would any of them have raised violent objection had a member of the party set the price at a million dollars? Yet this remarkably valuable screen asset fades into nothingness so silently that the average picturegoer is unaware of its passing.

In the minds of the screen's public, Keystone represents an individual. Take from behind the brand the person who is credited with creating it and the larger part of its importance is dissipated.

In the film business brand names are as valuable as property if and when they represent an institution and not an individual.

Without once mentioning Mack Sennett's name, the trade paper essentially acknowledged that *Keystone* and their *Cops* had passed into common, everyday usage when used to refer to any incompetent policemen completely independent of the film manufacturing firm that bore its name. *Moving Picture*

World was quite prescient, though one wonders if they imagined that "Keystone Cops" would still have currency a century later. The article is a testament to quickly evolving film conventions: a comic device popular just three or four years earlier was now being recalled with warm nostalgia.

Hidden historical gems like this are uncovered with regularity because comedy fans, film buffs, and serious historians now have at their fingertips an abundance of original source material concerning Mack Sennett, Keystone, and the creation of the Cops. Websites like the Media History Digital Library (www.mediaproject.org), the Internet Archive (www.archive.org), and YouTube contain fascinating primary and secondary source documents for the entire Keystone/Sennett story, from the beginning to its end.

From its founding in 1912 to the shuttering of Mack Sennett Studios and beyond, the Keystone company and its founder were mainstays in the industry and popular press. This chapter looks at the many resources available today for folks wanting to learn more about Mack Sennett, Keystone, and their times.

Glory Days

The first Keystone comedy was released by Mutual in September 1912 and the trades were thereafter fed a steady diet of press about the new company. Beyond simple blurbs about new releases, Sennett's staff provided readers with comic adventures about the making of the films. From *Moving Picture World* of October 26, 1912, is "Sennett and Mace Meet a Bear." This shaggy dog story consists of Mack Sennett and Fred Mace in disagreement as to whether they were chased over a cliff or devoured by a bear while on location, with the concluding punchline: "One suspects that it occurred to them when they were trying to figure out something for the press agent." This was the start of decades of skillful press agentry on the part of Sennett and his staff.

Two years later, the *Moving Picture World* caught up with Sennett, now the country's foremost comedy producer, in Fort Lee, New Jersey, to determine whether to acquire the Willat Studio as an East Coast production facility. He used the opportunity to gin up excitement about the soon-to-be-released *Tillie's Punctured Romance*: "I have put into it all that I've got," he stated proudly.

Sennett himself was a character that fan magazines and trade publications alike loved to profile. And Sennett understood that by presenting himself as "the world's best laugh tester," he "can bite into a joke and tell whether it is *really* funny or just a sort of bogus funny as accurately as the whiskey taster can tell the year of distilling" (*Photoplay*, May 1915). The line was an excellent hook to promote upcoming Keystone releases.

Gilbert Seldes's influential best seller of 1924, *The 7 Lively Arts*, was a paean to popular culture and an argument that "low" entertainments such as jazz, comic strips, vaudeville, and slapstick movies were uniquely American art forms that deserved to be held in as high esteem as traditional European high culture. Sennett was the perfect vehicle for Seldes to make his case and he declared that slapstick "had a fire, a driving energy of its own—and it was funny!" Comparing Sennett's output to that of his Triangle partners, Seldes wrote, "The Keystone comedies were consistently and almost without exception better . . . [it] is one of the few places where the genteel tradition does not operate, where fantasy is liberated, where imagination is still riotous and healthy." This would not be the last time a serious critic would attempt to elevate Sennett's brand of slapstick to the level of high art.

As the silent era was about to transition to talkies, Mack Sennett seemed to be reflecting on his role in the historical development of the industry he had pioneered. Small independent studios like his were becoming anachronistic as sound reinforced the growing trend toward factory-like studio industrialization. Novelist Theodore Dreiser (*Sister Carrie, An American Tragedy*) conducted an epic interview with Sennett for *Photoplay* magazine in August 1928. Dreiser presented Sennett as his peer in American Arts and Letters. Headlined "The Best Motion Picture Interview Ever Written: The Great American Master of Tragedy Brilliantly Interviews the Great American Master of Comedy," the piece recounts Sennett's discovery of Mabel Normand, Charlie Chaplin, and Harry Langdon, allowing Sennett to expound upon the changes in comedy style since the Keystone days. "Today an American comedy audience seems to want better surroundings or settings. And if the waiter is of the Ritz or Ambassador type, the customer a gentleman in evening clothes—or a lord—so much the better! But the spilling of the soup remains the same."

The Lion in Winter

One of Sennett's first projects after his studio closed in 1933 was to collaborate with Gene Fowler on a biography with the wistful title, *Father Goose*. Fowler was a fixture in the film industry as a journalist/screenwriter and famously became part of the alcohol-fueled Hollywood round table consisting of John Barrymore, W. C. Fields, John Decker, and other hangers-on. A newspaperman who had covered the wild-and-wooly days of Denver, Colorado, Fowler fashioned *Father Goose* as a comic novel starring Mack Sennett, fancifully mixing fiction, some facts, and legend. The book made no pretense of being an accurate history of the man and his times, with misremembered film titles, names,

Press book illustration courtesy of Scott MacGillivray.

Old-timers Hank Mann, Andy Clyde (with billy club raised and finger pointed), George Gray, James Finlayson, Chester Conklin, and Vernon Dent are on their way to see Down Memory Lane (1949). Photo courtesy of Bison Archive.

and events leaping across the decades with abandon. Sennett's career after 1917 becomes almost a footnote in the final few pages, as if the author and his subject instinctively understood that the producer's legacy would be those five Keystone years. Given Sennett's close collaboration with Fowler on the book, we must conclude that this is how he wished to be remembered.

The legend was cemented and Sennett's version of Keystone became the template for all accounts that followed. For the next twenty years, Sennett told his story through interviews, magazine profiles, newsreel reunions, and radio appearances.

The 20th Century-Fox Technicolor comedy-drama *Hollywood Cavalcade* (1939) was a lightly disguised *cinema-a-clef* story of the romance and careers of Michael Linnett Connors (the Sennett character, played by Don Ameche) and Molly Adair (a blonde version of Mabel Normand, played by Alice Faye). Sennett was hired as technical advisor, working on recreations of his silent comedies. Sennett even appeared on *The Texaco Star Theatre* radio program as himself to promote *Hollywood Cavalcade* and told host Ken Murray that the film was his "autobiography."

Ten years later, Sennett executive-produced *Down Memory Lane*, a compilation made up of edited versions of some of his best sound and silent work, hosted by L.A. disc jockey Steve Allen (yes, *that* Steve Allen), with newly filmed appearances by Sennett and Franklin Pangborn. *Down Memory Lane* was the first feature-length classic comedy compilation film and is a delight to watch, with clips taken from *The Pullman Bride* and *Home Talent* (thus preserving the only known footage), and sound clips featuring Bing Crosby in *Sing, Bing, Sing* and *The Blue of the Night*, and W. C. Fields in *The Dentist*.

While *Down Memory Lane* was still in general release, novelist James Agee's essay "Comedy's Greatest Era" was published as the copiously illustrated cover story for *Life* magazine's issue of September 5, 1949. This seminal essay reminded the country of what it had lost when the great visual comics of the silent and early sound eras were shunted aside for the rapid-fire verbal comics of the forties. *Life* was at the top echelon of American magazines with a circulation of well over a million readers per week. Agee's prose elegantly laid out the case for the great comics and comic films of the teens, twenties, and thirties, at a time when the films were virtually out of circulation except for very occasional re-releases and archival screenings in venues such as New York's Museum of Modern Art. For people who had only vague memories of the films upon original release, Agee brought them to life again: "... a profusion of hearty young women in disconcerting bathing suits, frisking around with a gaggle of insanely incompetent policemen and of equally certifiable male civilians sporting museum-piece mustaches. All these people zipped and caromed about the pristine world of the screen as jazzily as a convention of water bugs."

Down Memory Lane wasn't successful enough to warrant a follow-up, and septuagenarian Sennett put an official end to his career with the donation of his scripts, records, and contracts to the Motion Picture Academy in 1951. Soon thereafter, Sennett agreed to write his "as told to" autobiography with *Saturday Evening Post* writer Cameron Shipp. *King of Comedy* (1954) repeated many of the fanciful stories from *Father Goose*, but at least in Shipp he had a collaborator who made use of what research resources existed at the time, principally the uncatalogued Sennett papers recently donated to the Motion Picture Academy and interviews with veterans of the Sennett lot. At this relatively late date both Sennett and Shipp thought that the vast majority of Sennett's films were no longer extant. Walker Evans in the *New York Times* had qualms about the literary merit and historical accuracy of the book, even as he acknowledged its importance: "Mack Sennett tells his story not at all easily, and not funnily, really. . . . Now consider that students of 'cinema' have claimed Keystone Comedies were the only real film art done in America in their period; consider confusion as one of the contrivances of Sennett's works; then it may be excusable in his autobiography. It may even be appropriate."

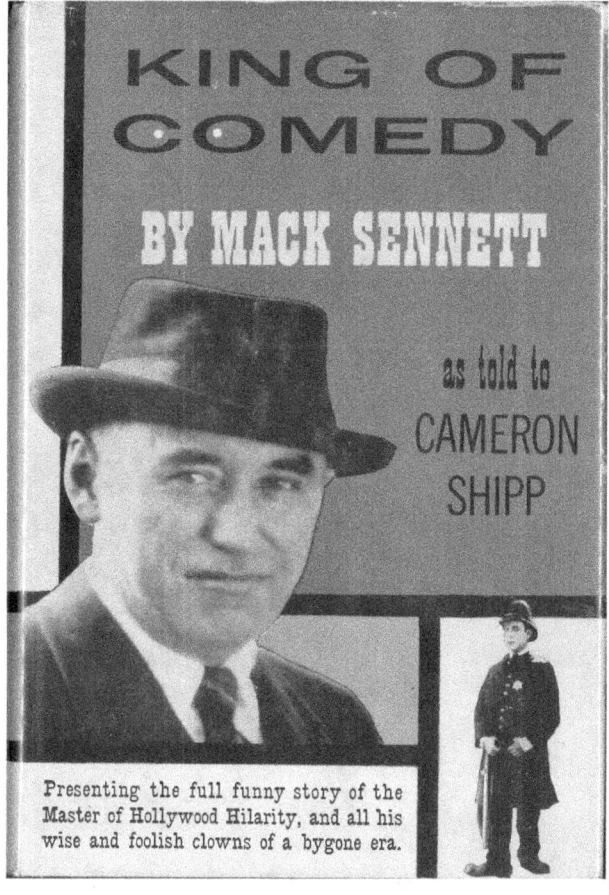

As Sennett neared the end of his life, historical documentarian Robert Youngson kept the Sennett legend alive in the popular imagination with compilation films such as *The Golden Age of Comedy* (1957) and *When Comedy was King* (1960). Youngson aimed at mainstream audiences and his challenge was to appeal to those who had firsthand recollections of the silent era and those who were too young to experience it. His loquacious narration may have featured one too many mother-in-law jokes, but his films triggered a lifelong fascination in a whole generation of classic comedy enthusiasts who would go on to write serious histories of Mack Sennett, his films, and his legacy.

Television programs such as *The Howdy Doody Show*, *Silents Please*, and *Fractured Flickers* relied on generous excerpts from Sennett comedies. And Blackhawk Films, of Davenport, Iowa, sold beautifully restored, complete versions of Keystone comedies to home collectors. Their fine-quality prints are collector's items to this day.

Press book illustration courtesy of Scott MacGillivray.

Keystone and Mack Sennett in Memory

One of the most vivid recollections of working with Sennett during his Keystone years came four years after the producer's death. Critics of Charlie Chaplin's *My Autobiography* (1964) were unanimous in their praise of his recollections of Mack Sennett's Keystone, which was more vividly drawn than later chapters about his life and career. A legend arose that Chaplin had been cast as a Cop soon after his arrival at Keystone, but since no film in his extensively researched filmography bore this out, it was written out of his official history. But in 2010, film historian Paul Gierucki bought an old reel at a flea market that contained Chaplin's performance as a Cop (in *A Thief Catcher*, just his fourth appearance) and it had its grand re-premiere at the Slapsticon Film Festival in Arlington, Virginia.

The late sixties and early seventies saw a nostalgia boom that seeded a cottage industry of books, TV shows, songs, and movies about pop culture from the first four decades of the century. While the vast majority of this product was fluff, the trend provided an outlet for film historians like Kalton C. Lahue, Sam Gill, and Leonard Maltin. Perhaps because they were too young to be nostalgic about the era, these historians, rather than accepting the legend, revisited the original sources, both oral and written, and produced the first serious scholarship in English about Sennett's contribution to film history.

The importance of fanzines (*Film Fan Monthly*), little film journals (*Films in Review*), and tabloids (*8mm Collector*, later known as *Classic Film Collector*, later known as *Classic Images*) to film scholarship cannot be understated. It was typical for today's young crop of historians to publish their first articles in these small-circulation journals, many of which were later reworked into books. Kalton C. Lahue was the most prolific of this group, turning out in quick succession first-rate volumes on Sennett and the Keystone years: *Kops and Custards: The Legend of Keystone Films* (1968) and *Mack Sennett's Keystone: The Man, the Myth and the Comedies* (1971).

When Sennett donated his papers to the Margaret Herrick Library of the

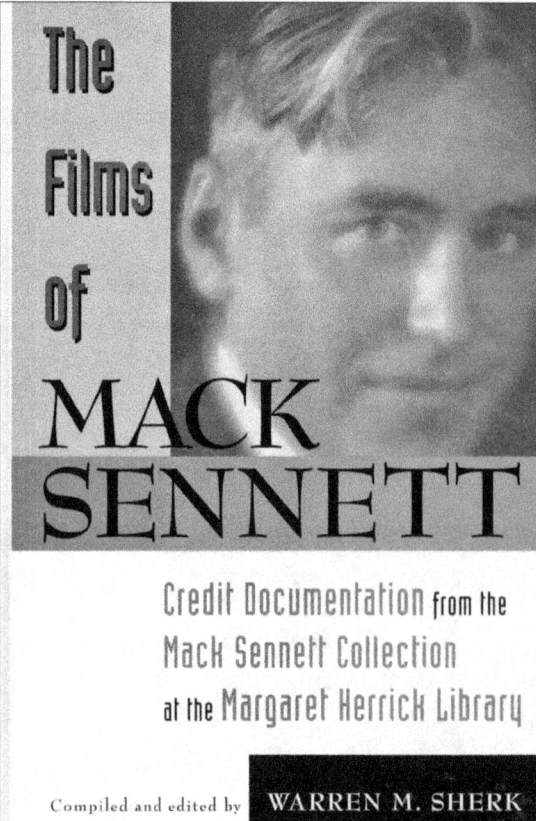

Academy of Motion Picture Arts & Sciences, he probably never imagined that it would take another four decades for the trove to be sorted, catalogued, and made available to researchers. In the introductions to both his Keystone books, Kalton C. Lahue lamented the fact that the Herrick was neither preserving the material nor allowing scholars to consult it. However, when it was finally catalogued, the event triggered the modern era of Sennett scholarship. Using the papers at the Herrick as his reference, Warren M. Scherk compiled *The Films of Mack Sennett: Credit Documentation from the Mack Sennett Collection at the Margaret Herrick Library*, the first book-length filmography of Sennett titles with accurate cast and crew credits.

Simon Louvish's popular study, *Keystone: The Life and Clowns of Mack Sennett*, was published in 2003 and was meant to appeal to a mass audience rather than scholars or a subset of silent comedy buffs. Louvish did a good job covering the whole of Sennett's life and career in just over three hundred pages, and his take on Sennett's police force is delightful: "Their entire existence seemed to be one huge, contagious twitch. . . . Marionettes of some malign force of anarchy, the Kops would leap into their car only to fall behind and be dragged along in a meandering daisy chain."

Chapter 13: Mack Sennett and Keystone in Print and Home Entertainment

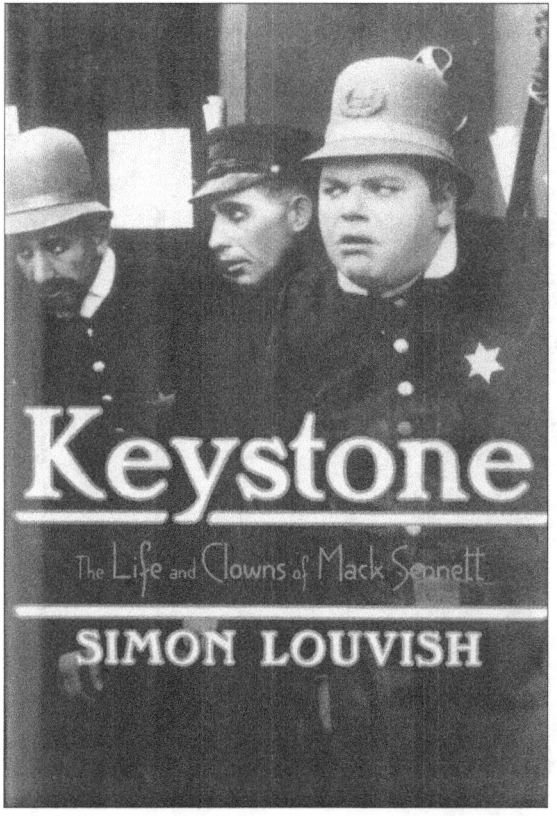

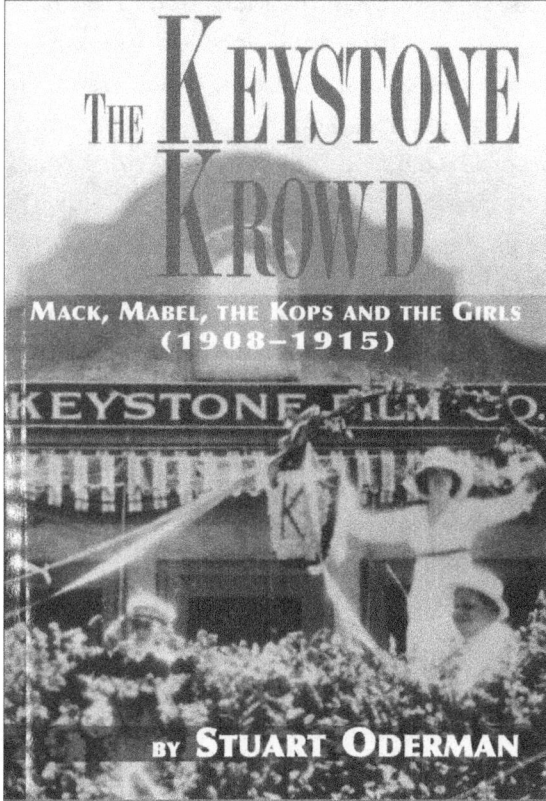

In 2001, Coy Watson Jr. released his memoir, *The Keystone Kid: Tales of Early Hollywood*, about his life in the film industry. Coy was but one of the large Watson family, a legendary group of nine child actors managed by their father. There was virtually no travel involved for Coy Sr.—a horse wrangler turned cowboy actor turned special effects man—to become an employee at Keystone; the Watson family home was located just six hundred feet from the Edendale studio. All told, the Watsons—known as "The First Family of Hollywood"—would go on to appear in an estimated one thousand films.

Another colorful, if lesser known, book is *The Keystone Krowd: Mack, Mabel, the Kops and the Girls (1908-1915)*, published by the silent film-friendly BearManor Media in 2007. It was written by the late Stuart Oderman who, for fifty years, was a silent film pianist for the Museum of Modern Art in New York City. Stuart was also a teacher, an author, and a personal friend of former Keystone players Minta Durfee Arbuckle, Chester Conklin, and Gloria Swanson.

Rob King, of Columbia University, published a sociological look at Sennett's work entitled, *The Fun Factory: The Keystone Film Company and the Emergence of Mass Culture* (2009). King makes the convincing case that the Cops were a logical outgrowth of Sen-

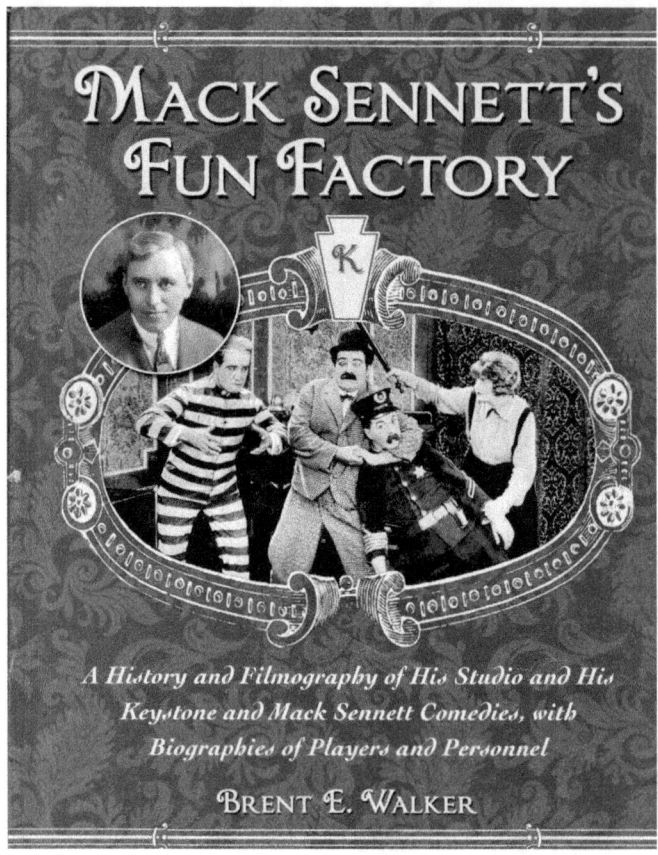

nett's apprenticeship with D. W. Griffith at Biograph. Griffith was an early pioneer of cross-cutting between two or more scenes of action unfolding simultaneously. Often this took the form of peril/rescuers. In Griffith's world this played out as life-and-death drama, but as seen through Mack Sennett's comic lens, the peril may have been life-and-death, yet the rescuers were comically inept. But somehow through the mayhem, love triumphed over evil.

The culmination of the Sennett literary canon was *Mack Sennett's Fun Factory* (2010). Brent E. Walker's 671-page magnum opus stands as the final word on Mack Sennett and the Keystone Studios. Work on the oversized book (since issued in paperback in two volumes) covered three decades and the result is an amazing piece of scholarship. Part I is a biographical and business history of Mack Sennett and his studios. Part II is a massive filmography, listing all of Sennett's 1,000+ films with cast and crew listings, filming dates, negative costs (when known), and a detailed synopsis of each film. Part III consists of biographies of Keystone and Mack Sennett personnel. Any student of Mack Sennett and his work must begin by reading Walker's book and keeping it nearby for reference while screening the films.

The Cops in Our Living Rooms

With the dawn of VHS home entertainment, the reluctance of studios to license their product at affordable prices led pioneering home video companies to look for public domain films that could be quickly marketed. Kartes Entertainment made use of the paper prints preserved by the Library of Congress and sold VHS packages of Sennett films through mall chains such as WaldenBooks. Other companies followed suit, and reasonably complete (if somewhat negligible quality) versions of Sennett's surviving shorts and features could be bought at Walgreen's Drug Stores and via mail-order firms throughout the country.

The DVD and laserdisc era brought improved visual reproduction, even if the titles were the same public domain films from the earlier era. This meant that while cheap discs of uncertain quality were readily available, discerning collectors could purchase stunning versions of titles such as *Tillie's Punctured Romance* from boutique distributors such as Kino Lorber and Flicker Alley. Over the years there have been many excellent collections of Sennett's work on DVD, one of the first being Image Entertainment's multi-volume *Slapstick Encyclopedia*, which had discs devoted to Keystone, Chaplin, and Harry Langdon. These came from David Shepard's Blackhawk Films Collection and were sharp, clear prints with original musical scores. (The rights to the late Mr. Shepard's personal collection of some ten thousand films are controlled by Lobster Films in Paris, France. The prints themselves are in the vast library of the Niles Essanay Silent Film Museum in Fremont, California, which regularly shows silent films with live piano accompaniment on Saturday evenings.)

A small independent label called Laughsmith, headed by Paul Gierucki, brought out a comprehensive collection entitled *The Forgotten Films of Roscoe "Fatty" Arbuckle*, which showcased Arbuckle's career with over thirty titles with Sennett and afterward, and was nothing less than a re-evaluation of Arbuckle's work as both an actor and director.

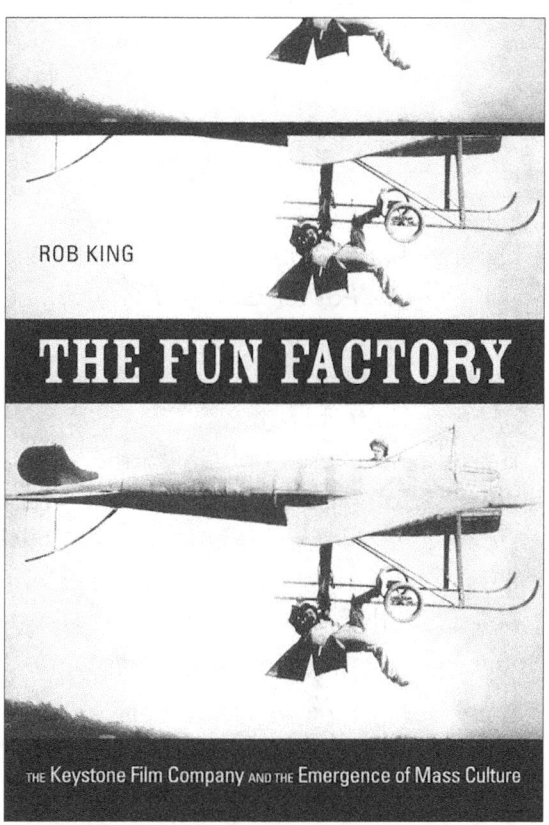

Someone else who received his first wide exposure through Sennett was Harry Langdon. David Kalat of ALLDAY Entertainment has done a fine job gathering a number of that great comedian's early films on *The Harry Langdon Collection, Lost and Found* DVD set.

Thanks to the combined sources of Association Chaplin, Lobster Films in Paris, the Blackhawk Films Collection, Cineteca Bologna, UCLA Film and Television Archive, the British Film Institute, and the distributor Flicker Alley in Los Angeles, *Chaplin at Keystone* is

one of the best silent-era Blu-ray sets released thus far. Included are excellent restorations of the thirty-five shorts and the six-reel feature that Charlie appeared in during his debut year of 1914.

Gierucki's CineMuseum is responsible for the most comprehensive collection to date: *Mack Sennett Collection, Vol. I: 50 Digitally Restored Classic Films*, a fifty-title collection of Sennett's work from Biograph to the sound era. A forthcoming *Volume II* promises at least as many titles, culled from archives and home collections.

We are living in the second Golden Age of Silent Film, when it is possible to see (and own!) more films than it was possible to see during the era in which they were first released.

Select Bibliography

Chaplin, Charles. *My Autobiography*. New York: Simon & Schuster, 1964.

Fowler, Gene. *Father Goose: The Story of Mack Sennett*. New York: Covici-Friede, 1934.

King, Rob. *The Fun Factory: The Keystone Film Company and the Emergence of Mass Culture*.
  Berkeley: University of California Press, 2009.

Lahue, Kalton C., and Terry Brewer. *Kops and Custards: The Legend of Keystone Films*. Norman: University of Oklahoma Press, 1968.

Lahue, Kalton C. *Mack Sennett's Keystone: The Man, the Myth and the Comedies*. South Brunswick, NJ: Barnes, 1971.

Louvish, Simon. *Keystone: The Life and Clowns of Mack Sennett*. London: Faber & Faber, 2003.

Oderman, Stuart. *The Keystone Krowd: Mack, Mabel, the Kops and the Girls (1908-1915)*. Albany, GA: BearManor Media, 2007.

Scherk, Warren M., compiler and editor. *The Films of Mack Sennett: Credit Documentation from the Mack Sennett Collection at the Margaret Herrick Library*. Lanham, MD: Scarecrow Press, 1998.

Sennett, Mack, and Cameron Shipp. *King of Comedy*. Garden City, NY: Doubleday, 1954.

Turconi, Davide. *Mack Sennett*. Rome: Edizioni dell'Ateneo, 1961.

Walker, Brent. *Mack Sennett's Fun Factory*. Jefferson, NC: McFarland & Co., 2010.

Watson, Coy Jr. *The Keystone Kid: Tales of Early Hollywood*. Santa Monica, CA: Santa Monica Press, 2001.

Select Videography

Chaplin at Keystone, directed by Charles Chaplin and others. 2010. Los Angeles: Flicker Alley, DVD set.

The Forgotten Films of Roscoe "Fatty" Arbuckle, directed by Mack Sennett and Roscoe Arbuckle. 2005. Laughsmith Entertainment/Mackinac Media DVD set.

The Harry Langdon Collection: Lost and Found, directed by Harry Edwards and others. 2007, Mack Sennett Films, ALLDAY Entertainment DVD set.

The Mack Sennett Collection, Vol. I: 50 Digitally Restored Classic Films, directed by Mack Sennett and others. 2014, Flicker Alley, Keystone Films, CineMuseum Blu-Ray set.

The Mack Sennett Collection, Vol. II: 50 Digitally Restored Classic Films, directed by Mack Sennett and others. Forthcoming CineMuseum Blu-Ray set.

The Slapstick Encyclopedia, directed by various. 2002. Image Entertainment DVD set.

ROB FARR teaches the History of World Cinema and early film at George Mason University in Fairfax, Virginia. He co-founded the Slapsticon, the world's first film festival devoted to silent and early sound films. Rob contributed commentary or liner notes for several DVD sets, including Kino Lorber's ultimate edition of Buster Keaton's *College*, Hesperus's versions of *The Mark of Zorro*, *Robin Hood*, and *Thelma Todd and ZaSu Pitts: The Hal Roach Collection 1931–33*. He is currently working on a book on the life and films of Mr. and Mrs. Sidney Drew.

Chapter 14
Top Cops:
Fifty-five Profiles of Original and Honorary Keystone Cops

By Lon Davis and Brent E. Walker

Keystone Cop police helmet on display at the Los Angeles County Museum, History Division, 1993. Courtesy of Bison Archives.

"Practically every actor whose movie career began in the dawn of screen history has claimed to be one of the original Keystone Kops," Kalton C. Lahue wrote in 1968. "So many have in fact claimed this distinction that in order to accommodate every claim, Sennett would have had to have hired a police force large enough for a city." That said, there were quite a few individuals who could truthfully make that claim. As Mack Sennett himself said, "I started every new man as a Keystone Cop to see how he worked out."

The following profiles encompass forty-five brave souls who appeared in uniform in the original Keystone and Keystone-Triangle comedies produced between 1912 and 1917. Their authenticity as Keystone Cops has been verified through trade magazines of the time and researched by Brent E. Walker for his book *Mack Sennett's Fun Factory*. The ten silent comedy veterans who took part primarily in later film tributes and reunions are included under the heading "Honorary Cops."

Dave "Andy" Anderson

Born in Sweden on July 23, 1883, David Carl Gustav Anderson was an ex-sailor and auto racer, the latter skill enabling him to take part in some alarmingly realistic chase scenes at Keystone, beginning in early 1913. He briefly left the Fun Factory in 1914, only to return the following year, remaining throughout the First National era. Utilizing the nautical skills he learned while in the navy, he became the skipper of Charlie Chaplin's yacht, *Panacea*, beginning in 1933. He eventually settled in Newport Beach, California, with his wife and four children. At the age of sixty-six, on November 18, 1950, he died of stomach cancer. David C. G. Anderson is interred at Westminster Memorial Park, Westminster, California, Garden of Harmony, Lot 89, Grave No. 1.

Roscoe Arbuckle

Born in Smith Center, Kansas, on March 24, 1887, Roscoe Conkling Arbuckle was forced to fend for himself from the tender age of twelve. He did so by singing in small-time vaudeville, where he met a chorus girl named Araminta (Minta) Durfee. The two married in 1908 and entered pictures together five years later by way of the Keystone Film Company. It was Mack Sennett himself who gave Roscoe his hated nickname. "Fatty" seemed an obvious choice as the rotund comic stood five-ten and weighed well over three hundred pounds. Despite his ample size, he was utterly graceful and could take the most breathtaking falls. After serving his time as a Cop, he was promoted to lead actor, often directing his own films. In one imaginative and poignant scene from the 1916 three-reeler *Fatty and Mabel Adrift*, Roscoe is shown kissing his wife (the radiant Mabel Normand) goodnight—in silhouette. So struck by this was the esteemed dramatic actor Hobart Bosworth, that he wrote Arbuckle the following note: "Many times since I saw 'Adrift,' I have said that the business of the shadowy goodnight kiss was the most touchingly poetic thing I have ever seen in a motion picture."

Roscoe, when out of character, was a complex man with his share of human weaknesses. His marriage to Minta became strained, leading to their divorce. As she recalled to Stuart Oderman: "Frankly, I was tired of picking up after him, of telephoning people he had offended the night before when he was drunk. . . . It was over. It was all over." After a brilliant career and a difficult personal life, Roscoe Arbuckle died, aged forty-six, of a heart attack at the Park Central Hotel in New York City. Survived by his third wife, actress Addie McPhail, he was cremated and his ashes were scattered in the Pacific Ocean. To learn much more about this complex individual, please read David Yallop's *The Day the Laughter Stopped* (St. Martin's Press, 1976).

Charles Avery

According to Mack Sennett, Charles Avery (Bradford)—born in Chicago, Illinois, on May 28, 1873—was one of the original seven Keystone Cops. And according to Minta Durfee Arbuckle, he was a total professional. "Avery was always very dependable," she told Stuart Oderman, "and he would turn out a satisfactory product, which was all that Mack really wanted." In a way, Sennett served as Avery's mentor the way D. W. Griffith had served as Sennett's. Charles Avery's death (in Los Angeles, reportedly by his own hand) occurred on July 23, 1926, when he was fifty-three. His cremains are inurned at Hollywood Forever Cemetery, in the Collonade, South Wall, Niche A [c].

Harry Bernard

Best remembered as an exasperated policeman in more than two dozen Laurel & Hardy films, Harold Bernard appeared in an estimated 150 movies. According to the preeminent Laurel & Hardy expert Randy Skretvedt, Harry (as he was billed) may actually have been born Frederick Owen Salmon, in Kensington, England, on January 13, 1878. He and his wife appeared in vaudeville together before he ventured into the movie business, via Keystone, in 1915. On November 11, 1940, following a lengthy battle with stomach cancer, he died at the age of sixty-two. Like many of his contemporaries, his final resting place is at Hollywood Forever Cemetery. His unmarked grave is in Section 10-W, Grave C-933.

Joe Bordeaux

A native of Canada, Joseph Emil Bordeaux was born on March 9, 1886. He was a Cop and stunt man at Keystone between 1914 and 1916, after which he left to begin a second (and far less dangerous) career as a property man, mainly for Republic. He still took on an occasional supporting role, co-starring on the Roach lot with Laurel & Hardy, Our Gang, and Charley Chase. He even put on his old uniform and helmet to participate in the 1935 short *Keystone Hotel*. On September 10, 1950, he died, aged sixty-four, in Los Angeles, California; he was survived by his wife and daughter. His body was cremated, and his ashes are inurned at the Chapel of the Pines Crematory in Los Angeles.

Jimmy Bryant

Very little is known about this particular Cop. What we *do* know is that Jimmy Bryant was one of Roscoe Arbuckle's sidekicks and was regularly cast in bit parts (particularly as policemen) in the star player's Keystone comedies of 1914–1916. When Arbuckle relocated to Paramount, he invited Jimmy to tag along. Bryant also found himself in supporting roles in the starring films of two other Arbuckle acolytes, Buster Keaton (including his 1926 Civil War masterwork, *The General*, in which Jimmy is one of the soldiers) and Al St. John (in *Stupid But Brave* [1924] and *The Iron Mule* [1925]). Unfortunately, this comic actor has a very uncomical stain on his reputation. Bryant and another man were suspected of having rolled a drunk in downtown

Los Angeles. Instead of prison time, he received probation, thanks to some highly influential character witnesses: Arbuckle, Sennett, and Chaplin.

Glen Cavender

Born in Tucson, Arizona, on September 19, 1883, Glen W. Cavender spent two seasons riding with Buffalo Bill's Wild West Show. Movies were an even more exciting way to make a living, particularly at Keystone, as he found out beginning in 1914. He proved his versatility by playing multiple minor roles in the ambitious production of *Tillie's Punctured Romance*. Hoping for the chance to play leading roles, this Keystone Cop and many of his fellow malcontents made the move to Fox Sunshine Comedies, where he was teamed with Jack Cooper. Never achieving stardom, Glen returned to the Sennett lot in 1924, this time as a gag man. From there, it was a series of bit parts and occasional jobs as a makeup artist at MGM. On February 9, 1962, the seventy-eight-year-old died at home, his wife and daughter by his side. He is interred in niche 20309 in the Columbarium of Dawn of the Great Mausoleum, in Forest Lawn Memorial Park, Glendale.

Charlie Chaplin

Regarding this one-time Cop (*A Thief Catcher*), very little is known about His Prehistoric Past, and even less about His Musical Career. He was considered by his fellow Keystone employees to be a Gentleman of Nerve and enjoyed various forms of Recreation. He was the kind of fellow often Caught in the Rain, or worse, Caught in a Cabaret. There, in His Trysting Place, he was known to sate Those Love Pangs and partake in His Favorite Pastime: Twenty Minutes of Love—Cruel, Cruel Love. Other sources show that he often ended up as just The Face on the Bar Room Floor. Then, Between Showers, he would continue A Busy Day in one of several jobs. He was ultimately The Masquerader, floating between being The Property

Man, The New Janitor, perhaps even A Film Johnnie—just a string of ventures that barely qualified as Making a Living. But, in general, information is sketchy regarding this now-obscure comic.

Charles Spencer Chaplin, of course, is the most revered (and most heavily documented) comedy filmmaker of all time. Although it was long believed that he was born in Lambeth, London, England, on April 16, 1889, new evidence (in the form of a handwritten letter discovered in his desk drawer in 1991) suggests that he was actually born in Smethwick, Staffordshire, England, in a gypsy queen's caravan. When he died, eighty-eight years later, he had come incredibly far from his impoverished beginnings. Knighted by Queen Elizabeth II in 1975, Sir Charles was a legendary, wealthy man.

On Christmas Day 1977 his passing made front-page news all around the world. His burial, a strictly private affair, was in a village cemetery in the hills above Lake Geneva, near Lausanne, Switzerland. Eight weeks later, two men robbed his grave and demanded $600,000 for the body's return. Oona, his widow, refused to pay anything, saying that her late husband, who was known for his parsimoniousness, would have found the sum "ridiculous." The culprits persisted, even making threats against the Chaplins' two youngest of their eight children. Five weeks of intense investigation led the police to two auto mechanics who, in turn, led the officers to the body, which they had buried in a cornfield, located approximately one mile from the Chaplin estate, the Manoir de Bain. The culprits were arrested for grave robbery and attempted extortion. Sir Charles, meanwhile, was reburied, this time in a concrete grave (in Cimetière de Corsier-sur-Vevey), to prevent any future such attempts. Oona, who died at the age of sixty-six in 1991, was laid to rest next to her husband of thirty-four years.

To learn more about this great filmmaker, the editors recommend an outstanding book, *The Art of Charlie Chaplin* (McFarland & Co., 2008), by Kyp Harness.

Eddie Cline

Born in Kenosha, Wisconsin, on November 7, 1892, Edward Francis Cline was raised in Edendale, not far from the Keystone studio. After serving his time as a Cop beginning in 1914, he was promoted to assistant director and by 1916 he became one of Sennett's most prolific directors, helming an estimated sixty comedies. He is also said to have been the architect of the Sennett Bathing Beauties concept. His career as a comedy director smoothly transitioned into the sound era, during which he managed to work harmoniously with the notoriously difficult W. C. Fields on some of his greatest films, including *The Bank Dick* (1940), the climax of which features a Keystone-style car chase. Eddie Cline died at the age of sixty-eight, on May 22, 1961, following a brief illness. Although predeceased by his second wife, he was survived by their daughter. He is interred at the San Fernando Mission Cemetery in Los Angeles, Section B, Lot 1048, Grave No. 1.

Nick Cogley

Some actors seem as though they are born old. That certainly seems to be the case with Nicholas Cogley, an old-timer born in New York City on May 4, 1869, who first entered films by way of the Selig Company beginning in 1909. By the time he joined Keystone in 1913, the heavyset, balding actor was typecast as grouchy authority figures in numerous split-reelers. Despite his weight and advancing age, the fifty-something actor was described by Donald MacKenzie (the director of the famed 1914 serial *The Perils of Pauline*) as "a feisty, fearless guy" who could still take falls with the best of them. There was one time, however, when he overestimated his flexibility. As Mack Sennett recounted in his autobiography: "One slimy day when the pavement was slick, Mr. Cogley was egged on too far . . . and did a back flip which gave him a compound fracture in his left leg. We kept Mr. Cogley on the payroll, but it was a matter of pride with my comedians not to break themselves." After a slow, painful recovery, Nick continued to portray (albeit more sedately) his stock authority figures, including the police chief in *Tillie's Punctured Romance*. Once he retired from knockabout comedy, he became a scenarist and assistant director—a trouper to the very end. Following an operation in May 1936, the sixty-seven-year-old Cogley died, leaving a wife and two children.

Chester Conklin

Born in Oskaloosa, Iowa, on January 11, 1886, Chester Cooper Conklin was working as a clown with the Al G. Barnes Circus in 1913, which wintered in Venice, California. It was then that he decided to take a chance and apply for a job

 at Keystone in nearby Edendale. Mack Sennett asked him point blank: "Are you funny?" Chester looked him straight in the eye and answered: "I'll leave that to you." He was hired on a day-rate basis (three dollars a day and a box lunch) and quickly became one of the Fun Factory's most dependable laugh-getters, playing two distinctive characters, "Walrus," a lascivious lecher, and "Droppington," a blustering bungler. Regardless of *what* he was playing, he wore his trademark bushy mustache. He also portrayed Cops in many early Keystone shorts, such as Charlie Chaplin's *Between Showers* (1914). In the 1915 one-reeler *Love, Speed and Thrills*, he is on the opposite side of the law when he kidnaps Ambrose's (Mack Swain's) wife (Minta Durfee) and takes her on a perilous ride in a motorcycle sidecar, with three Cops on foot in hot pursuit. "That chase was done all in one take," Conklin recalled with pride to writer Stuart Oderman some fifty-five years later. "I think we used all of it. We weren't conscious of any timing, of how long the sequence was taking, until we heard, '*Cut!*'" But nothing lasts forever, and Conklin gave his notice to Sennett. As the comic later explained, "I had to leave because I wanted to do other roles and not stay doing the same thing over and over again." He went on to star in the Fox Sunshine Comedies; he had a pivotal role in Erich von Stroheim's epic *Greed* (1924); he was teamed with W. C. Fields in three (now lost) silent Paramount comedies; and he supported The Three Stooges, Charley Chase, Harry Langdon, and others in sound two-reelers for Columbia. He also reunited with Chaplin for *Modern Times* (1936), playing a fellow factory worker, and *The Great Dictator* (1940), in which he is shaved by Charlie in precise time to Brahms's Hungarian Dance No. 5. But more than anything, Chester Conklin remained in the public eye as the ultimate Keystone Cop. Beginning in the 1940s, he, Hank Mann, Heinie Conklin, Snub Pollard, and Clarence Hennecke were on hand time and again for reunions and tributes, in films, on the stage, and on television. When these opportunities grew scarce in the mid-1950s, he took a job as a department store Santa Claus in Los Angeles and Long Beach. For several years, he was a resident of the Motion Picture and Television Country House and Hospital, Woodland Hills, California. On October 11, 1971, he died, aged eighty-five, although his national obituary gave his age as eighty-three. His body was cremated and the ashes were given to his fourth wife, retired screen actress June Gunther, with whom he eloped in 1965.

Robert Cox

Robert Cox is one of the least documented Keystone Cops. It was difficult to find *any* corresponding documentation to prove his authenticity, not just as a Cop, but as one of the famous lineup in the iconic still from *In the Clutches of a Gang*. (Indeed, the name given in the caption of Gene Fowler's 1934 book *Father Goose* was "Joe Demming," a name that has never been attributed in any other source). In the 1940s, film director and historian Robert Florey interviewed Keystone Cop Billy Gilbert, who recalled working with a Marvin Cox, which is apparently the name by which Robert Cox was known at that time. It was not until the publication of Brent Walker's definitive Keystone book in 2010 that some solid evidence was presented. Brent reproduced a page from a program for the "Picture Players Camera Men's Ball," dated January 16, 1914. There, among formal portraits of seven other noted original Keystone Cops (including Hank Mann and Al St. John), is a very young, very serious M. G. Cox (see accompanying photograph). Due to his having served in World War I, he was buried with military honors in Greenwood Memorial Lawn Cemetery, Phoenix, Maricopa County, Arizona; Plot Section 575, Block 12, Lot 4. Faded badly by Arizona's hot sun, his marker reads:

Robert Cox
M. Sgt. U. S. Army
May 12, 1896 † Sep 8, 1974

Bobby Dunn

Diminutive and cross-eyed, Robert Vivian Dunn was born in Milwaukee, Wisconsin, on August 28, 1887. Bobby, a gifted acrobat, was performing dangerous high dives when he was just nine years old. He was billed as "the champion high diver of the world" while appearing with Dr. Carver's Diving Horses. Repeated violent contact with the water cost the young man most of his front teeth. He also lost an eye in a diving stunt and was forced to wear a glass substitute, which he could adjust to make himself appear cross-eyed for comic purposes. Joining Keystone in 1915, he appeared in an estimated eighty films for Sennett over a nearly two-decade period. "There's a good reason Keystone was called 'The Fun Factory,'" said Babe London, the zaftig comedienne often referred to as the female Roscoe Arbuckle. "A lot of jokes and funny situations occurred. Everybody was a practical joker. . . . Bobby and Slim Summerville designed a water-bath trick to play on one of their co-workers. They somehow managed to get a cold bucket of water between the wall and top of the door. Whoever walked into that room or office would somehow tilt the bucket of water . . . you know the rest. But the person who was doused with the water was *Mack Sennett himself*!" Although it had nothing to do with that practical joke, Dunn's contract was not renewed. He went on to achieve greater recognition as a member of the Hal Roach stock company, occasionally co-starring with Laurel & Hardy. On March 24, 1937, his death, at age forty-six, was reported as a possible suicide. He is buried in an unmarked plot in Hollywood Forever Cemetery, Section 14, Grave 1431.

Ted Edwards

Maurice Edward Burrell (known professionally as Ted Edwards) was born on May 9, 1883, in Sheffield, England. He gained vast experience while playing comedy roles in British stock productions, which served him well when he went to work in American vaudeville in 1905. After touring the Midwest, he traveled to Los Angeles, where he successfully applied for work at Keystone. With his gray hair and light gray eyes, he was cast most often as clerics and policemen. The highlight of his career was appearing in two of Charlie Chaplin's short comedies, *A Busy Day* (Keystone, 1914) and *A Dog's Life* (First National, 1918). But Edwards was more than just an actor: he was a physical culture instructor and an accomplished building contractor and cabinetmaker. In 1922, he left the movie business for a far more lucrative (and much steadier) career in construction. Ted Edwards died, aged fifty-two, of a coronary occlusion, on September 29, 1945, leaving a wife and son. He is interred at Rose Hills Memorial Park in Whittier, California.

Chester Franklin

Born in San Francisco, California, on September 1, 1889, Chester Mortimer Franklin joined Keystone in 1912, becoming one of the very first Keystone Cops. Chester and his brother, Sidney, jointly helmed the Fox Kiddies series, directing feature-length versions of *Aladdin's Lamp* and *Jack and the Beanstalk*, with all-children casts. (Sidney Franklin would go on to become a major director in his own right.) Chester died on March 12, 1954, at the age of sixty-four. He is interred at Forest Lawn Memorial Park, Glendale, Sanctuary of Truth, GM, Memorial Terrace, Lot O, Space 5502.

Edwin Frazee

A number of fine directors were graduates of the Keystone Cop comedies, Edwin Frazee being a prime example. Born Edgar Allen Fraser in Lima, Ohio, on July 10, 1881, he had a circus background (another experience common to Sennett's knockabout comics) and fought in the Spanish-American War. Once he was back in civilian clothing, he appeared in stock in Seattle and San Francisco and also worked as a film exhibitor. He brought all of this experience with him when he joined Keystone in 1914, performing acrobatic stunts on camera and working behind the scenes as a prop man. After taking innumerable falls as a Cop (including in the climactic chase scene in *Tillie's Punctured Romance*), he was soon promoted to assistant director and, finally, to full-time Keystone director in the years 1915–1916. From there he went to Fox, L-KO, and Nestor, proving himself a first-rate director of comedies. In 1918, he set up his own production company in D. W. Griffith's former studio on Sunset Boulevard, although he is only known to have produced one film, a special-effects-laden mystery entitled *The Haunted House*. Always expanding his talents, he later owned a Hollywood-based company, Frazee Motion Picture Technical Research Laboratories. He died on February 20, 1937, at the age of fifty-five. A wife and two children survived him.

Billy Gilbert

An actual Los Angeleno, William V. Campbell was born on September 15, 1891. Billy began to develop a reputation as a stunt performer at the tender age of five. He was known to have been a high-dive champion (125 feet at Coney Island's Dreamland pier), a jockey, an acrobat, a clown, and a show manager. He joined Keystone in 1913, where his tiny frame earned him the nickname "Little Billy Gilbert." In 1917, Billy directed (or co-directed) some of Harold Lloyd's earliest "glass films" for Rolin. In 1921, he appeared onscreen with Pearl Shepard and Bud Duncan in a series of one-reel Aladdin Comedies for Reelcraft. There were a number of supporting roles as well. He later worked behind the camera—as property man—for Mascot serials. His last-known onscreen role was as a Cop in *Keystone Hotel*. Although no relation to the far better known—and far bigger physically—sound-era comedian Billy Gilbert (he of the famous sneezing routine), when Gilbert died at the age of sixty-nine in 1961, the more famous Billy received several messages of condolence.

George Gray

Another former high diver, George Gray (born in California on October 30, 1893), appeared with fellow future Cop Bobby Dunn in Dr. Carver's diving show. Gray earned the nickname "Sloppy" because of his tendency to splash as many spectators as possible when he performed his dives. He narrowly escaped serious injury in Reno, Nevada, when he struck his head and was knocked unconscious while performing a forty-foot drop. Joining Keystone sometime around 1914 seemed much safer by comparison. And it was, given his versatility. In addition to performing stunts, he worked as a writer, assistant director, and director. Gray freelanced as an actor for many years, including a five-year stretch for Sennett during the twenties; he also supported such well-known comics as W. C. Fields, Andy Clyde, and The Three Stooges, while moonlighting as a makeup man. He also had the distinction of being one of the authentic Cops in *Keystone Hotel*. After his good friend Andy Clyde passed away in May 1967, Gray married Clyde's widow, former Sennett Bathing Beauty Elsie Tarron. At the time, he was chairman of a committee for the acquisition of movie still photographs for the Hollywood Museum. He died on September 8, 1967, in Ashville, North Carolina, aged seventy-three, of a stroke. He is interred at Oakwood Memorial Park, Chatsworth, California, Section E, Lot 12, Space No. 5.

Eddie Gribbon

Born in New York City on January 3, 1890, Edward Gribbon joined Keystone in 1916, working as a Cop and doing stunt work (which, some might argue, is basically the same pursuit). After a stint with Al Christie's film comedy troupe, he served in World War I as an infantry drill sergeant. Returning to Sennett's employ in 1919, he began to take on more prominent roles, including one as a pasty-faced dolt. He was also in demand for roles as the bone-headed tough he resembled. He continued to work into the television era, performing vintage comedy routines on such programs as *The Colgate Comedy Hour*. Following a three-month illness, he died at home on September 29, 1965, simply falling asleep in his big easy chair; he was seventy-five. Eddie was survived by his wife, a brother, and a sister. (His older brother Harry, a fellow Sennett player, had predeceased him in 1961.) Eddie Gribbon is interred at Calvary Cemetery in East Los Angeles, Main Mausoleum, Block 64, Crypt E-1.

Bernard Harris

Born in New York City on February 23, 1892, Bernard Harris was destined to be a success, both professionally and personally. After his parents relocated to Venice, California, in 1906, Bernard worked in the family's small retail business. This proved a bit constraining for the athletic young man; he wanted to do something more interesting, more daring—something fun. Sometime around 1915, he stood in line at the Keystone gates, looking for work. Hired on the spot, Bernard would go on to appear in an estimated fifty films, as an extra, a bit player, and a Keystone Cop. In the latter capacity, he became attached to director Edwin Frazee's unit as part of a core group of the Cops known

Bernard Harris

as Frazee's Fearless Five; the other four were George Ramage, Frank Reynolds, Bill Weber, and Al Case. (*Photos courtesy of Michael Campino and* Slapstick! *Magazine.*) Given the perilous stunts these five Cops were forced to perform, they truly had to be fearless. Bernard described one such stunt for an interviewer: "Once, the force was exchanging smoke bombs with a group of robbers aboard a train when a bomb landed in the Cops' supply and blew the dump up. Four of the actors escaped with smoke damage, but a fifth, who had dived over the back of a moving car to escape, died of his injuries nine months later." Bernard had his own work-related injury when he fell through a weak stage plank. His parents became increasingly concerned about his safety, and even he was having second thoughts about risking his life for three dollars a day. His breaking point came when he was ordered to jump from the top deck of a steamship into the harbor. Although he had made similar jumps in previous films, this one seemed far too steep and far too dangerous. Reluctantly removing his cap and police jacket, he handed in his resignation. As Bernard's biographer, Michael Campino, points out, it would be more than fifty years before he put on the uniform again; that was in conjunction with one

George Ramage

Frank Reynolds

Al Case

Bill Weber

of Eddie LeVeque's Keystone Kop reunions, in 1970. In the intervening years, Bernard Harris had hardly been idle. He worked his way up to become vice president of the Utility Fan Corporation, a position that made him financially independent. So much so, in fact, that he and his wife, Rebecca, were able to build their dream home in Beverly Hills. Rebecca died in 1975, leading to Bernard's slow but steady decline. He died June 12, 1981, at the age of eighty-nine, on what would have been the couple's sixtieth anniversary. Bernard Harris, as mentioned earlier, was a successful individual. As he liked to say: "My greatest accomplishments were being a Keystone Cop and selling Utility cooling equipment to every citrus-packing plant in California."

Raymond Hatton

This well-known character actor got his start as a Keystone Cop beginning in 1913. Born in Red Oak, Iowa, on July 7, 1887, Raymond William Hatton entered the movies via the Biograph studio in 1909, appearing in several Griffith-directed films, some featuring Mack Sennett. Sennett obviously recognized Hatton's flair for comedy as he invited him to join the westbound company that would make up Keystone. A far more prestigious opportunity arose when he was signed by Famous Players–Lasky to appear in Cecil B. DeMille's earliest (and best) features: *The Squaw Man* (1914), said to be the first feature film shot in Hollywood; *Joan the Woman* (1917), starring the great opera diva Geraldine Farrar; and *Male and Female* (1919), with Gloria Swanson and Thomas Meighan. Although initially an uncredited bit player for DeMille, he began getting better roles and more screen time. That he was a funny man was readily apparent to audiences. He proved this in a series of silent Paramount comedies in which he was teamed with Wallace Beery (one of which, *Now We're in the Air* [1927], featuring Louise Brooks in a supporting role, was only recently rediscovered after having been lost for decades). In the early sound era, Raymond played the recurring character of tobacco-chewing Rusty Joslin in the popular B-Western series The Three Mesquiteers for Republic Pictures. Hatton kept turning up, whether in feature films (of which his filmography boasts nearly five hundred titles) and in every television program from *The Abbott & Costello Show* to *Gunsmoke* to *The*

Adventures of Superman. He never really retired—he simply aged out of show business. As late as 1967, he gave a highly credible performance as an ill, elderly Mexican hitchhiker in the stark film adaptation of Truman Capote's non-fiction novel *In Cold Blood* (1967). Raymond William Hatton died, aged eighty-four, in Palmdale, California, a week following the death of his beloved wife, Frances, and was inurned next to her at Joshua Memorial Park in Lancaster, California. This dependable, versatile player had a saying that should resonate with anyone wishing to join the theatrical profession: "A good actor carries his makeup box in his head."

Bill Hauber

Wisconsinite William Carl Hauber (born May 20, 1891) has been called "the greatest stunt man in all of silent comedy," and is known for his spectacular comic falls. On July 17, 1929, Bill Hauber, then only thirty-eight, was killed (along with cameraman Alvin Knetchel) in a plane crash near Van Nuys Airport while scouting locations for the First National feature *The Aviator*. Survived by his wife and son, he is interred at Forest Lawn Memorial Park, Glendale, Great Mausoleum, Sanctuary of Peace, Dahlia Terrace, Crypt No. 4008.

Frank Hayes

This comical-looking stage-trained actor would appear in more than forty comedies for Mack Sennett beginning in 1914. Sennett historian Kalton C. Lahue once wrote that Hayes "had no equal and was probably the most perfect Kop Keystone ever had." Frank Rowell Hayes was born in San Francisco on May 17, 1871, making him one of the older members of Sennett's rough-and-ready troupe. In 1918, he left Sennett's employ to join the Fox Sunshine Company; he also worked with Roscoe Arbuckle at Comique, and at Vitagraph with Larry Semon. Back with Sennett for the 1919 feature *Yankee Doodle in Berlin*, Hayes appears in drag, resembling what may well be the scariest-looking woman ever put on film. On December 28, 1923, he died of pneumonia at the age of fifty-two. He is buried in his hometown of San Francisco.

Clarence Hennecke

Born in Omaha, Nebraska, on September 16, 1884, Clarence R. Hennecke arrived in Los Angeles in 1913. At first employed by Vitagraph, he joined Keystone three years later, where he was cast as a Keystone Cop. A pugilist, he held the lightweight championship crown in the mid-twenties; he also worked as a boxing coach at the University of Southern California. After serving in World War I (during which he was a motorcycle dispatch rider in France and was twice cited for bravery), he briefly returned to Sennett in 1918. From there he went to Fox Sunshine, where he was teamed with Clyde Cook, the acrobatic Australian comedian known as "The Kangaroo Boy." Hennecke also worked as a gag writer for Will Rogers, Paul Parrott, and Stan Laurel (at Roach), Harry Langdon (at First National), and Mary Pickford (at United Artists). Managing to survive the transition to sound, he contributed to the short comedies of Karl Dane & George K. Arthur (at Paramount), George Sidney & Charlie Murray (at Universal), and performed bits in features. He died in Marin County, California, on August 28, 1969, at the age of seventy-four. Pierce Brothers Mortuary in Santa Monica was placed in charge of his final arrangements.

Bert Hunn

Illinois-born Albert W. Hunn joined Keystone in 1913. Possessing a keen sense of smell, he noticed the odor of smoke in the air, signaling a fire at the Keystone/Broncho/Kay-Bee lab in downtown Los Angeles. By alerting the fire department in time, Bert saved the negatives for the majority of Keystone films. (For once, a Keystone Cop genuinely came to the rescue.) He left Keystone briefly in 1914, only to return soon after. By 1930, he had given up on movies and was working as a tile setter and brick layer in Fresno, California. He died on October 3, 1964, at the age of eighty.

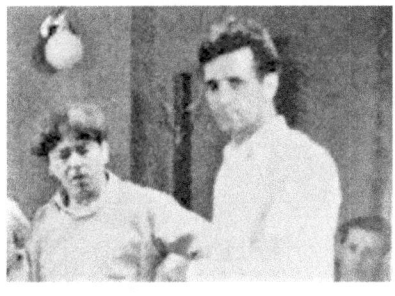

Ray Hunt

Born in Albuquerque, New Mexico, on November 11, 1892, Rae McKenzie Hunt was not only a Keystone Cop, he was an assistant director, a director, a cameraman, and a property man during his years with Mack Sennett. Later, he worked for Columbia's short subjects department, supplying props for The Three Stooges, Andy Clyde, Buster Keaton, Harry Langdon, and the other comedians working for that memorable unit. (A fuzzy, faded snapshot taken on the set of the 1935 Three Stooges two-reeler *Pardon My Scotch*, with Ray standing next to Moe Howard, is the only photo of Hunt that could be found. *Photo courtesy of ThreeStooges.net*). Columbia sound engineer and director Edward Bernds told authors Ted Okuda and Ed Watz (*The Columbia Comedy Shorts*, McFarland & Co., 1986): "Ray Hunt was a prop man who worked on all of the two-reelers. He was a wizard at special effects, supplying us with breakaway props, wire-belt rigging—and he was a great pie thrower. He had his own recipe for pies, which used shaving cream instead of whipped cream because it didn't stain like whipped cream did. Ray was a very valuable man; we were all indebted to him." Ray Hunt retired as property master of Columbia in 1960, after having served in that capacity for twenty years. He died of a heart attack the following year, on June 21, 1961, at the age of sixty-nine.

George Jeske

Salt Lake City, Utah, February 22, 1891, was the birthplace and birthdate for one of Mack Sennett's "original seven" Keystone Cops. George Washington Jaeschke described the working conditions for a movie actor in 1913 thusly: "We did *everything*. We handled lumber, built sets, acted, turned the camera—all for eighteen dollars a week. That was at first. When the money started rolling in, Sennett upped us. Pretty soon we were getting five dollars for an idea. That was the birth of the gag man." Jeske left Keystone for Sterling Comedies in 1914. There, he doubled for the missing-in-action Ford Sterling in a series of shorts. He later worked both as an assistant director and as a full-fledged director for various comedy outfits. For health reasons, Jeske left Hollywood for Indio, California, where he managed the Aladdin Theater. He died in Los Angeles on October 28, 1951, at the age of sixty. Survived by two sisters and two brothers, George Jeske is buried in Indio.

Edgar Kennedy

"Edgar Kennedy is one of the few silent film actors who was able to create and sustain an entire career from a single, simple gesture—the slow burn," Frank Capra told Stuart Oderman. "He was a one-faced, one expression guy, but what an expression!" Edgar Livingston Kennedy was born in the Northern California town of Veratina, on April 26, 1890. A stage-trained actor, he joined Chicago's Selig studio before signing with Keystone. During his Sennett years (1913–1919), the ruggedly built, six-foot-one, two-hundred-pound ex-boxer appeared in more than sixty Keystone films, usually playing Cops (at times even the chief) or jealous husbands. By the time he had become an established character actor, he had developed a paunch and lost most of his hair. His trademark expression, the slow burn, referred to above by Frank Capra, involved his slowly rubbing his hand down his baldpate and over his face, the very picture of exasperation. Ed used this schtick to brilliant effect as a foil for Laurel & Hardy (whom he also directed in two short subjects), Our Gang, and the Marx Brothers. Occasionally, he could be seen in a drama, such as *San Francisco* (MGM, 1936) and *A Star is Born* (Selznick, 1937). He starred in his own long-running series of shorts at RKO, in which he was the bungling victim of an annoying wife, a meddlesome mother-in-law, and a lazy brother-in-law. Edgar Kennedy was fifty-eight when he succumbed to throat cancer on November 9, 1948. He was survived by his second wife, a son, and a daughter. He is buried in Holy Cross Cemetery, Los Angeles; Section D, Lot 193, Grave No. 7. (For the full story on this great comedian and original Keystone Cop, please read Bill Cassara's book, *Edgar Kennedy: Master of the Slow Burn* [BearManor Media, 2017 edition].)

Eddie LeVeque

Born in Juarez, Mexico, on June 4, 1896, Edward LeVeque came from a distinctly mixed lineage: his father was a French American gentleman gambler from New Orleans; his mother was a Mexican from Chihuahua. Eddie's maternal granduncle Rito Armandariz, the acknowledged "black sheep" of the family, eked out a living touring Mexico and showing moving pictures to a curious public. At seven—with his parents' reluctant permission—Eddie joined Uncle Rito on the road, remaining with the old man until his death. By this time, Eddie was a full-blown movie fan, one who heavily favored the comedies of Mack Sennett. Determined to join the burgeoning film industry, he took a job carrying camera equipment to various battlegrounds in Mexico during the Madero revolution. Arriving in Edendale one day in 1917, he was hired as a prop boy by Keystone's Charles Avery. Eventually, the small-framed Eddie was called on to double some of the studio's actresses in stunts, such as jumping from a speeding automobile or trolley car. From there, he graduated to doing bits, and finally, he had the distinction of being one of the Keystone Cops. According to Eddie, the only direction he ever received was, "All right, boys, do what you want, do what's funny, only don't hurt yourselves." After Keystone was dissolved, LeVeque began to do bit parts (never "extra" work, he insisted) for other studios. He was honored to serve with his fellow Cops as Sennett's pallbearers upon the producer's passing in 1960. For a number of years thereafter, he made personal appearances at fairs, in nightclubs, and in parades, billed as "The Last of the Keystone Kops." Although there were those who doubted his veracity, he had affidavits regarding his authenticity from prominent Keystone players Chester Conklin and Minta Durfee. In 1961, he even purchased the rights to the police force's name for a mere two hundred dollars. An era officially ended when Eddie LeVeque passed away on January 28, 1989, at the age of ninety-two. He had been predeceased by his beloved wife, writer/artist Florence Gilbert, and was survived by a son, two daughters, and six grandchildren. He is buried alongside Florence in Hollywood Forever Cemetery (Section 8, Lot 128). Under his name, his marker proudly reads: KEYSTONE KOP.

Grover Ligon

This tall, bald, versatile Cop was also a bit player, an assistant director, a makeup man, and a stunt driver. Born Grover George Ligon in Kearney, Missouri, on February 1, 1885, he joined Keystone in 1913. His first and last film appearances were as Cops, the latter being in *Keystone Hotel* (1935). Not long after that, he turned his back on show business to manage his substantial real estate holdings. He died, aged eighty, in Hollywood, on March 3, 1965. Survived by his wife, he is entombed at Forest Lawn Memorial Park, Glendale, Court of Freedom 919-A, Map Page G35, Lawn Companion Crypt.

Del Lord

This handsome daredevil was born Delmer William Lord in Grimsby, Ontario, Canada, on October 7, 1894, and raised in Niagara Falls, New York. A natural athlete, he was both a speedboat racer and a football player. In 1913, he held the world record for the thirty-five-yard dash. In 1916, when he was in his early twenties, he began working as an extra at Keystone. Banking on his many skills, he became a stuntman, a bit player, a cameraman, and an assistant director. His particular specialty was driving the Cops' eight-foot-tall paddy wagon on the slickened streets of Eightieth and Figueroa. According to Mack Sennett, "He would sneak up on this location when the accommodating Los Angeles Police Department was looking the other way and spread a barrel of soap on the pavement. When he approached this at fifty miles per hour, slewed his wheels, and slammed on his brakes, the results were gratifying." Sennett also recalled: "The only Keystone Cops who suffered bruises and abrasions from working with Del Lord were those with faint hearts who leaped out of his careening wagons, racing automobiles, or pier-jumping contraptions ahead of time. When they stayed with Del they always lit safely." Del Lord went on to become Sennett's foremost director, turning out classic comedies from 1923-1928 and, later, from 1931-1932. He continued to stage breathtaking automobile chase scenes involving split-second timing. The most famous one can be found in the climactic second reel of *Wandering Willies*, a 1926 Billy Bevan–Andy Clyde farce that features a long string of Keystone Cops running after their speeding vehicle while holding onto one another's tailcoats.

Sennett declared bankruptcy in 1933, forcing Lord to find another occupation. While working as a used car salesman, he was approached by Jules White, head of the shorts subjects department at Columbia Pictures, to direct silent screen veterans Buster Keaton, Andy Clyde, Charley Chase, and Harry Langdon in their sound two-reelers. He also helmed some of The Three Stooges' most memorable shorts, including *Three Little Beers* (1935) and *An Ache in Every Stake* (1941), both of which feature gags, situations, and locations from the Sennett-Pathé period. In addition, he served as second-unit director on some of Frank Capra's features, including *Mr. Deeds Goes to Town* (1936). (Capra had previously written gags for Lord's comedies.) His final credited film was a 1952 industrial short starring Buster Keaton. Following his movie career, Del Lord returned to his first love, speedboat racing, winning various events with his type-51 hydroplane, *Midge*. At the age of seventy-five, on March 23, 1970, the seemingly indestructible Del Lord died, leaving a wife and son. He is interred at Olivewood Cemetery in Riverside, California, Section R, Division 1, Lot 260, Grave No. 2.

Fred Mace

This short, squat, tough-looking Irishman was a dentist in Pennsylvania, where he had been born Frederick W. Mace on August 22, 1878. After being bitten by the "acting bug," he established himself in stock, where he met Sennett. In 1911, he was at Biograph, appearing in several Sennett-directed comedy shorts. One of the original members of the Keystone company, he became its first popular comedian. Between shots, Mace sang with the Keystone Quartet, along with Roscoe Arbuckle, Charlie Murray, and Bob Albright. According to the *New York Daily Mirror* of June 30, 1915, "Mr. Mace left Keystone to make pictures for himself, but disastrous business conditions soon put an end to this. The star then assisted in the negotiations that brought about Evelyn Nesbitt Thaw's debut on the screen." He later appeared opposite Bud Duncan in the Apollo Comedies. Eventually, he focused his attentions on directing feature-length films. At the Astor Hotel in New York City, on the evening of February 21, 1917, the thirty-eight-year-old Mace suffered a major stroke and died. He is buried in New Jersey's Bordentown Cemetery, Section 7, Lot 106. Minta Durfee Arbuckle recalled that it was at Fred's recommendation that she and her husband, Roscoe, were hired by Keystone in the first place. "Mace was always looking out for other actors, trying to get them jobs," she said. "He was good to everyone but himself."

Hank Mann

Originally David W. Lieberman, he was born in Russia on May 28, 1887. David's parents immigrated to the United States in 1891, when their son was four. He later attended Morris High School in New York City, worked as a steeplejack, a sign painter, and, later still, as an acrobat on the Sullivan-Considine vaudeville circuit. In 1913, instead of walking through Keystone's front gate, he jumped the fence. Sennett, who just happened to be standing on the other side, chomping on an unlit cigar, was impressed: here was a fellow who knew how to command attention! Hired on the spot, the newly christened Hank Mann appeared at first in bits and supporting roles. When in character, he wore a push-broom-like mustache and a wig of straight bangs. And as Chester Conklin told writer Stuart Oderman, "The way he would use his eyes got laughs. He'd look like a beagle or a basset hound that was lost in the big city trying to find his way." Minta Durfee concurred: "Hank Mann had the camera *listen*, if you can understand my choice of word. It was something he knew wouldn't be done if he were front and center on the screen. He'd make a small gesture, a slight wave of the hand, and he'd take the scene away." In 1914, he defected to Universal, where he appeared in the Sterling Comedies and then Henry Lehrman's L-KO Comedies. Following a brief return to Keystone, he acted and directed in a number of Foxfilm Comedies. After serving in World War I, he returned to Sennett in 1918. From 1919–1920, he starred in his eponymous Hank Mann Comedies, which were produced by Morris Schlank and released by Arrow; this marked the highlight of his career as a two-reel comedian. His best features were those starring his fellow Keystone alum Charlie Chaplin, particularly *City Lights* (1931), in which Hank is Charlie's opponent in a hilariously choreographed boxing match. Appearing in small roles in an estimated five hundred pictures, Hank's familiar visage also added immeasurably to Hollywood films celebrating their own heritage. One of these was the Lon Chaney biopic, *Man of a Thousand Faces* (1957), in which Hank and Snub Pollard play Keystone-type chefs who engage in an on-set pie fight. James Cagney's most vivid memory of starring in that film was how impressed he was with the complete professionalism of these accomplished farceurs. When Hollywood stopped calling, Hank became the owner of a number of apartment buildings in Los Angeles; he also operated a malt shop in Sierra Madre, California. On November 25, 1971, he died in a convalescent center at the age of eighty-four. He was survived by his third wife and his daughter (by his second wife, who had died in 1948). He is interred at Hollywood Forever Cemetery, New Beth Olam, Corridor T-J-11, Crypt No. 7672.

Rube Miller

An aerialist with the Ringling Bros. beginning at the incredibly young age of six, Harry Carl Miller (born in Trotwood, Ohio, on January 27, 1887) seemed destined to become a Keystone Cop the moment he was old enough to drive to Edendale. He had other things to offer the Sennett company as well: he had been what was known as a "producing clown" with lesser-known circuses for eight years and had a distinctively odd face that only a camera could love. These traits and skills, along with the requisite ability to take dangerous-looking falls and still be able to get back up again, made him the perfect stuntman and, eventually, an ideal Cop. Indeed, he was one of the first, having joined the Keystone Film Company in its maiden year of operation, 1912. A restless soul, he departed Keystone just two years later and became a director (and occasional actor) in the Ham & Bud (Lloyd Hamilton & Bud Duncan) films for Kalem. He continued to work in that capacity at Vogue, megaphoning some of the Ben Turpin comedies, and from there went to L-KO. In 1919, he may have reached his creative peak by assisting Roscoe Arbuckle in the production of his brilliant Comique two-reelers, co-starring Buster Keaton and Al St. John. Miller's greatest contribution to that company may easily have been his ability with a bat and a ball, playing on Arbuckle's minor-league baseball team, the Vernon Tigers. Following this, there were notices in the trades that Miller was preparing to go into production with some ingénue or other, but no further work in motion pictures was credited. In 1929, however, there was a mention of a Rube Miller performing a comedic slack wire-walking act, as well as in a short-lived Wild West show, but neither of these appearances can be confirmed. The same can be said about his supposed involvement in Keystone Hotel, but his presence has not been detected by any Keystone expert thus far. Rube Miller died on January 1, 1944, at the age of fifty-three. He is interred at a cemetery in his hometown of Trotwood, Ohio.

Charlie Murray

One of eight children, Charles Murray was born in Laurel, Indiana, on June 22, 1872.

His first taste of show business was working for circuses and medicine shows; this was followed by appearances on stage. As half of various vaudeville comedy teams, he trod the boards for nearly two decades. Six feet tall, with red hair and light gray eyes, the forty-year-old Murray was an elder statesman when he officially joined the Keystone Film Company in 1912. According to Minta Durfee Arbuckle, "Charlie Murray was older than [the rest of] us, and we looked up to him like a father to listen to our problems." In addition to being a Keystone Cop, Murray developed his own character, that of a hard-drinking Irish laborer. His makeup and costume of choice included modified chin whiskers and a conductor's cap worn slightly off-center. From 1914 to 1921 (and, later, as a freelancer between 1924 and 1932), Murray was one of Sennett's top comedians, in both short subjects and features. He made films for other companies, including Universal, where he was teamed with George Sidney in *The Cohens and Kellys* (1926), a comedy revolving around two families, one Irish, the other Jewish. It proved so popular that it inspired a series. On July 29, 1941, Charlie Murray died in Hollywood of pneumonia; he was sixty-nine years old. Survived by his wife and daughter, he is entombed in the Inglewood Park Cemetery Mausoleum, Crypt No. 2230.

Charles Parrott

Born in Baltimore, Maryland, on October 20, 1893, Charley appeared in vaudeville and burlesque as a comic/dancer/singer/musician. He also had a part in at least one Broadway play before venturing west in 1912. After a stint with comedy producer Al Christie, he joined the much less subdued Sennett lot, where the unofficial slogan was, "You don't have to be crazy to work here, but it helps." Although it is uncertain if Parrott was ever a Keystone Cop, his biographers Brian Anthony and Andy Edmonds (*Smile When the Raindrops Fall*, Scarecrow Press, 1998) speculate that "he probably did don the uniform when reinforcements were needed." His roles at Keystone did not fall under the category of "grotesques" (as did those of Mack Swain and Chester Conklin, to cite but two examples); instead, he played handsome juvenile leads, particularly in films co-starring Fritz Schade and Mae Busch. One such title, *A Hash House Fraud* (1915), in which the Cops make an appearance in the final few minutes, was directed by him. Parrott left Keystone for FoxFilm, where he directed a series of shorts starring Lee Morris and original Cop Hank Mann. In 1921 he signed with Hal Roach, again as a director, this time for Snub Pollard. At Roach's behest, Parrott briefly assumed the character name Jimmy Jump and appeared in some shorts in 1924. He finally achieved success, only under a different name—Charley Chase. Transitioning well into sound films, Chase continued to work for Roach and was later hired as an actor/director for the Columbia shorts department. Sadly, Chase suffered from acute alcoholism. He was informed by his doctor that he had a choice to make—either stop drinking altogether or die. Unwilling (or unable) to stop, he passed away at the age of forty-six. He was survived by his wife and their two daughters. His brother James Parrott, a former comedian and director for Hal Roach, had predeceased him by thirteen months; like Charley, he was plagued by problems involving addiction. Both of the Chase brothers are interred at Forest Lawn Memorial Park, Glendale. Charley's grave is located on Sunrise Slope, Lot 147.

Fritz Schade

Born in Dresden, Germany, on January 19, 1879, this short (five foot tall) and solid (193 pounds), blond-haired, blue-eyed player first came to America to sing with the Olympia Opera Company on the West Coast. Turning to silent films, he worked for Al Christie at Universal before joining Mack Sennett's Fun Factory in 1913. During the next four years, "Keystone Fritz" was cast in a number of slapstick one- and two-reelers as comic leads and fierce rivals. Two of his regular co-stars were juvenile lead Charles Parrott and female firebrand Mae Busch. An excellent surviving example of their teamwork is on display in 1915's *For Better—But Worse*, in which Schade pompously struts around as the chief of the Keystone Cops. Joining the list of other injured Keystone players, Fritz broke his arm while filming a scene in 1916. It was a separate injury, though, one involving his leg, that led the portly comic to retire from performing altogether. On June 17, 1926, while undergoing surgery at Los Angeles's Methodist Hospital to remove a cyst on his brain, Fritz Schade died; he was forty-six. Survived by his wife of eleven years, he is interred at Evergreen Cemetery in Los Angeles.

Mack Sennett

The man who made the Keystone Cops and the Bathing Beauties household names was born Michael Sinnott in Danville, Quebec, Canada, on January 17, 1880. An ironworker, laboring for fifteen cents an hour (or nine dollars a week), he changed his name to Sennett because he thought *Sinnott* sounded too much like the vulgar word *snot*. After an unsuccessful attempt at becoming a singer on the legitimate stage, he took a job in silent movies with the American Biograph Company in New York City in 1908. No more gifted as a comic actor than a serious singer, Sennett took what supporting roles he was offered. Standing an impressive six-one, and weighing in at 210 pounds, he had dirty blond hair and long arms that (in his words) "almost touched the floor, even when standing erect." Mentored by the great D. W. Griffith, and as dedicated to slapstick as Griffith was to drama, Sennett received the needed financial backing of producers Adam Kessel and Charles Baumann to form the Keystone Film Company in Edendale, California, the first movie studio to produce only comedies. On screen, he specialized in playing oafish hicks opposite his on- and (for a while, at least) off-screen love, Mabel Normand. On occasion, he also filled in as a Cop. The concept of making fools out of authority figures like police officers had long been an obsession of his. He once described the essence of comedy as the "unseating of dignity." Although admired by the moviegoing public, there were those in the industry—particularly Griffith actress Lillian Gish—who felt "that Sennett will be a bad influence on children by seeing law enforcement as a subject for ridicule." Another dissenting voice belonged to one of his own discoveries, Gloria Swanson, who said of her one-time boss: "He was a penny-pinching, uneducated, vulgar man who constantly chewed tobacco and thought absolutely nothing about spitting it out, in any direction, and not giving a thought if you were in his way." But these rather haughty women were in the minority. When Mack Sennett died on November 5, 1960, at the age of eighty, his marker, located in Holy Cross Cemetery in Culver City, Section N, Lot 490, was engraved with the following words:

Mack Sennett
1880 † 1960
Beloved King of Comedy

Dick Smith

Born in Cleveland, Ohio, on September 17, 1886, actor/director/screenwriter Hiram Richard Smith began his eclectic career as a comedian in both vaudeville and burlesque. In 1910, he met and married the frouzy-haired comedienne Alice Howell when they were both appearing in a DeWolf Hopper production. The couple formed a two-act called Howell and Howell, a billing that was certainly more distinctive than Smith and Smith. Dick Smith, as he was known to movie industry insiders, was reportedly one of Mack Sennett's colleagues at the Biograph studio in New York City. Diagnosed with tuberculosis, Dick relocated with Alice to the much warmer Los Angeles, where they worked at Keystone in 1914. Dick was a Cop in *An Incompetent Hero* and *The Noise of Bombs*, and a customer in a restaurant scene in *Tillie's Punctured Romance*. The Smiths left Sennett for L-KO, where Dick and Alice had featured roles in some Keystone knockoffs. Dick also directed his first film for L-KO, the two-reel comedy *That Dawgone Dog*, starring vaudevillian Sammy Burns, in 1917. In 1920, Dick and Alice formed their own studio in Chicago, the Emerald Motion Picture Company, which soon merged into Reelcraft. When that concern went bankrupt, the couple pursued separate opportunities. It was during this period that Dick directed what would be his most discussed (if never seen) two-reeler, *Humor Risk* (1921), the infamously lost Marx Brothers' screen debut. At Universal, he was back to directing Alice, this time in a series that hit its mark with moviegoers in the more rural areas of the United States. Kalton C. Lahue and Sam Gill, in their book *Clown Princes and Court Jesters*, describe these collaborations as "some of the most memorable Universal comedies of the twenties." Dick Smith continued to direct, act, and began to write screenplays for a series called The Collegians. By decade's end, it is possible that his precarious health forced him into early retirement and may even have contributed to his untimely death, at age fifty, on February 7, 1937, in Los Angeles. Alice Howell, who left films in 1933 to manage her real estate holdings, died in 1961 at the age of seventy-two. Her surviving comedies have gained a select following in recent years.

Al St. John

Although his uncle Roscoe Arbuckle wanted to keep him out of the movies, Minta (Roscoe's wife) personally arranged a meeting with Mack Sennett to witness the acrobatic young man's prowess as a trick bicycle rider. Al was hired on the spot in 1913 (evidently, the demonstration was a success). Alfred St. John, born in Santa Ana, California, on September 10, 1892, was an unusual-looking man—five-eight, 140 pounds, splay-footed, and with large, bugged-out eyes. He was also perfectly suited to be a Keystone Cop: no stunt, it seemed, was too dangerous for him. When Arbuckle left Keystone to make his own comedies for his own production company, Comique, Al went with him. His onscreen persona became that of a "hick" character. His regular outfit became high-water, suspendered pants, extra-long shoes that curled up at the toes, a brimless hat, and a plaid shirt. Al was one-third of a comic ensemble with Arbuckle and Buster Keaton (one-fourth, if you count Minta's talented dog, Luke). Though never a star, he did have his own series of silent two-reelers (such as *The Iron Mule*, a satire on the John Ford–directed *The Iron Horse*) and helmed his own comedies for Fox Sunshine. His sound films were generally for such Poverty Row studios as Producers Releasing Company (PRC)—and almost always B-Westerns, in which he routinely portrayed a comic sidekick named "Fuzzy" Q. Jones, complete with chin whiskers. While visiting Lyons, Georgia, on a personal appearance tour on January 21, 1963, the seventy-year-old retired actor died of a heart attack in his wife's arms. His body was cremated, specifically at Vidalia, Georgia, and the ashes shipped to Double F Ranch, Homosassa Springs, Florida.

Ford Sterling

The actor best remembered as chief of the Keystone Cops was born in La Crosse, Wisconsin, in either 1880 or 1882. His diverse career included a stint as a boy clown in a circus, a vaudevillian acrobat, a dialectician, and, for a time, the world's most famous film comedian. Into the 1930s, Ford Sterling was still working, but poor health led to his early retirement in his mid-fifties. He passed away after having been hospitalized for sixteen weeks, during which time one of his legs was amputated. In a mausoleum at Hollywood Forever Cemetery, Colonnade 2, South Wall, "Dawn" community niche, a large bronze tablet reads:

FORD STERLING
(George Ford Stich, Jr.)
November 3, 1882–October 13, 1939
STAR OF THE SILENT SCREEN
ACTOR • COMEDIAN
KEYSTONE COP

Slim Summerville

A movie critic in the 1930s said that Bette Davis "has all the sex appeal of Slim Summerville." It was hardly meant as a compliment. George Summerville, born June 10, 1892, in Albuquerque, New Mexico, grew to be six-two, tipped the scales at only 164 pounds, had a large, bulbous nose and a gangly physique. A young runaway, he lived a nomadic existence until meeting Mack Sennett via

his friend Edgar Kennedy. "Slim"—his apt nickname—used his homeliness to comic advantage, beginning with Keystone in 1914. One of the most recognizable of the original Cops, he left Sennett in 1918 for Fox Sunshine Comedies. Around this time his interests shifted to behind-the-scenes work, leading him to direct other comics. He eventually returned to acting, bringing to life the comic-strip character Andy Gump. He also had some meatier roles, including one (in comic partnership with former Cop Mack Swain) in *The Beloved Rogue* (United Artists, 1927), starring "The Great Profile" John Barrymore. He scored a critical hit as Tjaden, a dramatic role, in *All Quiet on the Western Front* (Universal, 1930). He was also teamed with the equally gangly ZaSu Pitts in a number of popular comedy features for Hal Roach. A resident of Laguna Beach, California, he owned and managed an apartment building. On January 5, 1946, George "Slim" Summerville died, aged fifty-three, of a stroke. Survived by his second wife and a son, he is interred at Inglewood Park Cemetery, Utopia Plot, Lot 217, Division C.

Mack Swain

Known on the better vaudeville circuits as a surefire laugh-getter from the age of fifteen, Moroni "Mack" Swain (born in Salt Lake City, Utah, on February 16, 1876) and his comic partner, Knute Erickson, laid them in the aisles for six years. He later joined a West Coast stock company, where he met his future wife, actress Cora King. At one point, he even led his own stock company. Joining Keystone in 1913, Swain created a highly distinctive, if grotesque, appearance by wearing a wide mustache, heavily made-up eyes, and a straight spit of hair (one of the few he had left) down the middle of his forehead. This new Keystone Cop was also as tall as he was wide. Frank Capra, one of Sennett's gag writers in the twenties, told Stuart Oderman: "Mack Swain was the most visually arresting Mack Sennett player, but I doubt if anyone could identify him by name [today], the way they could identify Charlie [Chaplin]. Charlie was never a Keystone Cop in the ensemble way that Swain was." Eventually serving as a convincing bully in Chaplin's one- and two-reelers, he also co-starred with Chester Conklin in their own series. Mack's signature character, Ambrose, an eternally henpecked husband, and the lascivious Walrus (Conklin) proved especially popular with moviegoers. A supposed blacklisting by a well-known producer has been given as the reason for Mack Swain's absence from the big screen for a number of years. He was finally given a chance by his former co-star Charlie Chaplin when he was cast as Big Jim in *The Gold Rush* (United Artists, 1925). This solid performance in that epic film led to his being hired for other features, supporting such superstars as Greta Garbo (*The Torrent*), John Barrymore (*The Beloved Rogue*), and Mary Pickford (*My Best Girl*). When sound arrived, Mack Swain was nominated for an Academy Award for his performance in *Stout Hearts and Willing Hands* (1931), which featured a reunion of (mostly) original Keystone Cops. While traveling from Chicago to Hollywood, he was stricken during a stopover in Tacoma, Washington. On August 25, 1935, the fifty-nine-year-old was pronounced dead, a victim of an internal hemorrhage. He is buried in Huntsville, Columbia County, Washington State.

Josef R. Swickard

Born on June 26, 1886, in Coblenz, Germany, Josef's family immigrated to the U.S. in 1902. After more than fifteen years of stage experience, he signed with Keystone in 1912. One of the very first Cops, he even took a turn as the chief. After a brief initial stint with Keystone, he worked at Thanhouser and Majestic. He returned to the fold in 1914 and remained in Edendale for three additional years. In 1917, he had a major supporting role in Frank Lloyd's adaptation of Dickens's *A Tale of Two Cities*, made for Fox and starring William Farnum. The twenties saw Swickard as a major character actor. His credits included *The Four Horsemen of the Apocalypse* (Metro, 1921), in which he played Julio's (Rudolph Valentino's) father; *Don Juan* (Warner Bros., 1926), wherein he essayed the role of Duke Della Varnese; and *The Wizard of Oz* (Chadwick, 1925), in which he played Prime Minister Kruel. Less featured in the early sound era, his final onscreen appearance was a bit part in Frank Capra's *You Can't Take it with You* (Columbia, 1938). Josef Swickard died on March 1, 1940, aged seventy-three, from natural causes. He is interred at Hollywood Forever Cemetery, Section 1, Grave 440.

Arthur Tavares

Born Arturo Tavares in San Francisco, California, on January 10, 1884, this dark-featured photoplayer was one of the first Keystone Cops, appearing opposite his boss, Mack Sennett, in *The Stolen Purse* (1913). Within a year's time he had left Sennett for Universal, where he became a member of the Sterling Comedies unit. Then on to Essanay for a brief run before appearing in the Vogue Comedies in support of former Cop Rube Miller. Often typecast as Spaniards, Tavares acted in a number of feature films in the mid-teens. But acting was apparently not his true calling—*editing* was. On staff at First National, Tavares demonstrated his proficiency in cutting together pictures featuring such heavyweights as Corinne Griffith, Colleen Moore, and Milton Sills. In the late twenties he returned to his first employer and set about editing the feature-length Sennett comedy, *The Good-Bye Kiss*. (For whatever reason, the job was taken over by William Hornbeck.) The crowning glory of Tavares's editing career was Universal's Spanish-speaking version of *Dracula* (1931), which was filmed on the same impressive sets as the English-speaking company, only at night. In a mysterious downturn in his career, Tavares is listed as one of the extras in Sennett's final film, the seedy *Hypnotized*, in 1935. At least his final credit, as an editor on Paul Robeson's *The Song of Freedom* (1936) was one of prestige. But by the time his obituary appeared in late May of 1954, seventy-year-old Arturo Tavarez had been all but forgotten by the film industry.

And the Honorary Keystone Cops Are:

Billy Bevan

This brush-wearing comic began his career on stage in Orange City, South Wales, Australia, where he was born William Bevan Harris on September 29, 1887. In 1912, he immigrated to America—specifically Southern California—where he landed some supporting film roles for L-KO, Universal, and Christie. But it would be his ten years (1919–1929) with Mack Sennett that solidified him as a bankable comic, so much so that he was given his own series in 1921. These two-reelers, helmed by such expert comedy directors as Del Lord, Harry Edwards, Roy Del Ruth, and F. Richard Jones, are lightning paced and

full of gags. Indeed, many stock gags later used by Laurel & Hardy (two men, in this case Billy and Andy Clyde, carry a bulky object up a long flight of stairs), Curly Howard and Lou Costello (one man doing battle with a live oyster in a bowl of chowder), and Buster Keaton (an innocent man being chased by an army of policemen) were introduced by Billy. He did appear as a bungling officer in some Sennett offerings, but he worked alone, *not* in conjunction with a group. Still, that wonderfully expressive mustache of his stamped him as a pie-throwing Keystone Cop type, whether it was true or not. When sound entered the picture (literally), he became a dependable character actor (usually playing Cockney roles) in light comedies, horror films, and straight dramas. After retiring from acting in 1952, he devoted himself to his true passion: tending an avocado grove. He even took a class in citrus culture at the University of California at San Diego. Billy Bevan died, aged seventy, on November 26, 1957. He is interred in Oak Hill Cemetery in his adopted town of Escondido, California, Section 5, Lot 4, Grave 4.

Billy Bletcher

When eighty-four-year-old William Bletcher was laid to rest in the Rose Garden Plot of Los Angeles's Westwood Memorial Park in January 1979, he was leaving behind a show business career spanning nearly sixty years. Born in Pennsylvania on September 24, 1894, Billy would go on to become a dependable, if little-known, comic actor. In 1913, he received his first break at the Vitagraph Studio in Brooklyn, New York, as an actor and assistant director; in fact, as he later told Sam Gill: "I did anything that anyone wanted done." In early 1916, he and his wife relocated to Jacksonville, Florida, where he played supporting roles in the Vim Comedies and later for the Christie Brothers. It has also been said that Billy worked for Sennett between 1917 and 1918, although no titles have been verified. "I usually played character parts of old men with big beards and moustaches," he recalled, "—often a father or uncle comedy role." It was while wearing one of his impossibly long beards (and a not-quite-convincing bald cap) that he made his most memorable film appearance, as a patient/victim of *The Dentist* (1932), starring W. C. Fields, produced by Sennett and directed by Leslie Pearce. In the succeeding years, Billy participated in various Keystone Cop reunions and, in a particularly noteworthy turn, portrayed both a typical mustachioed Cop and a Ford Sterling lookalike in a 1968 Shasta Root Beer commercial. Accepting every acting offer that came his way, from voice-over work for Walt Disney and Warner Bros. to innumerable unbilled appearances in movies and on television, Billy was, you might say, still "doing anything that anyone wanted done."

Andy Clyde

It is fellow Scotsman James Finlayson who deserves the credit for bringing Andrew Clyde to the United States. Andy, who was born in Blairgowrie, Scotland, on March 25, 1892, was hardly an original Cop, but his likeable presence nevertheless earns him an honorary place in this section. Signing with Sennett in 1921, he soon proved a godsend to the cost-conscious producer. Andy's proficiency with makeup could transform him into just about any sort of character (unshaven tramps, bosses, professors, crazed scientists, eccentric kings, and, most of all, bewhiskered old men), allowing him to play multiple roles in the same film. He was also generous with his time and talent when helping his fellow players with their makeup. This, along with the fact that he was a kind and naturally funny individual, made him Mack Sennett's personal favorite among his many employees. For a time in the mid-twenties, Andy and leading Sennett comic Billy Bevan were teamed in a series of memorable two-reelers directed by Del Lord. Andy's rather tenuous connection to the Keystone Cops first came when he played a vice cop in the 1923 two-reeler *Nip and Tuck*, and (more interestingly) in the 1927 Sennett short *Love in a Police Station*, wherein Andy played the chief, à la Ford Sterling. In the sound era, the rustic Andy Clyde Columbia short subjects proved popular enough to keep the series going for twenty-two consecutive years, a record bested only by The Three Stooges (whose series lasted two years longer). In 1954, a noticeably older Andy donned the trademark Cop uniform once again, this time to perform a careful chase routine with a handful of other aging Sennett players as a tribute to their former boss on an episode of Ralph Edwards's *This is Your Life*. Andy served as the spokesman for the group, and his affection for Sennett and his old cronies was evident to all. He died on May 18, 1967, aged seventy-five, of a heart attack.

His place of interment is Forest Lawn Memorial Park, Glendale, Whispering Pines, Lot 102.

Pinto Colvig

This one-time Sennett animator later took part in the Keystone Cops reunions in the early 1960s. Born in Jacksonville, Oregon, on September 11, 1892, Vance DeBar Colvig sporadically attended Oregon State University in Corvallis from 1910 to 1913. After marrying, he relocated to San Francisco, where he worked as a newspaper cartoonist and as an artist and gagman at Animated Film Corp. It was there that he worked alongside Walter Lantz, the future creator of Woody Woodpecker. Both Lantz and Colvig worked as gagmen, animators, and title writers for Mack Sennett beginning in 1927. The early thirties saw Pinto (as he called himself) at the Walt Disney Studios, where he originated the voices for two cartoon canines, Pluto and Goofy. After a falling out with Disney, Pinto found work with Max Fleischer, for whom he voiced Popeye's burly nemesis, Bluto. He also lent his prodigious vocal talents to such radio programs as Jack Benny's, providing the vocal sound effects of the parsimonious star's Maxwell automobile, prior to Mel Blanc. In 1946, Capitol Records cast Pinto as Bozo the Clown, making him the first actor to play that immensely popular children's show character; he continued doing so for the next decade. Vance "Pinto" Colvig Sr. died, aged seventy-five, of lung cancer at the Motion Picture Country Hospital in Woodland Hills, California; he is buried in Culver City's Holy Cross Cemetery.

Charles "Heinie" Conklin

July 16, 1880 was the birthdate of this familiar-looking Cop, and San Francisco, California his place of birth. When in character as a latter-day Keystone Cop, he wore what has been described as a "Kaiser Wilhelm mustache worn upside-down," earning him the nickname "Heinie." Before entering films in 1913, he spent fifteen years on stage in stock, and in vaudeville with the prestigious Keith-Orpheum circuit. He made his mark at Keystone-Triangle from 1918 to 1919, teamed with Ben Turpin. Charles Conklin was in no way related to the better-known bearer of that surname, Chester Conklin. To avoid confusion, Charles temporarily went by the last name of Lynn. In the late forties and early fifties, Heinie was among the more recognizable Sennett veterans participating in various Keystone Cop reunions, both onscreen and onstage. On July 30, 1959, he died, aged seventy-nine. He was survived by two sons and a daughter. Charles Conklin's cremains are inurned at Chapel of the Pines Crematory, Los Angeles.

Jimmy Finlayson

The Scotland-born James Henderson Finlayson, who achieved cult-like status (albeit posthumously) as the foil for the team of Stan Laurel & Oliver Hardy, was born on August 27, 1887. When talkies came in, his thick Scottish brogue and the utter exasperation of his trademark "*D'oh!*" (later appropriated by voice actor Dan Castellaneta as Homer Simpson on the long-running Fox network cartoon series) endeared him to Laurel & Hardy aficionados, who affectionately refer to him as "Fin." Although he first joined Mack Sennett's stock company in 1918 (after having worked for Thomas Ince and L-KO), he was dissatisfied with his nondescript, secondary roles there and, in 1922, left for Metro, where he worked with Stan Laurel for the first time. When Stan was teamed with Oliver Hardy at the Hal Roach Studios in 1927, Fin was often cast as their squinty-eyed adversary, and always with hilarious results. Yet when the sixty-six-year-old died in his sleep on October 9, 1953, his nationally published obituary stressed his involvement as an "original Keystone Kop." His contribution to that fraternity did not actually begin until the early sound era, when he found himself in uniform in the nostalgic two-reeler *Stout Hearts and Willing Hands* (1931). He also appeared as a Keystone Cop in *Hollywood Cavalcade* (1939) and participated in Sennett tributes until the time of his death. James Finlayson's cremains are inurned at Chapel of the Pines Cemetery, Los Angeles.

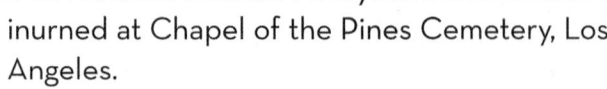

Tom Kennedy

No relation to the better known Edgar Kennedy, Thomas Kennedy was born in New York City on July 15, 1885. Like Edgar, Tom was a pugilist before entering films, and his imposing frame (over six feet tall, 210 pounds, with a nose that looked like it had been broken more than once in the ring), made him a perfect casting choice for rather dimwitted authority figures. His prior experience with show business came when he temporarily stepped in for heavyweight champion Jack Johnson's injured sparring partner in a vaudeville exhibition. When he arrived in California in 1915, Tom was hired as Douglas Fairbanks's trainer, which led to his appearance in the Fairbanks feature *Double Trouble*. His next stop was Keystone, where he stayed for four years. Even during this hectic period in his life, he kept his hand in the world of boxing, managing and training young fighters. Like many of Sennett's underpaid employees, he defected to Fox Sunshine and never looked back. Working steadily for several companies throughout the remainder of the silent era, he effortlessly made the transition to talkies, still playing dumb cops, prize fighters, and laborers. In the late forties and early fifties, he turned up in several of the Bowery Boys movies, filmed at the Poverty Row studio Monogram (which Bowery Boy Huntz Hall liked to refer to as "MGM spelled backward"). Tom's final film appearance, appropriately enough, was as an overzealous traffic cop in Stanley Kramer's *It's a Mad, Mad, Mad, Mad World* (1963). Married with three children, Kennedy died two years later, on October 6, 1965, at the Motion Picture and Television Country House and Hospital in Woodland Hills, a victim of bone cancer; he was survived by his wife and their three children. Although his turn with the Cops was limited to latter-day tributes and reunions, it was this connection that was stressed in his obituary. Tom Kennedy is interred at Hollywood Forever Cemetery, Abbey of the Psalms, Corridor B, Crypt 345.

Marvin Loback

A rotund, menacing-looking fellow who played his share of bullies and the occasional Keystone Cop, Oscar Marvin Loback was born in Tacoma, Washington, on November 21, 1895. In 1917, he worked at L-KO, and for Rolin in 1918. The following year, he was hired by Sennett. When the producer needed a fat guy, particularly in the post-Arbuckle era, he turned to Loback. The actor was no doubt grateful for the work, and always turned in a convincing performance, whether he was playing a good guy or a bad one. Teamed for a time with Snub Pollard by the studio-less Weiss Bros. Artclass comedy company, the two second-tier comics blatantly recreated some of Laurel & Hardy's routines, without the panache of the originals, of course. Sound didn't hurt Loback's career a bit. He had supporting roles at Columbia's Three Stooges and Andy Clyde shorts in the thirties; he also appeared in features, including *Hallelujah! I'm a Bum*

(1933), featuring Sennett graduate Harry Langdon, and *The Old-Fashioned Way* (1934), a starring vehicle for an even more recent Sennett veteran, W. C. Fields. Marvin Loback's career was cut short by his untimely death, on August 18, 1938, at the age of forty-two; he was survived by his wife. His body is interred at Hollywood Forever Cemetery, Section 2West, Grave 115 A.

Snub Pollard

Snub, whose real name was Harry Fraser, was born in Melbourne, Australia, on November 9, 1889. Immigrating to America, he attained his reputation as a dependable second banana in a series of Hal Roach one-reelers starring Harold Lloyd and Bebe Daniels, made between the mid- to-late teens. When Daniels was hired away by Cecil B. DeMille, and Lloyd began starring in his own shorts and features, Pollard was given his own series as well. The films in this series—many of which were directed by the great Charley Chase—had more than a hint of surrealism, and those which have survived still hold up beautifully. One 1923 short, *It's a Gift*, is certainly the most famous of his imaginative films. In it, he is Professor Pollard, inventor of a number of labor- and gas-saving devices, who also builds a strange-looking car that resembles a bullet. Seated in the single-seated vehicle, he uses an oversized magnet to follow whatever gas-run vehicle happens to be in front of him. It's a brilliant short, with typically witty titles by H. M. "Beanie" Walker and is known to silent comedy aficionados of every stripe. When sound came in and physical comedy went into decline, Snub began showing up in cameos for only the lowest-budget films, still wearing the long, pasted-on mustache associated with the "old-time" comics. As the years went by and more and more authentic Cops either retired or passed on, the still-working (though noticeably frailer) Snub Pollard would show up, often taking part in projects needing veteran Sennett players. In the early forties, he co-starred with perennial Cops Chester Conklin and Hank Mann in stage revues. He also played bit parts in countless films, *sans* his signature mustache. To cite just a few examples of his walk-ons from the early fifties, he is an uncredited stagehand in the film adaptation of Clifford Odets's play *The Country Girl* (1954); in *The Day the Earth Stood Still* (1951), he is a concerned (and, again, uncredited) family man listening intently to the car radio as the on-air reporter relates the incredible fact that a space ship has landed in the nation's capital; and he is the pedestrian to whom Gene Kelly hands over his umbrella in *Singin' in the Rain* (1952). In 1961, he had a brief walk-on in the Jerry Lewis–directed *The Errand Boy*, which takes place at a movie studio. At one point, Jerry is walking on the lot when he recognizes an old friend: "Hi, Snub!" he calls out. Pollard's last acting role was as a background extra on an episode of the popular Western television show *The Rifleman*. Johnny Crawford, who played the lead character's son Mark, always favored the antiquarian aspects of popular culture. Knowing exactly who Snub Pollard was, he asked him for an autographed picture. Snub, no doubt flattered by the young actor's attention, promised to bring one to the set. Sadly, he was unable to keep his word. He suffered a heart attack and died at the Magnolia Park Hospital in Burbank, California, on January 19, 1962, at the age of seventy-two. This gentle soul is buried at Forest Lawn Memorial Park, Hollywood Hills, on the Sheltering Hills, Lot 54.

Tiny Ward

When Mack Sennett resurrected the Keystone Cops for the 1927 two-reel homage *Love in a Police Station*, he cast this gentle giant in the role of original Cop Mack Swain. Ironically nicknamed "Tiny," Roscoe Samuel Ward stood a reported six-seven (or seven-six, if you believe the hype put out by one studio). He was born in Indian Point Township, Illinois, on January 2, 1883, and grew up on a farm in nearby Knox County. Attending military school and, later, Wesleyan University in Nebraska, he was a standout, not just due to his size, but for his ability to play football. He made his film debut in Charlie Chaplin's 1918 World War I comedy *Shoulder Arms*, in which he played a tall German officer standing in a trench. While working, on and off, for Mack Sennett's company between 1920 and 1932, during which he made an imposing figure in comedies featuring Harry Langdon and Ben Turpin, he moonlighted in shorts for Rolin, Bull's Eye, Century, Fox, and Bray, and in features starring Lon Chaney (*West of Zanzibar*, MGM, 1928) and Chaplin (*City Lights*, United Artists, 1931, pictured). In the sound era, he menaced the small-statured Three Stooges and El Brendel in a handful of their Columbia shorts, and made himself known in the Hal Roach series Taxi Boys, which starred Billy Gilbert and Ben Blue. In 1950, he made a memorable network television appearance with fellow Cops Chester Conklin, Heinie Conklin, Hank Mann, and Snub Pollard on Ed Wynn's variety program. Special guest star Buster Keaton smacked each of the Cops in the face with a pie, eliciting much laughter and applause from the studio audience. Like Chester Conklin, Ward was a department store Santa Claus in Los Angeles for a number of years following his film career. He died of a heart attack on September 12, 1956, at the age of sixty-three, and was survived by his wife. Roscoe "Tiny" Ward is buried in Abingdon Cemetery in his home state of Illinois.

Obituaries

For innumerable silent film actors, regardless of what they went on to accomplish in their careers (becoming a dramatic actor, a respected director, or even a successful businessman), the crux of their obituaries was always: "[Name], one-time Keystone Kop, has died." And beginning in the early seventies, there seemed to be a competition as to who the "last" Kop was.

Ford Sterling, One Time Film Comedian, Is Dead

Hollywood, Cal., Oct. 13 (AP).—Ford Sterling, 55 years old, one of motion picture's early day comedians, died tonight. He had been ill several months and physicians were forced to amputate his left leg last August. Cause of death was given as thrombosis. Teddy Sampson, his actress-wife, was at his bedside. Sterling, one of the original Mack Sennett Keystone Kops, was born at La Crosse, Wis. When a boy he ran away and joined a circus. Later he played in vaudeville and in musical comedies. He joined Sennett and Mabel Normand in organizing the Keystone comedies.

Ford Sterling (Chicago Tribune, Oct. 14, 1939)

Charley Chase, Keystone Kop of Other Days, Dies at 47

Veteran Comedian of Vaudeville and Screen Stopped on Way to Comeback as Director

Death stepped in yesterday to halt the comeback of Charley Chase, 47, veteran comedian of vaudeville and screen, writer and director, who was well on the road back to public favor from after appearances on the vaudeville stage in the East.

Born in Baltimore as Charles Parrott, he at first used that name in pictures, even after he was starring in Hal Roach comedies.

After leaving the Sennett lot he was under contract to Roach for 17 years. He was a contemporary of Harold Lloyd.

PERSONAL APPEARANCES

Later Chase became a writer and director for the studio and for several years had been making personal appearance tours in the East before he returned to begin the new series of comedies.

Chase leaves his widow, known professionally as Bebe Eltinge, and two daughters, Mrs. James Preshaw and Mrs. Donald Hargis, both of Hollywood.

Funeral arrangements, which will be in charge of the Pierce Brothers Mortuary, will be announced later.

Charley Chase

the obscurity into which talking films had thrust him.

Chase, whose two-reel comedies convulsed audiences in the days of silent films, died from a heart ailment in his home at 2157 N. Highland Ave.

He had completed four short comedies for Columbia studios since the first of the year and was scheduled to continue the series, the fifth of which was in preparation.

IN DECLINING HEALTH

He had been in declining health for several months, studio associates said, but his death came as a shock even to Del Lord, his producer, who was one of his closest friends.

With Lord, he was a member of the famous Keystone Kops in the Mack Sennett studio in 1914. He had come to Hollywood

Los Angeles Times 6/21/40

Charley Chase (Los Angeles Times, June 21, 1940)

"Slim" Summerville, Movie Comic, Dead

Hollywood, (AP)—George J. (Slim) Summerville, 51, one of the movies' top comics and character actors, died Saturday night at his home after suffering two strokes.

Confined to bed for several days on his doctor's orders, Summerville had shown a slight improvement just before his death.

He had appeared in few pictures recently. "Life's too short," he once explained, "to work all the time." All he wanted out of the movies was "just enough to cover expenses and let me get in some fishing."

"Slim," born Summerville, came to Los Angeles when he was 18. There wasn't much about the six-foot, two-inch skinny kid then to indicate he would die famous. But the boy must have had something. Edgar Kennedy saw it. Kennedy was playing bit parts in Mack Sennett's "Keystone Kop" comedies and "Slim" was a pool room porter, the only job he could get when he hit town hungry and broke. Kennedy liked the gangling kid and got him a job with Sennett.

It was after the talkies came in that he got his real break. The role of "Tjaden" in "All Quiet On The Western Front" won him a long-term contract. For a while he co-starred with Zasu Pitts.

He was twice married, first to Gertrude M. Roell, in 1927. Their son, Elliott George, was born in 1932. Divorced in 1936, he was married the following year to Eleanor Brown, a nurse who had attended him in an illness and was with him when he died.

Christian Science funeral services will be read at a Laguna Beach funeral home tomorrow afternoon and cremation will follow.

Slim Summerville (Times Record [Troy, NY], Jan. 7, 1946)

Jimmy Finlayson of Old Keystone Kop Fame Dies

Body of Famed Scottish Comedian of Films and Stage, 66, Found at Home by Friend

Jimmy Finlayson, one of the original Keystone Kops of the Mack Sennett slapstick comedy days, was found dead yesterday at his Hollywood home, 1966 N Beachwood Drive.

The body of the 66-year-old Scottish comedian was discovered by his old friend, English Actress Stephanie Insall. Finlayson had been in the habit of breakfasting with the actress for the past 20 years. When he didn't appear as usual at her home, 5959 Franklin Ave., she went to investigate.

International Success

The veteran actor was an international success between the world wars, appearing on the Broadway and London stages, starring for Sennett and Hal Roach comedies, and surviving the change from silent films to talkies in the early 1930s.

Born in Falkirk, Scotland, he was apprenticed to his father's iron foundry. But he rebelled at a business career because acting was in his blood, and ran away from home.

In 1912 he came to America as a juvenile player in a Scottish comedy that played Broadway for 18 months—"Bunty Pulls the Strings." With him came younger brother Bob, now a Hollywood camera technician.

The infant film industry was making its first strides to greatness when the actor stopped here on tour in 1916 and decided to stay.

In Many Comedies

He was under contract for three years to Sennett, appearing as one of the zany Keystone Kops and playing opposite Ben Turpin. Then came a four-year contract with Roach, followed by freelancing.

He also appeared in many of the early Laurel and Hardy comedies as the mustached heavy who was the butt of their escapades. In recent years these short-reelers were brought to life again by television.

DIES — Jimmy Finlayson, shown in one of early film comedy roles.

Through the years he worked for leading studios like MGM, 20th Century-Fox and RKO. Illness ended his career a decade ago and he went into retirement, living quietly by himself and occasionally showing up for reunions with filmland's old-timers.

Jimmy Finlayson (Los Angeles Times, Oct. 10, 1953)

Rites Saturday For Billy Bevan

Escondido —(P)— Funeral services will be held Saturday for veteran comedy and character actor Billy Bevan who died Tuesday at his home here. He was 70.

He had lived in Escondido 33 years but retired from films only in 1952.

Bevan began his film career as one of the famed Keystone Kops in 1912 and played in the series until 1922.

Billy Bevan (Times Standard [Eureka, CA], Nov. 29, 1957)

SNUB POLLARD

Burbank, Calif., Jan. 20 (UPI). —Harry (Snub) Pollard, 72, one of the original Keystone Kops and colorful star of old slapstick comedies, died last night at Magnolia Park Hospital of cancer.

From 1914 into the 20s Pollard appeared in nearly 500 comedies, most of them one-reelers, and had his own "Snub Pollard Comedies" produced by Hal Roach. He appeared with Charlie Chaplin, Bebe Daniels, Charles Ray, Harold Lloyd and Chester Conklin.

Snub Pollard

Pollard was known to movie audiences of 40 years ago as a little man with a deadpan expression whose black mustache twitched and was often reversed.

In recent years Pollard had played many bit movie and television parts. He was in TV's "Gunsmoke" series. His most recent part was in the movie "Pocketful of Miracles."

Pollard, who was born in Melbourne, Australia, leaves his widow, Gertrude.

Services were scheduled for Monday at Forest Lawn Memorial Park in the Hollywood Hills.

Snub Pollard (Daily News [NY], Jan. 21, 1962)

One Keystone Kop, Eddie Gribbon, Dies

HOLLYWOOD (AP) — Eddie Gribbon, one of the original Keystone Kops, died Tuesday after a bout with cirrhosis of the liver and congestive heart failure. He was 75.

"Eddie just fell asleep in his big easy chair and never woke up," said Mrs. Gribbon.

Gribbon, a big, New York-born Irishman noted for his comic mugging, came to Hollywood in 1916.

After World War I service he made a successful series of 36 war comedies with the late Slim Summerville. He also starred in the Joe Palooka movies.

Eddie Gribbon (Montgomery Advertiser [AL], Sept. 30, 1965)

Tom Kennedy, Keystone Kop

Hollywood, Oct. 7 ⟨AP⟩—Tom Kennedy, 80, one-time Keystone Kop whose career as a movie character actor spanned nearly 50 years, died last night of cancer.

Kennedy's hulking form and honest Irish face with the smashed nose made him familiar to generations of film fans as a portrayer of big, dumb cops, bartenders, taxi drivers and the like.

He came to Hollywood in 1915 from his native New York after a career as a heavyweight boxer.

His first job was as a trainer for Douglas Fairbanks, Sr. Later he worked for comedy producer Mack Sennett as a Keystone Kop and in the bathing beauty pictures.

He appeared in hundreds of movies and in recent years had been active in television. His last film was "It's A Mad, Mad, Mad, Mad World."

Tom Kennedy (Evening Sun [Baltimore, MD], Oct. 7, 1965)

Rites Pending for Hennecke, Keystone Kop

Private funeral services were pending Friday for Clarence R. Hennecke, 74, a member of the original Keystone Kops, who died Thursday at his home, 205 Washington Ave., Santa Monica, after a brief illness.

Mr. Hennecke was born Sept. 16, 1894 in Omaha, Neb., and attended schools in Chicago before moving to Los Angeles in 1913, where he briefly held the Southern California lightweight boxing championship.

He had just begun an acting career as a stuntman at Vitagraph Studios when World War I erupted. He served as a motorcycle dispatch rider in France and was twice cited for bravery.

Returning to California at the end of the war, Mr. Hennecke joined the Mack Sennett organization and appeared in more than 20 Keystone Kop comedies before moving to Hal Roach studios as a gagman and script writer.

He later directed several silent movies and wrote scripts for various studios. He was a boxing coach at

Clarence Hennecke (Los Angeles Times, Aug. 30, 1969)

OBITUARIES

Keystone Kop star Chester Conklin, 83

United Press International

HOLLYWOOD — Keystone Kop Chester Conklin, pioneer movie comedian in the slapstick era of two-reel silents, died yesterday at the age of 83.

Conklin was the daffy cop with the walrus mustache and a penchant for hitting the wrong man with his club. He also caught his share of pies in the face.

CHESTER CONKLIN
... 'Keystone Kop'

The long-time comedian appeared in hundreds of Mack Sennett shorts, often making two Keystone Kops pictures a week.

He starred in other two-reelers in the days when films were still a novelty and the accent was heavy on broad comedy.

One of his pictures, "Dough and Dynamite," co-starred, Charlie Chaplin who went on to become one of the great silent stars in motion picture history.

Conklin was born in Oskaloosa, Iowa, Jan. 11, 1888.

As a young man he joined a Barnum Circus as a clown. He began making movies in 1913 and amassed a considerable fortune, part of which went into a $70,000 Hollywood mansion — a great deal of money at the time.

With the advent of talkies, Conklin's career began to slide.

At one point he said, "talking pictures ruined comedy. Real laughs are based on pantomime. Everything was action, and audiences were forced to use their imagination."

Conklin gradually faded from pictures. For a time he lived in a small apartment in Long Beach, Calif., where he eked out a living playing bit parts in occasional movies and working as a department store Santa Claus during Christmas holidays.

In the late 1950s and 60s he was a resident of the Motion Picture Country House in the San Fernando valley for retired, indigent or ailing performers.

But in 1965 he suprised everyone by eloping with June Gunther to Las Vegas. He was 77. The bride was 65. They met while Miss Gunther was visiting the country home. Thereafter the couple settled in Van Nuys in the San Fernando valley.

Conklin had three previous marriages and was childless.

Rev. N. Boland, of St. John's

Chester Conklin (Boston Globe, Oct. 12, 1971)

HANK MANN
In a 1935 film

Keystone Kop Comic Hank Mann

SOUTH PASADENA — (AP) — Hank Mann, believed to be the last survivor of Mack Sennett's original Keystone Kops, has died here at the age of 84.

Entering motion pictures in 1912, Mr. Mann played one of the bumbling, bowler-hatted policemen in numerous movies and made occasional character actor appearances as late as 1960.

He died yesterday at the Braewood Convalescent Hospital. Funeral services will be private.

He is survived by his wife Dolly.

Hank Mann (San Francisco Examiner, Nov. 26, 1971)

Last Keystone Kop dies

PHOENIX, Ariz. (AP) — Robert "Bobby" Cox, last surviving member of the original Keystone Kops, is dead at the age of 79.

Cox, who had lived here since 1951, appeared in nearly 300 "one-reelers" in the four years he worked at Mack Sennett's Keystone Studio in Los Angeles. He died Sunday.

Cox was 17 and working as an extra on another film lot in 1917 when he heard Sennett was looking for 12 slapstick cops. He weighed less than 100 pounds during his movie days and, as the smallest of the cops, was the one most often swung from ladders in chase scenes.

Besides acting, Cox worked as assistant to such directors as John Ford and Cecil B. deMille.

After World War II service, Cox joined the U.S. Narcotics Bureau and worked in the Far East.

Cox, who was married three times, has no survivors, according to friends, Mr. and Mrs. Ed Sherman of Phoenix.

Robert Cox (Central Home News [New Brunswick, NJ], Sept. 9, 1974)

Abe Goldstein (Los Angeles Times, Feb. 15, 1990)

Last Keystone Kop dies at age 92

LOS ANGELES — Eddie LeVeque, the last of the original Keystone Kops, the troupe of slapstick gendarmes whose comic antics endeared them to a generation of silent film fans, has died at age 92.

LeVeque, who was born in Mexico, died Saturday, said his son, Gilbert.

The actor's first role in a major film was in 1914 in the D.W. Griffith classic "Intolerance."

He later joined the Keystone pro-

Eddie LeVeque (News-Press, Fort Myers [FL], Feb. 1, 1989)

Chapter 15.
The Keystone Cops on Film, Television, Radio, and Stage

By Brent E. Walker and Lon Davis

Photo by Matt Whittmeyer.

Unfortunately, due to neglect and nitrate decomposition, an estimated 75–80 percent of all silent films no longer exist.[1] Because of their immense popularity, however, Keystone comedies have a higher survival rate than those of competing film companies. Prints were duped and reduped, retitled and reissued, and thus are still with us in the 21st century, and, in certain cases, can now be viewed in all their digitally restored splendor. When applicable, a title is labeled as extant, meaning that a print of the film survives somewhere, either in an archive or readily available to the public in video or digital formats.

Special thanks to Michael J. Hayde, Steve Rydzewski, and Steve Massa for unearthing the reissue titles.

---

[1] David Pierce, *The Survival of American Silent Film Features, 1912–1929* (The Library of Congress, Washington D. C., September 2013.)

Keystone/Mutual Releases

Riley and Schultze 1/2 reel **(September 30, 1912)**
Director: Mack Sennett.
Cast: Fred Mace, Mack Sennett, Ford Sterling, Mabel Normand.
Observations: Sennett and Mace reportedly play police officers vying for the same girl in this early Keystone.

At It Again 1/2 reel **(November 4, 1912)**
Director: Mack Sennett.
Cast: Fred Mace, Mack Sennett, Ford Sterling, Mabel Normand, Alice Davenport.
Observations: Based on an extant scene still, this is the first verifiable Keystone Comedy to feature a group of comic cops.

A Temperamental Husband 1/2 reel **(November 11, 1912)**
Director: Mack Sennett.
Cast: Ford Sterling, Mabel Normand, Mack Sennett, Henry "Pathé" Lehrman, Laura Oakley.

Hoffmeyer's Legacy 1/2 reel **(December 23, 1912)**
Director: Mack Sennett.
Cast: Ford Sterling, Mack Sennett, Fred Mace.
Observations: Released as a split-reel with the Keystone comedy *The Drummer's Vacation*.

The Stolen Purse 1/2 reel **(February 10, 1913)**
Director: Mack Sennett.
Cast: Mack Sennett, Fred Mace, Ford Sterling, Henry "Pathé" Lehrman, Nick Cogley, Arthur Tavares, Chester Franklin.

Her Birthday Present 1/2 reel **(February 13, 1913)**
Director: Mack Sennett.
Cast: Fred Mace, Henry "Pathé" Lehrman, Ford Sterling.

A Landlord's Trouble 1/2 reel **(February 20, 1913)**
Director: Mack Sennett.
Cast: Ford Sterling, Mack Sennett.

A Rural Third Degree 1/2 reel (March 6, 1913)
Director: Mack Sennett.
Cast: Fred Mace, Dot Farley, Nick Cogley, Charles Avery, Raymond Hatton, Chester Franklin, Edgar Kennedy, Hal Studebaker.

The Man Next Door 1/2 reel (March 17, 1913)
Director: Mack Sennett
Cast: Ford Sterling, Dot Farley, Charles Avery, Bill Hauber, Edgar Kennedy, Dave "Andy" Anderson, Nick Cogley.
Observations: This extant film is believed to be the earliest surviving film that features the Keystone Cops. Prints are archived in the Library of Congress and the Motion Picture Academy. Although the film is only about five minutes in length, the Cops are fully realized, including a climax in which all four of them (Avery, Hauber, Kennedy, and Anderson) find themselves stuck in a large mud puddle. One scene that can still elicit a laugh is the Cops' initial entrance, when they have been called to handle a crisis of some kind. Their expressions of sheer earnestness are very funny indeed.

The Chief's Predicament 1/2 reel (March 24, 1913)
Director: Mack Sennett.
Cast: Ford Sterling, Nick Cogley, Charles Avery, Charles Franklin, Bill Hauber.

Hide and Seek 1/2 reel (April 3, 1913)
Director: Mack Sennett.
Cast: Mabel Normand, Ford Sterling, Nick Cogley, Hal Studebaker, Helen Holmes, Charles Avery, Bert Hunn, Dot Farley, Paul Jacobs.
Observations: This extant half-reeler was reissued by Blackhawk Films as one-half of *Keystone Tonight*, with a 1913 non-Keystone title from the American Film Company entitled *Courage of Sorts*.

A Life in the Balance 1 reel (April 14, 1913)
Director: Mack Sennett.
Cast: Ford Sterling, Dot Farley, Raymond Hatton, Laura Oakley, Dave "Andy" Anderson, Bert Hunn, Bill Hauber, Rube Miller, Coy Watson Jr.
Observations: This one-reel farce is a satire of D. W. Griffith's *The Miser's Heart* (Biograph, 1911). A reissue print bearing the title "Crashing Through" is held by the British Film Institute.

Murphy's I.O.U. 1/2 reel **(April 17, 1913)**
Director: Henry "Pathé" Lehrman
Cast: Fred Mace, Mack Sennett, Dot Farley, Henry "Pathé" Lehrman, Nick Cogley.

A Fishy Affair 1/2 reel **(April 24, 1913)**
Director: Mack Sennett.
Cast: Ford Sterling, Laura Oakley, Nick Cogley, Dot Farley, Bert Hunn, Bill Hauber, Rube Miller.

Bangville Police 1/2 reel **(April 24, 1913)**
Director: Henry "Pathé" Lehrman.
Cast: Fred Mace, Mabel Normand, Nick Cogley, Dot Farley, Raymond Hatton, Charles Avery, Rube Miller, Edgar Kennedy, Jack Leonard, Fred Happ.
Observations: This extant film, long mislabeled as the Keystone Cops' debut, was available from Blackhawk Films. An excellent transfer is included in Image Entertainment's *Slapstick Encyclopedia* DVD set. It is also on CineMuseum's *The Mack Sennett Collection, Vol. I* Blu-ray set.

Algy on the Force 1/2 reel **(May 5, 1913)**
Director: Henry "Pathé" Lehrman.
Cast: Fred Mace, Nick Cogley, Dot Farley, Edgar Kennedy, Charles Avery.

Mabel's Awful Mistake 1 reel **(May 12, 1913)**
Director: Mack Sennett.
Cast: Mack Sennett, Mabel Normand, Ford Sterling.
Observations: Re-released by W. H. Productions in 1919 as *Her Deceitful Lover*.

Their First Execution 1 reel **(May 15, 1913)**
Director: Mack Sennett.
Cast: Mack Sennett, Raymond Hatton, Ford Sterling, Charles Avery, Nick Cogley, Bert Hunn, Josef Swickard, Chester Franklin, Edgar Kennedy, Rube Miller, Bill Hauber, Dave "Andy" Anderson.

The Gangsters 1 reel **(May 29, 1913)**
Director: Henry "Pathé" Lehrman
Cast: Fred Mace, Nick Cogley, Evelyn Quick, Edgar Kennedy, Roscoe Arbuckle, Hank Mann, Charles Avery, Bill Hauber.
Observations: Extant.

Barney Oldfield's Race for a Life 1 reel **(June 2, 1913)**
Director: Mack Sennett.
Photographers: Walter Wright and Lee Bartholomew.
Cast: Mabel Normand, Mack Sennett, Ford Sterling, Barney Oldfield, Raymond Hatton, Helen Holmes, Carmen Phillips, Rube Miller, Engineer McNeil, Bill Hauber.
Observations: Barney Oldfield (January 29, 1878–October 4, 1946) was an American pioneer automobile racer in the first two decades of the 20th century. He was the first man to drive a car at sixty miles per hour on a circular track; as a result, his name was synonymous with speed itself. This was formerly available from Blackhawk Films. A fine transfer can be found on Image Entertainment's *Slapstick Encyclopedia*.

The Speed Queen 1 reel **(June 12, 1913)**
Director: Mack Sennett.
Cast: Mabel Normand, Ford Sterling, Nick Cogley.

Peeping Pete 1/2 reel **(June 23, 1913)**
Director: Mack Sennett.
Cast: Mack Sennett, Ford Sterling, Roscoe Arbuckle, Nick Cogley, Beatrice Van, Charles Avery, Bert Hunn, Bill Hauber, Edgar Kennedy, Rube Miller.
Observations: Extant; this genuinely funny short was once available from Blackhawk Films, coupled with *A Bandit*, another 1913 Keystone.

Safe in Jail 1 reel **(July 7, 1913)**
Director: Mack Sennett.
Cast: Ford Sterling, Edgar Kennedy, Raymond Hatton, Roscoe Arbuckle, Charles Avery, Bert Hunn, Arthur Tavares.

Love and Rubbish 1 reel **(July 14, 1913)**
Director: Henry "Pathé" Lehrman.
Cast: Ford Sterling, Charles Avery, Virginia Kirtley, Dave "Andy" Anderson, Alice Davenport, Roscoe Arbuckle, Paul Jacobs, Edgar Kennedy, Bill Hauber.
Observations: Extant; a print of this is held by the British Film Institute.

Just Kids 1 reel **(July 28, 1913)**
Director: Henry "Pathé" Lehrman.
Cast: Gordon Griffith, Thelma Salter, Paul Jacobs, Charles Avery, Edgar Kennedy.

A Game of Pool 1/2 reel **(August 7, 1913)**
Director: Wilfred Lucas.
Cast: Ford Sterling, Billy Gilbert, Edgar Kennedy, Fred Gamble.

The Riot 1 reel **(August 11, 1913)**
Director: Mack Sennett.
Cast: Roscoe Arbuckle, Mabel Normand, Charles Inslee, Alice Davenport, Charles Avery, Paul Jacobs, Gordon Griffith, Nick Cogley, Virginia Kirtley, Al St. John, Hank Mann, Bill Hauber, Edgar Kennedy.
Observations: Extant; a print is held by the British Film Institute.

A Chip Off the Old Block 1 reel **(August 14, 1913)**
Director: Henry "Pathé" Lehrman.
Cast: Nick Cogley, Gordon Griffith, Hank Mann, George Jeske, Bert Hunn.

The Fire Bug 2 reels **(August 21, 1913)**
Director: Mack Sennett.
Cast: Ford Sterling, Mack Sennett, Nick Cogley, Charles Avery, Alice Davenport, Arthur Tavares, Edgar Kennedy.

Mabel's New Hero 1 reel **(August 28, 1913)**
Director: Mack Sennett.
Cast: Mabel Normand, Roscoe Arbuckle, Charles Inslee, Virginia Kirtley, Charles Avery, Hank Mann, Edgar Kennedy.
Observations: Re-released by W. H. Productions in 1919 as *Fatty and the Bathing Beauties*. Extant; a print is held by the Museum of Modern Art.

Fatty's Day Off 1/2 reel **(September 1, 1913)**
Director: Wilfred Lucas.
Cast: Roscoe Arbuckle, Charles Avery, Grover Ligon, Fred Gamble, Bill Hauber.
Observations: Extant.

Mabel's Dramatic Career 1 reel **(September 8, 1913)**
Director: Mack Sennett.
Cast: Mabel Normand, Mack Sennett, Ford Sterling, Roscoe Arbuckle, Virginia Kirtley, Alice Davenport, Paul Jacobs, Charles Inslee, Charles Avery, Dave "Andy" Anderson, Edgar Kennedy, Billy Gilbert, Hank Mann, Grover Ligon, Bert Hunn, Bill Hauber.
Re-released by W. H. Productions in 1919 as *Her Dramatic Debut*.

Observations: This one-reeler is, in fact, a parody of the film industry and its principal players, made shortly after the introduction of the star system. An innovative effect involves the use of a superimposed movie screen in a nickelodeon, where a rube (played by Sennett) cannot distinguish reality from celluloid fantasy. The extant film is included on Image Entertainment's DVD set *Slapstick Encyclopedia*, and on the BFI's Blu-ray release of *Early Women Filmmakers, 1911-1940*. A restored version will be included on CineMuseum's forthcoming Blu-ray set *Mack Sennett Collection, Vol. II*.

When Dreams Come True 1 reel (September 22, 1913)
Director: Mack Sennett.
Cast: Ford Sterling, Mabel Normand, Roscoe Arbuckle, Hank Mann, Alice Davenport, Charles Inslee, Charles Avery, Emma Clifton.
Observations: Extant.

Mother's Boy 1 reel (September 25, 1913)
Director: Henry "Pathé" Lehrman.
Cast: Roscoe Arbuckle, Alice Davenport, Bill Hauber, Billy Gilbert, Edgar Kennedy, Nick Cogley, Al St. John, George Jeske.

Two Old Tars 1 reel (October 20, 1913)
Director: Henry "Pathé" Lehrman.
Cast: Roscoe Arbuckle, Nick Cogley, George Jeske.

A Quiet Little Wedding 1 reel (October 23, 1913)
Director: Wilfred Lucas.
Cast: Roscoe Arbuckle, Minta Durfee, Charles Inslee, Charles Avery, Edgar Kennedy, Rube Miller, Hank Mann, Billy Gilbert, Bill Hauber, Peggy Pearce, Virginia Kirtley, Emma Clifton.

The Janitor 1/2 reel (October 27, 1913)
Director: Wilfred Lucas.
Cast: Nick Cogley, Virginia Kirtley, Charles Avery, Minta Durfee, Fred Gamble, Bert Hunn, Rube Miller, Edgar Kennedy, George Jeske.

A Muddy Romance 1 reel (November 20, 1913)
Director: Mack Sennett.
Cast: Mabel Normand, Ford Sterling, Charles Inslee, Minta Durfee, May Wells, Harry Russell, Mack Swain, Charles Avery, Bill Hauber, Hank Mann, Rube Miller, George Jeske, Edgar Kennedy, Bert Hunn.

Observations: Long available in the home-movie market (from both Castle and Blackhawk Films), a restored print is included in Image Entertainment's DVD box set *Slapstick Encyclopedia*.

Fatty Joins the Force 1 reel (November 24, 1913)
Director: George Nichols.
Cast: Roscoe Arbuckle, Minta Durfee, Edgar Kennedy, Mack Swain, Dot Farley, George Nichols, Charles Avery, George Jeske, Billy White, Bill Hauber, Hank Mann, Bert Hunn, Harry De Roy.
Observations: An outstanding print of this extant film is available on Laughsmith Entertainment's *The Forgotten Films of Roscoe "Fatty" Arbuckle* DVD set.

The Gusher 1 reel (December 15, 1913)
Director: Mack Sennett.
Cast: Ford Sterling, Mabel Normand, Charles Inslee, Bert Hunn, Hank Mann, Mack Swain, Dot Farley, Peggy Pearce, May Wells, Bill Hauber, Edgar Kennedy, Harry Russell, Rube Miller, Charles Avery, George Jeske.
Observations: Extant; this is available on Kino-Lorber's 2008 DVD release of *The Extra Girl/The Gusher*.

Fatty's Flirtation 1/2 reel (December 18, 1913)
Director: George Nichols.
Cast: Roscoe Arbuckle, Minta Durfee, Mabel Normand, Hank Mann, George Jeske, Frank Cooley.
Observations: The original advertising for this now-lost film reads: "A Comedy of Merit with the Keystone Police force."

His Sister's Kids 1 reel (December 20, 1913)
Director: George Nichols.
Cast: Roscoe Arbuckle, Minta Durfee, Ford Sterling, Jack White, Gordon Griffith, Hank Mann, Al St. John, Charles Avery, Virginia Kirtley, Rube Miller.
Observations: Re-released by W. H. Productions in 1919 as *Fatty's Naughty Nephews*. Extant; a print is held by the Library of Congress.

He Would A-Hunting Go 1 reel (December 29, 1913)
Director: George Nichols.
Cast: Roscoe Arbuckle, Billy Gilbert, Hank Mann, Grover Ligon, Virginia Kirtley, Frank Opperman.

A Flirt's Mistake 1/2 reel **(January 12, 1914)**
Director: George Nichols.
Cast: Roscoe Arbuckle, Minta Durfee, Edgar Kennedy, Frank Cooley, George Nichols, Bill Hauber, George Jeske, Virginia Kirtley, Frank Opperman.
Observations: *A Flirt's Mistake* was later reissued by Blackhawk Films, coupled with *A Grocery Clerk's Romance*, under the joint title *Romance, Keystone Style*.

In the Clutches of a Gang 2 reels **(January 17, 1914)**
Director: George Nichols.
Cast: Ford Sterling, Hank Mann, Roscoe Arbuckle, Rube Miller, Al St. John, Edgar Kennedy, George Jeske, Marvin G. Cox [Robert Cox], George Nichols, Virginia Kirtley.
Observations: A fragment of this landmark film (considered lost for many decades) is held by the Academy of Motion Picture Arts and Sciences.

Double Crossed 1 reel **(January 26, 1914)**
Director: Ford Sterling.
Cast: Ford Sterling, Emma Clifton, Mack Swain, Chester Conklin, Hank Mann, Rube Miller, Al St. John, Frank Cooley.
Observations: Extant.

A Thief Catcher 1 reel **(February 19, 1914)**
Director: Ford Sterling.
Cast: Ford Sterling, Mack Swain, Edgar Kennedy, Charlie Chaplin.
Re-released by Tower Film Corporation in 1919 as *His Regular Job*.
Observations: A 16mm print of this previously lost film, featuring Chaplin as an authentic Keystone Cop, was discovered in 2010 by film historian Paul E. Gierucki at a garage sale in Michigan. It had its grand re-premiere at the Slapsticon Film Festival in Arlington, Virginia, in 2010. An excerpt from the one-reel film is included on Flicker Alley's *Chaplin at Keystone* DVD set, and a restored complete version appears on *The Mack Sennett Collection, Vol. I* Blu-Ray set. It is also included on *Behind Chaplin's Genius*, a European release of a limited-edition DVD.

Between Showers 1 reel **(February 28, 1914)**
Director: Henry "Pathé" Lehrman.
Cast: Charlie Chaplin, Ford Sterling, Chester Conklin, Emma Clifton.
Re-released by W. H. Productions in 1918 as *The Flirts*.
Observations: Charlie Chaplin famously boasted in 1914, "All I need to make a comedy is a park, a policeman, and a pretty girl." This extant one-reeler bears

that out. A beautifully restored copy of this one-reeler is included on Lobster Films' *Chaplin at Keystone* DVD set.

A False Beauty 1 reel (March 5, 1914)
Director: Ford Sterling.
Cast: Ford Sterling, Alice Davenport, Rube Miller, Mack Swain, Bill Hauber, Hank Mann, Frank Opperman.
Observations: A partial print of this film is held by the Library of Congress.

The Chicken Chaser 1 reel (April 2, 1914)
Director: Roscoe Arbuckle.
Cast: Roscoe Arbuckle, Charles Avery, Rube Miller, Bill Hauber, Eddie Cline.
Observations: Re-released by W. H. Productions in 1918 as *Fatty Chases Chickens*.

The Alarm 2 reels (May 28, 1914)
Director: Roscoe Arbuckle.
Cast: Roscoe Arbuckle, Mabel Normand.

The Knockout 2 reels (June 11, 1914)
Director: Mack Sennett.
Cast: Roscoe Arbuckle, Minta Durfee, Edgar Kennedy, Charlie Chaplin, Al St. John, Hank Mann, Grover Ligon, Mack Swain, Frank Opperman.
Re-released by W. H. Productions in 1918 as *The Pugilist*.
Observations: In addition to the sizable presence of Roscoe Arbuckle, the film gained added fame by the guest appearance of Charlie Chaplin. It also includes some of the liveliest footage ever taken of the Keystone Cops. A restored copy is included on Laughsmith's DVD set, *The Forgotten Films of Roscoe "Fatty" Arbuckle*, and on Lobster Films' *Chaplin at Keystone* DVD set.

Mabel's Busy Day 1 reel (June 13, 1914)
Director: Mack Sennett.
Cast: Mabel Normand, Charlie Chaplin, Chester Conklin, George "Slim" Summerville, Harry McCoy, Edgar Kennedy, Glen Cavender, Bill Hauber, Charles Avery, Edward Frazee, Mack Sennett, Billie Bennett, Charles Parrott, Frank Opperman, Alice Howell, Wallace MacDonald, Grover Ligon, Dan Albert, Dave Lewis, Lou Sorrell.
Observations: Extant; a restored print is included on Lobster Films' *Chaplin at Keystone* DVD set.

Love and Bullets 1 reel **(July 14, 1914)**
Director: Unknown.
Cast: Charlie Murray, Minta Durfee, Edgar Kennedy, Wallace MacDonald, Alice Davenport, George "Slim" Summerville, Fred Fishback, Charles Bennett, Roscoe Arbuckle, Billy Gilbert, Bill Hauber.
Observations: Re-released by W. H. Productions in 1919 as *The Trouble Mender*. Extant; a print is housed at the University of California, Los Angeles.

A Fatal Sweet Tooth 1 reel **(July 20, 1914)**
Director: Rube Miller.
Cast: Rube Miller, Wallace MacDonald.
Observations: Extant.

The Great Toe Mystery 1 reel **(July 25, 1914)**
Director: Unknown.
Cast: Charles Parrott.
Observations: Extant; a restored print is included on CineMuseum's *The Mack Sennett Collection, Vol. I* Blu-ray set.

Those Country Kids 1 reel **(August 20, 1914)**
Director: Roscoe Arbuckle
Cast: Roscoe Arbuckle, Mabel Normand, Al St. John, Chester Conklin, Jess Dandy, Minta Durfee, Frank Opperman, Harry McCoy, Charles Parrott, Alice Davenport, Josef Swickard, Frank Hayes, Billy Gilbert, George "Slim" Summerville, Fritz Schade.
Observations: Extant.

A Brand-New Hero 1 reel **(September 5, 1914)**
Director: Roscoe Arbuckle.
Cast: Roscoe Arbuckle, Harry McCoy.

The Love Thief 1 reel **(October 22, 1914)**
Director: Unknown.
Cast: Chester Conklin, Edgar Kennedy, Norma Nichols, Bill Hauber, Alice Davenport, Frank Opperman, Ted Edwards.

Stout Heart but Weak Knees 1 reel **(October 24, 1914)**
Director: Unknown.

Cast: Charlie Murray, Charles Parrott, Harry McCoy, Fritz Schade, Grover Ligon, George "Slim" Summerville, Alice Howell, Vivian Edwards, Cecile Arnold, Norma Nichols, Wallace MacDonald, Al St. John.

An Incompetent Hero 1 reel (November 12, 1914)
Director: Roscoe Arbuckle.
Cast: Roscoe Arbuckle, Edgar Kennedy, Lucille Ward, Minta Durfee, Al St. John, Josef Swickard, Ted Edwards, Dick Smith, George "Slim" Summerville.
Observations: Re-released by Tower Film Corporation in 1919 as *Fatty's Indiscretion*. Extant.

Fatty's Jonah Day 1 reel (November 16, 1914)
Director: Roscoe Arbuckle.
Cast: Roscoe Arbuckle, Norma Nichols, Al St. John, Frank Hayes, Ted Edwards.
Observations: Re-released by W. H. Productions in 1918 as *Fatty's Hoodoo Day*. Extant.

The Noise of Bombs 1 reel (November 19, 1914)
Director: Unknown.
Cast: Charlie Murray, Edgar Kennedy, Lucille Ward, Dixie Chene, Josef Swickard, Harry McCoy, Eddie Cline, Charles Parrott, Dick Smith.
Observations: Extant; a restored print is included on CineMuseum's *The Mack Sennett Collection, Vol. I* Blu-ray set.

The Sea Nymphs 2 reels (November 23, 1914)
Director: Mack Sennett.
Cast: Roscoe Arbuckle, Mabel Normand, Mack Swain, Minta Durfee, Alice Davenport, Charles Avery, James Bryant, Harry McCoy [disguised as Ford Sterling], Bill Hauber.
Observations: Re-released by W. H. Productions in 1918 as *His Diving Beauty*. Extant.

Fatty's Magic Pants 1 reel (December 14, 1914)
Director: Roscoe Arbuckle.
Cast: Roscoe Arbuckle, Minta Durfee, Harry McCoy, Alice Davenport, Phyllis Allen, Charles Parrott, George "Slim" Summerville, Eddie Cline, Frank Opperman, Glen Cavender, Dixie Chene, Al St. John, Bert Roach.
Observations: Re-released by W. H. Productions in 1918 as *Fatty's Suitless Day*. Extant; a paper print of this film is in the collection of the Library of Congress.

Tillie's Punctured Romance 6 reels **(December 21, 1914)**
Director: Mack Sennett.
Cast: Marie Dressler, Charlie Chaplin, Mabel Normand, Mack Swain, Charles Bennett, Douglas Banks, Chester Conklin, Edgar Kennedy, Charles Parrott, Glen Cavender, Harry McCoy, Phyllis Allen, Gordon Griffith, Rube Miller, Billie Bennett, Frank Opperman, Nick Cogley, Fritz Schade, Morgan Wallace, Charlie Murray, Minta Durfee, Hampton Del Ruth, Hugh Saxon, Fred Fishback, Ted Edwards, Hank Mann, George "Slim" Summerville, Al St. John, Edwin Frazee, Bill Hauber, Dan Albert, Billy Gilbert, Robert Kerr, Alice Howell, Eva Nelson, Dixie Chene, Wallace McDonald, Alice Davenport, Eddie Nolan, Grover Ligon, Josef Swickard, Frankie Dolan, Dick Smith, Meiklejohn and Hazel Allen, Helen Carruthers.
Observations: This 1914 six-reel comedy, starring the great stage actress Marie Dressler recreating the role she introduced on Broadway, has gained massive recognition as the screen's first feature-length comedy. *Tillie's Punctured Romance* was such a hit with the public that it generated two non-Sennett sequels, *Tillie's Tomato Surprise* and *Tillie Wakes Up*, although neither generated much interest. Miss Dressler, who is hardly presented at her best in the original *Tillie* film, went on to give some truly hilarious performances in such MGM offerings as *The Patsy* (1927), co-starring Marion Davies, and in the sound films *Anna Christie* (1930), co-starring Greta Garbo; the Dressler–Wallace Beery vehicle *Min and Bill* (for which she won the Best Actress Academy Award for 1930–1931); and especially the all-star comedy-drama *Dinner at Eight* (released in 1933, just a year before her death). Despite its creaky plot and Miss Dressler's grotesque overacting, the original *Tillie's Punctured Romance* remained in the public's collective memory and was continuously re-released well into the sound era. A pristine restoration of the complete six-reeler is included on Lobster Films' *Chaplin at Keystone* DVD set.

Gussle the Golfer 1 reel **(December 28, 1914)**
Director: F. Richard Jones.
Cast: Syd Chaplin, Mack Swain, Dixie Chene, Josef Swickard, Eddie Cline, Dick Smith, George "Slim" Summerville, Bobby Dunn, Ted Edwards, Grover Ligon, Dan Albert.
Observations: A paper print of this film is in the collection of the Library of Congress.

Giddy, Gay and Ticklish 1 reel **(January 7, 1915)**
Director: F. Richard Jones.

Cast: Syd Chaplin, Phyllis Allen, Edgar Kennedy, Dixie Chene, Grover Ligon, Edwin Frazee, Dan Albert.
Observations: Re-released by W. H. Productions in 1919 as *A Gay Lothario*. Extant.

Love, Speed and Thrills 1 reel (January 18, 1915)
Director: Walter Wright.
Cast: Mack Swain, Chester Conklin, Minta Durfee, Josef Swickard, Edwin Frazee, Billy Gilbert, Grover Ligon.
Observations: This extant one-reel film, once available from Blackhawk Films, ran on a loop at Disneyland's Main Street Cinema for years. It will be included in CineMuseum's forthcoming Blu-ray set, *Mack Sennett Collection, Vol. II*.

Mable (sic), Fatty, and the Law 1 reel (January 28, 1915)
Director: Roscoe Arbuckle.
Cast: Mabel Normand, Roscoe Arbuckle, Harry Gribbon, Minta Durfee, Frank Hayes, Joe Bordeaux, James Bryant, Bill Hauber, Al St. John, Eddie Cline, Ollie Carlyle, Glen Cavender, Josef Swickard, Alice Davenport, Billie Bennett.
Observations: Re-released by W. H. Productions in 1918 as *Fatty's Spooning Days*. Extant; a paper print is in the collection of the Library of Congress.

Peanuts and Bullets 1 reel (January 30, 1915)
Director: Nick Cogley.
Cast: Fritz Schade, Charles Parrott, Dora Rodgers, Harry McCoy, Billie Bennett, Eddie Cline, James Bryant, Grover Ligon, Ted Edwards, Bill Hauber.
Observations: Extant; a paper print of this film is in the collection of the Library of Congress.

The Home Breakers 2 reels (February 1, 1915)
Director: Walter Wright. **Assistant Director:** Fred Fishback.
Cast: Mack Swain, Chester Conklin, Alice Davenport, Dora Rodgers, George "Slim" Summerville, Ollie Carlyle, Fred Fishback, Ted Edwards.
Observations: Re-released by W. H. Productions in 1918 as *A Mix-Up in Affinities*. Extant; a paper print is in the collection of the Library of Congress.

Fatty's New Role 1 reel (February 1, 1915)
Director: Roscoe Arbuckle.
Cast: Roscoe Arbuckle, Mack Swain, George "Slim" Summerville, Bobby Dunn, Glen Cavender, Frank Hayes, Frank Opperman, Charles Lakin, Edgar Kennedy, Al St. John, Joe Bordeaux, James Bryant, Luke the dog.
Observations: Extant; a paper print is in the collection of the Library of Congress.

Ambrose's Nasty Temper 1 reel (April 17, 1915)
Director: Dell Henderson.
Cast: Mack Swain, Cecile Arnold, Louise Fazenda, Dave Morris, Dixie Chene, Josef Swickard, Harry McCoy, William A. Sheer, Billie Walsh, George Ovey, Ted Edwards. Extant.

Wished on Mabel 1 reel (April 19, 1915)
Director: Roscoe Arbuckle.
Cast: Mabel Normand, Roscoe Arbuckle, Alice Davenport, Joe Bordeaux, Edgar Kennedy, Glen Cavender, Billy Gilbert, James Leslie.
Observations: A paper print is in the collection of the Library of Congress.

Love, Loot and Crash 1 reel (April 24, 1915)
Director: Frank C. Griffin.
Cast: Charles Parrott, Dora Rodgers, Josef Swickard, Fritz Schade, Bill Hauber, Harold Lloyd, Robert Kerr.
Observations: Extant; this one-reeler was available from Blackhawk Films.

Our Dare-Devil Chief 2 reels (May 10, 1915)
Director: Ford Sterling.
Cast: Ford Sterling, Harry Bernard, Minta Durfee, Eddie Cline, Al St. John, Grover Ligon, James Rowe, Vivian Edwards, William A. Sheer, Charles Lakin.
Observations: Extant; this was available from Blackhawk Films.

He Wouldn't Stay Down 1 reel (May 20, 1915)
Director: Ford Sterling.
Cast: Ford Sterling, Minta Durfee, Charles Parrott, Frank Hayes, Dixie Chene, Harry Bernard, Dan Albert, William A. Sheer.
Observations: Extant.

For Better—But Worse 1 reel (May 22, 1915)
Director: Dell Henderson.
Cast: Harry McCoy, Fritz Schade, Mae Busch, Dell Henderson, Venice Hayes, Hugh Fay.
Observations: Dell Henderson, a former member of D. W. Griffith's Biograph unit, helmed this hilariously funny film, and has a leading part in it as well, that of a married man who is flirting with the police chief's daughter, played with gusto by Mae Busch. The police chief, incidentally, is Keystone regular Fritz Schade. Extant.

A Hash House Fraud 1 reel **(June 10, 1915)**
Director: Charles Parrott.
Cast: Louise Fazenda, Hugh Fay, Fritz Schade, Harry Bernard, Billie Brockwell, Chester Conklin, Harold J. Binney, Fred Fishback, Billy Gilbert, Glen Cavender, Charles Lakin.
Observations: Extant; formerly available from Blackhawk Films.

The Cannon Ball 2 reels **(June 14, 1915)**
Director: Walter Wright.
Assistant Director: Fred Fishback.
Cast: Chester Conklin, Charles Arling, Harry Booker, Fred Fishback, James Rowe, Ted Edwards, Charles Lakin, Grover Ligon, Bobby Dunn, George Ovey.
Observations: A print of this extant (and explosively funny) comedy was available for many years from Blackhawk Films.

Dirty Work in a Laundry 2 reels **(July 19, 1915)**
Director: Ford Sterling.
Cast: Ford Sterling, Minta Durfee, Harry Bernard, Harry McCoy, Alice Davenport, Josef Swickard, Grover Ligon, Dan Albert, Glen Cavender, Bobby Dunn, James Bryant, Ollie Carlyle.
Observations: Re-released by W. H. Productions in 1918 as *A Desperate Scoundrel*. As late as December 1976, Blackhawk Films was offering prints of this film under the reissue title. A restored print of this extant two-reeler will be included in CineMuseum's forthcoming Blu-ray set *Mack Sennett Collection, Vol. II*.

Fatty's Tintype Tangle 2 reel**s (July 26, 1915)**
Director: Roscoe Arbuckle.
Cast: Roscoe Arbuckle, Norma Nichols, Louise Fazenda, Edgar Kennedy, May Wells, Josef Swickard, Bobby Dunn, Glen Cavender, Frank Hayes, Joe Bordeaux, Grover Ligon, Charles Lakin, Ted Edwards.
Observations: In 1995, *Fatty's Tintype Tangle* was selected for preservation in the National Film Registry by the Library of Congress as being "culturally, historically, or aesthetically significant." An excellent, restored print is included in Laughsmith's DVD box set, *The Forgotten Films of Roscoe "Fatty" Arbuckle*.

A Lover's Lost Control 2 reels **(August 5, 1915)**
Directors: Syd Chaplin and Charles Avery.
Cast: Syd Chaplin, Phyllis Allen, Frank Alexander, Joy Lewis, Wayland Trask, Wesley Ruggles, Jay Belasco, Billie Bennett, Josef Swickard, Charles Lakin, Grover Ligon, Minnie Chaplin.

Observations: Extant; a restored print is included on *The Mack Sennett Collection, Vol. I* Blu-ray set. Syd Chaplin, of course, was Charlie's half-brother. He was offered a place with Keystone after his superstar sibling defected to Essanay.

No One to Guide Him 2 reels (August 30, 1915)
Director: F. Richard Jones.
Cast: Syd Chaplin, Phyllis Allen, Edgar Kennedy, Josef Swickard, George "Slim" Summerville, Edwin Frazee, Ted Edwards, Charles Lakin, Cecile Arnold, Billy Gilbert, Dixie Chene, Grover Ligon, Joe Bordeaux, Eddie Cline.
Re-released by W. H. Productions in 1919 as *Looking Them Over*.
Observations: Extant. Initially a three-reeler, *No One to Guide Him* was later re-edited and released in two reels.

Keystone/Triangle Releases

A Janitor's Wife's Temptation 2 reels (December 5, 1915)
Director: Dell Henderson.
Supervisor: Mack Sennett.
Cast: Fred Mace, Marta Golden, Betty Marsh, Harry Gribbon, Joy Lewis, Ivy Crosthwaite, Harold J. Binney, Harry Bernard, Billie Bennett, Harry McCoy, Frank Hayes, James Donnelly, Eddie Cline, Frank Alexander, Bobby Dunn, Fred Fishback, Billy Gilbert, Robert Kerr, Lige Crommie [Lige Conley], Erle C. Kenton, Fred Huntley.
Observations: Extant.

Fatty and the Broadway Stars 2 reels (December 15, 1915)
Director: Roscoe Arbuckle.
Cast: Roscoe Arbuckle; Broadway stars: Weber & Fields, Sam Bernard, William Collier Sr., Joe Jackson, Bert Clark; Sennett personnel: Ivy Crosthwaite, Mack Sennett, Ford Sterling, Fred Mace, Chester Conklin, Harry Gribbon, Mack Swain, Mae Busch, Hank Mann, Charlie Murray, Glen Cavender, Harry Booker, Louis Hippe, Polly Moran, Slim Summerville, Bobby Vernon, Tom Kennedy, Charles Baumann, Al St. John, Frank Hayes, Joe Bordeaux, Jimmy Bryant, Nick Cogley, the Keystone Cops (billed as the Keystone Police Force).
Observations: In this unusual attempt to mix the lights of Broadway with the dim bulbs of Keystone, Fatty plays a janitor who dreams of success on the Great White Way. When he rescues stage actress Ivy Crosthwaite from a fire, he is rewarded with a contract.

Fatty and Mabel Adrift 3 reels **(January 9, 1916)**
Director: Roscoe Arbuckle.
Assistant Director: Dave "Andy" Anderson; supervised by Mack Sennett.
Cast: Roscoe Arbuckle, Mabel Normand, Al St. John, Frank Hayes, May Wells, Wayland Trask, Glen Cavender, James Bryant, Joe Bordeaux, Luke the dog.
Observations: This three-reel film, one of the best Sennett ever produced (or Arbuckle ever directed) was cut into brief segments which were then duped countless times, given various titles (appearing on television in the 1950s as "Mabel's Jealous Romeo"), and released on the 8mm home-movie market in the 1960s (including such Atlas Films' cut-downs as "Farmer Boy," "Concrete Biscuits," and "Adrift on Honeymoon"). A fine, complete print of *Fatty and Mabel Adrift* is available on Image Entertainment's DVD box set *Slapstick Encyclopedia*, and a restored, tinted version appears on *The Mack Sennett Collection, Vol. I* Blu-Ray set.

Because He Loved Her 2 reels **(January 16, 1916)**
Director: Dell Henderson.
Supervisor: Mack Sennett.
Photographer: George C. "Duke" Zalibra.
Supervising Editor: William Watson.
Cast: Sam Bernard, Mae Busch, Glen Cavender, Harry McCoy, Walter Klintberg, Alice Davenport, Fritz Schade, Harry Gribbon, Charlie Murray, Ford Sterling, Charles Lakin, Billy Gilbert, Eddie Cline, James Bryant, Joe Bordeaux, Luke the dog.

His Pride and Shame 2 reels **(February 27, 1916)**
Director: Ford Sterling.
Assistant Director: Charles Parrott.
Supervisor: Mack Sennett.
Cast: Ford Sterling, Juanita Hansen, Bobby Vernon, Bobby Dunn, Guy Woodward, Robert Eddy, James Rowe, Frank Hayes, James Donnelly, Clarence "Clarry" Lyndon, George Allen.

Cinders of Love 2 reels **(February 27, 1916)**
Director: Walter Wright.
Supervisor: Mack Sennett.
Cast: Chester Conklin, George "Slim" Summerville, Claire Anderson, Billie Bennett, Lois Holmes, William Mason, Harry McCoy, Frank Alexander.

Wife and Auto Trouble 2 reels **(March 5, 1916)**
Director: Dell Henderson.
Assistant Director: Eddie Cline.
Scenarist: Hampton Del Ruth.
Photographer: Fred W. Jackman.
Cast: William Collier Sr., Del Lord (Collier's stunt double), Blanche Payson, Joseph "Baldy" Belmont, Alice Davenport, Mae Busch, Fritz Schade, Wayland Trask, Eddie Cline, Hugh Fay.
Observations: This one-reel short featuring stage star William Collier includes an especially effective chase sequence featuring the "Tri-Stone Cops," in order to remind audiences of the time that they were watching a Keystone-Triangle production. (Needless to say, the new name did not catch on.) A print was long available from Blackhawk Films. A new transfer will be included on CineMuseum's forthcoming Blu-ray set *Mack Sennett Collection, Vol. II*.

A Village Vampire 2 reels **(March 12, 1916)**
Director: Edwin A. Frazee.
Assistant Director: Walter Reed.
Supervisor: Mack Sennett.
Cast: Fred Mace, Anna Luther, Josef Swickard, Earle Rodney, Dale Fuller, Billie Brockwell, Frank Hayes, Charles Arling, Hugh Fay, Bill Hauber, Al Case, Bernard Harris, George Ramage, Frank Reynolds, Bill Weber, Billy Gilbert.

Maid Mad 2 reels **(September 3, 1916)**
Director: Frank C. Griffin.
Assistant Director: Jack Scharrer.
Supervisor: Mack Sennett.
Photographer: Leon Loeb.
Cast: Charlie Murray, Sylvia Ashton, Louise Fazenda, Harry Booker, Wayland Trask, Frank Hayes, Vera Steadman.
Observations: Extant; this was available from Blackhawk Films.

Dollars and Sense 2 reels **(September 10, 1916)**
Director: Walter Wright.
Assistant Director: Dave "Andy" Anderson.
Supervisor: Mack Sennett.
Cast: Ora Carew, Joseph "Baldy" Belmont, Nick Cogley, Blanche Payson, Malcolm St. Clair, Lige Crommie [Lige Conley], Joseph Callahan, Pat Kelly.
Observations: Extant; this was available from Blackhawk Films. The Keystone Cops—known in this instance as "Mountain Police"—make a perilous trip to

save a couple from a huge bear (or a large man in a bear suit). At one point, the Cops dangle precipitously from a rescue ladder that has been dropped down the face of a cliff.

Keystone-Triangle Resolution

Stars and Bars 2 reels **(February 18, 1917)**
Director: Victor Heerman.
Cast: Ford Sterling, Harry Gribbon, Gene Rogers, May Emory, Hugh Fay, James Donnelly.

Pinched in the Finish 2 reels **(April 1, 1917)**
Director: Harry Williams.
Cast: Ford Sterling, Mary Thurman, Harry Gribbon, Guy Woodward, Alice Davenport, Myrtle Lind.

Her Torpedoed Love 2 reels **(May 13, 1917)**
Director: Frank C. Griffin.
Assistant Director: Harry Williams.
Supervisor: Mack Sennett.
Photographer: G. Felix Schoedsack.
Cast: Louise Fazenda, Ford Sterling, Wayland Trask, Harry Booker, Glen Cavender, Tom Kennedy, Frank Hayes, Harry McCoy, Al Kaufman, Wesley Ruggles, Grover Ligon, Edith Valk.
Observations: Chase footage used in Robert Youngson's *The Days of Thrills and Laughter* (1961). The complete film was available from Blackhawk Films. A fine transfer is included on CineMuseum's *Mack Sennett Vol. II* Blu-ray set.

Mack Sennett Comedies, Released by Associated First National Pictures, Inc.

Love, Honor and Behave 5 reels **(November 22, 1920)**
Directors: F. Richard Jones and Erle C. Kenton.
Supervisor: Mack Sennett.
Scenarist: Mack Sennett.
Photographers: J. R. Lockwood and Perry Evans.
Film Editor: Allen McNeil.
Cast: Charlie Murray, Ford Sterling, Phyllis Haver, Marie Prevost, George O'Hara, Billy Bevan, Eddie Gribbon, Kalla Pasha, Fanny Kelly, Billy Armstrong, Charlotte Mineau, Joseph "Baldy" Belmont, Raymond Griffith, Sibye Trevilla

[Sybil Seely], James Finlayson, Dave "Andy" Anderson, John Rand, Gordon Lewis, Al Cooke, Virginia Fox, Garry O'Dell, Pat Kelly, Marvin Loback, Hal Haig Prieste, George "Sloppy" Gray, Lige Crommie [Lige Conley], Frank Earle, Jane Allen, Elva Diltz, Mildred June, Eva Thatcher.
Observations: This film exists only partially in clips used for the 1940s Vitaphone retrospective shorts.

Call a Cop 2 reels (June 26, 1921)
Director: Mal St. Clair.
Photographers: Fred W. Jackman and Robert Walters.
Cast: Marie Prevost, George O'Hara, Pat Kelly, John J. "Jack" Richardson, Eddie Gribbon, Roscoe "Tiny" Ward, Kalla Pasha, John Rand, Eddie Fitzgerald, Fanny Kelly.
Observations: Extant.

Be Reasonable 2 reels (October 31, 1921)
Director: Roy Del Ruth.
Producer: F. Richard Jones.
Photographers: Fred W. Jackman and Perry Evans.
Cast: Billy Bevan, Mildred June, Eddie Gribbon, Ethel Teare, Bobby Dunn, Horace "Kewpie" Morgan, Al Cooke, Billy Armstrong, Marvin Loback, Clarence Hennecke, Stanley "Tiny" Sandford, Pat Kelly, Silas D. Wilcox, Floy Guinn.
Observations: A large portion of this wonderful comedy was included in the 1945 Warner Bros. short *Good Old Corn*. The complete film will be included on CineMuseum's *Mack Sennett Collection, Vol. II*. *Be Reasonable*, one of Sennett's true audience pleasers, features a hilarious scene in which petty thief Billy Bevan is chased through Los Angeles's downtown streets by an entire police force. Incidentally, Buster Keaton's classic 1921 short *Cops* featured a virtually identical version of this comedic concept.

On Patrol 2 reels (March 12, 1922)
Director: Roy Del Ruth.
Production Manager: F. Richard Jones.
Photographers: J. R. Lockwood and W. W. Padgett.
Film Editor: Allen McNeil.
Cast: Billy Bevan, Mildred June, James Donnelly, Kalla Pasha, Horace "Kewpie" Morgan, Fanny Kelly, Marvin Loback, Al Cooke, Larry McGrath, Andy Clyde, Pat Kelly, Sibye Trevilla [Sybil Seely].
Observations: This film survives only in fragments in the 1940s Vitaphone retrospective shorts.

Mack Sennett Comedies, Released by Pathé

Nip and Tuck 2 reels **(August 12, 1923)**
Director: Roy Del Ruth.
Supervisor: F. Richard Jones.
Title Writers: John A. Waldron, Arthur MacArthur, H. Lee Hugunin.
Photographer: Robert Walters.
Cast: Billy Bevan, Harry Gribbon, Horace "Kewpie" Morgan, Alberta Vaughn, Mildred June, Marvin Loback, Andy Clyde, Billy Armstrong, Al Cooke, Cameo the dog.
Observations: In this highly enjoyable comedy (due, primarily, to the remarkably well-trained Cameo), a crooked poker game leads the culprits to be chased by the Keystone Cops. Crystal-clear footage from the film is included in Robert Youngson's *The Golden Age of Comedy* (1957).

Wandering Willies 2 reels **(March 28, 1926)**
Director: Del Lord.
Supervisor: J. A. Waldron.
Story: Gus Meins.
Title Writer: A. H. Giebler.
Photographer: Ernest A. "Hap" DePew.
Film Editor: William Hornbeck.
Cast: Billy Bevan, Andy Clyde, Ruth Hiatt, Horace "Kewpie" Morgan, Bobby Dunn, Dave Morris, Ruth Taylor, Marvin Loback, William McCall, Billy Gilbert, Charles Force, Danny O'Shea, Marion McDonald, Barney Hellum, Leo Sulky.
Observations: The composite opening of the early 1960s syndicated television show *Comedy Capers* included the famous scene of the Cops being dragged by their own paddy wagon in a cut-down version entitled "The Hoboes," referring to its stars Billy Bevan and Andy Clyde. A new transfer of this latter-day Cops comedy is included in its entirety on Image Entertainment's DVD set *Slapstick Encyclopedia* and on CineMuseum's forthcoming Blu-ray set *Mack Sennett Collection, Vol. II*.

Love in a Police Station 2 reels **(December 25, 1927)**
Director: Earle Rodney.
Supervisor: J. A. Waldron.
Story: Harry McCoy and Phil Whitman.
Title Writers: A. H. Giebler and Jimmy Starr.
Photographers: William "Billy" Williams and Earl L. Stafford.
Film Editor: William Hornbeck.

Publicist: Agnes O'Malley.
Cast: Andy Clyde, Madeline Hurlock, Eddie Quillan, Barney Hellum, Alice Ward, Johnny Burke, Jo Kessel, William Armstrong, Roscoe "Tiny" Ward, Bobby Dunn, Alice Belcher, William McCall, George "Sloppy" Gray, Gordon Lewis.
Observations: Extant.

Tribute Films Featuring One or More Original Keystone Cops

Easy Street 2 reels **Lone Star–Mutual Film Corporation (January 22, 1917)**
Producer/Writer/Director: Charles Chaplin.
Photographer: Roland Totheroh.
Cast: Charlie Chaplin, Edna Purviance, Eric Campbell, Henry Bergman, Albert Austin, James T. Kelley, John Rand, Frank J. Coleman, Stanley Sanford, Loyal Underwood.
Observations: Charlie Chaplin, a one-time Keystone Cop, always professed his admiration for Mack Sennett's comedy creation. And in *Easy Street*, hailed as one of Chaplin's most brilliant short films, there is more than a passing resemblance to the Keystone Cops in the unit Charlie joins. The Cops wear the traditional helmets that the Sennett players had worn (although Charlie and his fellow officers more accurately resemble the British bobbies of Chaplin's youth). Their onscreen antics are unmistakable, however, particularly in the sequence when Easy Street's powerful bully, Big Eric (Campbell), who had been anesthetized with a broken gas lamp by recruit Charlie in the previous scene, finds himself handcuffed in the station. Slowly coming to, he seems impervious to the entire force beating him with their billy clubs all at the same time. After freeing himself through sheer brute force, he proceeds to pummel the cops, throwing one around like a rag doll and knocking over the others. *Easy Street* and the eleven other Chaplin-Mutual two-reelers have been beautifully restored and are available on Blu-ray from Flicker Alley.

The Rough House 2 reels **Famous Players-Lasky (June 25, 1917)**
Producer: Joseph M. Schenck.
Directors: Roscoe Arbuckle, Buster Keaton.
Scenario: Roscoe Arbuckle, Buster Keaton, Joseph Anthony Roach.
Camera: Frank D. Williams.
Cast: Roscoe Arbuckle, Buster Keaton, Al St. John, Alice Lake, Joe Bordeaux, Glen Cavender, Agnese Neilsen, Josephine Stevens.
Observations: Buster Keaton, an admitted fan of the Keystone Cops, makes his first appearance in police garb in this two-reel comedy also starring Roscoe Arbuckle and Al St. John. Engaged in a brawl, Buster and Al are arrested and

told they have a choice to make—either go to jail or join the force; they choose the latter. Their first case involves a valuable necklace that is stolen during a dinner party. Someone phones for the police, resulting in the inevitable race to the scene of the crime. Buster and Keystone veterans Al St. John and Joe Bordeaux are dazzlingly acrobatic as the novice officers, with their stunts expertly filmed in longshots. Incidentally, during that period in filmmaking, questionable scenes were subject to censorship by city and state censorship boards. The Chicago Board of Censors, in fact, demanded that the act of stealing the necklace be cut. Extant; a 35mm transfer of *The Rough House* is included on the Image Entertainment DVD set, *The Best Arbuckle/ Keaton Collection*, and on Kino-Lorber's DVD/Blu-ray release of *Buster Keaton: The Shorts Collection, 1917–1923*.

Cops 2 reels **First National Pictures, Inc. (March 11, 1922)**
Producer: Joseph M. Schenck.
Director: Buster Keaton, Edward F. Cline.
Camera: Elgin Lessley.
Cast: Buster Keaton, Joe Roberts, Virginia Fox, Eddie Cline.
Observations: The Keystone Cops were no doubt Buster Keaton's inspiration when he made this two-reel comedy classic. Buster, a poor schnook trying to make an honest living, is mistaken as an anarchist during a policemen's parade, thereby incurring the ire of the entire Los Angeles force. The film moves at the speed of light and features hilarious run-ins, and running from, the dogged police force. Buster's co-director (as well as a supporting player) was original Keystone Cop Eddie Cline. Excellent 35mm transfers of Cops are included on two DVD/Blu-ray releases from Kino-Lorber: *Buster Keaton: The Shorts Collection, 1917–1923*, and *Buster Keaton: Short Films Collection, 1920–1923*.

Cleaning Up 2 reels **Paramount Pictures (September 27, 1930)**
Producer: Phil L. Ryan.
Director: Harry Edwards.
Cinematographers: Jack Breamer and Gus Peterson.
Film Editor: Arthur Huffsmith.
Cast: Chester Conklin, Mack Swain, Estelle Bradley, Gibson Gowland.
Observations: This early sound two-reeler effectively recreates the look and feel of silent film comedy, even using intertitles to advance the narrative. Two bumbling street sweepers—Chester Conklin and Mack Swain—inadvertently save the local police commissioner's life and are rewarded with jobs as policemen. Their first assignment reflects the commissioner's faith in them: they are to find and arrest Public Enemy No. 1. (This premise, with minor variations,

had been used previously by Roscoe Arbuckle in his 1917 Keystone Cops tribute *The Rough House*; W. C. Fields later added new life to the plot device in his 1940 comic masterpiece *The Bank Dick*.) The climax features a wild race through the downtown streets in a horse-drawn wagon. Naturally, despite their seeming incompetence, the two recruits get their man. (Incidentally, the man is played by Gibson Gowland, who portrayed the leading character McTeague in Erich von Stroheim's *Greed*.) *Cleaning Up* was released on DVD in 2006 as part of an anthology of early talkie shorts called *Cavalcade of Comedy*.

Stout Hearts and Willing Hands 2 reels **RKO Pathé Pictures (June 15, 1931)**
Director: Bryan Foy.
Production Company: Masquers Club.
Story and Screenwriters: Albert Austin and Walter Weems.
Cast: Frank Fay, Lew Cody, Laura LaPlante, Alec B. Francis, Mary Carr, Owen Moore, Tom Moore, Matt Moore, Georgie Harris, Eddie Quillan, Matthew Betz, Maurice Black, Benny Rubin, Bryant Washburn, Mack Swain, Chester Conklin, James Finlayson, Hank Mann, Clyde Cook, Bobby Vernon, Ford Sterling.
Observations: Featuring veteran vaudevillians and some former silent film stars, this was the first in a series of sound movie parodies produced by the Masquers Club. The Academy of Motion Picture Arts and Sciences nominated the twenty-minute film for Best Short Subject of 1931 (as well as a nomination for co-star Mack Swain), but the nominations were ultimately withdrawn, with no explanation given.

Keystone Hotel 2 reels **Warner Bros. Vitaphone (September 21, 1935)**
Director: Ralph Staub.
Story and Screenwriter: Joe Traub.
Cinematographer: William Rees.
Art Director: Esdras Hartley.
Film Editor: Frank McGee.
Music: Howard Jackson.
Cast: Ford Sterling, Ben Turpin, Chester Conklin, Marie Prevost, Hank Mann, Vivien Oakland, Dewey Robinson, Joseph Belmont, Joe Bordeaux, Glen Cavender, Heinie Conklin, Carrie Daumery, Jack Duffy, Bobby Dunn, Billy Engle, June Gittelson, Sol Gorss, Sheldon Jett, Jack "Tiny" Lipson, Henry Otho, Paul Panzer, Bert Roach, Henry Roquemore, Leo White, Roger Williams, Tom Wilson, Billy Gilbert, George Gray, Grover Ligon.
Observations: This was an experiment by producer Ralph Staub to reunite as many former Keystone players in one two-reel sound film as possible. A screening of the completed film proved so successful that a series was sug-

gested. The actors involved, however, insisted on a hefty pay raise, which effectively quashed the deal. The film ultimately fell into the public domain and has been passed off countless times since then as authentic silent movie footage, particularly the well-staged race-to-the-rescue and climactic pie-fight. The rear-screen footage used to replicate an amusement park roller coaster was later used by director Mal St. Clair in the 1943 Laurel & Hardy Fox feature *The Dancing Masters*. Ken Films, a home-movie outfit located in New Jersey, issued a silent, one-reel 8mm edition of *Keystone Hotel*, which evidently sold very well. They continuously show up on eBay.

Hollywood Cavalcade 97m **20th Century-Fox (October 13, 1939)**
Director: Irving Cummings; chase sequence directed by Malcolm St. Clair.
Producer: Darryl F. Zanuck.
Story: Hilary Lynn and Brown Holmes.
Screenwriter: Ernest Pascal.
Cinematographers: Allen M. Davey and Ernest Palmer.
Film Editor: Walter Thompson.
Cast: Alice Faye, Don Ameche, J. Edward Bromberg, Alan Curtis, Stuart Erwin, Jed Prouty, Donald Meek, George Givot, Al Jolson, Eddie Collins, Russell Hicks, Robert Lowery, Ben Welden, Willie Fung, Paul Stanton, Mary Forbes, Joseph Crehan, Irving Bacon.
Silent film guest stars: Mack Sennett, Buster Keaton, Hank Mann, Heinie Conklin, James Finlayson, Snub Pollard, Ben Turpin, Chester Conklin, Marjorie Beebe.
Observations: A beautiful transfer of *Hollywood Cavalcade* is available on DVD from 21st Century Fox Video.

Meet the Stars: Stars—Past and Present 6:39m **(July 24, 1941)**
Cast: Harriet Parsons (hostess/narrator), Mack Sennett, William Farnum, Mae Busch, Richard Bennett, Dorothy Davenport (Mrs. Wallace Reid), Charlie Murray, Chester Conklin, Edgar Kennedy, Andy Clyde, Heinie Conklin, John Wayne, Ann Miller, Judy Canova, among many others; ***archival footage:*** Mabel Normand.
Observations: Newsreel footage showing the dedication of the Mabel Normand Soundstage at Republic Pictures in Glendale, California, the former location of the Mack Sennett studio, on December 27, 1940. This historic record is included as an extra on volume one of the Mack Sennett Blu-ray collection, produced by CineMuseum, LLC and Keystone Films, LLC.

Trouble at the Beach 1 reel **R. M. C. Productions, Inc. (1942)**
Producer: Sam Coslow.
Director: Josef Bernie.
Cast: The "Original Keystone Kops" Chester Conklin, Eddie Gribbon, Hank Mann, Snub Pollard, Bill Irving.
Observations: A definite rarity, this takeoff on silent comedies was printed in reverse for rear projection and was issued as a "Soundie," viewable exclusively via the Mills Panoram machine—essentially a jukebox for short films. This historic record is included as an extra on CineMuseum's forthcoming Blu-ray set *Mack Sennett Collection Vol. II.*

Merton of the Movies 82m **Metro-Goldwyn-Mayer (October 11, 1947)**
Producer: Albert Lewis.
Director: Robert Alton.
Writer: Lou Breslow and George Wells, based on the 1922 novel by Harry Leon Wilson and the 1923 play by George S. Kaufman and Marc Connelly.
Cinematographer: Paul C. Vogel.
Music: David Snell and Robert Franklyn.
Cast: Red Skelton, Virginia O'Brien, Gloria Grahame, Leon Ames, Alan Mowbray, Charles D. Brown, Hugo Haas, Harry Hayden, Tom Trout, Douglas Fowley, Dick Wessel.
Observations: *Merton of the Movies* was initially a comic novel written by Harry Leon Wilson and published in 1922; millions of copies were sold. It told the story of a nebbish named Merton Gill, who dreams of becoming a famous dramatic film star. The only thing is, he is a hopeless ham who insists on mugging his way through a role. A film producer reasons that the neophyte actor is so bad that he might be considered funny. Merton is then cast in a comedy, although the hapless young man is led to believe he is starring in a drama. The great playwriting team of George S. Kaufman and Marc Connelly adapted this premise for the Broadway stage, where it made its debut in 1923, followed by a successful run of 392 performances. In 1924, it was made as a silent film starring Glenn Hunter, the actor who introduced the role on stage. In 1932, a sound version starring Stuart Erwin was released to theaters, this time bearing the title *Make Me a Star.* Eventually, the story was purchased by MGM as a vehicle for Red Skelton. Buster Keaton, then a gag writer for MGM, coached Skelton and others in the cast on silent comedy technique. He also no doubt contributed gags to a very funny sequence featuring Jack Sterling, King Mojave, Robert Milasch, and four Keystone Cops—Chester Conklin, Heinie Conklin, Clarence Hennecke, and Vernon Dent—in an undercranked silent comedy recreation. The 1947 film, under the original title *Merton of the Movies*, was a critical and

commercial failure, with a loss to the studio of $367,000. (It was released by MGM on VHS in 1994; there is yet to be an official DVD or Blu-ray release.) In 1957, a live adaptation of *Merton of the Movies* opened at Hollywood's Huntington Hartford Theatre. Its star was none other than Buster Keaton.

Erskine Johnson's Hollywood Reel 3m Johnson-Watson Productions (January 17, 1950)

Observations: Newsreel of Mack Sennett's seventieth birthday celebration includes a recreation of a silent comedy featuring James Finlayson and Hank Mann. Also on hand are well-wishers Chester Conklin, Minta Durfee, Andy Clyde, Ora Carew, Blanche Payson, Ruth Hiatt, Elva Taylor, Julie Faye, Babe Evans, and many others. This footage (and several minutes of outtakes) can be found as a bonus extra on Disc 2 of the Blu-ray set *The Mack Sennett Collection, Vol. I.*

Joe Palooka in Humphrey Takes a Chance 62m Monogram Pictures (June 4, 1950)

Producer: Hal E. Chester.
Director: Jean Yarbrough.
Cast: Leon Errol, Joe Kirkwood Jr., Robert Coogan, Lois Collier, Gil Lamb, Tom Neal, Jack Kirkwood, Mary Margaret Robinson, Andrew Tombes, Iris Adrian.
Observations: A minor political satire, based on the once-popular comic strip, "Joe Palooka," which was introduced in 1930. The only distinctive element of this low-budget film is its climactic pie fight, staged with excellent timing (no doubt) by four guest stars: Chester Conklin, Hank Mann, Heinie Conklin, and Clarence Hennecke, billed as Members of the Original "Mack Sennett Keystone Kops." Grapevine Video released a sharp 16mm transfer on DVD in 2016.

Bud Abbott and Lou Costello Meet the Keystone Kops 79m Universal-International (February 25, 1955)

Producer: Howard Christie.
Production Manager: Foster Thompson.
Director: Charles Lamont.
Assistant Director: William Holland.
Second Unit Director: Tom Shaw.
Story: Lee Loeb.
Scenarist: John Grant.
Script Supervisor: Adele Cannon.
Musical Director: Joseph Gershenson.
Music: William Lava, Henry Mancini, and Herman Stein.

Cinematographer: Reggie Lanning, A.S.C.
Film Editor: Edward Curtiss.
Art Directors: Alexander Golitzen and Bill Newberry.
Set Decorators: Russell A. Gausman.
Costume Designer: Jay A. Morley Jr.
Make-up Artist: Bud Westmore.
Hair Stylist: Joan St. Oegger.
Cast: Bud Abbott, Lou Costello, Fred Clark, Lynn Bari, "Slapsie" Maxie Rosenbloom, Roscoe Ates, Doris Barton, Margaret Eubank, Peggy Gordon, Barbara Jones, Dorothy Martinson, Beverly Snyder, Marjorie Bennett, Joe Besser, Ralph Brooks, Forest Burns, Colin Campbell, Carl Christian, Carole Costello, Jack Daly, Joe Devlin, Charles Dorety, Paul Dubov, Sam Flint, Bess Flowers, Slim Gaut, Joe Gilbert, Kit Guard, William Haade, Frank Hagney, Don House, Bob Jellison, Byron Keith, Donald Kerr, Henry Kulky, Murray Leonard, William H. O'Brien, Allen Ray, Houseley Stevenson Jr., Jack Stoney, Harry Tyler, Billy Varga, Frank Wilcox. **Silent film guest stars:** Heinie Conklin, Hank Mann, Herold Goodwin.
Observations: This penultimate Abbott & Costello Universal film features a cameo by Mack Sennett himself, who throws a pie with precision into Bud Abbott's face. The story, which takes place in 1912, has Bud and Lou being tricked into buying Thomas Edison's embryonic Black Maria studio before making the trek to Hollywood, where they meet the Keystone Kops. Although the film itself is rife with anachronisms, it is redeemed by the climactic, well-staged Keystone Kops chase sequence involving automobiles, a train, and a motorcycle and sidecar, all of which is beautifully staged by silent comedy veteran Charles Lamont. The working title, "Bud Abbott and Lou Costello Meet the Stunt Men," was considered by the studio's top brass as they felt the name "Keystone Kops" would be meaningless to contemporary moviegoers. Perhaps due to the success of Sennett's autobiography, *King of Comedy*, published the same year the film went into production (1954), it was decided to revert to the now-familiar title. Sennett was reportedly paid five hundred dollars from Universal for use of the name.

Have Badge, Will Chase, a one-reel version of the feature's madcap chase sequence, was readily available for home-viewing use from Castle Films, a mail-order company based in New York City. It was not uncommon for camera stores back in the sixties and early seventies to include a complimentary print of *Have Badge, Will Chase* (the "streamlined," fifty-foot, silent version, which ran for approximately three minutes, not the two-hundred-foot "complete" version, which ran for around eight) when selling an 8mm projector. In the years since, the entire film (soundtrack and all) has been twice released on Universal

DVD, in 2005 and 2009. In 2019, Shout! Factory released a Blu-ray set containing immaculate transfers of twenty-eight Bud and Lou films for Universal, *Bud Abbott and Lou Costello Meet the Keystone Kops* included. The feature's original theatrical trailer will be included as a bonus extra on the forthcoming *Mack Sennett Collection, Vol. II*.

Won Ton Ton, the Dog Who Saved Hollywood 91m **Paramount Pictures (May 26, 1976)**
Director: Michael Winner.
Writer: Arnold Schulman.
Cinematographer: Richard H. Kline.
Music: Neal Hefti.
Cast: Madeline Kahn, Bruce Dern, Art Carney, Ron Liebman, Teri Garr, Ronny Graham, Phil Silvers, and seventy guest stars in cameos.
Observations: The best thing about this sometimes-lurid, occasionally hilarious satire of 1924 Hollywood (in addition to Neal Hefti's wonderful score, Madeline Kahn's performance as Estie, an aspiring actress who adopts a scraggly German Shepard, Won Ton Ton, played to perfection by Augustus von Schumacher) is trying to name all the once-famous actors and actresses who turn up in bit parts. In fact, this marked the final film appearance of scores of former 20th Century-Fox stars, including Richard Arlen, Carmel Myers, Stepin Fetchit, Rudy Vallee, George Jessel, Ann Rutherford, Andy Devine, Barbara Nichols, Johnny Weissmuller, William Demarest, Jack LaRue, Benny Rubin, Dennis Morgan, and the Ritz Brothers (Harry and Jimmy, as cleaning women no less). There is the obligatory pie fight near the conclusion, with some imitation Keystone Cops (played by Morey Amsterdam, Eddie Foy Jr., and Peter Lawford), although the director does not bother to show us their faces, which is no great loss as they are covered in custard. Incidentally, this is the last motion picture to feature an original Keystone Cop, eighty-year-old Eddie LeVeque. *Won Ton Ton, the Dog Who Saved Hollywood* was released on DVD by Legend Films in 2008.

Theatrical Films Featuring Imitation Keystone Cops

Big Moments from Little Pictures 2 reels **Hal Roach/Pathé (March 30, 1924)**
Director: Paul Clements.
Title Writer: H. M. Walker.
Cinematographers: Robert Doran and Otto Himm.
Film Editor: T. J. Crizer.

Cast: Will Rogers, Marie Mosquini, Earl Mohan, Guinn "Big Boy" Williams, Noah Young, Charlie Hall, Carmencita Johnson, Billy Engle.

Observations: Will Rogers pays an homage to his contemporaries (Douglas Fairbanks, Rudolph Valentino, and Ford Sterling) by way of hilarious parodies of their signature roles. Doing a spot-on impersonation of Ford Sterling as Chief Teheezel, he is more than ably supported by various Roach stock players replicating the Cops. A generous portion of the film is highlighted in Robert Youngson's *The Golden Age of Comedy* (1957). A more complete print (including close-ups of some Sennett doppelgängers) is available on Image's *Slapstick Encyclopedia*, Vol. VI: "The Hal Roach All-Stars."

Show People 79m Metro-Goldwyn-Mayer (November 20, 1928)
Producers: Marion Davies, Irving Thalberg (uncredited), and King Vidor.
Director: King Vidor.
Screenwriters: Agnes Christine Johnston and Laurence Stallings.
Title Writer: Ralph Spence.
Cast: Marion Davies, William Haines, Dell Henderson, Paul Ralli, Tenen Holtz, Harry Gribbon, Sidney Bracey, Polly Moran, Albert Conte; **special guest stars:** Charlie Chaplin, Douglas Fairbanks, William S. Hart, Lew Cody, John Gilbert, and Renée Adorée.

Observations: This wonderful silent comedy, released during the dawn of the talkies, is loosely based on Gloria Swanson's rise from a girl in the lowly Sennett comedies to Cecil B. DeMille's top dramatic star. In a wonderfully evocative depiction of the Keystone Cops, there is the obligatory chase sequence that perfectly captures their era. The scene (as well as the entire film) benefits by Photoplay Production Ltd.'s employment of Maestro Carl Davis, who composed the ultimate Cops-style chase music. In 2003, *Show People*—deemed by the Library of Congress to be "culturally, historically, or aesthetic importance"—was selected for preservation in the National Film Registry. It is currently available on DVD (with William Axt's original synchronized score) by Warner Archive collection.

The Stolen Jools 2 reels Masquers Club of Hollywood/Paramount Pictures (April 4, 1931)
Producer: Pat Casey.
Directors: William C. McGann, John C. Adolfi, Thomas Atkins, Harold S. Bucquet, Victor Heerman, Russell Mack.
Screenwriters: Edwin J. Burke, Percy Heath.
Cast: Norma Shearer, Polly Moran, Gary Cooper, Joan Crawford, William Haines, Charles Butterworth, Richard Barthelmess, Richard Dix, Jack Oakie,

Fay Wray, Loretta Young, Douglas Fairbanks Jr., George "Gabby" Hayes, Joe E. Brown, Laurel & Hardy, Wheeler & Woolsey, Our Gang, and many others.

Observations: This meandering two-reeler was produced for the purpose of raising funds for the National Vaudeville Artists Tuberculosis Sanitarium. Ironically, it was co-sponsored by Chesterfield cigarettes. Built on the tiny premise that MGM's Norma Shearer's jewels had been reported stolen, the short opens in the Los Angeles Police station, where the curmudgeonly desk sergeant (Wallace Beery) summons the force (a bumbling group of Keystone Cops, featuring Buster Keaton, Jack Hill, and J. Farrell MacDonald), who set off to catch the culprit. Although lost for decades, prints eventually turned up in the UK (where the film was released as *The Slippery Pearls*) and the U.S. It can be viewed on public domain DVDs and YouTube.

Mickey's Gala Premier 7m **Walt Disney Productions/United Artists (July 1, 1933)**

Producer: Walt Disney.

Director: Burt Gillett

Cast: *In caricature form:* Sid Grauman (host), Mickey Mouse, Minnie Mouse, Pluto, Horace Horsecollar, Clarabelle Cow (Disney characters); guest celebrities: John, Ethel, and Lionel Barrymore (dressed in their costumes from *Rasputin and the Empress*), Joan Crawford (dressed as Sadie Thompson in *Rain*), Eddie Cantor (as the bogus bullfighter in *The Kid From Spain*), Bela Lugosi (as Dracula), Boris Karloff (as Frankenstein's monster), Fredric March (as Mr. Hyde), Will H. Hayes (dressed as a king, a reference to his being the industry's Censorship Czar), Laurel & Hardy, the Marx Brothers, Maurice Chevalier, Jean Harlow, Janet Gaynor, Harold Lloyd, Clark Gable, Edward G. Robinson, Adolphe Menjou, George Arliss, Joe E. Brown, Charlie Chaplin, Buster Keaton, Helen Hayes, William Powell, Chester Morris, Wallace Beery, Marie Dressler, Rudy Vallee, Myrna Loy, Ed Wynn, Wheeler & Woolsey, Douglas Fairbanks, Constance Bennett, Warner Baxter, Walt Disney, Greta Garbo.

Observations: In this star-studded animated musical short, Mickey Mouse interacts with humans for the first time as the biggest names in Hollywood arrive in their limousines at Grauman's Chinese Theatre to celebrate the premiere (although the title card reads *premier*) of his latest cartoon. The traffic is so congested that the Keystone Cops—Ben Turpin, Ford Sterling, Mack Swain, Harry Langdon, and Chester Conklin—are called in to control it. This entertaining cartoon is included on the DVD *Walt Disney Treasures: Mickey Mouse in Black & White*.

Who Killed Cock Robin? 8m **Walt Disney Studios (June 26, 1935)**
Producer: Walt Disney.
Director: David Hand
Writers: William Cottrell, Joe Grant, Bob Kuwahara.
Animators: Norman Ferguson, Clyde Geronimi, Hardie Gramatky, Joe Grant.
Music: Frank Churchill.
Cast: Billy Bletcher, Pinto Colvig, Clarence Nash, Purv Pullen, Martha Wentworth.
Observations: An intriguing aspect of this vintage Walt Disney cartoon concerns the involvement of two Sennett veterans, Billy Bletcher and Vance "Pinto" Colvig. Bletcher's
career in silent comedy dated back to 1916; Colvig worked as an animator for Sennett in the twenties. In later years, both Colvig and Bletcher happily participated in Keystone Kop reunions.

Matthew Hahn, author of the excellent *Animated Marx Brothers* (BearManor Media, 2018) vividly describes this rather violent depiction of the Keystone Kops in bird form.

> A Silly Symphony based on a nursery rhyme. All characters are anthropomorphic birds. Cock Robin, a caricature of Bing Crosby, serenades Jenny Wren, a caricature of Mae West. Someone shoots him with an arrow, and he plunges to the ground in front of The Old Crow Bar. The avian Keystone Kops arrive and start rounding up the usual suspects: a mentally handicapped cuckoo, caricaturing Harpo Marx; a gangster, Legs Sparrow; and a blackbird, caricaturing Stepin Fetchit. A Kop beats on the bird's head, dissolving to Judge Owl pounding his gavel. Court is now in session. Paul Parrot is prosecuting. Cock Robin's body is Exhibit "A." Merritt and Kaufmann write that Joe Grant said William Cottrell's story was inspired by Gilbert and Sullivan, "But the court scene is closer to the rough-and-tumble world of minstrelsy, slapstick burlesque, and the Marx Brothers—particularly *Duck Soup* [1933]—than to the refined topsy-turvy of nineteenth century operetta." The blackbird is the first witness, as the Kops beat him mercilessly. After he says he knows nothing, he is thrown back into "Sing-Sing," the Kops beating him all the way there. Next up is Legs. Two Kops beat him on the way to the witness stand, but . . . Legs refuses to talk. Finally, the cuckoo gives his wordless testimony. He then implicates Judge Owl, then Paul Parrot, then both, then himself. "He don't know a thing," says Parrot.

Suddenly Jenny Wren enters the courtroom, seeking justice for her dead lover. "These birds look guilty," she says. The Judge, smitten, says, "Hang 'em all!"

An arrow pierces the Judge's mortarboard. It was first fired by Dan Cupid, who also shot Cock Robin—not, it turns out, fatally, but just with an arrow of love. When Robin fell from the tree, he was knocked cold. He now comes to and kisses Jenney Wren, The Kops apologize for profiling based on priors, mental defect, and race. Just kidding.

Who Killed Cock Robin? was released in 2001 as part of the DVD release *Walt Disney Treasures Wave One: Silly Symphonies* and was introduced by film historian Leonard Maltin.

The *Hollywood Cavalcade* Opening Night 83s Fox Movietone News (October 13, 1939)

Cast: In attendance at the film's major premiere are the producer Darryl F. Zanuck and his wife; director Irving Cummings and his mother; Ben Turpin, looking quite normal, with his gray hair combed neatly and sans his paste-on mustache; Mr. and Mrs. Jean Hersholt; Linda Darnell; Tyrone Power; Sonja Henie; Jane Withers; Cesar Romero and Joan Crawford; Don Ameche; Alice Faye and Tony Martin.

Observations: Newsreel taken outside the 4 Star Theatre at 5112 Wilshire Boulevard in Los Angeles. In the nostalgic spirit of the evening, it opens with eight uniformed Keystone Cop ringers pulling up in a Model T Ford.

The Adventures of Ichabod and Mr. Toad 68m Walt Disney Pictures /RKO Radio Pictures (January 6, 1950)

Producer: Walt Disney.
Directors: Clyde Geronimi, Jack Kinney, James Algar.
Cast: Basil Rathbone, Bing Crosby (narrators); Eric Blore, J. Pat O'Malley, Claude Allister.
Observations: One of the most delightful of all Walt Disney animated films, this contains two classic tales for children: *The Wind in the Willows* (1908), by Kenneth Grahame, and *The Legend of Sleepy Hollow* (1820), by Washington Irving. The one pertinent to this study is the former; it stars the hilarious anthropomorphic character Mr. Toad (voiced by British character actor Eric Blore). At one point, the reckless amphibian is on the lam, being chased by none other than the Keystone Cops. One of the animators on this film, Clyde Geronimi, also worked on Disney's *Who Killed Cock Robin?* (1935), which features the Cops in avian form. *The Adventures of Ichabod and Mr. Toad* was

released on Blu-ray, DVD, and Digital HD and in a two-film collection with *Fun and Fancy Free* (1947) in 2014. It is also available to stream on Disney+ since that service began in 2019.

Keystone Kops Intermission Cartoons (1959-1969)

Observations: Anyone old enough to remember family outings to a drive-in movie theater is sure to recall the intermission ads touting snacks. Two such enticements feature the Keystone Kops in animated form. The first, a thirty-eight-second entry from 1959, is drawn in the abstract style of that period. The film opens inside a warehouse where inept burglars are bungling an attempt to find the refreshments stored therein. The scene switches to a police station, where an emergency call comes through, reporting the robbery in progress. A tiny, mustachioed police chief summons his officers and leads them to the warehouse, where they catch the crooks red-handed. Another intermission ad (this one apparently from the late 1960s and featuring both live-action footage and animation) is specifically advertising Coca-Cola. A blonde model (shot in close-up) reacts inanely to the pop-art version of the Keystone Cops around her. Even at forty-eight seconds it feels too long.

Casino Royale 131m **Columbia Pictures (April 13, 1967)**

Producers: Charles K. Feldman, Jerry Bresler.
Directors: Ken Hughes, John Huston, Joseph McGrath, Robert Parrish, Val Guest, Richard Talmadge.
Screenwriters: Wolf Mankowitz, John Law, and Michael Sayers (based on the novel *Casino Royale* by Ian Fleming).
Music: Burt Bacharach (Academy Award winner, "The Look of Love").
Cast: Peter Sellers, Ursula Andress, David Niven, Woody Allen, Joanna Pettet, Orson Welles, Daliah Lavi, among many, many others.
Observations: Overlong, overstuffed James Bond satire, featuring innumerable celebrities in cameo roles. The one scene that pertains to this study involves a riot breaking out at a large upscale party and someone yelling, "POLICE!" The next shot (in black & white with tinkly piano music) is of the Keystone Cops jumping into their patrol car, ready for action. Twenty-two-year-old Geraldine Chaplin (wearing a paste-on toothbrush mustache) is one of the Cops. So, not only did Charlie Chaplin once join the force, his daughter did as well. *Casino Royale* was released by MGM Video in 2001; a collector's edition Blu-ray (20th Century Fox Home Entertainment) followed a decade later, in 2012.

Silent Movie 87m **20th Century–Fox (June 16, 1976)**
Producer: Michael Hertzberg.
Director: Mel Brooks.
Screenwriters: Mel Brooks, Rudy DeLuca, Barry Levinson, Ron Clark.
Music: John Morris.
Cast: Mel Brooks, Marty Feldman, Dom DeLuise, Sid Caesar, Harold Gould, and several guest stars, both vintage (Fritz Feld, Harry Ritz, Henny Youngman, stunt man Harvey Parry) and contemporary (Paul Newman, Burt Reynolds, James Caan, Liza Minnelli).
Observations: Nineteen seventy-six was a banner year for old Hollywood. Eighty-year-old George Burns won a Best Supporting Actor Oscar for Neil Simon's *The Sunshine Boys* (1975). *Won Ton Ton, the Dog Who Saved Hollywood* had cameos by seventy former stars. Theaters were showing such biopics as *Gable and Lombard*, *W. C. Fields and Me*, and the MGM musical compilation *That's Entertainment, Part II*. Perhaps the most significant tribute came from filmmaker Mel Brooks. *Silent Movie*, an Academy Award–nominated parody of silent comedies, has several moments of inspired slapstick and a Sennett-style chase sequence, featuring a group of black-suited corporate bad guys jumping and running à la the Keystone Cops. Although *Silent Movie* was both a critical and commercial success for Brooks and 20th Century–Fox, the concept of a mainstream film without dialogue would not be attempted again until *The Artist*, which won the Academy Award for Best Picture of 2011. *Silent Movie* was released on DVD by 20th Century Fox Home Entertainment in 2009; *The Mel Brooks Collection*, a Blu-ray collector's set containing *Silent Movie* and eight other films by the director, followed in 2017.

Gilbert & Sullivan's Pirates of Penzance 112m **Universal Pictures (February 18, 1983)**
Producer: Joseph Papp.
Lyrics: Sir William Schwenck Gilbert.
Music: Sir Arthur Seymour Sullivan.
Screenwriter/Director: Wilford Leach.
Cast: Kevin Kline, Angela Lansbury, Linda Ronstadt, George Rose, Rex Smith.
Observations: Based on the theatrical production by Joseph Papp, *Pirates of Penzance* is a film adaptation of the 1879 Gilbert & Sullivan musical comedy. One of the key elements of this particular operetta is the policemen's chorus, a group of comical cops. It is possible that Mack Sennett, a confirmed aficionado of musical theatre, had seen this show at one time or another and was influenced by the device, although he generally stated that the Keystone Cops were his answer to the early French comedy films. Comedy historian Trav S.D.

(*Chain of Fools*, BearManor Media, 2013) has pointed out that a major revival of *Pirates of Penzance* was staged at Broadway's Casino Theatre in 1912, the same year the Keystone Cops made their film debut. But, as he is quick to add, that's just a theory.

Dot Goes to Hollywood 73m **Yoram Gross Films (1987)**
Producer/Director: Yoram Gross.
Writers: Rod Hay, John Palmer.
Music: Guy Gross.
Observations: This low-budget animated children's feature, made in Australia, is based on a beloved Australian children's book, *Dot and the Kangaroo*, written by Ethel Pendley in 1899. The 1987 film continues the story by featuring Dot, a little girl with big dreams, in a classic Hollywood setting. Several vintage characters appear in caricature, including Laurel & Hardy, Groucho Marx, and Charlie Chaplin, the latter of whom interacts with W. C. Fields and the Keystone Cops. *Dot Goes to Hollywood* was released on DVD (Region 4) in 2014.

Chaplin 143m **Tri-Star Pictures (December 18, 1992)**
Producer/Director: Richard Attenborough.
Screenwriters: William Boyd, Bryan Forbes, William Goldman (based on *My Autobiography* by Charles Chaplin, and *Chaplin: His Life and Art* by David Robinson).
Cast: Robert Downey Jr., Dan Ackroyd, Geraldine Chaplin, Kevin Kline, Anthony Hopkins, Milla Jovovitch, Moira Kelly, Penelope Ann Miller.
Observations: Lugubrious biopic of Charlie Chaplin, with an Academy Award–winning performance by Robert Downey Jr. in the title role. In the story (as in life), Chaplin began his film career at the Keystone Film Company in late 1913. Mack Sennett (Dan Ackroyd) is depicted, as are, of course, the Keystone Cops. The film has since been released by StudioCanal in a deluxe edition on Blu-ray.

Theatrical Compilations Featuring the Keystone Cops

The Movies March On 22m **RKO Radio Pictures (July 7, 1939)**
Cast: Jackson Beck (narrator); *archival footage:* Renée Adorée, Gilbert M. Anderson, Theda Bara, Lionel Barrymore, Cecil B. DeMille, Walt Disney, Douglas Fairbanks, Greta Garbo, Mary Garden, John Gilbert, Lillian Gish, Al Jolson.
Observations: A documentary short (part of RKO's *March of Time* series) featuring film clips from *The Great Train Robbery* (1903) to the present day (1939). The Keystone Cops are represented by a clip from *Tillie's Punctured Romance*.

Happy Times and Jolly Moments 2 reels **Warner Bros. "Broadway Brevities" Featurette (July 10, 1943)**
Cast: Lou Marcelle (narrator); ***archival footage:*** Ben Turpin, Harry Langdon, Slim Summerville, Mack Swain, Charlie Murray, Chester Conklin, Mabel Normand, Louise Fazenda, Gloria Swanson, Polly Moran, Mildred June, James Finlayson, Roscoe Arbuckle, Billy Bevan, Charley Chase, Eddie Gribbon.
Observations: Joke-laden narration mars this retrospective containing some Sennett–First National releases and their imitators. The Cops are represented by a chase scene from *On Patrol* (1922) and the pie-fight sequence from the non-Sennett sound short *Keystone Hotel* (1935). A one-reel silent edition of *Happy Times and Jolly Moments* was available for home use in 8mm from Ken Films in the 1970s.

Once Over Lightly 2 reels **A Warner Bros. "Broadway Brevities" Featurette (October 14, 1944)**
Director: James Bloodworth.
Music: William Lava.
Film Editor: Doug Gould.
Cast: Knox Manning (narrator); ***archival footage:*** Billy Bevan, Andy Clyde, Louise Fazenda, James Finlayson, Marvin Loback, Ben Turpin, the Keystone Cops.

Good Old Corn 2 reels **A Warner Bros. "Broadway Brevities" Featurette (November 24, 1945)**
Cast: Knox Manning (narrator); ***archival footage:*** Billy Bevan, Mildred June, Harry Gribbon, Monty Banks, the Keystone Cops.
Observations: Another jokey lookback at "old-time" comedies, with the police chase from Sennett's *Be Reasonable* (1921). Like *Keystone Hotel* and *Happy Times and Jolly Moments*, a one-reel 8mm silent version of *Good Old Corn* was made available for home use by Ken Films in the 1970s.

Down Memory Lane 72m **Eagle-Lion (September 23, 1949)**
Executive Producer: Mack Sennett.
Director (of newly filmed sequences): Phil Carlson.
Supervisor: Aubrey Schenck.
Photographer: Walter Strenge.
Film Editor: Fred Allen.
Musical Director: Irving Friedman.
Additional Music: Sol Kaplan.
Scenarist: Steve Allen.

Cast (new footage only, shot over a two-day period): Steve Allen, Franklin Pangborn, Frank Nelson, Yvonne Peattie, Renny McEvoy, Jo Ann Joyce, Rowland McCracken, **special guest star:** Mack Sennett.

Observations: This was an early attempt to showcase Mack Sennett comedies, with an uncharacteristic emphasis on his sound films (including Bing Crosby's *Sing, Bing, Sing*, and W. C. Fields's *The Dentist*, both of which are shown almost in their entirety). The much earlier silent footage briefly shows Officer Billy Bevan's violent encounter with a call box, unidentified clips of the Keystone Cops in the police station, and a chase involving a horse-drawn fire engine.

All in Good Fun 50m Butchers Film Service, UK (1955)

Producer: Henry E. Fisher

Writer/Director: James M. Anderson.

Cast: Bob Monkhouse (host); **archival footage:** John Bunny, Charlie Chaplin, Marie Dressler, Max Linder, Fred Mace, Mack Sennett, Ford Sterling.

Observations: British-made compilation featuring silent film comedians, including Dressler, Chaplin, and the Cops in *Tillie's Punctured Romance*.

Lifetime of Comedy 59m D. U. K. Films, UK (1960)

Writer: Sid Stone.

Cast: Kent Walton (narrator); **archival footage:** Charlie Chaplin, Buster Keaton, Harold Lloyd, Eddie Quillan, Ben Turpin, the Keystone Cops, Bing Crosby, Billy Bevan, Danny Kaye, Harry Langdon, Mack Sennett, Ford Sterling.

Observations: Advertised with the tagline "One Hour of Backaching Laughs," this compilation proved that old clips mixed with corny narration and Mickey Mouse music were no longer enough for discerning film buffs—not when Charlie Chaplin, Harold Lloyd, and Robert Youngson were assembling first-rate compilations of their own, complete with restored prints and orchestral scores. Another oddity concerning this British import is the use of sound Educational shorts, presented as though they were silents.

When Comedy Was King 81m 20th Century–Fox (February 29, 1960)

Producer and Scenarist: Robert Youngson.

Music: Ted Royal.

Sound Effects: Ralph Curtiss.

Cast: Dwight Weist (narrator); **archival footage:** Roscoe Arbuckle, Wallace Beery, Charlie Chaplin, Buster Keaton, Edgar Kennedy, the Keystone Cops, Harry Langdon, Laurel & Hardy, Mabel Normand, The Sennett Girls, Gloria Swanson, Ben Turpin, Billy Bevan, Andy Clyde, Chester Conklin, Vernon Dent,

Stu Erwin, James Finlayson, Madeline Hurlock, Mabel Normand, Daphne Pollard, Snub Pollard, Al St. John, Mack Swain, Keystone Teddy, Bobby Vernon.

Observations: Robert G. Youngson (1917–1974), a Harvard University graduate who went on to become a two-time Academy Award–winning documentarian of historical news footage, indulged his unending passion for silent comedy by producing a string of feature-length theatrical films, the first being *The Golden Age of Comedy*, released by Distribution Corporation of America (DCA) in late 1957. Due to an aggressive promotional campaign, enthusiastic endorsements from the likes of talk show hosts Jack Paar and Steve Allen, as well as a two-page, ten-photo spread in *Life* magazine entitled "Sight Gag Revival," *The Golden Age of Comedy* helped to generate a resurgence in the popularity of silent comedy stars, Laurel & Hardy in particular. The Cops were represented by the 1924 Hal Roach–produced two-reeler *Big Moments from Little Pictures*, starring Will Rogers as Ford Sterling. The second in the series, *When Comedy Was King*, is the best of the Youngson compilations. In a memorable sequence from *Wandering Willies* (1926), a Sennett-produced Billy Bevan–Andy Clyde two-reeler, some latter-day Keystone Cops are memorably dragged behind their patrol wagon. The series' third installment, *The Days of Thrills and Laughter* (1961), also had a tip of the helmet to the Cops by including a snippet from the 1917 Keystone comedy *Her Torpedoed Love*. These family-friendly anthologies also turned up regularly on television in the sixties and seventies, introducing a new generation to the silent comedians in their best moments. It is gratifying, therefore, to see these special films being released on DVD. *The Golden Age of Comedy* and *When Comedy Was King*, for example, were released under the title *The First Kings of Comedy* by Genius Entertainment in 2007. A separate DVD of *When Comedy Was King* was released by VCI Video in 2017; this is worth having as well: the film was restored from the original negative, allowing for a stunning viewing experience. For more information on the late Mr. Youngson and his contribution to silent film preservation, there is a fascinating chapter on him in Scott MacGillivray's splendid *Laurel & Hardy: From the Forties Forward* (iUniverse, Second edition, 2009).

Television Documentaries/Compilations Featuring the Keystone Cops

The Fun Factory 30m **Paul Killiam Productions (1960)**
Producers: Paul Killiam and Saul J. Turrell.
Director and Scenarist: Saul J. Turrell.
Research: William K. Everson.

Observations: This fine educational film details the history of Mack Sennett and his silent comedies. The Keystone Cops are discussed in some detail, beginning with clips from *A Muddy Romance*, *Bangville Police*, and *Tillie's Punctured Romance*.

Comedy Capers 15m **National Telepix (1960–1962)**
Cast: Laurel & Hardy, Ben Turpin, Harry Langdon, Billy Bevan, the Keystone Cops, among others.
Observations: This kiddie-oriented program, consisting of ninety-one episodes, ran in syndication throughout the sixties, usually during the daytime. The show opened with a sequence featuring the above-mentioned comedians, including the Keystone Cops in the famous "dragged from the patrol wagon" routine from *Wandering Willies* (1926). That film, which stars Billy Bevan and Andy Clyde, was cut down by approximately half its length and retitled "The Hoboes."

The Funny Manns 15m **New Merritt Enterprises (1960)**
Observations: Designed for the same juvenile audience as *Comedy Capers*, the show is comprised of silent comedy snippets and encompasses 130 episodes. The novelty of this program is the presence of comic actor Cliff Norton, who portrays several of his fictional relatives who had graced the silent screen, all of whom shared the last name Mann: Police Mann, Circus Mann, Fisher Mann, et al. One wonders if he was ever tempted to play Hank Mann.

The DuPont Show of the Week: "Laughter USA," 60m **(September 17, 1961)**
Director: Donald B. Hyatt.
Screenwriters: Richard Hansen and Rod Reed.
Cast: George Burns (narrator); ***archival footage:*** Clark & McCullough, Weber & Fields, Laurel & Hardy, Eddie Cantor, Bob Hope, the Marx Brothers, Ben Turpin, Phil Silvers, Jonathan Winters, the Keystone Cops.

The DuPont Show of the Week: "Merrily We Roll Along," 60m **(October 22, 1961)**
Director: Robert L. Bendick.
Writer: Philip H. Reisman.
Cast: Groucho Marx (narrator), Skitch Henderson (bandleader); ***archival footage:*** Ben Turpin, Will Rogers, the Keystone Cops.

Hollywood and the Stars: **"The Funny Men, Part I,"** 30m **NBC/UA (December 9, 1963)**
Producer: David Wolper.
Director: Jack Haley Jr.
Theme Music: Elmer Bernstein.
Narrator: Joseph Cotten.
Observations: This elegant series details Hollywood's history by way of half-hour episodes focusing on either a star or a genre. Encompassing thirty-one episodes, it ran in prime time from September 30, 1963, to May 18, 1964, and continued in occasional daytime reruns until the late sixties. Part I of the two-part examination of movie comedians begins, not surprisingly, with Mack Sennett and the Keystone studios, with ample footage of the usual suspects: Turpin, Arbuckle, Chaplin, Sterling, Summerville, Conklin, and others of the Keystone gang.

Fractured Flickers 25m **Jay Ward Productions/Desilu (1963–1964)**
Creator: Chris Hayward.
Screenwriters: Allan Burns, Chris Hayward, George Atkins, Bill Scott.
Host: Hans Conried.
Observations: In a desecrating presentation of some of the silent era's greatest stars (including Lon Chaney, Rudolph Valentino, Douglas Fairbanks, and Conrad Veidt), comedy music, cartoon sound effects, and ludicrous dialogue (voiced by June Foray, Paul Frees, and Bill Scott) make a complete mockery of films once considered to be serious dramas. Several Sennett comedies are also ridiculed (something akin to a parody of a parody), including *A Muddy Romance* and *Our Dare-Devil Chief,* both of which feature the Keystone Cops. The Cops are also seen in cartoon form during the show's animated opening. All twenty-six episodes of this series were released on DVD in 2004.

Hollywood: The Pioneers: **"Comedy—A Serious Business," Photoplay Productions (1980)**
Producers, Writers, and Directors: David Gill and Kevin Brownlow.
Observations: This brilliant thirteen-part series is essentially a love letter to American silent films. Featuring stunning archival footage (accompanied by Carl Davis's glorious music) and firsthand accounts by surviving actors, directors, and technicians, this truly is a one-of-a-kind viewing experience. Episode no. 7, "Comedy—A Serious Business," opens with a twelve-minute history of Mack Sennett, who Americanized the primitive trick films from the Pathé Freres company in France and made millions of moviegoers laugh in the process. The Keystone Cops, naturally, are featured in a bounty of clips, along

with reminiscences by rival producer Hal Roach, British comedian George Harris, gag writer Frank Capra, stunt man Harvey Parry, and film editor William Hornbeck. In production for several years, the episodes were originally aired in weekly installments on public television stations during 1980. Although the entire series was released in the VHS format, no plans—unfortunately—are imminent regarding a DVD/Blu-ray release.

The Muppets Go the Movies 60m **TV movie, Henson Associates (May 20, 1981)**
Producer: Jim Henson
Director: Peter Harris.
Writers: Jim Henson, Jerry Juhl, Chris Langham.
Cast: Dudley Moore, Lily Tomlin, Kermit the Frog, Miss Piggy, Fozzie Bear, et al.
Observations: As a plug for their forthcoming feature *The Great Muppet Caper* (1981), Jim Henson's lovable characters celebrate classic cinema with recreations and vintage clips. The first clip shown is of the Keystone Cops performing the slalom gag in their patrol car.

Make 'Em Laugh 12 episodes, 20m each, **British Broadcasting Company (1982–1984)**
Director: Bruce Rawlings.
Writer/Presenter: Mark Curry.
Cast: (first season); **archival footage:** Harry Langdon, Lupino Lane, Buster Keaton, Larry Semon, Laurel & Hardy, the Keystone Cops. The second season deals less with individual performers and focuses on the themes "Trains," "Fighting Mad," "Cars," "Boats," "Houses," and "Keep Moving."
Observations: The first episode of this British import is titled "The Keystone Days." It originally aired on April 23, 1982.

Legends of Comedy 165m **The Disney Channel (1992 TV movie)**
Producers: Charles Grinker, Edward Murphy, and Gary Theroux.
Film Editor: Gary Theroux.
Cast: Abbott & Costello, George Burns & Gracie Allen, Edgar Bergen & Charlie McCarthy, Martin & Lewis, Red Skelton, The Three Stooges, Mae West.
Observations: An ambitious look at comedy, from vaudeville to silent films to television to home video. The segment dedicated to silent comedy features Roscoe Arbuckle, Charley Chase, Charlie Chaplin, Harry Langdon, Buster Keaton, Harold Lloyd, Laurel & Hardy, Mabel Normand, Will Rogers, and—of course—the Keystone Cops. When this documentary film first aired on the Disney Channel in 1992, it was that network's highest-rated program.

SlapHappy 30m each episode, **PBS series (July 15, 2001–2003)**
Producers: Paul Lisy, Chris Mohr, Laurence Stefan.
Screenwriters: Richard M. Roberts, Laurence Stefan.
Film Editor: Chris Mohr.
Music: Vince Giordano.
Cast (*via archival footage*): Charlie Chaplin, Buster Keaton, Harold Lloyd, Charley Chase, Lupino Lane, the Keystone Cops, and countless other silent comedians and comediennes.
Observations: Initially a Public Broadcast Station series (2001–2003) and, later, a ninety-minute anthology movie, *SlapHappy*, according to its executive producer Laurence Stefan, features "superb print quality, rare stills, anecdotal narration, and a scintillating hot jazz soundtrack from the acclaimed Stomp Off Records." The Keystone Cops are seen in clips from *Love, Loot and Crash* (1915). *The SlapHappy Collection* (consisting of 900 minutes of footage) was released as a ten-disc set by Fishigan Films; *SlapHappy the Movie* is available on DVD as well.

The Birth of the Tramp 91m **Steamboat Films/Lobster Films/Arte France (2014)**
Directors: Serge Bromberg, Eric Lange.
Narrator: Peter Hudson.
Cinematography: Jean-Louis Sonzogne.
Music: Robert Israel.
Cast: Antoine Lange (boy watching silent films in the prologue and epilogue); Kate Guyonvarch (Roy Export Associate); David Robinson (author, *Chaplin— His Life and Art*); Kevin Brownlow (documentarian, *Unknown Chaplin*); archival footage: Charlie Chaplin, Mabel Normand, Eric Campbell, Henry Bergman, Max Linder, Mary Pickford, Douglas Fairbanks, the Keystone Cops (*Tillie's Punctured Romance*).
Observations: Commissioned to celebrate the centennial of Charlie Chaplin's iconic character, *The Birth of the Tramp* is an especially interesting and delightful look at Chaplin's tenure with Keystone in 1914. One of the on-camera commentators is Kevin Brownlow, who smilingly describes the cathartic release experienced by nickelodeon patrons (many of whom were immigrants, like Chaplin) by seeing the Keystone Cops reduce the image of policemen to buffoonery: "In that era, which was a very strait-laced era, discipline was the watchword. People worked through fear a lot of the time. If they could see a policeman get kicked up the rear—that was something they would never even imagine! And to see it being done very amusingly was tremendous!"

Silent Legend: The Mack Sennett Story 50m **Prairie Coast Films, Canada (April 19, 2016)**
Writer/Director/Editor: Sean Patrick Shaul.
Associate Producer: Stan Taffel.
Cast: Robert S. Birchard, Jan-Christopher Horak, Brian McIlroy, Ann Naymie, Kliph Nesteroff, Jesse Rogg, Warren Sherk, Stan Taffel, Michael van den Bos, Brent E. Walker; ***archival footage:*** Mack Sennett, Charlie Chaplin, Harry Langdon, Andy Clyde, Mabel Normand, Charlie Murray, W. C. Fields, Bing Crosby, Dell Henderson, the Keystone Cops.
Observations: Film historians discuss Mack Sennett's life, career, and lasting impact on comedy. A comparison is made between Sennett and Lorne Michaels, the veteran producer of NBC's *Saturday Night Live*. Like Michaels, Sennett had an uncanny knack for discovering funny people and successfully presenting them to a discerning public. The Keystone Cops are referred to numerous times by the talking heads while footage from *A Lover's Lost Control*, *The Noise of Bombs*, and *The Great Toe Mystery* shows them in action. This documentary on one of Canada's favorite sons is the first such film to focus specifically on Mack Sennett.

Television Programs Featuring Actual Keystone Cops

The Ed Wynn Show (Camel Caravan) 30m **CBS (July 6, 1950)**
Cast: Ed Wynn (host); guests: Buster Keaton, Hank Mann, Heinie Conklin, Chester Conklin, Tiny Ward, Snub Pollard.
Observations: Filmed before a live audience in New York City and then filmed on a monitor (otherwise known as a kinescope) to be shown on the West Coast in prime time, *The Ed Wynn Show* was one of network television's earliest variety shows. Wynn was still playing "The Perfect Fool" at this point in his long career and surrounding himself with seasoned vaudevillians like The Three Stooges and Buster Keaton. In this episode, Buster teaches Ed the art of pie throwing, using as human targets five Keystone Cops (Chester Conklin, Hank Mann, Heinie Conklin, Snub Pollard, and Roscoe "Tiny" Ward). Wynn was even made an honorary Cop following the skit.

This is Your Life: Mack Sennett 30m **NBC Kinescope, (March 10, 1954)**
Cast: Ralph Edwards (show creator and host), Mack Sennett, Cameron Shipp (*Saturday Evening Post* writer who actually penned Sennett's autobiography), Rose Guilfoil (Sennett's first sweetheart), Fritzi Scheff (opera singer and one-time Sennett girlfriend), Dell Henderson (actor and director), Phyllis Haver (Bathing Beauty, actress), Franklin Pangborn (comic actor featured in Sennett's

early talkies), Minta Durfee (actress, Roscoe Arbuckle's one-time wife), Alberta Vaughn (actress), Jack Mulhall (actor, matinee idol), Sally Eilers (actress featured in Sennett talkies), Louise Fazenda (former Keystone player, wife of producer Hal Wallis), Harold Lloyd (retired filmmaker, one-time Keystone bit player), Chester Conklin, Hank Mann, Vernon Dent, Andy Clyde, Heinie Conklin (Keystone Cops).

Observations: Once-popular reality program allows (or forces) celebrities to revisit their pasts with the assistance of old friends and former colleagues. Mack Sennett, who was told he was going to be on a program with Cameron Shipp, the writer of Sennett's autobiography, is genuinely gobsmacked by the surprise appearance of Ralph Edwards at El Capitan Theater in Hollywood. In a (literal) running gag, Del Lord (who staged some of the most eye-popping Sennett-style chases in the 1920s) is chased around the stage by Keystone Cops Chester, Hank, Andy, Vernon, and Heinie.

The Danny Thomas Show 30m **"Danny Lands in Pictures" (November 2, 1954)**
Producer/Director: Sheldon Leonard.
Writer: Mac Denoff.
Cast: Danny Thomas, Jean Hagen, Rusty Hamer, Sherry Jackson.
Observations: In this Hollywood-based episode of the sitcom also known as *Make Room for Daddy*, Chester Conklin and Hank Mann appear in a cameo as Keystone Cops.

***Playhouse 90:* "The Big Slide,"** 90m **CBS-TV (November 8, 1956)**
Producer: Martin Manulis.
Director: Ralph Nelson.
Screenwriters: Edmund Beloin, Dean Reisner.
Cast: Red Skelton, Shirley Jones, Murray Hamilton, Eddie Firestone, Jack Albertson, Jack Mulhall, Fay Spain, Victor Sutherland, Lyn Osborn.
Observations: *Playhouse 90*, an American television drama anthology which ran from 1956 to 1960 and encompassed 134 episodes, was one of the reasons the 1950s were often called "The Golden Age of Television." In this show business drama, a second-rate vaudevillian (Red Skelton, in an Emmy-nominated performance) becomes a silent film star, leading to overwhelming crises in his personal life. Hank Mann, Clarence Hennecke, and Heinie Conklin turn up briefly as Keystone Cops.

To Tell the Truth 30m **A Goodson-Todman Production CBS-TV (April 16, 1957)**
Cast: Bud Collyer (host), Kitty Carlisle, Polly Bergen, Ralph Bellamy, and Hy Gardner (celebrity panelists).

Observations: On this episode of the long-running game show, three jolly elves each claim to be original Keystone Cop Chester Conklin. The real Mr. Conklin wins three votes, primarily because he recalled that Wallace Beery, before his days as a dramatic character actor, had worked in drag in one-reel comedies.

People in the News: "Keystone Cops Reunion" 69s **(1962)**
Observations: Outtakes from an advertisement for the fortieth anniversary of Gibraltar Savings and Loan in Los Angeles, California, features Chester Conklin, who comments unfavorably about the new breed of comedian. "We used to get a lot more laughs than they do today!" he says, chuckling proudly. This fascinating footage (from the Richard M. Roberts collection), in both silent and sound, is on Disc 3 of *The Mack Sennett Collection, Vol. I.*

The Merv Griffin Show: "A Salute to the Silent Screen" 90m **CBS (January 14, 1971)**
Cast: Merv Griffin (host), Lillian Gish, Chester Conklin, Babe London, Beverly Bayne, Betty Blythe, Jackie Coogan, Minta Durfee, Jack Mulhall, Ken Maynard, Buddy Rogers, Mary Pickford (by telephone, although that brief interview was deleted prior to the broadcast), Richard Arlen, Viola Dana, Neil Hamilton, Eddie Quillan, Vivian Duncan, Dorothy Devore, Carter DeHaven, and Betty Bronson.
Observations: Merv Griffin hosts this remarkable gathering of silent film actors and actresses, all of whom were senior citizens by that time. The Keystone Cops are well represented by Chester Conklin, who is introduced by way of a crystal-clear clip from 1914. He makes his entrance slowly, wearing a derby and his famous paste-on mustache. "You've given every single one of us an awful lot of laughs," Merv says with sincerity. "And what a *thrill* to be able to say that to you in person!" Sadly, this was Chester's final major appearance; he died on October 11, 1971, less than a year after the program was taped. A black & white copy of "A Salute to the Silent Screen" is held by the Library of Congress but has yet to be made available to the public. Information on this show came from Steve Randisi, who made copious notes when viewing it during its sole telecast. Randisi also personally interviewed Griffin's talent coordinator Don Kane, who more than anyone was responsible for booking the guests on that historic episode. A detailed account of the behind-the-scenes machinations of "A Salute to the Silent Screen" can be found in Randisi's excellent book *The Merv Griffin Show* (BearManor Media, 2018).

To Tell the Truth 30m **A Goodson-Todman Production (December 31, 1974)**
Cast: Garry Moore (host), Bill Cullen, Peggy Cass, Orson Bean, Kitty Carlisle (celebrity panelists).

Observations: In one of the two segments of this episode, three elderly gentlemen all claim to be Keystone Cop Robert Cox. Archival footage from *Keystone Hotel* is shown silent with live piano accompaniment.

Television Tributes to the Keystone Cops

There have been countless homages to Mack Sennett's police on television since its very inception. On November 24, 1956, for instance, the British television variety show *Saturday Spectacular* presented a 90-minute adaptation of the 1947 Broadway show *High Button Shoes*, an acclaimed musical comedy set in 1913 and prominently featuring the Keystone Cops.

Buster Keaton found himself being chased by a determined group of Cops in a silent-film-style commercial for the Ford Motor Company in 1964. A second minute-long Ford van commercial with Buster, this one filmed in 1965 for the new 1966 model, shows him demonstrating the vehicle's ample storage space by loading it up with a couch, a moose head, and a live lion on a leash. Eventually, a stray Keystone Cop makes a brief appearance for a final, pie-in-the-face gag.

British comedian Benny Hill (1924–1992) had a remarkably long run playing to a massive television audience (his eponymously named show was broadcast to 140 countries in some form or other from 1955 to 1989). Hill was obviously a huge admirer of slapstick comedy—with more than a touch of burlesque. Countless episodes of his show end with various cops (or bobbies, to use the British term) chasing bikini-clad girls. When one or more of the cops are female, they invariably wear mini skirts. As popular as these shows were in their time, they are unlikely to see a resurgence in the current "Me Too" era.

UPA's 1961 animated series *The Dick Tracy Show*, based on the long-running comic strip by Chester Gould, featured a group of Keystone-type Cops who called themselves "The Retouchables," a takeoff on the then-popular series *The Untouchables*. *Cool McCool* (1967–1969), another cartoon series, centered on a super-hip secret agent who would occasionally reminisce about his father—his "pop, the cop"—Harry McCool, who decades earlier was a member of "Komedy Kops," a three-man squad of pie-throwing policemen.

Batman (1966–1968), of course, was an incredibly popular prime-time, live-action television series based on the iconic superhero created by Bob Kane, the man who also brought us Cool McCool. In the episode "Death in Slow Motion" (original airdate: April 27, 1966), Bruce Wayne/Batman (Adam West) and his hypomanic sidekick Dick Grayson/Robin (Burt Ward) attempt to put an end to a series of robberies committed by the Riddler (Frank Gorshin). In the show's first shot, a black & white scene from a Keystone Cops film is shown at the newly opened Gotham movie theater as part of a silent film festival sponsored by the wealthy collector Mr. Van Jones (Francis X. Bushman). In the theater's lobby following the screening, the high-toned guests are entertained by the surprise appearance of a Charlie Chaplin imitator (Gorshin, again), his sexy moll Pauline (Sherry Jackson), and some ersatz Keystone Cops performing a pantomime arrest of Charlie the thief. This, in fact, is a clever ruse by the Riddler and his henchmen to commit an actual robbery—out of view of the delighted onlookers—of the box office take of two hundred dollars.

One of the most entertaining commercials ever made (at least for those of us who love silent comedy) was for Shasta Root Beer. The color, sixty-second-long film was shot in Los Angeles in 1968 and ran on daytime television through 1971. Featuring former Sennett actor Billy Bletcher as a Keystone Cop (and as a Ford Sterling lookalike), this mini-masterpiece perfectly captures the bounce of silent comedy, with a tip of the derby to Laurel & Hardy's 1927 two-reeler *The Battle of the Century* (except that the flying pies are replaced with root beer foam). The jingle "Shasta! It has to be Shasta!" is sung by an actress in the style of Helen Kane (voice of Betty Boop) to a Charleston beat. Fortunately, the commercial has survived and will be a bonus extra on the Blu-ray set *The Mack Sennett Collection, Vol. II*.

During the 1970s, a time when nostalgia was a marketable commodity, American variety programs such as *The Lawrence Welk Show, The Sonny & Cher Comedy Hour,* and particularly *The Carol Burnett Show* featured "silent movie" sketches and dances featuring both male and female Keystone Cops.

In more recent times, the Cops have been referenced in some unexpected places, like outer space and Portland, Oregon. *Portlandia* (2011-2018), a quirky sketch comedy series created by and starring Fred Armisen and Carrie Brownstein, often deals with the inner workings of the Portland city council. In season two's fifth episode, "Cops Redesign," the city's airheaded mayor (Kyle MacLachlan) suggests that in order to make the Portland police more likeable to the public, the word "*cops* should be spelled *kops*, like the silent movie Keystone Kops." *Star Wars: The Clone Wars* (2008-2020), an animated series based on the blockbuster theatrical franchise, features a group of police 'droids which, according to the supervising director Dave Filoni, were designed along the lines of Keystone's finest.

Radio Tributes to the Keystone Cops

Given that the Keystone Cops' appeal is exclusively visual, radio has hardly been the medium to best exploit them. One of the rare exceptions to this rule is a long-forgotten Los Angeles–based radio program, *Stars of Yesterday*, hosted by former silent film vamp Louise Glaum and broadcast each Sunday evening on local station KMTR (later KLAC) in the mid-thirties. On one episode, broadcast August 23, 1936, Glaum welcomed as her guests four Sennett veterans: Chester Conklin, Dot Farley, Minta Durfee, and Vernon Dent. *Los Angeles Times* show business columnist Philip K. Scheuer was evidently quite moved by the show. As he wrote, "It is the crowning irony that these dismembered voices, audible at last, are in many cases the sole means of expression left to those who in all their long screen careers never uttered a sound." Although this makes for a potent statement, it is not accurate. Conklin, Dent, and Farley each had several speaking roles in talkies prior to 1936.

Mack Sennett took his turn before the microphone during a December 13, 1939 appearance on the *Texaco Star Theater* program on the NBC network. Sennett was there to be interviewed by Ken Murray (of *Blackouts* fame) about the just-released *Hollywood Cavalcade*, the 20th Century-Fox Technicolor feature, which the King of Comedy described as his "autobiography." The film includes an eight-and-a-half-minute recreation of a Keystone Cops chase sequence. Sennett's interview (which has survived in complete form) took place in the first half of the hour-long episode. It is included as an extra on CineMuseum's Blu-ray set of *The Mack Sennett Collection, Vol. I.*

On February 2, 1993, the British Broadcasting Company (BBC) presented an audio dramatization entitled *Keystone, The Movie*, a well-crafted ninety-minute radio play directed by Matthew Walters and based on the 1983 novel *Keystone*, by British author Peter Lovesey. *Keystone* tells the fictional story of Warwick Easton, a British vaudevillian who applies for work at the Mack Sennett studio in 1916. As is his wont, Sennett hires him on a trial basis as a Keystone Cop. After one of his fellow Cops dies in a tragic accident, evidence begins to point to the fact that foul play had been involved. Easton (or Keystone, his newly coined nickname) risks his own life to solve the mystery and bring the culprit to justice. As an online description for the play states: "Being a Keystone Cop is bound to be dangerous, but murder is another thing." Featuring actors portraying real-life Cops Frank Hayes, Chester Conklin, and Slim Summerville, this highly entertaining program was uploaded to the internet on May 21, 2016.

Stage Shows Featuring Keystone Cops, Both Real and Imitation

When talkies hit, the entire film industry panicked. According to a headline in the February 1, 1928 issue of *Variety*, "Film Names Stampede Towards Vaudeville." The article then proceeded to list the recognizable silent players who had defected for the stage, including George Walsh, Ben Turpin, Ian Keith,

Ethel Clayton, Irene Rich, and Renée Adorée. Two months later, *Variety* listed more such photoplayers-turned-vaudevillians, including one original Keystone Cop, Hank Mann, and one future member, Snub Pollard. Unfortunately, talkies (and radio) eclipsed not only silent films but vaudeville as well.

April 30, 1939, the 150th anniversary of George Washington's inauguration, marked the official kickoff day of the World's Fair, held at what is now Flushing Meadows Park, in Queens, New York. The theme of the fair was "The World of Tomorrow." And while many exhibits pointed toward the future, one entitled "George Jessel's Old New York," was a six-week-long celebration of the past. Ann Pennington, the pint-sized (four-foot-nine) Jazz Age "shake and quiver" dancer who had begun her career on Broadway in 1911 and who had popularized the notorious "Black Bottom" back in 1926, was the star of Jessel's revue. Pennington, now forty-five, was wearing the same type of "barely there" costume she had worn in the Ziegfeld *Follies* and the George White *Scandals* more than twenty years earlier. As the Caucasian dancer gyrated her hips and kicked her legs while performing the African-inspired dance (all the while showing off her once-famous dimpled white knees), the Keystone Cops (Chester Conklin, Al St. John, Heinie Conklin, Hank Mann, and Snub Pollard) showed up to haul her black bottom offstage, thus keeping the fair family-friendly. All of this was done tongue-in-cheek, of course, and audiences were delighted to see their favorite comic policemen in person and still clowning expertly. (Home movie footage of Pennington and the Cops performing for the crowds has survived and can be viewed on YouTube.) Conklin, Conklin, Mann, and Pollard later performed a variation of the sketch, this time with the Gaiety Girls, at the Gaiety Theater. Long since demolished, the historic theater was located at 523 South Main Street in downtown Los Angeles.

High Button Shoes was a successful Broadway show with music by Jule Styne, lyrics by Sammy Cahn, and a book by George Abbott and Stephen Longstreet, based on Longstreet's semi-autobiographical 1946 novel *The Sisters Liked Them Handsome*. The story has two conmen hounding an All-American family from their home in New Brunswick to Atlantic City, New Jersey, in 1913. There, they must contend with an odd assortment of bathing beauties, lifeguards, fellow criminals, identical twins—and a gorilla. But when the Keystone Cops arrive on the scene in the frenzied climax, the jig is up, and all ends happily for the Longstreet family. Up-and-coming choreographer Jerome Robbins staged the climactic number featuring the Cops along the lines of a Mack Sennett silent-film comedy, with split-second timing, pratfalls, and plenty of slamming doors. This nostalgic show, which made its debut at Broadway's New Century Theatre in 1947, was warmly received by critics and audiences alike, with comic actor Phil Silvers a standout as conman Harrison Floy. It closed after a respectable run of 727 performances. *High Button Shoes* continues to be staged by regional companies.

Mack and Mabel, a two-act musical comedy/drama, opened at Broadway's Majestic Theatre on October 6, 1974. Despite the best efforts of the highly respected leads Robert Preston (portraying Mack Sennett) and Bernadette Peters (as Mabel Normand), composer Jerry Herman (*Hello, Dolly!*, *Mame*) book writer Michael Stewart, producer David Merrick, and director Gower Champion, the show's original run lasted only sixty-six performances and five previews. Fortunately, the original cast recording of *Mack & Mabel* (which has since been reissued on the Broadway Gold MCA Classics label) stands as a testament to the show's beautiful music. Preston (Broadway and film's *The Music Man*) sings a poignant composition entitled "I Won't Send Roses." And two numbers— "When Movies Were Movies" and "My Heart Leaps Up"/"Hit 'em on the Head"—feature a group of singing-and-dancing Keystone Cops. Despite its initial failure, *Mack and Mabel* has been revived several times to great acclaim, particularly in the UK. On February 21, 1988, a second recording of the score, supervised by Jerry Herman, was performed in concert at the Theatre Royal Drury Lane in London.

Keystone, a much lower-profile attempt to turn Mack, Mabel, and the Cops' story into musical magic, made its debut at the McCarter Theatre in Princeton, New Jersey, in January 1982. The show featured a cast of versatile if unknown actors, some of whom took on multiple roles (one corpulent thespian, Thomas Lee Sinclair, portrayed both Roscoe Arbuckle and Marie Dressler). In his *New York Times* review, Mel Gusso pointed out that "the approach [to presenting Mack Sennett's comedy] demands a much keener sense of style than is demonstrated . . . [o]n a very basic level, 'Keystone' is just not funny enough." Videotaped in its entirety during a live performance, *Keystone* was broadcast on the Arts & Entertainment (A&E) network in the late eighties.

The Eugene (Oregon) Ballet Troupe was brave enough to tackle the genre in a one-act piece, *Silent Movie*, which made its debut (c. 1990) at the city's Hult Center for the Performing Arts. The dancers portraying such iconic characters as Charlie Chaplin (danced by a petite young lady) and the Keystone Cops did an admirable job of capturing the comics' distinctive mannerisms along with the requisite pliés and pirouettes. In an attempt at a multi-media presentation, a black-and-white silent film featuring the cast in a park setting was shown as a link between dances.

Appendix A
Keystone, an Illustrated Chronology, 1912–1917
By Marc Wanamaker

1912

In August, Adam Kessel and Charles O. Baumann, two ex-bookmakers who have become successful movie distributors, join with producer Fred J. Balshofer of the Bison Film Company to form the Keystone Film Company under the umbrella of the New York Motion Picture Corporation. The trademark for the new company is the familiar Pennsylvania Railroad "keystone" logo.

Kessel and Baumann sign the Biograph comedy star-director Mack Sennett, who will have creative control over stories and methods of operation. The rough-hewn thirty-two-year-old is not noted for his businesslike methods or smooth organization. His principal actors are his colleagues from Biograph—Mabel Normand, Ford Sterling, and Fred Mace.

The first Keystone comedy is *At Coney Island*, a split-reeler (occupying approximately five hundred feet of a thousand-foot roll of film), shot on location at the famous East Coast amusement park on the Fourth of July (it is not released until October 28). Another early Keystone release is *The Water Nymph* (September 23). The plot has Mack Sennett, a practical joker, encouraging his girlfriend (Mabel Normand) to flirt with his father (Ford Sterling), whom she has never met. Mabel shows off her shapely curves when wearing the kind of one-piece swimsuit worn by Australian swimming champion Annette Kellerman. This approximately five-minute-long film is considered to be a forerunner to the Mack Sennett Bathing Beauties concept.

Another embryonic production, *Riley and Schultze* (September 30), concerns a constable and his sergeant (Mack Sennett and Fred Mace) vying for the same girl (Mabel). This is likely the first Keystone film to feature comedic policemen, making it the predecessor of the Keystone Cops.

On August 28, the Keystone troupe arrives in Los Angeles, where they set up their headquarters in the former Bison Film Company Studio in Edendale at 1712 Allesandro Boulevard. The studio, which had been built in 1909, is the former site of a grocery store. (Edendale is a historical name for a district northeast of downtown Los Angeles, in what is currently known as Echo Park, Los Feliz, and Silver Lake. Allesandro Street became Glendale Boulevard in the 1920s; a smaller nearby street took on the name Allesandro.) Some in Hollywood consider the ramshackle Keystone studio a madhouse, while others find it a good place to work—at least initially. Sennett, calling himself the director-general, runs the place with an iron hand.

More players are added to the Keystone roster, including Dot Farley, Victoria Forde, Evelyn Quick, Alice Davenport, and Henry "Pathé" Lehrman.

1913

Keystone's first outdoor stage, 1912.

Lehrman becomes Keystone's second unit director, and Charles Avery and Betty Schade are signed as his principal players. Among those leaving are Dot Farley, Fred Mace, Evelyn Quick, and writer Karl Coolidge. Their replacements include Roscoe "Fatty" Arbuckle, Minta Durfee, Mack Swain, Chester Conklin, Harry McCoy, Al St. John, Phyllis Allen, Charles Parrott, directors Robert Thornby, Rube Miller, George Nichols, and Wilfred Lucas.

New innovations are constantly being attempted. In *A Noise From the Deep* (July 17), for instance, there occurs an event of some historical importance: the first documented instance of a Keystone pie being thrown, in this case by Arbuckle into the face of character actor Nick Cogley.

Mack Sennett's Keystone Studio, Edendale, California, 1912.

About this time, a new series, informally known as "Keystone Kiddies," is headed by Vitagraph veteran Robert Thornby. The short comedies star three-year-old Paul Jacobs, known professionally as "Little Billy."

The Keystone Cops are now fully established with a roster that includes Ford Sterling as either the chief of police or the villain, along with Chester Conklin, Grover Ligon, M. G. Cox, George Jeske, Hank Mann, Billy Gilbert, Al St. John, Bill Hauber, and Bert Hunn.

1914

Twenty-four-year-old British music hall artiste Charles Chaplin makes his film debut with *Making a Living* (February 2), although he isn't seen wearing his soon-to-be famous "Tramp" outfit. That costume actually comes about by chance one day, when Lehrman assists Chaplin in gathering all sorts of ill-fitting clothes from the wardrobe department. Chaplin goes on to make thirty-five more films for Keystone, including *A Thief Catcher*, in which he is cast as a Keystone Cop.

Marie Dressler is hired by Keystone at $2,500 per week to star in *Tillie's Punctured Romance*, adapted by Hampton Del Ruth from one of Miss Dressler's stage successes. The massive popularity of this first full-length comedy feature is due to the presence of Charlie Chaplin as a city slicker out to cheat the naïve country girl Tillie. Chaplin is soon directing himself in films, including the two-reel hit *Dough and Dynamite*, in which he and Chester Conklin play dueling chefs. During this period, Chaplin devises his oft-copied system of editing his own work by ending a scene with a shrug, a twist of the lip, or some other eas-

Charlie Chaplin (in full makeup) and Mabel Normand on the set of Caught in a Cabaret *(Keystone, 1914).*

Pictured (left to right) are Fred J. Balshofer, Ford Sterling (center, in his trademark "Dutch" makeup), Universal founder Carl Laemmle, unknown, and director Henry Lehrman, 1914.

ily recognizable mannerism. After fourteen months with Keystone, he leaves the company to join the Essanay Film Manufacturing Company in Chicago.

Balshofer leaves Keystone with Ford Sterling, Paul Jacobs, Henry Lehrman, and others to establish the Sterling Film Company in Hollywood. The producer later claims that both Lehrman and Sterling are impossible to work with, leading to their dismissals. The series manages to continue without either the director or star's cooperation. This is accomplished by editing together outtakes and using a body double, Keystone Cop George Jeske, wearing Sterling's trademark top hat, overcoat, and makeup. According to Balshofer, one of the comedies made in this unconventional way is perhaps the best of the series. What's more, the ruse goes completely undetected by moviegoers.

1915

More new actors and actresses enter the revolving door at Keystone, including Louise Fazenda, Polly Moran, Harry P. Gribbon, and Mae Busch.

All production on the lot halts during July when the distribution contract with Mutual expires. George Stout becomes the studio manager, and by September Sennett begins production of his Mack Sennett Comedies after negotiating a contract with the New York Motion Picture Corporation, Keystone's parent company. Meanwhile, Harry Aitken forms the Triangle Film Corporation in New York, so named for its three famous directors: Sennett, Thomas Ince, and D. W. Griffith. Triangle's backers include Kessel and Baumann of the NYMPC. Its headquarters are established in the Brokaw Building on 42nd Street in New York City.

Sennett continues working for Keystone and signs the Broadway stage stars Eddie Foy and the Seven Little Foys, along with Weber & Fields. The salaries are high, the box-office returns low.

Actors and directors, not to mention personnel at every level, continue to come and go. Sydney Chaplin, Charlie's brother, signs on as a director and actor.

Ford Sterling returns to Keystone and, despite their previous differences. Lehrman and he resume their collaboration. Lehrman produces his own L-KO (Lehrman Knock-Out) Comedies, which are out-and-out imitations of Sennett's work. Moviegoers prefer the originals, however, and express their displeasure in letters to fan magazines.

Business is good and getting better. The New York money men come across with approximately $100,000 for improvements to Edendale's physical plant.

Charles Baumann and Mack Sennett supervise the studio's expansion as employees look on, 1915.

The new concrete stage at Keystone, 1915.

Its dilapidated wooden structures, which have become known to locals as the "Pig Sty," are replaced with concrete and brick buildings. The first concrete interior stage built in Los Angeles is located on the Keystone lot. (In 2020, this building is occupied by a storage company, its walls adorned by plaques and memorabilia commemorating its significance to motion picture history. The exterior of the building proudly bears the legend Mack Sennett Studios.)

1916

Fifteen companies are shooting at the studio. There are three studio lots, two of which are on the west side of Allesandro Street facing the main lot. Occupying the annex lot to the south is the famous turntable cyclorama. Used for action shots, chases, and other stunts, it gives the theatrical illusion of scenery passing by—essentially, an early "process" shot. No other studio has a piece of special-effects equipment that is so unique and effective.

The famous Keystone Cyclorama, 1916.

Hampton Del Ruth is now the story editor, and the new directors include J. F. MacDonald, Victor Heerman, Fred Fishback, and one-time Keystone Cop Glen Cavender. Mabel Normand returns from the Eastern studios with Arbuckle to find that Sennett has finally persuaded Adam Kessel of the NYPC to establish her very own company, with the right to choose her own stories, writers, and directors. A four-acre plot of land at Bates and Effie Streets off Fountain Avenue in East Hollywood had been used by the Keystone Company as a location annex for a couple of years. Sennett has a proper studio built and equipped on the site, and shooting soon begins on *Mickey*, written by J. G. Hawks and directed by James Young (the latter is soon replaced by F. Richard Jones). Mabel is suffering from health problems at the time, but the company works for eight months to produce a six-reel feature, which Keystone promptly shelves. (When it is finally released in 1918 by Hiller & Wilk, *Mickey* is a runaway hit.)

1917

Directors Harry Williams and Clarence Badger arrive at Keystone in January. Meanwhile, Roscoe Arbuckle leaves to direct his own films at Paramount.

The Mack Sennett Bathing Beauties (also known as The Sennett Girls), each of whom is paid twelve dollars a day, prove to be worth many times that in free publicity. Sennett knows intuitively that newspapers can boost sales by publishing photos of pretty girls in bathing suits. The first of these knee-baring lovelies are Evelyn Lynn, Cecile Evans, and Marie Prevost. Some future stars who start out by posing in the one-piece (although still daring) bathing suits of the time are Juanita Hansen, Claire Anderson, Mary Thurman, Phyllis Haver, Myrtle Lind, Carole Lombard, and Gloria Swanson (although Swanson vehemently denies that she was *ever* a Bathing Beauty).

Sennett is frustrated by his relationship with the Kessel-Baumann (NYMPC) distribution network and tries to make an end run around them by offering his comedies to any exhibitor who would have them. They counter by limiting his productions to two-reelers. It seems they need Keystone for their block-booking scheme, whereby distributors who want one part of their

Phyllis Haver and Gloria Swanson smile enticingly for the cameras in this 1917 cheesecake shot.

The thriving Keystone Studios and a foretelling of the parking shortage in Los Angeles.

product have to take all—or nothing. Tempers are brought under control by an agreement that Sennett will be given greater freedom of production if he keeps out of the distribution business altogether. Baumann soon retires, and Kessel, though now ill, forms an executive committee of Triangle with C. M. Parker and Harry E. Aitken.

Ben Turpin brings his crossed eyes and backward somersaults to Keystone, and production continues apace.

Sennett wants a showdown with the New York group, and he gets it. The board agrees that it is time for a parting, and with that, they buy up Sennett's stock, with a bonus. All they want is the Keystone trademark. When Sennett keeps silent, they agree to throw into the deal the Edendale studio and any rights they might have to the name Mack Sennett. The deal is made, with both sides breaking into smiles of victory. Sennett signs a contract with Paramount for a single two-reel Mack Sennett Comedy every other week. Some of the Keystone group stay with him, and others depart for the Triangle lot in Culver City, to work under H. O. Davis.

The year 1917 is Keystone's most prolific in terms of new releases—125 titles. The last Sennett Keystone comedy is *The Sultan's Wife* (September 30), a two-reeler directed by Clarence Badger. The stars are Bobby Vernon, Gloria Swanson, and Teddy the dog.

Marc Wanamaker was born in Los Angeles and grew up in Beverly Hills. He has worked in many aspects of film production, exhibition, and research. In 1971, he formed Bison Archives, a research and informational collection documenting the history of the motion picture industry. Marc co-produced a commercial documentary on movie history, *Ticket to Hollywood*, and has worked on more than a hundred documentaries and feature films. He is an associate of the Los Angeles County Museum, The Academy of Motion Picture Arts and Sciences, and the State Library in Sacramento, and is a consultant for more than twenty historical societies in Southern California. A writer as well, Marc has had articles published in *Architectural Digest*, *Los Angeles Magazine*, the *Los Angeles Times*, *American Cinematographer*, *The Hollywood Reporter*, and *Daily Variety*.

All photos in the chronology are courtesy of Bison Archives.

Appendix B
"Putting the Key in Keystone."

The following article, "Putting the Key in Keystone," was written by Stanley W. Todd for the January 1917 issue of *Motion Picture Classic*. It is being reprinted here as it gives a remarkable first-hand account of taking a guided tour of the Keystone studio when it was at its apex. An original issue of the vintage magazine was provided by our friend and fellow author Tim Lussier.

Appendix B: "Putting the Key in Keystone"

Putting the Key in Keystone

By Stanley W. Todd

IT is not an easy matter to break into the Keystone studio. Of course, anybody in Los Angeles filmdom can tell you what car will take you to Edendale. They will at once recognize "Allesandro Street" as one of the important points on the "movie map." But as to getting inside — that is quite another proposition.

Not that you will have difficulty in recognizing the studio when you reach it. The miscellaneous collection of low buildings, cottages, and broken "sets" sprawls out on both sides of the street for a full city block. The automobiles parked along the curbs make the daily output of a flivver factory seem insignificant. But if this be not enough, until recently the largest structure generously was labeled with two names: Mack Sennett-Keystone.

That, however, is as it should be, for the names are interchangeable. What would Keystone have been without this genius of comedy film? Strangers from the East rush in where local photoplay devotees fear to tread. But the very efficient sentry on guard at the studio entrance is blind to anything but a "pass" from headquarters. If you are one of these misguided but persistent persons, you will be at once referred to a trim cottage across the street where the powers that be hold forth.

Before you go over there, take a look at one of the small structures sandwiched in between the Administration building and the business office. This mission-like section is captioned simply: "Emergency Hospital." If this does not convince you that making "Keystone stuff" is a serious business, you need not go far for further proof. Beside the studio building there is a row of small, typical California bungalows, each one of them bearing the shingle of some registered physician or surgeon!

As we make our way towards the unassuming cottage wherein we are to present our credentials for admission, we may have to jump out of the path of some picture-making party madly turning things all topsy-turvy for the benefit of the camera. We finally locate the official bungalow, which looks like a "cottage built for two," but is really somebody's former home transformed into a cold, businesslike film headquarters, with separate rooms for the department heads. Here the scenario experts frequently congregate, while the managerial forces of the big plant also hold conferences in it.

While our credentials are being examined under a high-power microscope by the high potentates of the establishment, we have an opportunity to review rapidly the remarkable story of Mack Sennett and how he won the niche he now occupies in the Moving Picture Hall of Fame. It brings one's memory back to old Biograph days, when the distinctive style of film that Mr. Sennett has made his own—"slapstick with a point to it"—first showed its head. Biograph was scraping the bottom of the pot for its dramatic company, headed by Mary Pickford and Arthur Johnson, and comedy was regarded somewhat as a filler-in. Biograph was the dominating figure in the Moving Picture business then, and David Griffith was first giving evidences of his genius. Every once in a while Griffith conscripted Sennett for his dramatic company, but comedy seemed to be the latter's forte, and, under Dell Henderson, the present Keystone chief, developed his funmaking talents. Few picture "fans" in those days suspected for a moment that the boobish actor, who always wore a light-gray derby and tight-fitting clothes, and was a mighty good shot in those pie-throwing battles, would later contribute so much to the lighter side of Motion Picture entertainment.

If we recall rightly, it was about five years ago that Mack Sennett broke away from Biograph affiliations and tried his Keystone experiment. Sennett interested Kessel and Baumann in his enterprise, but their New York Motion Picture Company had a dramatic company under Tom Ince out in Santa Ynez Cañon, near Los Angeles, and money was scarce. The Ince output was called "Bison 101," because he had leased the cañon from Miller's 101-Ranch, where he was having troubles of his own.

Keystone was really born in the old film colony across the river from New York—Fort Lee, N. J. —and Sennett's early experiences were heartrending, indeed. On one occasion, he "fell for" the boastful assurances of an alleged camera-man, who looked like the Count de Kackyack, and professed to have an encyclopedic knowledge of the baby Motion Picture industry. Sennett did not discover the vacuum in the pseudo camera-man's mind until it was apparent that scenes had been taken all day without film in the camera!

The "company" could not then afford the luxury of motor-cars, and there was no recourse but to "hoof it" for locations. Yes, Mabel Normand and Ford Sterling, who had just forsaken the vaudeville stage, were "among those present." One day a photoplayer, whose name shall be omitted, drove along in a fine new car, remarking sarcastically as he went by: "Hello, Sennett, how's Keystone getting along?" The director said nothing, and it is an interesting commentary on Sennett's persistence that the day came when this self-same actor condescended to apply for a job in Mr. Sennett's present headquarters in Edendale.

Kessel and Baumanr both stuck by Sennett, wit the result

MACK SWAIN AND POLLY MORAN

that the Keystone Company in toto was shipped out to Los Angeles and transplanted. The "studio" was set up at Allesandro Street, and this was used chiefly as a place where actors could report mornings and collect their salaries on Saturdays. But the genius of Sennett began to show itself; back of all that animated nonsense devised by Sennett's active brain there was something that stuck, while other comedy companies appeared and disappeared with startling regularity. Soon the Keystone had won its place in the affection of the photoplay "fans," at a time when feature reels had not been attempted. Even in those days a Keystone was a synonym for a really "funny picture."

And so the Keystone infant, under Mack Sennett's careful tutelage, slowly grew. Ford Sterling, Fred Mace, and Mabel Normand, together with Mr. Sennett, who appeared occasionally in his own pictures, kept up a fast pace, and the output of Keystones of the kind that has established their reputation was regular. But Mr. Sennett was not content with following along beaten trails. Charlie Murray forsook the Biograph and continued his same line of "goods" with Sennett, other prominent additions to the original company being made from time to time. Dell Henderson became a Keystone producer—another Biograph recruit.

But the Keystone chief looked into the future. He saw that the senseless "chase" and the "pie-slinging" stunts were becoming hoary with age. He sensed the demand of the public for something new along the comedy line, and set about to find it. Then came the Keystone Cops, the fast parlor-comedy and film tricks, and the Keystone chase, which must be classified differently from the sort of "chase" which Mr. Sennett had discarded.

About this time Charlie Chaplin came along. The little comedian had been playing in a knockabout English music-hall skit in vaudeville, which he effectively picturized in his Essanay production, "A Night at the Show," several years later. Chaplin got his Keystone try-out and first came to attention in a picture showing the filming of the Santa Monica automobile races. In the world-famous get-up which he originated—baggy trousers, clodhopper shoes, derby, cane, mustache et al., Chaplin was the irrepressible straggler who persisted in getting in the way of the camera.

Perhaps no one in the "picture game" can so quickly appraise an actor's possibilities in film comedy as Mr. Sennett. Before anybody else, he realized that Chaplin had hit upon something which was certain to make a hit. Charlie Chaplin teamed with Mabel Normand in numerous film absurdities under the Mutual banner, under which Keystone was then releasing. His Keystone experience culminated with the champion long-distance film farce, "Tillie's Punctured Romance," in which Marie Dressler was featured as an arch-conspirator, and in which several of the present Keystoners had a hand.

At the same time, Ford Sterling was shining as the Chief of the justly famous Keystone police, while Fred Mace and Charlie Murray were following along in characters peculiarly their own. With the exception of brief periods, during which they were able to prove to their own satisfaction there was little for them outside of the Keystone banner, most of these original players have stuck with Sennett. And if the director-general of Keystone—and Mr. Sennett was the "general" in every sense—did nothing else for Moving Picture comedy, his fame could rest on the fact that he first of all was

A BIRD'S-EYE VIEW OF THE KEYSTONE PLANT

responsible for Charlie Chaplin; that he struck out along original lines, and brought forth such comedians as Roscoe Arbuckle and several other former Keystonites whose fame, achieved under that banner, has enabled them to go out and "paddle their own canoes." Among these might be included Mabel Normand, except for the fact that she is still under Mr. Sennett's tutelage, with a studio and a company all her own, and her latest effort, "Mickey," and, incidentally, her first "honest-to-goodness" five- or six-reeler, being awaited by everybody generally.

"SHOOTING" THE WATER STUFF IN A PORTABLE TANK

KEYSTONE MID-SKY COMEDY

It is due, too, to Mr. Sennett's quick perception of their comic possibilities along original lines that many of the present Keystone stars have become identified before the tremendous Motion Picture audience in the United States, to which we could add, were it not for the war, thruout the world. Mack Swain, the doughty "Ambrose," and Chester Conklin, the well-known "walrus," are the best examples that come to mind, but lesser lights who might be included are easy to name—Polly Moran, Louise Fazenda, Harry Booker, Harry Gribbon, Harry McCoy, Bobby Vernon, "Slim" Summerville, Phyllis Allen, and any number of others who might be named on reflection.

WE GO INSIDE OF THE STUDIO

A sudden commotion, following the entrance into the cottage headquarters of a rather heavy-set young man wearing green-colored eyeglasses, arouses us from our reverie. It is Mr. Hampton Del Ruth, adjutant of Mr. Sennett, incidentally general manager, scenario editor, etc., and his aides have many matters of detail to bring to his immediate attention. A word of advice here and there satisfies the various men buzzing around him, and then Mr. Del Ruth is able to take up your particular case. He scrutinizes you keenly and then probably decides you are perfectly harmless, rather reluctantly signing a white slip of paper, which he turns over to Frank Buck, the genial publicity scout of the plant.

CARL'S CANDY-STAND OUTSIDE THE STUDIO

And before we leave the cottage, it might be well to remark, regarding the scenario end of the comedy business, that script-writers thruout the country are convinced that Keystone buys nothing, altho it sends out some very pretty rejection slips. But that is a fact—it buys few, if any, scripts, and sometimes "there aint no such animule." It is some time since that the scenario department abandoned the job of going thru a haystack to find a needle—in other words, an "original" idea. Mr. Sennett has gotten together a coterie of comedy-writers, jokesmiths and song-writers, who have a session every once in a while. Believing, possibly, that a man who can write a popular song and make sense out of it possesses a virile imagination, the Keystone commander-in-chief has chosen well. Given a central idea for a story, these conferences develop some of the craziest ideas of which the human mind is capable. Sometimes a stenographer will take notes, so that nothing suggested is forgotten, but more often a director will sit in and, having been given the assignment, will throw the script aside and go in to produce the story with all the "pep" that's in him. And if by chance the comedy dopesters hit upon something that "has never been done before," you can take it for granted it will be adapted to the screen, if it doesn't kill the actors to do it.

But we're going into the studio and mustn't lose any more time. It is no little satisfaction to feel that you are outwitting the grim sentry in "horning into" the studio. He takes the "pass" from Buck and examines it top and bottom, just as tho Buck himself is an intruder. This precaution to keep Keystone methods away from the general public—and others —is entirely justified. Still, it is strange, despite all of the changes in personnel of actors and directors that the Keystone, as well as other studios, experience, no one has been able to make "Keystone stuff."

THE KEYSTONE TANK IN ACTION

A NEW SENNETT COMEDY IDEA

A FAST-MOVING RAILROAD COMEDY

huge hole in the stage floor. The aldermen do not show sufficient amazement, much to the despair of the rapid-fire director, who shouts: "Come, come, I'll throw you into it, if you dont watch out!" It was in outdoor scenes of this picture, in which shoes which "walk on water" were introduced, that an actor jumped from a bark chartered by Mr. Sennett in San Pedro harbor. Incidentally, from the yardarm to the water was only 110 feet, and the actor was laid up for a week. Just one sample of "Keystone stuff."

In another set, Director Fred Fishbeck is supervising a scene in which moon-eyed Ambrose or even to imitate it successfully, away from this big Edendale plant. Which is another evidence of the dominating genius of Sennett.

The interior of the Keystone is the same as you would expect to find any up-to-date, efficient Motion Picture plant. The open-air stages cover five acres. Many industries of a small-sized town are to be found here—planing-mill, carpenter's shop, plumbing establishment, wall-paper and designers' department; paint- and sign-shops, prop-room, buildings with many tiers of dressing-rooms, and a "light studio." The latter is of concrete, covering 15,000 square feet, a marvel of electrical ingenuity, where work can be done at night and when the weather gets eccentric. With other producers, Mr. Sennett has learnt by experience that Los Angeles is not a land of perpetual sunshine, altho it is a city where rightly many Easterners long to live.

"This is a man's studio," says your guide, Frank Buck. "We dont have so many girls here."

Evidently Buck hasn't been with Keystone for very long, or else this is "ladies' day." At least, the men are decidedly in the minority—perhaps most of them are working on "locations." Here and there you will see a vision all dressed up in some filmy costume waiting for a call; perhaps this is the day when the Keystone bathing-girls disport; there is almost an army of girls, their features accentuated or spoiled by the hideous make-up both sun and mercury-light require. Everything hums with activity.

If you are lucky you will see two or three directors working in different sets at the same time. For instance, Director Victor Herman is putting a group of long-whiskered city fathers thru a scene in "She Loved a Sailor," and there is a and Polly Moran—perhaps the best eccentric film comédienne in the game—are having a little set-to. Polly is caught in the wood-bin, and Ambrose brings a load of wood—all of it hollow—and dumps it on her. If any one has any complaint to make, she'll probably remark: "What are you kicking about? Gee-whiz! just see what I've been thru!" And Mack Swain hasn't much to say. He, too, has had his experiences.

Or perhaps you will see Charlie Murray, all in his Irish janitor make-up, chatting with the camera-man, while Director Frank Griffin is putting Louise Fazenda and Harry Booker in some film absurdity in which Murray is buffeted around. Murray was one of the particular stars of the old Biograph Comedy Company, and his work with Keystone has added to his reputation.

The mere appearance of Chester Conklin in make-up is a laugh in itself, without "adding insult to injury" by watching him perform. "Perform" is right, for there is little short of sure death that Conklin ever balks in the hands of Director Harry Williams, who has forsaken song-writing and taken to "movie" production like a duck to water.

Then, there is Ford Sterling and his company, usually under the watchful eye of Director Herman, as well as the group of players in the hands of Director Clarence Badger, principally Gloria Swanson and Bobby Vernon. And it is significant of

CLASSIC

Mr. Sennett's policy in recognizing and rewarding merit, that one of these directors was his former office-boy, who now, under twenty-five, is earning $200 or $300 a week as a director. With all of these companies working, to say nothing of the mechanical and scenic staffs, it is not surprising that the Keystone family should number nearly a thousand.

You would appreciate how big a crowd this is if you should take luncheon in the studio cafeteria, on the second floor of one of the buildings facing Allesandro Street. The rush is on at noon-hour, but be careful that you dont fall into the Keystone tank! It is in the middle of the studio, and not half so large or impressive as the pictures would lead you to believe. But it has seen faithful service in many

DRESSING-ROOM ROW FOR KEYSTONE GIRLS

KEYSTONE FIREMEN IN ACTION

Keystone hits. But on to the restaurant—the hungry picture-players will not leave anything, if you dont hurry! Almost everybody is in make-up of some sort, from the cowboy with hair chaps to the actor who looks like Villa. It is, indeed, a rare experience to have luncheon with such an odd-looking set, but a spirit of good-fellowship seems to prevail, and while there is much joking and jibing, nobody loses much time in satisfying the inner man.

MACK SENNETT'S DEN

"Supervised by Mack Sennett," in connection with the Triangle-Keystone comedies, meant just what it said. Mr. Sennett worked hard and long, and his supervision was not merely superficial. The chief has a wonderful capacity for developing bits of comedy where no one would imagine any possibilities existed. In overseeing the production of a scene by one of his directors, Mr. Sennett watched for a while, and, after it had been "shot," went over the action and offered suggestions that made it threefold as amusing.

In the same way, he may witness the showing of a completed production and, catching an opportunity lost for more comedy business, Mr. Sennett will order several scenes entirely remade

to get in the added action. We refer to all of his activities as of the past, as the Big Chief has recently left Keystone and has set up his own shop in the old Biograph studio. Some of his comedy stars have followed him.

It is probably as a monument to the memory of the early days, that one very small portion of the studio is not as up-to-date as it might be. This is a little wooden hut or cabin, centrally located near the different stages, without a single redeeming feature as far as appearances go. But this is Mr. Sennett's "den" and is where he communed with himself when directing almost all the pictures himself, when Keystone was in its swaddling-clothes. It was not so very long ago that Mr. Sennett gave in to the urgent pleas of General Manager Del Ruth, and now a suitable office for the director-general has risen in its place, with a switchboard like a battle-ship's outfit.

WATER-SHOES AS A COMEDY THEME

No need to tell the average "movie fan" just what "Keystone stuff" is like, for he knows it only too well. He knows that only a Sennett could have devised the "comedy cops"; those thrilling automobile chases in which pursuing cars barely miss being run over by trolleys and railroad-cars; the toboggan-slide in bathing-suits; the smash-ups; dazzling stunts on the tops of high buildings—or any of the hundred and one hazardous tricks that have set the whole world holding its side from laughter.

Index

Numbers in **bold** indicate photographs

Abbott, George 174, 296
Academy Award® 47, **123**, 231, 258, 280, 281, 282, 285
Academy of Motion Picture Arts and Sciences 30, 32, **33**, 151, 254, 270, 307
Ache in Every Stake, An 221
Adler, Felix 86
Adventures of Ichabod and Mr. Toad, The filmography information 279
Agee, James 43, 190
Aitken, Harry E. 128, 129, 133, 134, 137, 139, 140, 303, 306
Al G. Barnes Circus 206
Aladdin Theater (Indio, CA) 218
Alarm, The filmography information 255
Albert, Dan 255, 258, 259, 260, 261
Albright, Bob 221
Alexander, Frank 261, 262, 263
Algy on the Force **102**, filmography information 249
Algy the Watchman 2
Alias Jimmy Valentine 11
Alice in Wonderland (1933) 61
All in Good Fun 176, filmography information 284
All Quiet on the Western Front 230
Allen, George 263
Allen, Hazel 258
Allen, Meiklejohn 258
Allen, Phyllis **192**, 257, 258, 259, 261, 262, 300
Allen, Steve 124, 182, 190, 283, 284, 285
Ambrose's Nasty Temper filmography information 260
American Biograph Company 2, 3, 5, 6, 7, 8, 9, 14, 18, 128, 196, 198, 214, 221, 226, 227, 248, 260, 299
Anderson, Dave "Andy" **4**, 104, (bio) **201**, 248, 249, 250, 251, 263, 264, 266
Andre, Lona **119**
Anna Christie 258
Apollo Comedies 161, 222–229, 237
Arbuckle, Roscoe "Fatty" 20, **26-27**, **28**, 29, **32**, 33, 35, 42, 45, **48**, 66, 69, **71**, **74-75**, 104, 105, 108, 111, **129**, 130, **142**, **144**, 148, 149, 167, 182, **192**, 197, (bio) **201**-202, 203, 204, 209, 215, 221, 223, 249, 228–229, 237, 249, 250, 251, 252, 253, 254, 255, 256, 257, 259, 260, 261, 262, 263, 268, 269, 270, 283, 284, 287, 288, 297, 300, 301, 304, 305
Arizona Magazine 144, 156
Arling, Charles 261, 264
Armstrong, William "Billy" 167, 265, 266, 267, 268
Arnold, Cecile 257, 260, 262
Art of Charlie Chaplin, The (Harness)
Arthur, George K. 216
Arts & Entertainment network (A&E) 35, 297
Asher, Max **174**
Association Chaplin 197
At It Again **2**, 103, filmography information 247
At Twelve O' Clock 10
Atlas Films 138, 263
Au Telephone (André de Lorde) 7
Austin, Albert 268, 270
Avery, Charles **4**, 23, **24-25**, **102**, 104, (bio) **202**, 219, 248, 249, 250, 251, 252, 253, 255, 257, 261, 271, 300
Aviator, The 215

Bacon, Lloyd 97
Badger, Clarence **70**, **72**, 97, 305, 306
Baker, Kenny 116–117
Bakhtin, Mikhail 11, 14
Ball, Lucille 159
Bandit, A 250
Bangville Police **7**, 11, 23, **24-25**, 26, 42, 103, 104, 137, filmography information 249, 286
Bank Dick, The 206, 270
Banks, Douglas 258
Barber Shop, The 96, 115, **116**, 169
Bari, Lynn 176, **177**, 274
Barnes, "Slim" Ray 198,
Barney Oldfield's Race for a Life **3**, 24, 53, 137, filmography information 250
Bathing Beauties, The (see Sennett's Bathing Beauties)
Battle of the Century, The 294
Baumann, Charles O. 127–128, 133, 145, 227, 262, 298, 299, **303**, 305–306
Be Reasonable 165, **166**, 174, filmography information 266, 283
Beaudine, William 30, 97

Because He Loved Her 121, 173, filmography information 263
Beck, Jackson 282
Beebe, Marjorie 115, 271
Beery, Wallace 169, **172**, 214, 277, 258, 284, 292
Behind the Green Lights 61
Belasco, Jay 261
Belcher, Alice 92, 268
Bellamy, Madge 155
Belmont, Joseph "Baldy" 264, 265, 270
Beloved Rogue, The 230, 231
Bennett, Alma 93-94
Bennett, Billie 255, 258, 259, 261, 262, 263
Benny, Jack 180, 235
Bergman, Henry 268, 289
Bernard, Harry (bio) **202**, 260, 261, 262
Bernard, Sam 262, 263
Bernds, Edward 217
Best Arbuckle/Keaton Collection (Image) 269
Best of Enemies, The 151, 152
Between Showers 207, filmography information 254-255
Bevan, Billy 77, 78-79, 80-**81**, 82, 84, 86, 96, 165, 167, **185**, **186**, 221, (bio) **232**-233, 234, 242, 265, 266, 267, 283, 284-285, 286
Big Moments from Little Pictures **60**, 96, 166, **167**, 176, filmography information 275-276, 285
"Big Slide, The" (episode of *Playhouse 90*) filmography information 291
Binney, Harold J. 261, 262
Birth of a Nation, The 128, 134
Bison Film Company 298, 299
Bitzer, G. W. "Billy" 7, 70
Bitzer, J. C. **70**
Blackhawk Films 40, 134, **136-137**, 139, 143, 191, 197, 248, 249, 250, 253, 254, 259, 260, 261, 264, 265
Blanc, Mel 235
Bletcher, Billy 178, **180**, 181, (bio) **233**-234, 294
Blue of the Night, The 190
Blue, Ben 239
Booker, Harry 261, 262, 264, 265
Bordeaux, Joe 104, **147**, **171**, (bio) **203**, 259, 260, 261, 262, 263, 268-269, 270
Bosworth, Hobart 201
Bow, Clara **155**
Bowery Boys, The 237

Brand-New Hero, A filmography information 256
Bray Comedies 239
Brendel, El 239
Bright Eyes **76**, 77, 88
British Broadcasting Company (BBC) 295
Brockwell, Billie 261, 264
Broke in China 88, 93
Broken China 93
Broncho Film Company 129, 132, **300**
Brooks, Louise 60, 214
Brownlow, Kevin 106, 182, 287, 289
Bryan, Vincent **72**
Bryant, James 104, (bio) **203**-204, 257, 259, 261, 263
Bud Abbott & Lou Costello Meet the Keystone Kops 96, **108**, 124, **150**, **175-177**, filmography information 273-275
Buffalo Bill's Wild West Show 204
Bull's Eye Comedies 239
Burns, Sammy 228
Busch, Mae 225, 226, 260, 262, 263, 264, 271, 302
Bushman, Francis X. 180, 294
Buster Keaton: The Shorts Collection, 1917-1923 (Kino-Lorber) 269
Busy Day, A 209
Butcher Boy, The 125
Byrd, Aaron **83**

Cagney, James 223
Cahn, Sammy 174, 296
Call a Cop filmography information 266
Callahan, Joseph 264
Camel Caravan (The Ed Wynn Show) 125, filmography information 290
Cameo the dog 165, **167**, 267
Campbell, Eric 268, 289
Campino, Michael 213
Cannon Ball, The filmography information 261
Capra, Frank 83, 84, 97, **123**, 218, 221, 230, 288
Carew, Ora 264, 273
Carlyle, Ollie 259, 261
Carnival Films 138
Carr, Harry 72
Carruthers, Helen 258
Carver, Louise 89, 92-93
Case, Al **213**, 264

Casino Royale (1967) filmography information 280
Castle Argyle Apartments **49-50**
Castle Films **135**, 274
Castle Sans Souci **50**
Caught in a Cabaret 134, **302**
Cavender, Glen 104, 108, **180**, (bio) **204**, 255, 257, 258, 259, 260, 261, 262, 263, 265, 268, 270, 304
Century Comedies 239
"Chain Gang Man"/"I Laughed You Cried" 179
"Charge of the Keystone Kops, The" (unproduced play) 181
Chaplin (née O'Neil), Oona 205
Chaplin at Essanay (Neibaur) 31
Chaplin at Keystone (Flicker Alley) 40, 197, 254, 255, 258
Chaplin, Charles 12, 21, 22, 27, 28, 30, **31**, 32, **34**, 35, 36, 37, 38, 39, **40**, 41, **43**, **44**, 45, **48**, 51, 66, 67, 68, 69, 70, 75, 81, 82, 84, 89, 96, 97, 100, 104, 128, 129, **133**, 134, **150**, 151, 155, 161, 163, 169, **185**, 188, **192**, 193, 197, (bio) **204**-205, 207, 222, 230, 231, **239**, 254, 255, 258, 268, 276, 277, 280, 282, 284, 287, 288, 289, 290, 294, 297, 301, **302**
Chaplin, Geraldine 280, 282
Chaplin, Minnie 261
Chaplin, Syd 134, 258, 261-262
Charley, the Gang Leader **31**-33
Charlie Chaplin (Huff) 38, 69
Chase, Charley (see also Parrott, Charles) 96, 150, **185**, 203, 207, **225**, **241**, 283, 286, 289
Chased Into Love 22
Chene, Dixie 257, 258, 260, 262
Chesterfield Cigarettes 169, 277
Chicago Board of Censors, The 269
Chicken Chaser, The filmography information 255
Chief's Predicament, The filmography information 248
Chip Off the Old Block, A filmography information 251
Christie, Al 96, 111, 135, 225, 226
Christie Brothers Comedies 61, 93, 96, 111, 232, 233
Cinefest (Syracuse, NY) 35
CineMuseum 8, 35, 38, 39, 84, 139, 174, 176, 198, 249, 252, 256, 257, 259, 261, 264, 265, 266, 267, 271, 272, 295
Cineteca Bologna 197
Cirque Medrano 125
City Lights 22, 222, **239**
Clansman, The (Dixon) 134
Clark, Bert 176, 262
Clark, Fred **177**, 274
Classic Film Collector 193
Cleopatra (1917) 34
Clifton, Emma 252, 254
Cline, Eddie 90, 92, 94, 97, 104, (bio) **205**-206, 255, 257, 258, 259, 260, 262, 263, 264, 269
Clown Princes and Court Jesters (Lahue/Gill) 228
Clyde, Andy **61**, 90, 91, 92, **108**, 110, 165, **167**, 175, **189**, 211-212, 217, 221, 233, (bio) **234**, 237, 266, 267, 268, 271, 273, 283, 284-285, 286, 290, 291
Cogley, Nick 4, 23, **102**, 104, (bio) **206**, 247, 248, 249, 250, 251, 252, 258, 262, 264, 301
Cohens and Kellys, The 224
Cohens and Kellys in Trouble, The 96
Coleman, Frank J. 268
Colgate Comedy Hour, The 212
Collegians, The (series) 228
Collier, William Sr. 262, 264
Collings, Pierre 58
Collins, Eddie **119**, 122, 123, 173, 271
Colonna, Jay 178
Columbia Comedy Shorts, The (Okuda/Watz) 217
Columbia Pictures 96, 180, 207, 217, 221, 225, 231, 234, 239, 280
Colvig, Vance "Pinto" 178, **180**, (bio) **235**, 278
"Comedy's Greatest Era" (Agee) 190
Comique Film Corporation 105, 215, 223, 228
Conklin, Charles "Heinie" 86, **119**, 121, 125, 125n, **172**, 173, **174**, 175, 176, 207, (bio) **235**-236, 239, 270, 271, 272, 273, 274, 290, 291, 296
Conklin, Chester 62, 67, 68, 104, 110, 111, 117, **118**, 123, 125, 125n, **145**, **148**, 158n, 169, **170**, **171**, **172**, **173**, 174, 175, 178, **180**, **189**, 195, (bio) 206-**207**, 219, 222, 225, 231, 235, 238, 239, 240, **244**, 254, 255, 256, 258, 259, 261, 262, 263, 269, 270, 271, 272, 273, 277, 283, 284, 290, 291, 292, 295, 296, 300, 301
Conley, Lige (a.k.a. Lige Crommie) 262, 264, 266
Conried, Hans 179, 287
Conversion of Frosty Blake, The 132

Cook, Clyde 96, 169, **170**, 216, 270
Cool McCool 180, **181**, 293
Cooley, Frank 253, 254
Cooper, Jack 121, 204
Cope Studio 135
Cops (1922) 165, **166**, 266, 269
"Cops Redesign" (episode of *Portlandia*) 294
Cox, Robert (Marvin) 29, 104, **105**, **142**-158, (bio) **208**, 245, 254, 293, 301
Crawford, Johnny 239
Crosby, Bing 115, 169, 190, 278, 279, 284, 290
Crosthwaite, Ivy 262
Crowd, The **49**, 59
Cruel, Cruel Love 51
Cruze, James 152

Dancing Masters, The 120n
Dandy, Jess 266
Dane, Karl 216
Daniels, Bebe 238
"Danny Lands in Pictures" (episode of *The Danny Thomas Show*) filmography information 291
Dare-Devil, The 81
Davenport, Alice "Mother" 67, 68, 145, 247, 250, 251, 252, 255, 256, 257, 258, 259, 260, 261, 263, 264, 265, 271, 300
Davies, Marion **168**, 258, 276
Davis, Bette 229
Davis, Carl 168, 276
Dawgone Dog, That 228
Day Dreams 165
Day of Thrills and Laughter, The 135, 139, 178, 265, 285
Day the Laughter Stopped, The (Yallop) 202
"Death in Slow Motion" (episode of *Batman*) 179, 293-294
de Forest, Lee 44
De Roy, Harry 253
Del Ruth, Hampton **72**, 97, 258, 264, 267, 301, 304
Del Ruth, Roy 232, 266
DeMille, Cecil B. 74, 118, **153**, 214, 238, 282
Dent, Vernon 175, **189**, 272, 284, 291, 295
Dentist, The 190, 234, 284
DePew, Ernest A. "Hap" 267
Desperate Scoundrel, A (see also *Dirty Work in a Laundry*) 38
Dick Tracy Show, The 293
Dictator, The 152, **153**

Diltz, Charles 178
Diltz, Elva 266
Dinner at Eight 258
Dirty Work in a Laundry 51, filmography information 261
Disneyland's Main Street Cinema 176-177, 259
Dixon, Thomas E. 134
Dog's Life, A 209
Dolby Theatre (Hollywood, CA) 47
Dollars and Sense 138, filmography information 264-265
Donnelly, James **147**, 262, 263, 265, 266
Double Crossed filmography information 254
Double Trouble 237
Dough and Dynamite 301
Down Memory Lane 124, **189**, 190, filmography information 283-284
Dr. Carver's Diving Horses 208, 211
Dreiser, Theodore 188
Dressler, Marie 45, **46-50**, 109, 136, 258, 277, 284, 297, 301
Drummer's Vacation, The 247
Duncan, Bud (see also Ham & Bud) 211, 222, 223
Dunham, Phil 161
Dunn, Bobby 29, 104, 145, **147**, 167, **171**, (bio) **208**-209, 211, 258, 259, 261, 261, 263, 266, 267, 268, 270
Durfee, Minta 25, 26-27, **133**, 148, 195, 201, 202, 207, 219, 222, 224, 252, 253, 254, 255, 256, 257, 258, 258, 260, 261, 273, 291, 292, 295, 300
Dutiful but Dumb 196
Dwan, Allan 57

Earle, Frank 266
Easy Street filmography information 268
eBay 39, 43, 271
Echo Park Lake 63, **64-65**, 146
Eddy, Robert 263
Edgar Kennedy: Master of the Slow Burn (Cassara) 218
Edlin, Ted 143
Educational Pictures 35, 119, 120, 284
Edwards, Harry 232, 234, 269
Edwards, Jack **182**
Edwards, Ralph 124, 174, 234, 290-291
Edwards, Ted (bio) **209**, 256, 257, 258, 259, 260, 261, 262

Edwards, Vivian 257, 260
Eisenstein, Sergei 6
Emerald Motion Picture Company 228
Empress Theatre (Grundy Center, IA) 82
Engle, Billy 170, 171, 270, 276,
Enright, Ray 97
Erickson, Knute 230
Erskine Johnson's Hollywood Reel filmography information 273
Escaped Lunatic, An 5
Essanay Film Manufacturing Company 21, 31, 43, 69, 151, 161, 232, 262, 302
Evans, Perry 265, 266
Evans, Walker 191
Everson, William K. 43, 285
Exhibitor's Trade Review 22
Exhibitors Herald 22, 98
Extra Girl, The 253

Fabray, Nanette 174
Fairbanks, Douglas 128, **163**, 276, 277, 282, 287, 289
False Beauty, A filmography information 255
Famous Players-Lasky 55, 152, 165, 214, 268
Farley, Dot 23, 24, 25, 77, 78, 79, 248, 249, 253, 295, 300
Farnum, William 231, 271
Farrar, Geraldine 214
Fatal Hour, The 6, 10
Fatal Sweet Tooth, A filmography information 256
Father Goose (Fowler) 115, 169, 188, 190, 208
Fatty and Mabel Adrift 32, 74-**77**, **78**, 97, 201, filmography information 263
Fatty and the Broadway Stars filmography information 262
Fatty Joins the Force **17**, 24-**27**, 42, 161, filmography information 253
Fatty's Day Off filmography information 251
Fatty's Flirtation filmography information 253
Fatty's Jonah Day filmography information 257
Fatty's Magic Pants filmography information 257
Fatty's New Role filmography information 259
Fatty's Plucky Pup **48**
Fatty's Tintype Tangle filmography information 261
Fay, Hugh 112, 260, 261, 264, 265
Faye, Randall 88
Fazenda, Louise 110, 112, 260, 261, 264, 265, 283, 291, 302

Fields, W. C. 90, 96, 115, **116**, **123**, 169, 188, **189**, 190, 206, 207, 211, 234, 238, 270, 281, 282, 284, 290
Film Daily, The 58
Film Fan Monthly 193
Film Johnnie, A 82
Films in Review 193
Films of Mack Sennett, The (Scherk, ed.) **194**
Fine, Larry 96
Finlayson, Jimmy 37, **119**, 121, 122, 123, 169, **170**, **173**, **174**, 175, **189**, 234, (bio) **236**, 242, 265, 270, 271, 273, 283, 285
Fire Bug, The 251
First National Pictures 31, 61, 139, 165, 173, 201, 209, 215, 216, 232, 265, 269, 283
Fishback, Fred 256, 258, 259, 261, 262, 304
Fishy Affair, A 249
Fitzgerald, Eddie 266
Fixer, The 22
Fleischer, Max 235
Flicker Alley 139, 197, 268
Flirt's Mistake, A 254
Florey, Robert 208
Foolish Age, The 22
For Better—But Worse 226, filmography information 260
Foray, June 179, 287
Force, Charles 267
Ford Econoline 126, 179
Ford Model T 167, 279
Ford, Glenn 182
Ford, John 96, 154, **155**, 229
Forde, Victoria 300
Forgotten Films of Roscoe "Fatty" Arbuckle, The (Laughsmith) 27, 35, 197, **198**, 253, 255, 261
Four Horsemen of the Apocalypse, The 231
Fowler, Gene 66, 115, 169, 171, 188, 208
Fox Film Corporation 22, 210, 231, 239
Fox Kiddies series 210
Fox Sunshine Comedies 204, 207, 215, 216, 229, 230, 237
Fox, Virginia 266, 269
FoxFilm 222, 225
Fractured Flickers 112, 179, 191, filmography information 287
Franklin, Chester **103**, (bio) **210**, 212, 247, 248, 249, 259
Frazee, Edwin (bio) **210**, 258, 262
"Frazee's Fearless Five" 214
Frees, Paul 179, 287

Freuler, John R. 131
Fuller, Dale **148**, 264
Fun Factory, The (King) 15, 195, **197**
Funny Manns, The 112, 176, filmography information 286

Gamble, Fred 251, 252
Gangsters, The filmography information 249
Garbo, Greta 258
Garmes, Lee 58
Garnett, Tay 97
Geduld, Harry 68
General, The 122, 203
"George Jessel's Old New York" (1940 World's Fair exhibit) 296
George White Scandals 296
Gertie's Gasoline Glide **162**
Giddy, Gay and Ticklish filmography information 258-259
Giebler, Al 86, 91, 267
Gilbert & Sullivan's Pirates of Penzance filmography information 281-282
Gilbert, Billy 104, **171**, **105**, 208-209, (bio) **211**, 251, 252, 253, 256, 258, 259, 260, 261, 262, 263, 264, 267, 270, 301
Gilbert, Billy (sound-era comedian) 61, 211, 239
Gilbert, Florence 219, 233
Gill, Sam 28, 193
Gish, Lillian 18, **19**, 227, 282, 292
Gladysz, Thomas 60
Glaum, Louise 295
Gold Rush, The 231
Golden Age of Comedy, The 96, 139, 176, 191, 267, 276, 285
Golden, Marta 262
Goldstein, Abe **245**
Good and Naughty 55
Good Old Corn **138**, 173, 266, filmography information 283
Good-Bye Kiss, The 232
Goodwin, Herold 274
Gorshin, Frank 179, 293-294
Grapevine Video 273
Grauman's Chinese Theatre 46, 47, 169, 277
Gray, George **147**, **171**, **189**, (bio) **211**-212, 270
Great Movie Shorts, The (Maltin) 172
Great Toe Mystery, The filmography information 256, 290
Grey, John **180**

Gribbon, Eddie **124**, 175, 178, (bio) **212**, 243, 265, 266, 272, 283
Gribbon, Harry 165, 167, 212, 259, 262, 263, 265, 267, 276, 283
Griffin, Frank C. 260, 264, 265
Griffith, Corinne 232
Griffith, D. W. 3, 6, 7, 8, 9, 10, 11, **12**, 13, 15, 18, 19, 20, 21, 65, 66, 67, 69, 70, 96, 97, 104, 118, 128, 196, 202, 214, 227, 303
Griffith, Gordon 250, 251, 253, 258
Griffith, Raymond 265
Grocery Clerk's Romance 254
Guinn, Floy 266
Gusher, The filmography information 253
Gussle the Golfer filmography information 258
Gusso, Mel 297
Gymnasium Jim **81**

Haines, William 168, 276
Hal Roach Studio 76, 203, 209, 216, 225, 230, 236, 238, 239, 275-276
Hale, Alan 152
Halfback of Notre Dame, The 82, 102
Hall, Huntz 237
Hallelujah! I'm a Bum 237
Ham & Bud (see also Hamilton, Lloyd, and Duncan, Bud) 223
Hamilton, Lloyd 223, 115
Hamilton, Shorty 129
Hammond, Harriet 77, 78
Hammons, Earle W. 120
Handler, A. L. 161
Hansen, Juanita **52**, 263, 305
Happy Times and Jolly Moments 138, 173, filmography information 283
Hard Luck 93
Hardy, Oliver 236
Harris, Bernard (bio) 212-214
Harry Langdon Collection, The (ALLDAY) 197
Hart, Sunshine 94
Hart, William S. 128, 129, **131**, 276
Hash House Fraud, A 112, 138, 225, filmography information 261
Hats Off 34
Hatton, Raymond **3**, 104, **214**-215, 248, 249, 250
Hauber, Bill **4**, 104, **105**, 149, 161, (bio) **215**, 248, 249, 250, 251, 252, 253, 254, 255, 255, 256, 257, 258, 259, 260, 264, 301

Haunted House, The (1918) 210
Haunted Spooks 93
Have Badge, Will Chase (see also *Bud Abbott & Lou Costello Meet the Keystone Kops*) 274
Haver, Phyllis 78, 79, 80, 265, 290, **305**
Havez, Jean **77**
Hawks, Howard 96
Hayes, Frank 104, (bio) **215**-216, 256, 257, 259, 260, 261, 262, 263, 264, 265, 295
Hayes, Venice 260
He Who Gets Slapped 55
He Wouldn't Stay Down filmography information 260
Headline Woman, The 61
Heckler, The 96
Heerman, Victor 97, 265, 276, 304
Heisler, Stuart 71, 97, 98
Hellum, Barney 167, 267, 268
Help! Help! 9, 10, 11
Henderson, Dell 175, 260, 262, 263, 264, 276, 290
Hennecke, Clarence 88, **180**, 207, (bio) **216**, 243, 266, 272, 273, 291
Her Birthday Present filmography information 247
Her Deceitful Lover **127**, filmography information 249
Her Majesty, Love 61
Here Come the Co-eds 96
Herman, Jerry 182
Hiatt, Ruth 82, 267, 273
Hide and Seek 11, 248
High Button Shoes 182, 293, 296-297
Hiken, Nat 178
Hill, Benny 293
Hill, Jack 169, 277
Hill, Thelma 91
Hirschfeld, Al 183
His First Flame 93
His Musical Career 69
His Prehistoric Past 68
His Pride and Shame **52**, 263
His Sister's Kids 13, 253
His Trysting Place 134
Hitchcock, Alfred 96
Hoffmeyer's Legacy 2, filmography information 247
Hold Everything 96
Holderness, Fay **116**
Hollywood: The Pioneers filmography information 287-288
Hollywood Bowl 46
Hollywood Cavalcade 22, 96, **116**-123, **159**, 172, 190, 236, filmography information 271, 279, 295
Hollywood Museum 212
Holmes, Helen 248, 250
Holmes, Lois 263
Home Breakers, The filmography information 259
Home Talent 190
Hornbeck, William 232
Howard, Jerome "Curly" 96, 233
Howard, Moe **217**
Howard, Shemp 96
Howdy Doody Show, The 191
Howell, Alice 227, 228, 255, 258
Huff, Theodore 38
Hugunin, H. Lee 267
Humor Risk 228
Hunn, Bert **105**, (bio) **216**-217, 248, 249, 250, 251, 252, 253, 301
Hunt, Ray (bio) **217**
Huntley, Fred 262
Hurlock, Madeline **83**, 85, 86, 88, 89, 90, 91, 94, 110, 268, 285
Hutton, Betty 174
Hypnotized 114, 232

Idle Class, The 89
Image Entertainment 60, 197, 249, 250, 252, 253, 263, 267, 269, 276
In Cold Blood (Capote) 215
In the Clutches of a Gang **28**-33, 53, 104, 111, 133, **142**, 144, 208, 236, filmography information 254
Ince, Thomas **12**, 66, 128, 303
Incompetent Hero, An 228, filmography information 257
Inslee, Charles 3, **64**, 251, 252, 253,
Internet Movie Database (IMDb) 29
Intolerance 47, 128
Iron Horse, The 154-**155**, 229
Iron Mule, The 203, 229
Irving, Bill 272
It's a Gift (1923) 238
It's a Mad, Mad, Mad, Mad World 237

Jackman, Fred W. 264, 266
Jackson, Joe 262

Jackson, Sherry 291, 294
Jacobs, Paul 248, 250, 251, 301, 302
Janitor, The 252
Janitor's Wife's Temptation, A filmography information 262
Jazz Singer, The 156
Jeske, George 29, 104, 105, 161, (bio) **217**–218, 251, 252, 253, 254, 301, 302
Joan the Woman 214
Joe Palooka in Humphrey Takes a Chance filmography information 273
Johnson, Cole 29
Jolly Jilter, The 95
Jolson, Al 156, 271, 282
Jones Family series 122
Jones, F. Richard 232, 258, 262, 265, 266, 267, 305
Jones, Grover 88
Jones, Spike 177
June, Mildred 266, 267, 283
Just Kids filmography information 250

Kalat, David 197
Kalem Company, The 233
Kane, Bob 180, 293
Kane, Eddie 169
Kane, Helen 294
Karen, James 179
Kartes Entertainment 196
Katchem Kate 2
Kaufman, Al 265, 216
Kay-Bee Pictures 129, 216
Keaton, Buster 28, 44, 82, 84, 90, 91, 100, **105**, **106**, 108, 117, **118**, **119**, **120**, 121, **122**, 123, **124**, 125, 125n, 126, 165, **166**, 169, 172, 178, 179, 181, **192**, 203, 217, 221,223, 229, 233, 239, 268, 269, 271, 272, 273, 277, 284, 288, 289, 290, 293
Kelley, James T. 268
Kelly, Fanny 265, 266
Kelly, Gene 233
Kelly, George 55, 58
Kelly, Pat 264, 266
Ken Films 138, 271, 283
Kennedy, Edgar 23, 25, **26**-**27**, 29, 86, **102**, 104, 111, 144, 161, **192**, (bio) **218**, 230, 236, 248, 249, 250, 251, 252, 253, 254, 255, 256, 257, 258, 259, 260, 261, 262, 271, 284
Kennedy, Tom **124**, 178, **180**, (bio) **236**-237, 243, 262, 265
Kenton, Erle C. 262, 265

Kerr, Robert 258, 260, 262
Kessel, Adam 127–128, 227, 298, 304
Kessel, Charles 127–128
Kessel, Joe 167
Keystone (Lovesey) 295
Keystone Cops Band, The **163**
Keystone Cyclorama **304**
Keystone Film Company 1, 13, 29, 111, 201, 223, 224, 227, 282, 298, **300**, **301**, **303**
Keystone Hotel **61**, 96, 122, 122n, 138, **171**–172, 174, 203, 211, 212, 220, 224, filmography entry 270–271, 283
"Keystone hop" **108**
"Keystone Kapers" (Jones) 176–177, **179**
"Keystone Kapers" (video game)
Keystone Kid, The (Watson) 112, 195
Keystone Kiddies series 301
Keystone Komical Kops 109
"Keystone Kops Capture Virginia Richmond, The" (unproduced play) 181
Keystone Kops Dixieland Band 178–179
"Keystone Kops Theme (for orchestra)" (Davis) 168
Keystone Krowd, The (Oderman) **195**, 198
Keystone Quartet 221
Keystone Tonight 248
Keystone, The Movie 295
Keystone: The Life and Clowns of Mack Sennett (Louvish) 112, 194, **195**
Keystone-Triangle 152, 200, 235, 262, 264, 265
King of Comedy (Sennett/Shipp) 124, 160, 175, 190-**191**, 274
King of Kings, The 153
King, Cora 230
Kino-Lorber 60, 139, 197, 253, 269
Kirtley, Virginia 29, 250, 251, 252, 253, 254
Kismet (1930) 61
Kitchen, Fred 69
Kleine, George 22
Kleptomaniacs 22
Klintberg, Walter 263
Knockout, The 108, filmography information 255
Koenekamp, Hans F. 97, **145**
Kops and Custards (Lahue) **193**, 198
Korda, Alexander 97

Laemmle, Carl **302**
Lahue, Kalton C. 29, 43, 73, 133, 193–194, 200, 215, 228

Lake, Alice 268
Lakin, Charles 259, 260, 261, 262, 263
Lamont, Charles 176, 273-274
Lane, Nora 115
Langdon, Harry 81, 96, 98, 161, **171**, 188, 197, 207, 216, 217, 221, 237, 239, 277, 283, 284, 286, 288, 299
Lanning, Cheryl 143, 156
Lantz, Walter 98, 235
Lasky, Jesse 152
Laughing Gas 48
Laurel & Hardy 38, 100, 122n, 175, **192**, 202, 203, 209, 218, 233, 236, 271, 277, 282, 284, 285, 286, 288
Laurel, Stan (see also Laurel & Hardy) 169, 216, 236
Lawrence, William C. 85
Lawson, Stan 178
Lee, Lila 152
Lehrman Knock-Out (L-KO) Comedies 111, 161, 162, 210, 222, 223, 228, 232, 236, 237, 303
Lehrman, Henry "Pathé" 11, 23, **103**, 161, 247, 249, 250, 251, 252, 254, 300, 301, **302**, 303
Leonard, Jack 249
Leonard, Marion **7**
Leslie, James 260
Lessley, Elgin 97, 269
LeVeque, Eddie **124**, 175, 178, 179, **180**, 181, (bio) **219**, 245, 275
Lewis, Dave 255
Lewis, Gordon 167, 266, 268
Lewis, Joy 261, 262
Library of Congress 4, 196, 246n, 248, 253, 255, 257, 258, 259, 260, 261, 276, 292
Life in the Balance, A 11, filmography information 248
Life magazine 178, 190, 285
Lifetime of Comedy filmography information 284
Ligon, Grover 104, **171**, 105, (bio) **220**, 251, 253, 255, 257, 258, 259, 260, 261, 262, 265, 270, 301
Lind, Myrtle 265, 305
Lipson, Jack "Tiny" **108, 171**, 270
Little Annie Rooney 30
Lizzies of the Field 82
Lloyd, Frank 97, 231
Lloyd, Harold 22, 28, 76, 84, 151, 238, 260, 277, 284, 288, 289, 291

Loback, Marvin **167**, (bio) **237**-238, 266, 267, 283
Lobster Films 34, 40, 197, 255, 258, 289
Lockwood, J. R. 265, 266
Loeb, Leon 264
London After Midnight 34
London, Babe 209, 292
Lonely Villa, The **7**, 8, 9
Long, Walter 152
Looney Tunes 65
Lord, Del 82, 91, 97, 175, **180**, (bio) **220**-221, 232, 234, 264, 267, 291
Los Angeles Athletic Club 151
Los Angeles Coliseum 173
Los Angeles Police Department 160, 220, 277
Los Angeles Times 175, 241, 242, 243, 245, 295
Lost Child, The 5
Loud Mouth, The 96
Love and Bullets filmography information 256
Love and Rubbish filmography information 250
Love in a Police Station **61, 108**, 110, 111, 167, 172, 234, 239, filmography information 267-268
Love Thief, The 256
Love, Honor and Behave 165, filmography information 265-266
Love, Loot and Crash 137-138, 161, filmography information 260, 289
Love, Speed and Thrills **137**, 161, 207, filmography information 259
Lover's Lost Control, A filmography information 261-262, 290
Lucas, Wilfred 251, 252, 300
Luke the dog (a.k.a. Fido) 74-**75**, 259, 263
Lynch, Charles **174**
Lyndon, Clarence "Clarry" 263

Mabel at the Wheel **146**
Mabel Normand Soundstage 271
Mabel's Busy Day 255
Mabel's Dramatic Career 66, 137, filmography information 251
Mabel's New Hero 20, 22, 24, filmography information 251
Mable (sic), Fatty and the Law filmography information 259
MacArthur, Arthur 267

MacDonald, Wallace 258
Mace, Fred 2, **8**, 9, 10, 23, **103**, 104, 145, 160, 161, 187, (bio) **221**-222, 247, 248, 249, 262, 264, 284, 299, 300
Mack and Mabel (Broadway show) **182**, 297
Mack, Charlie 114
Mack Sennett Collection, The: Vol II (CineMuseum) 252, 259, 261, 264, 265, 266, 267, 272, 275, 294
Mack Sennett Collection, The: Vol. I (CineMuseum) **185**, 249, 254, 256, 257, 262, 263, 273, 292, 295
Mack Sennett Studios 96, 115, 187, 271, 304
Mack Sennett's Fun Factory (Walker) 41, 53, 62, 111, 112, **196**, 200
Mack Sennett's Keystone (Lahue) 73, 193, **194**, 198
Mack Sennett's The Fun Factory (Killiam Shows) filmography information 285-286
Mack, Marion 122
MacKenzie, Donald 206
Maid Mad filmography information 264
Maines, Don 92
Majestic Pictures, Inc. 133, 231
Majestic Theatre (New York, NY) 297
Making a Living 301
Male and Female 214
Maltin, Leonard 172, 193, 279
Mann, Hank **28**, 29, 61, 62, 104, 105, 117, **119**, 121, 123, 125, 144, 149, 161, 169, **170**, 171, 172, **173**, **174**, 175, 176, **189**, 207, 208, (bio) **222**-223, 225, 238, 239, **244**, 249, 251, 252, 253, 254, 255, 258, 262, 270, 271, 272, 273, 274, 286, 290, 291, 296, 301
Man Next Door, The **4**, 10, 11, filmography information 248
Man of a Thousand Faces 223
Margaret Herrick Library (Mack Sennett papers) 97-98, 151, 187, 193, 194
Marriage Circus, The **83**, 84, 87, 98
Married Life 174
Marsh, Betty 262
Marshall, George 174
Marx Brothers, The 94, 218, 228, 277, 278, 286
Mascot Studios 21, 61
Mason, William 263
Masquerader, The 82,
Masquers Club 169, 170, 175, 270, 276
Massa, Steve 112, 160, 246
McBride, Joseph 85

McCabe, John 38
McCall, William 267, 268
McCoy, Harry 67, 88, 104, 256, 257, 258, 259, 260, 261, 262, 263, 265, 267, 300
McDonald, J. Farrell 169, 277
McDonald, Marion 267
McFadden, Bob 180
McNeil, Allen 265, 266
McPhail, Addie 202
Media History Digital Library 62, 187
Meet the Stars: Stars—Past and Present filmography information 271
Meighan, Thomas 214
Meins, Gus 267
Melford, George 154
Méliès, Georges 102
Merton of the Movies filmography information 272-273
Metro Pictures 122, 231
Metro-Goldwyn-Mayer (MGM) 119, 125, 168, 204, 218, 237, 239, 258, 272, 273, 280, 281
Mickey **132**, 133, 305
Mickey's Gala Premier (sic) 169, **171**, filmography information 277
Miller, Rube 23, 29, 104, 149, 161, (bio) **223**-224, 232, 248, 249, 250, 252, 253, 254, 255, 256, 258, 300
Min and Bill 258
Mineau, Charlotte 265
Miser's Heart, A 11
Mishaps of Musty Suffer, The 22
Monkhouse, Bob 176
Monogram Pictures 134, 237
Moore, Colleen 232
Moran, George 114
Moran, Polly 262, 276, 283, 302
Morgan, Kewpie 82, 165, 167, 266, 267
Morris, Dave 260, 267
Morris, Lee 225
Morris, Reggie 86
Mother's Boy 252
Mothering Heart, The **18-19**
Motion Picture and Television Country House and Hospital 143, 207, 237
"Moving Picture Hero of My Heart" (Lewis/Erdman) 163
Motion Picture Classic 161, 308
Motion Picture News 13, 22, 77, 115, 130
Motion Picture Relief Fund 175
Movieland Wax Museum 124, 178

Moving Picture World 5, 10, 22, 30, 33, 60, 109, 185-186, 187
Movies March On, The 173, filmography information 282
Moving Picture World 5, 10, 22, 30, 33, 60, 109, 112, 185, 187
Mr. Deeds Goes to Town 221
Muddled in Mud (see also *Muddy Romance, A*) **135**
Muddy Romance, A 3, **64-65**, 96, 135, filmography information 252-253, 286, 287
Murphy's I.O.U. filmography information 249
Murray, Charlie 27, 96, 110, 111, **150**, 165, 173, 216, 221, (bio) **224**, 256, 257, 258, 262, 263, 264, 265, 271, 283, 290
Murray, Ken 190, 295
Murtagh, Jack 30
Museum of Modern Art 190, 195, 251
Mutual Film Corporation 31, 37, 44, 69, 128, 131, 187, 247, 268, 303
Mutual's Strand Comedies 22
My Autobiography (Chaplin) 67, 193, 198, 282
"My Heart Leaps Up" (Herman) 182, 297
My Wonderful World of Slapstick (Keaton/Samuels) 120, 126

Napoleon the Great 29
National Variety Artists (NVA) 169
Neilsen, Agnese 268
Nelson, Eva 258
Nestor Studio 210
New Century Theatre (New York, NY) 174, 296
New Janitor, The 32, 205
New York Daily Mirror 221
New York Motion Picture Company (NYMP) 127, 298, 303
New York Times 14, 123, 175, 191, 297
New York World's Fair (1940) 156, 173, 296
New Zealand Film Archive 30
Nichols, George 24, 29, 253, 254, 300
Nichols, Norma 256, 257, 261
Night at the Opera, A 94
Niles Essanay Silent Film Museum 197
Nip and Tuck 165, **167**, 176, 234, filmography information 267
No One to Guide Him filmography information 262
Noise of Bombs, The 228, filmography information 257, 290

Normand, Mabel **3, 7**, 9, 10, 11, 20, 23, **24, 25**, 45, **46, 64**, 66, **67**, 69, 74-**75, 76**, 81, 116, 118, **120**, 124, **133, 135**, 145, **146**, 147, 160, 169, 172, 182, 188, 190, **192**, 195, 198, 201, 227, 247, 248, 249, 250, 251, 252, 253, 255, 256, 257, 258, 259, 260, 263, 271, 283, 284, 288, 289, 290, 297, **299, 302**, 304, 305
Norris, Eleanor 125
Novis, Donald 115
Now We're in the Air 214
Nugent, Frank 123
Number, Please? 22

O' Hara, George 265, 266
O'Shea, Danny 267
Oakley, Laura 247
Oderman, Stuart 195, 202, 207, 218, 222, 230
Oettinger, Malcolm 55
Olde Time Movies (home movie distributor) **135**-136
Old-Fashioned Way, The 237
"On a Sunday by the Sea" (Styne/Cahn) 174
On Patrol 266, 283
Once Over Lightly 173-174, filmography information 283
Opperman, Frank 253, 254, 255, 256, 257, 258, 259
Our Dare-Devil Chief 54, 137, filmography information 260, 287
Our Gang 143, 203, 218, 277
Ovey, George 260, 261

Padgett, W. W. 266
Palmer, Frederick **72**
Pangborn, Franklin 115, 124, 190, 284, 290
Pantages Theatre (Hollywood, CA) 175
Paolo Cherchi, Usai 80
Paramount Pictures 61, 148, 167, 169, 174, 203, 207, 214, 216, 269, 275, 276, 305, 306
Pardon My Scotch 217
Parrott, Charles (see also Chase, Charley) 150, (bio) **225**, 226, **241**, 255, 256, 257, 258, 269, 260, 261, 263, 300
Parrott, James 225
Parrott, Paul 216
Parry, Harvey 106, 266, 281, 288
Parsons, Harriet 271
Pasha, Kalla 78, 80, 265
Pathé Exchange 76, 84, 95, 165, 167, 169, 241, 267, 275
Pathé Freres 1, 2, 160, 287

Patsy, The 258
Paul, Robert W. 102
Peanuts and Bullets filmography information 259
Pearce, Leslie 234
Peeping Pete 250
Pennington, Ann 296
Perils of Pauline, The (1914) 164, 206
Perils of Pauline, The (1947) **173**, 174
Personal 5
Peters, Bernadette 182, 297
Phillips, Carmen 250
Phoenix Gazette 143
Photoplay magazine 187, 188
Photoplay Productions, Ltd. 168, 276, 287
Pickford, Mary 7, 30, 128, 216, 231, 289, 292
Pictorial History of the Silent Screen, A (Blum) 29
Picture-Play Magazine 55, 57, 58
Pinched in the Finish 161, filmography information 265
Pitts, ZaSu 230
Police (1916) 31
Policemen's Little Run 1, **2**, 102
Pollard, Snub 117, 125, **172**, 173, 174, **192**, 207, 223, 225, 237, (bio) **238**–239, **242**, 271, 272, 285, 290, 296
"Poor Pauline" (McCarron) 164
Portlandia 294
Potterton, Gerald 181
Preston, Robert 182, 297
Prevost, Marie 61, 62, 265, 266, 270, 305
Price, Oscar 133
Pride of Pikeville, The **84**
Priest, Hal Haig 266
Producers Releasing Company (PRC) 229
Property Man, The **34**
Prouty, Jed **117, 119**, 122, 123, 172, 271
Pullman Pride, The 190
Purviance, Edna 268

Quick, Evelyn 249, 300
Quiet Little Wedding, A filmography information 252
Quillan, Eddie **108**, 110–111, 167, 268, 270, 284, 292

Railrodder, The 181
Ramage, George **213**, 264
Rand, John 266, 268
Reckless Romeo, A 44
Reelcraft Comedies 211, 228

Reid, Wallace 152, 153
Reisner, Charles **72**
Reisner, Dean 291
Reliance-Majestic Pictures 128
Republic Pictures 203, 214, 271
Reynolds, Frank **213**, 264
Richardson, Jack 77, 78, 79, 266
Rides, Rapes and Rescues 176
Rifleman, The 239
Riley and Schultze 2, 103, filmography information 247, **299**
Riley, Mack 104
Ringling Bros. Circus 223
Riot, The filmography information 251
Ripley, Arthur 88
Ritchie, Billie 161
RKO 61, 173, 218
RKO-Pathé 169, 270
RKO Radio Pictures 279, 282
Roach, Bert 62, 161, 257, 270
Roach, Hal 115, 135, 139, 150, 166, 167, 169, 176, 285, 288
Robbins, Jerome 174, 296
Roberts, Joe 269
Robeson, Paul 232
Robinson, David 21, 282, 289
Rodgers, Dora 259, 260
Rodney, Earle 88, 264, 267
Rogers, Will **60**, 166, **167**, 169, 216, 276, 285, 286, 288
Rolin Film Company, The 211, 237, 239
Roosevelt Hotel 46
Rosemary Clooney Show, The 126
Rosenbloom, "Slapsie" Maxie **177**, 274
Ross, Budd 77, 78, 79
Rough House, The 44, **105**, 108, 268–269, 270
Rounders, The 69
Ruggles, Wesley 261, 265
Ruman, Sig 61
Rural Third Degree, A filmography information 238
Russell, Harry 252, 253
Ruth, Marshall 118
Ryan, Phil L. 269

Safe in Jail filmography information 250
Sally 22
Salter, Thelma 250
"Salute to the Silents, A" (episode of *The Merv Griffin Show*) filmography information 292

San Francisco (1936) 218
San Francisco Call-Bulletin 88
San Francisco Post 88
Sanford, Stanley J. "Tiny" 119, 268
Sargent, Epes W. 60
Saturday Afternoon 94
Saturday Evening Post 190, 290
Saxon, Hugh 258
Schade, Betty 300
Schade, Fritz 104, 225, (bio) **226**, 256, 257, 258, 259, 260, 261, 263, 264
Scharrer, Jack 264
Scheming Gambler's Paradise, The 102
Schenck, Aubrey 283
Schenck, Joseph M. 268, 269
Scheuer, Philip K. 295
Schloesser, Dr. A. G. R. 49
Schoedsack, G. Felix 265
Scott, Bill 179, 287
Sea Nymphs, The 257
Seely, Sybil (see also Trevilla, Sibye) 266
Seldes, Gilbert 188
Selig Polyscope Studios 48, 49, 206, 218
Semon, Larry 161, 215, 288
Sennett Bathing Beauties (a.k.a. The Sennett Girls) 82, 103, 110, 115, 117, 118, 119, 124, 143, 151, 169, 190, **192**, 205, 212, 226, 251, 284, 290, 296, 299, **305**
Sennett, Mack 12, **63**, **103**, **120**, **123**, **145**, **146**, **174**, **176**, **185**, **191**, **196**, **194**, **226**, **303** (actor) 2, 3, 7, 8, 10, 65, 103, 145, 187, 214, 232, 247, 249, 250, 251, 255, 262, 271, 274, 284, 299; (bio) 226-227; (director) 20, 145, 200, 201, 207, 247, 248, 249, 250, 251, 252, 253, 255, 257, 258, 299; (Hollywood legend) 116, 118-126, 135, 139, 169, 174, 175, 176, 188, 191, 193, 271, 274, 284, 290-291, 295, 297 (producer) 29, 44, 61, 109, 114, 115, 116, 120, 145, 146, 151, 165, 168, 178, 185, 196, 235, 239, 258, 283, 303; (scenarist) 7, 63, 65, 81, 265; (style of comedy) 1, 10, 12, 65, 93, 96, 101, 115, 117, 130, 151, 177, 183, 273, 284, 286, 287, 290, 296, 299 (supervisor) 117, 145, 206, 220, 262, 263, 264, 265, 303
Sennett-Color 115
7 Lively Arts, The (Seldes) 188
Sheer, William A. 260
Shepard, Pearl 211
Sherlock Jr. **122**
Shipp, Cameron 101, 175, 190, 290-291
Shivering Sherlocks 96

Shoulder Arms 239
Show Off, The 55-62
Show People **168**, filmography information 276
Shriners, The 160, **178**, 179, 224
Sidney, George 96, 216
Sight & Sound 37-38
Silent Legend: The Mack Sennett Story (Prairie Coast Films) filmography information 290
Silent Movie (Eugene Ballet Company) 297
Silent Movie (1976) 281
Silents, Please (Killiam Shows) 191
Sills, Milton 232
Silvers, Phil 174, 275, 286, 296
Simmonds, Joseph 129, 139
Sing, Bing, Sing 190, 284
Skelton, Red 272, 288, 291
Slapstick Encyclopedia (Image) 197, 249, 250, 252, 253, 263, 267, 276
Slapstick! Magazine 29, 213
Slapsticon Film Festival (Arlington, VA) 38, 193, 254
Smile When the Raindrops Fall: The Story of Charley Chase (Anthony/Edmonds) 225
Smith, Dick **227**-228, 257, 258, 104
Smith, Vernon 81, 84
Smith's Family (series) 110
Social Pirates 22
"Son's (sic) of the Keystone Kops" 179
Song of Freedom, The 232
Sorrell, Lou 255
Spectrum Theater (Arlington, VA) 38
Speed Queen, The 250
Squaw Man, The (1914) 214
St. Clair, Malcolm (Mal) 55, 57, 58, 59, 79, 97, 117, 121, 122n, 264, 266, 271
St. John, Al **28**, 29, **32**, 75, 104, **105**, 108, 111, 142, 144, **148**, 149, 172, 173, 203, 208, 223, (bio) **228**-229, 251, 252, 253, 254, 255, 256, 257, 258, 259, 260, 262, 263, 268, 269, 285, 296, 300, 301
Stafford, Earl L. 267
Stage Struck 55, 57
Star Is Born, A (1937) 218
Star Wars: The Clone Wars 294
Starr, Jimmy 267
Stars and Bars filmography information 265
Stars of Yesterday 294-295
Staub, Ralph 171, 172, 270
Steadman, Vera **174**, 264

Step Forward 135
Sterling Comedies 218, 222, 232
Sterling, Ford 2, **3**, 4, 11, 21, 27, 28, 30, 37, 42, 44, **52**-**62**, **64**, 66, **103**, 109, 111, 119, 122, 135, 144, 145, 149, 160, 161, 166, 167, 169, **170**, **171**, 172, 218, (bio) **229**, 234, 241, 247, 248, 249, 250, 251, 252, 253, 254, 255, 257, 260, 261, 262, 263, 265, 270, 276, 277, 284, 285, 294, 299, 301, **302**, 303
Stevens, George 97
Stevens, Josephine 268
Stolen Jools, The 169, filmography information 276-277
Stolen Purse, The 2, **103**, 232, 247
Stooges: The Men Behind the Mayhem (Laughsmith) 25
Stout Heart but Weak Knees filmography information 256-257
Stout Hearts and Willing Hands 169, **170**, 231, 236, filmography information 270
Stroheim, Erich von 34, 207, 270
Stromberg, Hunt 22
Studebaker, Hal 248
Stupid But Brave 203
Styne, Jule 174, 296
Sulky, Leo **174**, 267
Sullivan, Ed 126
Sullivan-Considine vaudeville circuit 222
Sultan's Wife, The 306
Summerville, George "Slim" 104, **147**, 209, 229-**230**, 241, 255, 256, 257, 258, 259, 262, 263, 283, 287, 295
Super-Hooper-Dyne Lizzies 84
Survival of American Silent Film Features, 1912-1929, The (Pierce) 246n
Sutherland, A. Edward (Eddie) 97, 311
Swain, Mack 69, 104, 110, 150, 161, 167, 169, **170**, **171**, **185**, **192**, 225, (bio) **230**-231, 239, 252, 253, 254, 255, 257, 258, 259, 260, 262, 269, 270, 277, 283, 285, 300
Swanson, Gloria 55, **70**, 168, **192**, 195, 214, 227, 283, 284, **305**, 306
Swickard, Josef R. **70**, **231**, 249, 256, 257, 258, 259, 260, 261, 262, 264

Tarron, Elsie 212
Tavares, Arthur **103**, 104, (bio) **232**, 250, 251, 257
Taxi Boys, The 239
Taylor, Ruth 89, 90, 91, 267
Teare, Ethel 266

Technicolor 116, 118, 161, 174, 190, 295
Temperamental Husband, A 2, filmography information 247
Texaco Star Theatre 116, 190, 295
Thatcher, Eva 266
Thaw, Evelyn Nesbitt 221-222
Their First Execution filmography information 249
Thief Catcher, A **36**-**44**, 161, 193, 204, filmography information 254, 301
This is Your Life 124, 175, 234, filmography information 290-291
Those Country Kids filmography information 256
"Those Keystone Comedy Cops" (McCarron) 163-165
Those Love Pangs **48**
Three Ages (1923) 90
Three Little Beers (1935)
Three Mesquiteers, The 214
Three Stooges, The 97, 98, 207, 211, 217, 221, 234, 237, 239, 288, 290
Thundering Taxis 96
Tillie Wakes Up 258
Tillie's Punctured Romance (1914) 21, **45**-51, 109, 129, **133**, 134, 136, 138, 187, 197, 204, 206, 210, 228, filmography information 258, 282, 284, 286, 289, 301
Tillie's Tomato Surprise 258
Timid Young Man, The **119**, 120
To Tell the Truth 156, **157**, filmography information 291-293
Todd, Stanley W. 308, 309
Totheroh, Roland 268
Tower Film Corporation 36, 37, 129, **133**, 254, 257
Trask, Wayland 261, 263, 264, 265
Trevilla, Sibye (see also Seely, Sybil) 265, 266
Triangle Motion Picture Company 82, 128, 133, 134, 152, 163, 165, 188, 200, 235, 262, 264, 265, 303, 306
Triple Trouble **31**
Tri-Stone Pictures 133, **134**, 264
Trouble at the Beach filmography information 272
Trouble with Wives, The 55
Turner Classic Movies (TCM) 42
Turpin, Ben 21, **61**, 62, 77, 78, 79, 80, 81, 82, **83**, **84**, 85, 86, 87, 88, 90, 91, 92, 93, 94, 95, 117, 118, 123, 135, **149**, 161, 166, 167, 169, **171**, 172,

173, **185**, **192**, 223, 235, 239, 270, 271, 277, 279, 283, 284, 286, 287, 295, 306
20th Century-Fox 96, 116, 122, 123, 159, 172, 190, 271, 275, 281, 284, 294
Two Old Tars filmography information 252
UCLA Film and Television Archive 197
Underwood, Loyal 268
Unfortunate Policeman, The 101-102
Unger, J. J. 133
United Artists 133, 216, 230, 231, 239, 277
Universal Pictures 281

Valk, Edith 265
Van, Beatrice 250
Vaughn, Alberta 267, 291
Velarde, Gloria **116**
Vernon, Bobby 169
Vidor, King 49, 54, 59, 168, 276
Village Vampire, A filmography information 264
Vitagraph Company of America 161, 215, 216, 233, 301
Vogue Comedies 223, 232

W. H. Productions 129, 130, 131, 132, 133, 137, 251, 253, 254, 255, 256, 257, 259, 261, 262
Waley, Hubert D. 37, 38
Walker, H. M. "Beanie" 238, 275
Wallace, Morgan 258
Wallington, Jimmy 116-117
Walsh, Billie 260
Walt Disney Studios 93, 234, 235, 277, 278-279
Walters, Robert 266, 267
Wandering Willies 82, **83**, 96, **107**, 110, 165, 176, 221, filmography information 267, 285, 286
Ward, Burt 293
Ward, Jay 179, 287
Ward, Lucille 257
Ward, Tiny 92, 125n, 167, (bio) **239**-240, 266, 268, 290
Warner Bros. 61, 122, 138, 139, 171, 173, 231, 234, 266, 270, 283
Water Nymph, The **299**
Watson, Coy Jr. 108, 195
Watson, William 73, 263
Weber & Fields 151, **152**, 262, 286, 303
Weber, Bill **213**, 264
Weber, Lois 50
Weiss Bros. Artclass 237

Wells, May 252, 253, 261, 263
West of Zanzibar 239
West, Adam 293
West, Billy 39
West, Ford 122
Western Import Company 129, 133
When Comedy Was King 96, 178, 191, **192**, filmography 284-285
"When Movies Were Movies" (Herman) 182, 297
White, Billy 253
White, Jules 221
White, Leo 32, 270
Whitman, Phil 88, 267
Who Killed Cock Robin? filmography information 278-279
Wife and Auto Trouble 138, 161, filmography information 264
Wilcox, Silas D. 266,
Wild Oranges 54
Williams, Frank D. 268
Williams, Harry **75**, 265, 305
Wilson, Lois 55, **56**
Winick, Hyman 129, 132
Wished on Mabel filmography information 260
Wizard of Oz, The (1925) 231
Won Ton Ton, the Dog Who Saved Hollywood filmography information 275, 281
Woodward, Guy 263, 265
Work 31
World of Laughter (Lahue) 29
Worst of Friends, The 152
Would-Be Shriner, The 160
Wright, Walter 250, 259, 261, 263, 264
Wulze, Harry **72**
Wynn, Ed 125, 239, 277, 290

Yankee Doodle in Berlin **137**, 216
Yarbrough, Jean 273
Youngson, Robert 96, 135, 139, 176, 178, 191, 265, 267, 276, 284

Zalibra, George C. "Duke" 263
Zanuck, Darryl F. 116, 271, 279
Zecca, Ferdinand 1, 102
Zepped 39, **42-43**
Ziegfeld Follies 296

www.ingramcontent.com/pod-product-compliance
Lightning Source LLC
Chambersburg PA
CBHW081346230426
43667CB00017B/2733